Modes of Thought

Modes of Thought

ESSAYS ON THINKING
IN WESTERN AND NON-WESTERN
SOCIETIES

Edited by

ROBIN HORTON and
RUTH FINNEGAN

WIPF & STOCK · Eugene, Oregon

Wipf and Stock Publishers
199 W 8th Ave, Suite 3
Eugene, OR 97401

Modes of Thought
Essays on Thinking in Western and Non-Western Societies
By Finnegan, Ruth and Horton, Robin
Copyright©1973 by Finnegan, Ruth
ISBN 13: 978-1-5326-1761-4
Publication date 2/2/2017
Previously published by Faber and Faber, 1973

To
Sir Edward Evans-Pritchard

Contents

Contents

Preface

This book focuses on one central question: *Is there a basic difference in modes of thought (both in content and, more especially, in logic and formulation) as between Western and non-Western societies?* (*or as between 'traditional' and 'modern', 'pre-scientific' and 'science-orientated', literate and non-literate, industrial and non-industrial, 'developed' and 'developing' etc. etc.?*). Or—following on from this basic question—is there perhaps no significant difference that can be pointed to in this context? Or, again, is this perhaps not a feasible or a single question at all? Questions like this are not of merely anti-quarian or exotic interest but relevant for modern Western society today: for any attempt to define or place contemporary Western thinking involves not only a view of this in historical and geographical context but also, implicitly at least, some assumption(s) about its contrast with other societies.

At first sight the obvious group who have dealt with this basic question might seem to be the social anthropologists through their wide interests in societies of many periods and areas (with Evans-Pritchard as one of their most stimulating exponents). But it is increasingly clear that this is also a matter of interest to philosophers, psychologists, social theorists, historians, linguists, sociologists and many others—indeed that they have, implicitly or explicitly, been as much concerned with this topic as those who term themselves social anthropologists. It is clear too that there is now far more reliable data from research in all these fields than was available to earlier writers on this kind of subject (Lévy-Bruhl for instance) and that all sides have suffered from lack of contact between the different disci-plines concerned with it.

The collection is dedicated to Sir Edward Evans-Pritchard, till recently Professor of Social Anthropology at the University of Oxford. It is not intended as a *Festschrift* in the sense of meditations

11

Preface

on his work by friends and colleagues. Rather, this volume is an occasion for two things: first, to take further a problem with which Evans-Pritchard has concerned himself—and to which he has made an influential contribution; and second, to pursue the kind of approach for which he himself has always been noted: a fruitful refusal to throw strict barriers round his own subject, and a sympathy with an interdisciplinary and wide-ranging approach to the study of man and his thought. Though this collection of essays does not try to give any comprehensive coverage of the central question (the reader will note, for example, that—somewhat to our surprise—none of the contributors elected to take up a thorough-going Lévi-Straussian line), it is nevertheless grouped round a common theme and presents a series of individual analyses, arising from the basic question of the volume, set within an interdisciplinary framework. It seems to us that this type of volume may perhaps be seen as constituting a real and constructive salute to a great scholar and a great thinker—and one conveying as much respect as a series of sincere but unrelated personal tributes.

R.H.
R.F.

NOTE:

We would like to thank the Open University for help towards preparing the manuscript, and Doreen Beacham and Frances Gurney for their speedy and efficient typing of it.

12

Introduction

Ruth Finnegan and Robin Horton

The central question with which this collection is concerned has been explained briefly in the Preface. The contributors to this volume have many different approaches to, and opinions about, this central question in the light of their own research and interests—including some who consider it ultimately not a clear or sensible question at all (for various thought-provoking reasons). The purpose of this introduction is therefore not to state firm conclusions but to point to such themes as can be discerned and to the kinds of controversies that have been taken up for discussion—or that remain to be further pursued elsewhere.

The first part of the introduction draws together the major themes and questions that emerge in the various essays in this volume. In the second part, there is a more detailed discussion of the contribution of Evans-Pritchard's own work to the analysis of modes of thought and of the relationship of several of the essays in this volume to his ideas; this section also points to the many implications of his writings for the sociology of thought more generally.

I. Some Themes and Questions

The central question necessarily implies the idea of contrast: opposing one type of society (or groups of society) to another in respect of modes of thought; and following up the various possible character-istics by which these contrasts are to be assessed. It also involves the concept of 'modes of thought' and the notion that the whole question is one worth considering.

13

Introduction

In all these respects, interesting differences have emerged among the contributors.

(A) CONTRASTS BETWEEN WHAT?

First, then, what is being set up as a contrast to what? What kinds of societies/areas/periods are seen as opposable to each other either in the light of empirical evidence or as a useful heuristic device?

Here one of the interesting points to emerge is the diversity of views among the contributors. It is true that many contributors speak of 'modern', 'scientific' societies as opposed to 'traditional' (or 'primitive') 'pre-scientific' ones as being clear enough categories at least to start off from. But these terms, it becomes clear, cover some diverse cases. Nagashima, for instance, sees his own point of departure in the difference between Japanese and European modes of thinking. But, as he goes on to point out, the contrast could equally well have been (indeed, must be seen in the context of) that between Japan and China; or, again, that between Africa and the West. Colby and Cole, on the other hand, concentrate on possible contrasts between modern industrial America (or, rather, one group of American children in southern California) and, first, a particular group in West Africa (the Kpelle of Liberia), then various non-literate groups in Guatemala and Yugoslavia, widening this to a general possible contrast between a literate culture (primarily modern America) and an oral one. For Jenkins, the contrast is between two traits—secularism and religion— within Western European culture, both in the present and viewed in the context of its historical developments. Both Wolfram and Gellner explicitly pose the problem of how to delimit the opposing poles in any such contrast. Wolfram leaves it an open question for each analyst ultimately to settle for himself, but also specifically points to the dangers of committing oneself to 'all-embracing divisions of societies' and, in another context, expresses doubts about one common notion of 'the Western World . . . on the same side of a fence . . . and all other societies, past and present, hand in hand on the other'. Gellner, on the other hand, points out that for analytic purposes it may be convenient to posit two extremes: 'the modern' (belonging to modern technological society) and 'the savage'. He argues that it may be useful for analysis to assume each of these extremes to be homogeneous, but that at the same time one must explicitly state that the assumptions of both homogeneity and contrast are not self-evidently true and,

14

furthermore, that 'the enormous middle ground [between these two] . . . covers perhaps the most interesting part of human history.'[1] And yet other contrasts are invoked or implied by other contributors.

The significant thing here is the lack of clear agreement among the authors despite the apparent similarities with which a number started off. One is inevitably led, in reading through these essays, to an awareness both of the problematical nature of the terms in any such opposition and that, even when the poles are clearly stated or assumed, the homogeneity of each cannot be taken as self-evident.

This consciousness of the problems involved as to *what* is being differentiated contrasts with the self-confidence of many analysts in earlier decades. We have not lost the preoccupation with dichotomies that characterized writing at the end of the nineteenth century—in fact this interest runs through the volume—but we have come to be somewhat more cautious than some of the (still influential) writers in what has often been termed the formative era of modern social theory about the exact terms and definitions of these dichotomies. In the far-reaching oppositions between, say, *Gemeinschaft* and *Gesellschaft*, or societies with mechanical and those with organic solidarity, it is not now absolutely self-evident to which groups one should unquestionably apply these terms and in respect of what. It is not just that we now have access to dependable information (and the wish to use it) about many areas where before speculation was acceptable—though this is one dimension. It is also that some of our lack of certainty must be put down as an inevitable result of historical process—what could be dubbed for short our expanding horizons. For the late nineteenth-century European, no doubt, it was easier than now to see Europe as the focus, as the standard by which other cultures must be judged and distinguished. Nowadays—when we think about it at least—it no longer seems so obvious that one pole in any opposition must always and inevitably be 'modern Western Europe'—and not, say, China.

This lack of certainty about exactly where the contrasts lie comes in even when our motive in looking for oppositions is really, at root, to find out something about *ourselves* rather than about others—and to find out who *we* are by distinguishing ourselves from who we are *not*.

---

[1] His analytic extremes would, then, probably exclude a number of the other cases discussed, under one head or the other, in some other essays in the volume—Japan, for instance, rural Yugoslavia or Thai peasants.

Here, it is reasonable and essential to assume that we have to take 'ourselves' as one of the opposing poles. But we still have to remember two things. First, if one extreme is to be 'ourselves' and 'ourselves' happens to coincide with 'modern Western Europe'[1]—then we must say so, and make whatever definition or delimitation we are using an explicit one. And second, related to this, we have to remember that the particular opposition we have fixed on is only one of many possible ones, for there is nothing immutable and self-evident about it which gives it absolute priority for analytic purposes.

Where our motive is the more general one of looking for illuminating contrasts between societies which may throw light on, or be connected with, differing modes of thought then we may indeed find that a contrast between, say, Britain in the 1970s and Zande society in the Sudan in the 1930s, is a useful one; or we may find more fruitful a wider-scale one which contrasts the sweep of intellectual development in Western Europe since (say) the fifth century B.C. with either a similar period in India or with intellectual development (or what is known about it) in certain rural areas in Africa over the last century or so. But we have to admit that there is nothing in the nature of the facts themselves which inevitably and unquestionably makes such contrasts more interesting than those between, say, intellectual development in China and in Japan at certain periods, or between the thought of two different centuries in Greek culture (say, the seventh contrasted with the fourth century B.C.) or between the views of the world implied in Hinduism in contrast to Islam. This is not to say that the more popular contrasts between 'modern West' (in various interpretations of this) and 'others' is not a useful and an illuminating one—merely that we can no longer assume that this is the only one of interest.

(B) WHAT ARE SEEN AS THE DIFFERENTIATING CHARACTERISTICS ?
The polar terms in the opposition between areas with potentially different modes of thought are, then, not in themselves self-evident and are taken up differently by different contributors. The same also applies to the various differentiae used by the contributors to delineate these possible differences. Logically, two rather different aspects are involved here: one, the criteria by which the opposites are to be

---

[1] In so far as even that is a clear term.

defined,[1] and the other, the empirical properties which are discovered through research to belong to already defined and known opposites. Whatever the strict logic, however, these two aspects in practice often seem to shade into each other, and the purpose here is not to follow up this distinction (which can be pursued, where appropriate, in individual essays), but to point to some of the main characteristics fixed on by writers.

The various contributors focus on different factors here as being of the greatest significance in their particular approaches, but it is interesting to note one general point. This is that the characteristics most concentrated on tend to coincide with those which have for many years been taken as the typical differences between what have been termed 'primitive' and 'civilized' societies. A number of these date back to points made in nineteenth-century discussion of this topic. It is unlikely that the contributors would necessarily accept all the implications of the popular image of 'the primitive' but it is no surprise that some of the strands which make up this composite picture should have been selected for further analysis and query. Among the characteristics frequently discussed here are the following (some of them overlapping obviously): rationality (sometimes equated with scientific method) as opposed to non-rationality; the findings of science (usually identified with 'Western science' and sometimes defined as 'true') as against non-science/mistaken notions/false ideas; openness as against closure in thought systems; secularism (sometimes equated with scientific method or findings) as against religiousness and/or magic; high as against low division of labour (more relevant for modes of thought than may at first appear); and the dominance of tradition (including rote-learning) as against creativity and individual expression.

Perhaps the single most important characteristic picked on is that of 'rationality' (often equated with 'scientific'). Exactly what quality this is being opposed to varies from essay to essay, and at times is left implicit only. Sometimes it seems to be seen in opposition to magic or to non-empirically verifiable modes of thought, at others to mistaken explanations, or, yet again, to a meaningful personal view of the universe (as in Gellner) or to Horton's 'lost world'. In each case

---

[1] This sense obviously involves an overlap with the problem discussed in the previous section.

'scientific/rational' acquires different connotations depending on what it is being opposed to. One of the main points of disagreement here is between those who would regard as part of the definition of 'scientific' (and hence, in *some* cases, of 'rational') its verifiability and falsifiability by the test of the empirical facts (implied in, for instance, Horton and Lukes), and Barnes, who, in his discussion of the nature of Western science, rejects this 'empiricist model of scientific rationality' in favour of a presuppositionalist and analogical view of science[1] —a point that will be returned to later. 'Scientific-rational' is thus being used by contributors with slightly different meanings. The term is, indeed, not a self-evident one. Wolfram, as so often in her valuable essay, sums up some of the problems when she writes

> Scientific thinking is sometimes supposed to characterize our society. What however does this mean? We might take 'scientific thinking' to be, let us say, the acceptance of evidence or, more narrowly, the attempt to discover natural laws, or perhaps, more narrowly still, the attempt to discover those natural laws which will enable us to manipulate nature. . . . Then, what allows us to say that a society thinks scientifically? Is it that there should be a body of knowledge . . . or . . . that the society should conduct its affairs on a scientific basis, or that its members . . . have a penchant for 'scientific' support for beliefs they may hold . . .?

Despite these problems and differences between different writers, however, the general tendency seems to be to regard 'rationality' and/or 'science' as an obvious candidate for differentiating modes of thought—one at least that must be considered seriously. On this point, contributors give different answers. Some by and large would consider that this is indeed a mark of difference between modes of thinking in different societies (these include Lukes, Gellner and Horton), while others seem to suggest doubts about this (for example, Nagashima and Barnes). These cases are worth noting for it is not only a difference of definition but also of differing interpretations of the available evidence.

A further point to notice in this connection is the implication that sometimes appears that rationality/science is in some sense a good thing, a move in a progressive direction. This is sometimes justified in terms of the greater explanatory power of modern science, sometimes by the test of a somewhat positivist model of scientific method

---

[1] Explained further in Barnes's essay, pp. 182 ff.

Introduction

and achievement. As against this, Jenkins reminds us that some have doubted the value of at least certain attributed properties of rationality, and Horton speaks of the romantic view which rejects science in favour of the vision of the 'lost world'. Barnes also adds to this by the way he queries the whole empiricist model of science. On these points there is no need to take up one side or the other, but it is relevant to point to such evaluative overtones and the need (as indeed Horton makes clear in his essay) to make them explicit.

Much more could obviously be drawn out of this debate on rationality, and many controversies and problems are not followed up here.[1] However it does at any rate emerge clearly from the differing views in the essays here that the concept is a problematic one with several possible meanings. It is no longer easy to assert confidently that we can clearly measure the progress of a known and self-evident variable termed 'rationality' and know just where and how it can be applied. Where, just to take one example, should one place the striking development of Chinese science, documented with such detailed erudition by Needham?[2] The controversies involved in discussing the problems of definition and application of such terms ('rational', 'science' and so on) can lead to fruitful enquiry, but the conclusions are by no means yet self-evident.

When we move from consideration of scientific *method* or outlook as a characteristic to that of scientific *findings* (sometimes equated with 'truth') we encounter another suggested mark of differentiation in modes of thought: that between 'true' and 'false' beliefs. Questions about how far this factor is relevant in analysing differing modes of thought have preoccupied a number of contributors. Here again one can discern disagreement. Barnes on the one hand explicitly considers this point and concludes that the truth or falsity of beliefs is not and cannot be a criterion for differentiation in modes of thought. He discards, he says, 'the dichotomy between "truth" and "falsehood"', central to so much anthropology and sociology' and prefers 'the possibility . . . of treating all beliefs, preliterate or scientific, apparently true or apparently false, within a single framework'. Those who do not introduce questions of truth and falsity into their discussions

[1] Certain aspects of the problem of 'rationality' are discussed further in a recent collection of papers (B. R. Wilson (ed.), *Rationality*, Blackwell, Oxford, 1970).
[2] J. Needham, *Science and civilisation in China*, University Press, Cambridge, 1954 and following.

19

presumably tend to the same opinion as Barnes in so far as this particular characteristic is concerned. Lukes, on the other hand, explicitly rejects Barnes's view and argues that there are and must be universal criteria for the truth of beliefs and that a sociologist or anthropologist must be prepared to use these to make cognitive judgements about the modes of thought he studies. Indeed he, like Horton, is prepared to speak of the 'superior cognitive powers' of 'science-orientated' modes of thought as against traditional or 'prescientific' ones. Similarly Horton speaks of the 'cognitive forms of the modern West' as constituting 'forms of explanation, prediction and control of a power unrivalled in any time or place'. In each case it is the criterion of 'truth' as against 'falsity' that is primarily emphasized in reaching such judgements.[1]

The next characteristic is one that can be summed up briefly as 'religiousness', but seems sometimes to be stretched to include many things: emphasis on religion, magic, an 'enchanted' view of life (as in Gellner) or even interest in poetic and symbolic modes of expression. The counter-terms vary: sometimes 'rationality' or 'science', sometimes a 'mechanistic' view of the world, sometimes the increasing secularization said to characterize 'modern' life in contrast to the all-pervasiveness of religion once believed to mark out 'primitive' society. All or any of these are sometimes thought relevant for characterizing different modes of thought. Within this general area there are a number of different approaches. Jenkins throws doubt on some confident interpretations in the light of his discussion of Newman's writings on this. As emerges clearly in Jenkins's essay, the idea that religion and secularism (or religion and rationality) are self-evidently and unchangingly opposites can be challenged, for differing polarities and syntheses can be discerned. Indeed perhaps a whole new language is needed to interpret the new relationship and the older interpretations of opposition are outdated. Jenkins appositely quotes Newman:

> Nor do I aim at more than ascertaining the sense in which the words Faith and Reason are used by Christian and Catholic writers. . . . Half the controversies in the world are verbal ones; and could they be brought to a plain issue, they would be brought to prompt termination.[2]

[1] This point is taken up further below, p. 27.
[2] J. H. Newman, *Sermons . . . before the University of Oxford*, London, 1843, p. 192 (quoted by Jenkins, p. 346).

20

Introduction

Many would agree with at least one aspect of this, pointing to the difficulty of defining or measuring 'religion' and hence of using it as a touchstone in any contrasts without very critical analysis of its exact sense and application. Another approach is to point to poetic or symbolic thought in certain cultures (as, albeit from different viewpoints, in the essays by Nagashima, Finnegan and Whiteley) and query whether this aspect is something which necessarily must disappear with the spread of scientific and mechanistic modes of thought (as would seem to be suggested, say, in Gellner). Another interesting point in this connection comes out in Whiteley's detailed and meticulous account of colour concepts among the Gusii of Kenya. This is his tentative conclusion that, among at least this people of East Africa, the evaluative tone of colour concepts is important only in ritual contexts and not in everyday usage, where the terms 'are simply neutral'. He stresses that the concepts lack value without the ritual matrix—'just as the associations of whiteness in the ceremonial Lily do not influence the house-decorator'. If Whiteley is justified in his conclusion here this may make some analysts want to adopt a somewhat more sceptical approach to other accounts of symbolic classifications connected with colour among East African (and other) peoples, accounts which, deliberately or not, somehow give the impression of an all-pervasive and deeply symbolic approach to the world. In the light of Whiteley's evidence, it may be possible to argue that such interpretations conceivably rest on a mistaken analysis of the evidence and, if so, that we may need to reconsider certain impressions about the profound part played by symbolism in the everyday life of these and similar peoples.

Another way of approaching this particular aspect is to take the religious (or magical) behaviour as something given in its own right —a particular pattern of thought-action—and analyse its logic. This is done in an illuminating way by Tambiah. His essay points, as it were, in two interesting directions. First he emphasizes the *similarities* between what he terms scientific and magical thought—both are based on analogy. This point fits well with the use of analogy in scientific procedures discussed in Barnes's provocative and (many will think) convincing essay. It recalls too Geoffrey Lloyd's celebrated discussion of early Greek thought[1] in which he speaks of one of the two main

---

[1] G. E. R. Lloyd, *Polarity and analogy: two types of argumentation in early Greek thought*, University Press, Cambridge, 1966.

21

types of argumentation being that based on analogy. Lloyd's general conclusion is worth quoting here—that it is not in fact easy to distinguish a sharp break between such argumentation and later more 'logical' and 'empirical' procedures in science:

> So far from inhibiting the growth and development of scientific thought, the two general modes of explanation we have been considering [polarity and analogy] provided essential vehicles for the expression of ideas in the debates that were conducted on fundamental problems in each of the physical and biological sciences.[1]

This might seem to fit with Tambiah's insistence that the basic intellectual procedures in scientific and what some term 'magical' activities may be more similar than sometimes supposed—or that, at any rate, it is difficult to detect a sharp *a priori* break between them.[2]

Tambiah however would not go so far as this. Having pointed out the similarity in terms of use of analogy, he then goes on to the second interesting theme of his essay: making a radical distinction between different ways of using analogy. The empirical mode of science, he argues, must be set against the persuasive, ritual 'performative' mode. Here are *two* modes of thought, differing in this respect, and it is misleading to try to apply the criteria of the one to the other—for example to judge magical thought-action by the standards of empirically verifiable scientific usage of analogy. The differences between the two modes of thought may then be more striking than the similarities and they must not be assessed by the same criteria—a conclusion that is in turn disputed by, for instance, Lukes and Horton. Tambiah also follows up his distinction by querying the common assumption (more often a preconception than explicitly stated) that all development must follow that supposed to be true of Western Europe (a development, broadly, from magic to science, from pervasive religion to increasing secularization) and suggests that assumptions of this kind may result from too narrow a concentration on the experience of only one particular civilization—a conclusion in which our other contributor who shares Tambiah's acquaintance with Eastern civilizations concurs.

[1] Ibid., p. 439.
[2] Though here again the terms must be looked at carefully—is this to be applied to 'poetic' thought? metaphysical? cosmological speculation in general? or what else? The equation of all these terms is hardly self-evident.

22

Introduction

The suggested quality of 'open' as against 'closed' systems of thought is another recurring theme, the former characterized by an awareness of alternative possibilities, the latter not. This is discussed more fully in the second part of the Introduction in the context of Evans-Pritchard's writing, but it is worth noting here briefly that several contributors fix on this as a crucial quality for characterizing differing modes of thinking. Barnes and Gellner for instance are both centrally concerned with the ideas of 'closure' and 'openness'. Unlike Horton, however, they are doubtful whether the awareness of alternative possibilities of explanation can really be a crucial factor in the transition from one type of thought system to another. Barnes argues that scientists are not in practice typically and consistently aware of the existence of alternatives in any case, while Gellner gives various examples in which awareness of alternatives does not in practice result in 'open' or 'science-orientated' modes of thought. Gellner indeed sheds doubt on the whole assumption that in 'traditional' societies there are necessarily no possibilities of choice between alternatives. 'Frankly I do not believe this. Some savages may live in a unique, option-less world. Many do not.'

Another possible characteristic seized on by several contributors is that in terms of differential 'role specialization' or 'division of labour' in different communities. This can be looked at from the point of view of its relevance for modes of thought. This line is pursued in particular in the essays by Barnes and by Gellner. Their suggestions are discussed at some length in Part II of the Introduction.

One final possible characteristic taken up by a number of contributors is the implication for thinking of the contrast between, on the one hand, dominance of tradition and, on the other, the opportunity for individual creativity. Colby and Cole, for instance, consider how far rote-learning (sometimes supposed to be the characteristic type of learning and transmission among non-literates) applies to certain non-literate groups and conclude that in many cases the postulation of rote memory is not sufficient to explain the facts. They discuss some of the general characteristics of oral transmission and composition as exemplified in particular in work on rural Yugoslavia, and show how far this is from word-for-word repetition by rote. The same point comes out in Finnegan's discussion, where the significance of creativity and individual expression in oral composition is stressed and the idea that 'tradition' necessarily plays the predominant part in oral cultures

23

firmly rejected. On the other hand those who stress the importance of 'closed' as against 'open' systems of thinking in certain cultures might take the line that in certain respects the possibility of change is more limited in the 'closed' cultures and to this extent 'tradition' must necessarily be regarded as more important there. There is therefore room for real disagreement in this area, and the need for much more detailed and empirical research on the topic.

For all these possible characteristics (among others) discussed by the various contributors to this volume, there are varying answers not only about the relevance of each in principle but about the empirical evidence for its existence and its significance in various contexts. But one final point of dispute must be mentioned here. This is the fundamental one of how far these differing characteristics can be seen as going together, either necessarily or in common practice. How far can one identify a kind of syndrome in systems of thought by which such things as high role specialization, openness, scientific methods and findings, rationality and individual creativity go together, as against an opposing syndrome characterized by 'closure', magical or non-rational orientation, dominance of tradition and low division of labour? Some authors, like, say, Gellner or Horton, would tend to an affirmative answer here, others, like Nagashima or Finnegan, would reject it or at least regard it as unproven. This links in turn with the problem raised earlier: if there *are* these syndromes, can we predict which societies will be marked by which syndrome, or is this too a further question to be investigated? Or, alternatively, do *some* of these characteristics go together (say, openness and a high division of labour) but not all? Or is there not necessarily even this amount of convergence? And finally, how far do any or all of these go with particular social institutions not mentioned so far at all (a point raised in, for instance, Colby and Cole, Nagashima and Whiteley)?

These are all questions to which the contributors here tend to give different answers. They are also questions which lay themselves open as the basis for much future investigation.

(C) WHAT ARE 'MODES OF THOUGHT'?

So far in this introduction the meaning of this key term has been taken as given. It must however be discussed, if only briefly, for the term is certainly an ambiguous one and the various contributors here have interpreted it in various ways.

Introduction

Some writers are concerned primarily with *processes* of thinking. Colby and Cole in particular insist on a distinction between the *content* of cognitive activity and its *processes*. They are concerned with *how* people think as distinct from the things they think *about*. They argue indeed that till recently at least most social anthropologists have taken less interest in this particular aspect, tending to leave it to psychologists in favour of concentrating on the *content* of thought.

Within this general sphere of thought processes, there are various possible strands one could enquire about. There was the nineteenth-century view that equated cognitive activity with the processes of formal logic. Again, there is the more recent identification of thinking with 'problem solving'. Colby and Cole choose to follow up one particular aspect of problem solving: the cognitive skill involved in 'deutero-learning'—learning how to learn—and it is this which they compare across various cultures in their essay.

Other contributors are concerned to compare different aspects of thought processes (and do not all necessarily insist on such a clear content/processes distinction as Colby and Cole). Tambiah, for instance, is interested in the kind of *logic* involved in magical activity. He sees this as proceeding very much through the argument from analogy, and as something, furthermore, which cannot be divided into *thinking* as against *action*, for the two are intimately connected through the concept of 'performative utterances'. To discuss thinking in this context, therefore, it is necessary to discuss action also. Starting from a different point, Barnes also holds that a valid analysis of thinking must include reference to actual practice and not just to ideal models of that thinking. He argues pertinently that to understand the nature of scientific thought one must look at what actually happens in science—i.e. the proceeding on an analogical or metaphorical basis —rather than at what Barnes regards as a misleading *ideal*: 'empiricist models of scientific rationality' which suggest an inductive mode of logic. Barnes makes it clear that he considers that *in practice* the paradigms that form the basis of science are not rationally demonstrated by the test of 'the facts' but are passively received and accepted within the group. 'Rather than the paradigm being believed because nature, as it were, insists, the natural world is seen through the paradigm (in terms of atoms for instance, or fields) and its behaviour is interpreted to accord with this perception.' He would conclude from this (in opposition to Tambiah) that when comparable items are compared (i.e. actual practice compared with actual practice rather than—when science is involved—with a misleading ideal model) there is no clear and radical distinction between 'scientific' and 'non-scientific' thinking. To those writers in this volume and elsewhere who take an opposite line he would retort that they are falling into the error of measuring against each other two incomparable things: on the one hand an *ideal* model of scientific thought, on the other the *actual* procedures of 'non-scientific' peoples. In such cases, he would argue, the 'difference' in mode of thinking that emerges is predetermined by the terms of the question. What is needed for valid comparison is to treat all modes of thinking in the same framework: looking at the actual processes in the context of the social structure in which they occur.

Another way of proceeding would be to follow up the distinction between actual procedure and ideal model of thinking and compare the *latter* across different societies (recognizing that these models may or may not correspond to actual practice). This indeed seems to be one of the contrasts some contributors here sometimes have in mind, though the point is not always very explicitly spelt out. Gellner for example contrasts the mechanistic disenchanted outlook of the 'modern mind' with the personal and 'meaningful-cosy' view of 'the savage'. The ideal used to represent one's processes of thinking may indeed be of greater significance than Barnes would perhaps allow. It is true that, as Wolfram points out, one must distinguish between the accepted manner of justifying beliefs and their actual basis—the first by no means necessarily equals the second. Nevertheless, even when the ideal does not accord with actual practice, the model is likely to have some influence on behaviour; it will certainly affect the kinds of grounds which people tend to employ (whether validly or not) to justify their beliefs and their conclusions.

A number of the writers here have pointed to the mechanistic idiom which in one way or another seems to pervade many aspects of modern Western thought. How far this idiom—or this model—is in contrast to other comparable idioms and models in other places or at other periods is a topic well worth following up (some hints are given in certain essays here but the subject is not very fully or systematically explored). It may be that, in terms of actual procedures, actual modes of thinking will turn out to be far less different than are the ideal models of thinking prevalent in given societies, and that the comparative investigation of these models in their own right may be of great interest.

The original distinction between content and processes of thinking has, by now, become somewhat blurred. The aspects discussed so far tend to fall more on the side of 'processes', but it is difficult completely to exclude 'content'. However, there are some approaches which do imply much more focus on the actual content of thought in various societies. There is, understandably, little interest in compiling lists of beliefs as such, but the relationship of different beliefs (or thoughts or sets of symbols, etc.) to each other or to other social institutions is sometimes explored. Whiteley for instance treats of the relations between symbolic concepts and lexical sets in the realm of colour among the Gusii, and also raises the question of how these relate to social change. Horton and others point to the significance of the existence (or otherwise) of alternative beliefs in a given society as a crucial variable for the openness or closedness of belief-systems. Again the nature and interrelationships of beliefs may be connected with the extent of division of labour in particular societies, as discussed in Gellner and Barnes. The question of truth or falsity also comes in here, for in the last analysis it is to the actual content of thought, not the process of reaching a conclusion, that these criteria must be applied.

The aspect of 'content' can spill over into the more intangible and, as it were, adverbial aspects of thinking—what could be summed up (not very satisfactorily) as the quality of thought. This aspect is stressed in such questions as, for instance, Finnegan poses in her essay. Can non-literates think detachedly, critically, or with self-awareness? Do they, in particular, have the intellectual and artistic experience of literature—an experience which, we would normally accept, can both express and mould thought? Such a question—discussed both in Finnegan's essay and, by implication, in those by Nagashima and by Colby and Cole—is on the face of it at least relevant for considering modes of thought, and yet is not quite synonymous with either enquiries about thought *processes* proper or those about the *content* of thought. It clearly bears some relation to both these enquiries, but exactly what this relation is perhaps still remains to be explored.

Another problematical sphere is the question of *who* is pictured as doing the thinking when 'modes of thought' are being discussed. This again is sometimes a crucial factor when comparison and contrast are involved; for unless the variables remain the same any valid comparison is difficult. Is it individuals? societies? in some sense whole 'thought systems' (as Gellner, taking issue with Horton, suggests)? How far is it valid (as Barnes, for one, asks) to look at individual actors rather than social structure? This then is another point on which there are explicit and implicit divergences among a number of contributors here.

Another way of approaching the whole question of 'modes of thought' is to see this in the context of how people and societies (or, rather, people-in-societies) make sense of the world, structure the reality around them. This is an aspect touched on in a number of essays in one way or another (Colby and Cole, for instance, Barnes, Horton and Finnegan), and one which fits well with current interest in phenomenology and the sociology of knowledge. Looking at the problem from this point of view one may be impressed by how *all* societies (the people in them, that is) build up what has been termed their own 'social construction of reality'.[1] This is often defined in terms of meanings—meanings *to the people concerned*—rather than as something susceptible to the test of absolute 'objective truth'; for in this approach the whole concept of 'objective reality outside' tends to be denied.

This is one point at issue among some of the contributors here. Barnes, for one, is doubtful about the relevance of any idea of objective reality 'out there', and his approach would probably find some sympathy from at least some other contributors. Lukes on the other hand specifically rejects this and points to the dangers inherent in embracing epistemological or logical relativism and thus refusing to make cognitive judgements about people's beliefs. Horton and perhaps others too would ultimately fall in with this judgement.

Here then is yet another area of disagreement—not so much about the differences between potentially differing 'modes of thought' in themselves, but about the whole approach to and definition of what 'thought' is, and its relation to social perceptions and/or external reality. This whole question *need* not impinge on the problem of how, within this, different modes of thought are or are not differentiated in this or that respect—but, as the discussion in, for instance, Lukes, Barnes or Gellner indicates, it *may* do so. Questions of this kind, then,

---

[1] As it is termed in the book of that name by P. L. Berger and T. Luckmann, Allen Lane, London, 1967.

may need to be faced, if only to be finally rejected as irrelevant by some, as part of the wider framework of the basic problem treated in this volume.

Here again then, on the general problem of what exactly is meant by 'modes of thought', we end up with questions and a number of different possible strands rather than with firm conclusions. But pinpointing what questions to ask and the differences between them may be, after all, a mark of progress. Though not all would accept Colby and Cole's particular interpretation, it is easy to agree with one main point they make: that before we can try to construct any general theory of intellectual development we must sort out which cognitive skills we want to enquire about and compare.

> At the moment we are nowhere near the identification of evolutionary sequences; what we are nearing is a way in which we can specify the important kinds of cognitive structures and skills that different peoples possess.

(D) WHY ASK THE BASIC QUESTION?

A final theme must be noticed. This is what could be referred to as the *point* of drawing contrasts in modes of thought (or any other sphere) at all.

Obviously there are many answers to this in the usual terms of our desire for greater knowledge for its own sake or for the sake of better-informed action. But in this particular context, a further reason must be looked at. As is pointed out in several essays (for instance Gellner, Nagashima, Ita and Horton), one of the major motives in such contrasts is to help us recognize *ourselves*—the common process of defining something by contrasting it to its presumed opposite. In this process what sometimes happens is that 'the other' is seen as the mirror image of ourselves (the 'reversed world' as Nagashima calls it), the terms of this image often being derived not from actual enquiry but from introspection or wishful thinking about how we would ideally like to see ourselves; this mirror image of ourselves is then projected onto 'the other'. This process may be a complex and ambivalent one. Speaking of Japanese images of 'the other', for example, Nagashima speaks of 'the tendency among various peoples to regard other cultures as a reversed world to their own in terms of their value system. The Japanese image of the West is thus a mixture of Utopia and the world of witches, or of monsters of excessive rationality.'

Again, Ita shows clearly how one of the main motives in Frobenius's interpretation of various African modes of thought was his attempt to reassert 'German mysticism' against what he regarded as the French cultural domination of Germany; the contrasts he supposedly found within Africa were thus projections of his desire to define himself and his own national spirit as distinct from others.

This general process seems to be a common one. When the aim is obviously for literary or artistic purposes (some of Senghor's writings, say) rather than for scientific enquiry, this is one thing. As Horton points out, the Surrealists would probably be quite happy to admit to dreaming up most of their ideas about the non-Western world. But basing serious investigation on this sort of process is another matter. Horton speaks of the influence of this on scholarly and apparently well-based accounts of the matter. Even in some orthodox anthropological approaches, the 'lost world' or 'the other', 'being a world in which every frustrated yearning of the West is fulfilled and every malaise of the West banished, is inevitably defined as an inverted image of Western culture'. This kind of process does not just take place in supposed contrasts between 'ourselves' (in the sense of modern Westerners) and 'the primitive'. It also, as indicated earlier, applies to Japanese contrasts of themselves and Western Europe, or to the double contrasts which modern West African students sometimes draw between themselves and, on the one hand, 'modernized Europeans', on the other, 'our traditional ancestors'. Again, a recent book demonstrates the series of images held of 'Sparta' in different eras of Western thought, images which fluctuated and changed throughout many centuries according to the outlook and self-image of those doing the looking.[1] 'The other'—whatever it is—can all too readily become only the symbol of one's own hopes and desires expressed in an upside-down form.

This points to a possible ambiguity that one needs to be aware of in all attempts to tackle the central question of this volume. Instead of the surface and apparent sense of the question being treated, the question that is *really* being answered may be in fact 'Who are we?', 'How can we define ourselves?'. It is true that this is a perfectly proper enquiry and one on which other approaches to the central question

---

[1] E. Rawson, *The Spartan tradition in European thought*, Clarendon Press, Oxford, 1969.

may indeed throw much light. But it may be that in the last analysis a satisfying answer to it can only be found by laying aside the more speculative aspects of this enquiry and first analysing the problem and the evidence in a more matter-of-fact and open-minded way. Indeed, even in trying to understand *ourselves* it may be necessary—if Barnes is right about the misleading nature of our ideal model of rationalistic science as a guide to actual practice—to take a cool and critical look at our ideal image even of ourselves. It is one of the virtues of a number of the essays in this volume that, by showing how our perceptions are moulded by our assumptions about *ourselves*, they make us explicitly aware of the possible ambiguities and thus more able to make a more dispassionate analysis of both ourselves and others.

After this quick discussion of some of the themes in this volume (and some of the disagreements that emerge from them) we will pursue some of these points further in the following discussion of the relevance of Evans-Pritchard's writing to the basic question of this volume.

II. Evans-Pritchard and 'Modes of Thought'

Perhaps the most apt characterization of Evans-Pritchard's work is the one given by his student David Pocock, who points out that, in recent British social anthropology, he has been the real leader of the movement from concern with social function to concern with meaning.[1] Although Evans-Pritchard's *Witchcraft, oracles and magic among the Azande* and *Nuer religion* are obvious pioneers in this sphere, even the more apparently 'sociological' works like *The Nuer* and *Kinship and marriage among the Nuer* show the same cast of thought.[2] More than anyone else in Britain, Evans-Pritchard has brought scholars back to a realization that an adequate phenomenology of alien concepts, beliefs and cosmologies is the prerequisite to an adequate sociology of such things—the same realization that now, from another

---

[1] D. Pocock, *Social anthropology*, Sheed and Ward, London, 1961, pp. 72–83.
[2] E. E. Evans-Pritchard, *Witchcraft, oracles and magic among the Azande*, Clarendon Press, Oxford, 1937, (abbreviated as WOM); *Nuer religion*, Clarendon Press, Oxford, 1956 (abbreviated as NR); *The Nuer*, Clarendon Press, Oxford, 1940; *Kinship and marriage among the Nuer*, Clarendon Press, Oxford, 1951.

side, is being increasingly applied to the study of the familiar, in the work of the phenomenological sociologists.[1] Outstanding in the phenomenological tradition to which Evans-Pritchard himself has given rise are the works of various of his associates or pupils such as Lienhardt, Middleton and Douglas.[2] Most of the essays in the present collection follow on from this approach in their focus on the meaning of cultural phenomena, not to the exclusion of their sociology, but as an indispensable prelude to it.

(A) MEANING AND THE PROBLEM OF TRANSLATION

Evans-Pritchard's interest in the interpretation of alien concepts, beliefs and cosmologies led him early on in his career to an interest in the difficulties and complexities of the translation process. In shorter essays such as his 'Zande theology',[3] as well as in his major monographs, one is made constantly aware of translation as something problematic rather than as something to be taken for granted. And in the introduction to his later critical review of previous work in the field of 'primitive religions', he has some trenchant, if all too brief, comments on the nature of the problem.[4] Thus, on the one hand, he has repeatedly stressed the dangers of the forcible and unreflective imposition of one's own conceptual categories upon the alien conceptual material one is concerned to interpret.[5] Yet, on the other hand, he has several times stressed the analyst's need to be as fully as possible acquainted with the complete range of conceptual categories carried by his own culture if he is to perform adequately

---

[1] See, for instance, the concern with meaning in works of such writers as Howard S. Becker (see e.g. *Sociological work: method and substance*, Allen Lane, London, 1971); Alfred Schutz (*Collected papers*, Nijhoff, The Hague 1962–4); the younger British phenomenologists (e.g. S. Cohen (ed.), *Images of deviance*, Penguin, Harmondsworth, 1971); and the symbolic interactionists generally.

[2] J. Middleton, *Lugbara religion*, Oxford University Press, London, 1960; G. Lienhardt, *Divinity and experience: the religion of the Dinka*, Clarendon Press, Oxford, 1961; M. Douglas, *Purity and danger*, Routledge and Kegan Paul, London, 1966.

[3] In his *Essays in social anthropology*, Faber, London, 1962 (abbreviated as ESA).

[4] E. E. Evans-Pritchard, *Theories of primitive religion*, Clarendon Press, Oxford, 1965 (abbreviated as TPR).

[5] See for instance TPR, pp. 24, 43, 47, 108–9.

as a translator.[1] Yet again, he has drawn attention to the fact that, if translation is to be possible at all, there must be some minimal continuities between the conceptual apparatus of the ethnographer and that of his subjects.[2]

Though he himself has never gathered together and amplified his insights in this sphere into a full-scale essay on the problem of translation, the various hints he has thrown out in the course of his work have provided a tremendous stimulus both to philosophically minded anthropologists and sociologists and to anthropologically minded philosophers. Thanks largely to this stimulus, the philosophy of intercultural translation is now a fashionable and flourishing sub-discipline.[3]

Several of the essays in the present collection deal with various aspects of this problem. Finnegan, Horton and Tambiah draw attention to the dangers of using one's own categories to interpret foreign meanings—though they disagree as to where the dangers lie. Barnes, Horton and Tambiah point out the degree to which adequate translation depends on the range of concepts in his own culture which the translator is able to bring into play. Here again, there is considerable disagreement as to the deficiencies and strengths of scholars currently working in the field. Thus Barnes and Horton attribute inadequate interpretation of 'traditional' magico-religious thought to an inadequately informed notion of Western science, while Tambiah feels that Horton's use of scientific concepts for the translation of magico-religious ideas involves unjustified imposition of our own conceptual apparatus and that it is better to look to the category of 'performative

---

[1] For the thesis that the Western anthropologist's interpretation of a primitive religion often suffers from the fact that he is not equipped with the conceptual apparatus of the religion of his own culture, see TPR, p. 17. For a more general statement, see ESA, p. 61.

[2] ESA, p. 61; TPR, p. 87.

[3] See for instance, E. Gellner, 'Concepts and society', *Transactions of the Fifth World Congress of Sociology*, I, Washington D.C., 1962; E. Gellner, 'The new idealism', in I. Lakatos and A. Musgrave (eds.), *Problems in the philosophy of science*, North-Holland Publ. Co., Amsterdam, 1968; A. MacIntyre 'Is understanding religion compatible with believing?', in J. Hick (ed.), *Faith and the philosophers*, Macmillan, London, 1966; P. Winch, 'Understanding a primitive religion', in D. Z. Phillips (ed.), *Religion and understanding*, Blackwell, Oxford, 1967; S. Lukes, 'Some problems about rationality', *European Journal of Sociology*, 8, 1967; M. Hollis, 'The limits of irrationality', *European Journal of Sociology*, 8, 1967; M. Hollis, 'Reason and ritual', *Philosophy*, 42, 165, 1968.

33

utterances' for analysing both Western and 'traditional' thought-action.[1]

Though the disagreement is a profound one, what is perhaps more important is that both parties are drawing long-overdue attention to the fact that the most serious single source of misinterpretation of the concepts of alien cultures is inadequate mastery of the concepts of one's own culture. The essay by Lukes draws attention to the third main feature of the translation process: the fact that translation depends on the existence of certain minimum logical and conceptual continuities between the languages and thought-traditions involved. In particular, Lukes puts up a strong case for the view that certain basic criteria of truth and falsity are common to all human cultures and that the existence of such common criteria is a vital prerequisite to communication between cultures.

In these essays we can, albeit dimly, discern the emergence of some guiding principles. At the same time, there are strong disagreements as to what constitutes apt or inept application of these principles. Here, clearly, is something that needs a lot more thought.

(B) THE INFLUENCE OF IDEOLOGY ON INTERPRETING
MODES OF THOUGHT

Evans-Pritchard's awareness of the problems of translation has inevitably brought him hard up against the factor of ideological influence. More than any other anthropologist of his generation, he has insisted that 'theories purporting to explain the religious beliefs and practices of primitive peoples cannot adequately be appreciated without reference to the social milieu in which they were propounded.'[2]

Evans-Pritchard and his associates have been concerned, above all, with ideological influences on nineteenth-century writers such as Tylor and Frazer; and, thanks to them, we now have a full picture of the various subtle and not-so-subtle ways in which Victorian ideology competed with ethnographic data in determining the image of

---

[1] The distinction between statements and 'performative utterances' is worked out in detail in J. L. Austin, *How to do things with words*, Clarendon Press, Oxford, 1962.

[2] Preface to ESA, p. 10. For similar caveats by close associates of Evans-Pritchard see G. Lienhardt, *Social anthropology*, Oxford University Press, London, 1964 (especially chapter 7); P. Bohannan, *Social anthropology*, Holt, Rinehart and Winston, New York, 1963, p. 339.

Introduction

'primitive thought'.[1] Perhaps because this has been the consumingly real battle for their generation, Evans-Pritchard and his associates have given less attention to the influence of later ideological currents. In some of Evans-Pritchard's writings, it is true, the use of such epithets as 'savage' and 'primitive' would seem to be more than anything else a device 'pour épater les libéraux'.[2] And in Lienhardt's more programmatic work, we find warning remarks about the dangers both of sentimental liberalism and of romanticism.[3] On the whole, however, Evans-Pritchard and those most closely associated with him have left others to apply their characteristically watchful attitude to the newer trends in the sociology of thought. Ernest Gellner has been one of the first to take up this challenge. In his 'Concepts and society', we find a brief but searching examination of the influence of twentieth-century liberal ethos on the characterization of 'traditional thought'.[4]

Most of the essays in this collection show some degree of concern with the ideological problem. Finnegan, writing on oral literature, and Tambiah, writing on magic, feel that current interpretations of these phenomena are still bedevilled by traces of the ethnocentric arrogance so typical of nineteenth-century scholars. Barnes, Lukes, Gellner and Horton, on the other hand, see a sentimental liberalism as the current ideological enemy. Horton, in addition, points to the powerful distorting influence of that twentieth-century romanticism which is the obverse of disillusionment with modernity. He suggests that the current scholarly image of 'traditional' magico-religious thought is above all else the result of a projection onto non-Western societies of an essentially Western vision of a pre-industrial, pre-scientific 'lost paradise'. Ita, writing on Frobenius, shows that scholarly romanticism can take yet more complex forms. She shows how Frobenius, having first made the Germans the only remaining European guardians of the lost heritage of pre-modern thought, and the French the foremost destroyers of this heritage, goes on to attribute German romanticism to the indigenous 'Ethiopian' peoples of Africa, and French rationalism to the invading 'Hamites'. Self-styled

---

[1] 'Religion and the anthropologists', in ESA; chapters 1, 2, 5 in TRP.

[2] *Social anthropology*, Cohen and West, London, 1951 (abbreviated as SA); also TPR, *passim*.

[3] Lienhardt, op cit., 1964, ch. 7; also the remarks at the beginning of his 'Modes of thought', in E. Evans-Pritchard (ed.), *The institutions of primitive society*, Blackwell, Oxford, 1954.

[4] Gellner, op. cit., 1962.

'sober empiricists' may laugh at the antics of Frobenius; but these are no more than their own antics, presented in caricature.

These essays confirm what Gellner suggested in his 'Concepts and society': that the intensive fieldwork enjoined by the modern social-anthropological establishment is far from being the ideological purgative it is so often made out to be.[1] But if fieldwork won't do the trick, what will? Can we invoke the old Socratic slogan 'Know thyself?'. Alas, the psychoanalysts have shown us just how difficult this is. And as for 'Know thyself with the aid of psychoanalysis', who in his senses now trusts the psychoanalysts that far? Maybe there is no real solution. But perhaps the mere recognition that the problem of ideological influence is as acute in the twentieth century as it was in the nineteenth is at least a first step.

(C) EVANS-PRITCHARD, THE FRENCH MASTERS AND THE SOCIOLOGY OF THOUGHT

Evans-Pritchard has played a valuable part in keeping before British scholars the works of the great French philosopher-sociologists of the late nineteenth and early twentieth centuries—notably those of Lévy-Bruhl, Durkheim, Mauss and Hertz.[2] He has also followed up this advocacy by personal example. The work of Lévy-Bruhl and Durkheim, in particular, was an important stimulus for the writing of his two great studies of African world-views: *Witchcraft, oracles and magic among the Azande* and *Nuer religion*. All too often, these books are regarded purely and simply as triumphs of descriptive ethnography based on intensive participant observation. In fact, however, both are as much reports on field tests of the Masters' theories as they are descriptive monographs. Hence both are as

[1] The same could be said of the emphasis laid on prolonged participant observation by sociologists of a symbolic interactionist bent.

[2] See for instance his sponsorship of research on the intellectual biography of Durkheim by Steven Lukes and of a series of translations from the French (E. Durkheim, *Sociology and philosophy*, trans. by D. F. Pocock with an introduction by J. G. Peristiany, Cohen and West, London, 1953; M. Mauss, *The gift*, trans. by Ian Cunnison with an introduction by E. Evans-Pritchard, Cohen and West, London, 1954; R. Hertz, *Death and the right hand*, trans. by R. and C. Needham, with an introduction (including a glowing estimate of the *Année Sociologique* school) by E. Evans-Pritchard, Cohen and West, London, 1960; E. Durkheim and M. Mauss, *Primitive classification*, trans., edited, and with an introduction by R. Needham, Cohen and West, London, 1963; H. Hubert and M. Mauss, *Sacrifice*, trans. by W. D. Halls, with a foreword by E. Evans-Pritchard, Cohen and West, London, 1964).

pregnant with theoretical significance as are most of the inflated tomes of self-styled 'sociological theory'.

In the case of *Witchcraft, oracles and magic*, it is Lévy-Bruhl's early theory that is under test. Whilst writing up his material for this study of the Azande people of the Nile–Congo divide, Evans-Pritchard was clearly stimulated by the writings of his French predecessor. A long essay, written three years before the book was published, is devoted to a critical yet sympathetic analysis of Lévy-Bruhl's theories.[1] In the introduction to the book itself, Evans-Pritchard writes that he is going to abjure any discussion of the relevance of Zande data to more general anthropological theory, and refers those interested to a series of articles which includes his essay on Lévy-Bruhl. Yet many features of the book suggest that it is a response, at once appreciative and critical, to the stimulus of the latter's work.

On the appreciative side, Evans-Pritchard develops Lévy-Bruhl's insistence that people of other cultures believe the things they do believe first and foremost because they have been brought up to believe them—just as *we* believe most of the things we believe because *we* have been brought up to believe them. Evans-Pritchard also accepts and develops the related proposition that people of alien cultures think neither more nor less intelligently and efficiently than ourselves, but merely live out their lives in the light of different initial premises. Finally, he accepts Lévy-Bruhl's radical contrast between 'the empirical' (a category in which he lumps together both commonsense and science) and 'the mystical' (a category which includes all beliefs involving unobservable entities).[2]

There are also, however, a number of fundamental criticisms. First, Evans-Pritchard shows that Azande, and by implication other 'primitives', are not in a state of constant 'mystical orientation'. They spend much of their time at the level of commonsense, only moving to the level of the 'mystical' in those situations where commonsense fails to provide an adequate causal placing of some misfortune. Again, he shows that, when they do move to the 'mystical' level, the move is not accompanied by any special feelings of awe. There is no

---

[1] E. E. Evans-Pritchard, 'Lévy-Bruhl's theory of primitive mentality', *Bulletin of the Faculty of Arts*, Egyptian University (Cairo), 2, 1934.
[2] WOM, pp. 8–12.

trace of Lévy-Bruhl's *catégorie affective du surnaturel*, or, for that matter, of Otto's *mysterium tremendum et fascinosum*. The Zande 'does not become awe-struck at the play of supernatural forces. He is not terrified at the presence of an occult enemy. He is, on the other hand, extremely annoyed.'[1] The sense of awe and mystery has no place in the reaction, because what is at work is not one of Lévy-Bruhl's uncanny and unpredictable influences, but a force which operates along reasonably well-charted lines, and hence can be dealt with by following appropriate procedures. Yet again, he shows that, in their deployment both of witchcraft theory and of magical beliefs, Azande are not subject to a Lévy-Bruhlian *imperméabilité à l'expérience*. Though their 'mystical' beliefs involve predictions, and the predictions are frequently falsified, Azande do not just leave the matter there. Rather, they invoke other premisses of their belief-system to explain away the falsifications and so preserve the major premisses of the system intact.

Evans-Pritchard, then, shows that Azande, in deploying their 'mystical' beliefs, take as much account of experience as do modern Westerners. At the same time, there are some important differences. For whereas Azande seem to spend most of their time (albeit unconsciously) *defending* beliefs about the causes of sickness and misfortune *against* experience, Western medical scientists seem more ready to *expose* equivalent beliefs *to* the possibly destructive effects of experience.

In his characteristically unobtrusive way, Evans-Pritchard slips into his description some thought-provoking passages which sketch out a possible explanation of this very important difference. He says of Azande:

There is no incentive to agnosticism. All their beliefs hang together, and were a Zande to give up faith in witch-doctorhood, he would have to surrender equally his faith in witchcraft and oracles . . . In this web of belief, every strand depends upon every other strand, and a Zande cannot get out of its meshes because it is the only world he knows. The web is not an external structure in which he is enclosed. It is the texture of his thought and he cannot think that his thought is wrong.[2]

[1] WOM, pp. 64–5.
[2] WOM, p. 194.

And again, later on,

> And yet Azande do not see that their oracles tell them nothing!
> Their blindness is not due to stupidity, for they display great
> ingenuity in explaining away the failures and inequalities of the
> poison oracle and experimental keenness in testing it. It is due
> rather to the fact that their intellectual ingenuity and experimental
> keenness are conditioned by patterns of ritual behaviour and
> mystical belief. Within the limits set by these patterns, they show
> great intelligence, but it cannot operate beyond these limits. Or,
> to put it in another way: they reason excellently in the idiom of
> their beliefs, but they cannot reason outside, or against, their
> beliefs because they have no other idiom in which to express their
> thoughts.[1]

An additional clue as to the kind of explanation he is suggesting is
provided by a passage on 'closed' societies in his *Theories of primitive
religion*:

> Everyone has the same sort of religious beliefs and practices,
> and their generality, or collectivity, gives them an objectivity
> which places them over and above the psychological experience
> of any individual, or indeed of all individuals . . . Apart from
> positive and negative sanctions, the mere fact that religion is
> general means, again in a closed society, that it is obligatory, for
> even if there is no coercion, a man has no option but to accept
> what everybody gives assent to, because he has no choice, any
> more than of what language he speaks. Even were he to be a
> sceptic, he could express his doubts only in terms of the beliefs
> held by all around him. And had he been born into a different
> society, he would have had a different set of beliefs, just as he
> would have had a different language. It may here be noted that the
> interest shown by Durkheim and his colleagues in primitive
> societies may well have derived precisely from the fact that they are,
> or were, closed communities. Open societies, in which beliefs may
> not be transmitted and in which they are diversified, and therefore
> less obligatory, are less amenable to sociological interpretations on
> the lines pursued by them.[2]

Here, it is evident, we have the raw materials for a general theory
of 'closure' and 'openness', with unawareness of alternative conceptual

[1] WOM, pp. 337–8.
[2] TPR, p. 55.

possibilities as the basic factor in 'closure', and a developed awareness of alternative possibilities as the basic factor in 'openness'.

Even from the hasty and superficial sketch we have given here, it will be clear that, only a little way beneath the surface of descriptive ethnography, there lies a fund of general ideas relating to the phenomenology and the sociology of belief. Precisely because these ideas lie a little buried, and have not been put into a balloon, puffed up with a lot of air, and floated into the academic skies with a large label attached, they have received nothing like the attention they deserve. Rather, *Witchcraft, oracles and magic* has stimulated a large number of intensively researched, detailed monographic studies in the sociology of witchcraft and sorcery—studies which, for all their worth, have not done justice to the depth and breadth of its underlying themes.[1]

During the last fifteen years, however, things have begun to change, for the book has begun to circulate outside the narrow circle of the social anthropologists. As we said earlier, the philosophers have taken it up as providing rich material for a discussion of how the anthropologist translates and finds meaning in ideas whose validity he denies and whose very sense he may not find immediately apparent.[2] Again, the philosophers and sociologists of science have begun to find in it a source of inspiration. Thus Michael Polanyi, in his *Personal knowledge*, uses Evans-Pritchard's descriptions and insights for a thorough-going critique of Lévy-Bruhl's position. He not only argues with great cogency that African doctrines about supra-sensible entities have much the same logical structure as Western scientific doctrines about theoretical entities, but even uses Zande data to throw light on the relation of theory to experience in the sciences.[3] Polanyi's thesis gains authority from the fact that, before turning to the philosophy, psychology and sociology of science, he was a successful physical chemist. Though some would say that he depicts science and scientists in an unfortunately conservative mood, his writing has been one of the sources of inspiration for the influential work of

---

[1] On this, see Mary Douglas's thoughtful and appreciative introduction to M. Douglas (ed.), *Witchcraft confessions and accusations*, Tavistock, London, 1970.
[2] Many of the authors cited in note 3 on p. 33 make specific use of material drawn from WOM.
[3] M. Polanyi, *Personal knowledge*, University of Chicago Press, Chicago, 1958, pp. 286–94.

Introduction

Ziman and, above all, of Thomas Kuhn.[1] More recently, Barry Barnes, another scientist turned philosopher/sociologist of science, has also made effective use of the Zande material to draw attention to continuities between 'mystical' and scientific theories. He insists that, in the modern West as in traditional Africa, theories relating to the central concerns of a society are carefully defended against refractory experience by a web of secondary elaborations. Even in the sciences, there are more of such defences than is commonly supposed; and where scientists consistently manage to break through them, this is largely in areas of experience which impinge but lightly on the central concerns of the society involved.[2]

So much for continuities between pre-scientific and science-oriented thought. Evans-Pritchard's remarks on the nature of 'closure' and 'openness' have also begun to stimulate further reflections on the basic differences between the two streams of thought sometimes called 'pre-scientific' and 'science-oriented', and on the consequences of such differences.

The philosopher Alasdair MacIntyre, for example, has proposed a threefold typology in an important essay on the relation of ideas to behaviour: (1) Closed Societies, of which he takes the Azande as his example; (2) Open Societies, amongst which he would appear to count at least some of the Western nations; and (3) Open Societies whose leaders are trying to force them back into the closed predicament, of which he takes the Soviet Union under Stalin as his example.[3] Though MacIntyre cites Bergson and Popper as originators of the concepts of 'closure' and 'openness', many features of this seminal essay suggest the influence of Evans-Pritchard. There is the use of Azande as the prime example of the closed society, and the comparison between closure in Zandeland and attempted closure in the Soviet Union.[4] There is also the stress on alternative possibilities of explanation as crucial to the transition from the closed to the open predicament.[5]

---

[1] T. Kuhn, *The structure of scientific revolutions*, University of Chicago Press, Chicago, 1962; J. Ziman *Public knowledge: the social dimension of science*, University Press, Cambridge, 1968.

[2] S. Barnes, 'Paradigms—scientific and social', *Man*, N.S., 4, 1969.

[3] A. MacIntyre, 'A mistake about causality in social science', in P. Laslett and W. Runciman (eds.), *Philosophy, politics and society* (second series), Blackwell, Oxford, 1967.

[4] See the remark at the end of SA.

[5] See WOM, pp. 194, 338.

Introduction

Horton has attempted to co-ordinate Evans-Pritchard's insights in this sphere with both the ideas of his pupil Mary Douglas and the independently developed ideas of Mircea Eliade.[1] He takes Evans-Pritchard's presentation of the relation between Zande beliefs and experience as applicable to closed cosmologies generally, and he goes on to suggest that the bearers of such cosmologies attempt to defend them against recalcitrant reality, not only by secondary elaboration (the means stressed in *Witchcraft, oracles and magic*), but also by taboo reactions, and by rituals designed to annul the passage of time and the occurrence of non-repetitive change. Indeed, he regards the three phenomena as complementary defence-mechanisms. Like MacIntyre, he follows Evans-Pritchard in stressing the awareness of alternative possibilities of explanation as crucial to the transition from the closed to the open predicament; and he tries to suggest some of the social circumstances in which this awareness is likely to emerge.

From *Witchcraft, oracles and magic*, let us turn to *Nuer religion*. Here again, we have a monograph which, though overtly merely descriptive of the ideas and actions of this by now well-known pastoral people of the southern Sudan, nonetheless conceals within its pages both a report on field tests of established theories and a number of suggestions for the formulation of new theories. *Nuer religion* is concerned with the theories both of Lévy-Bruhl and of Durkheim.

Earlier it was Lévy-Bruhl's conception of the relation of the empirical to the 'mystical' that was being examined. In *Nuer religion*, the scrutiny is transferred to Lévy-Bruhl's idea of 'participation'. The essence of this idea is that, whereas the empirically oriented Western observer sees most things as clear-cut, distinct objects, the 'mystically oriented' observer sees most things as at once themselves and as things which to the empirical eye seem quite different. Trees are seen as spirits and spirits as trees, men are seen as cockatoos and cockatoos as men, Bororos as araras and araras as Bororos.[2] Now, as Evans-Pritchard shows, the Nuer copula *e* can be translated without too much

---

[1] R. Horton, 'African traditional thought and Western science', *Africa*, 37, 2, 1967; Douglas, op. cit., 1966; M. Eliade, *The myth of the eternal return*, Pantheon Books, New York, 1954.

[2] For the theory of 'participation', see L. Lévy-Bruhl, *Les fonctions mentales dans les sociétés inférieures*, Presses Universitaires de France, Paris, 1951, pp. 68–110.

distortion by the English 'is'; and if this translation equivalence is accepted, there are many occasions on which Nuer appear to be subject to 'participation'—i.e. to be asserting that a thing is at once itself and something quite different from itself. However, the situation here is both more complex and more subtle than Lévy-Bruhl would allow.[1]

In some cases, 'is' has a simple metaphorical significance: 'X is Y' is shorthand for 'X (in virtue of direct resemblance) is symbolic of Y.' In other cases 'is' has a more complex metaphorical significance: 'X is Y' is shorthand for 'X (because it stands in the same relation as Y to a third term Z) is symbolic of Y.' Thus, in ritual contexts, a cucumber 'is' an ox, because both are equivalent as offerings in the eyes of God. Again, twins 'are' birds, because both stand in relations of special closeness to God.

In addition to these largely metophorical senses of 'is', there are others which imply more substantial identifications. Thus heavy, unseasonal rain 'is' Unitary Spirit in a sense which requires no further qualifications; crocodiles 'are' a particular clan spirit; various air-spirits 'are' Unitary Spirit. However, although these identities are substantial rather than metaphorical, they are nonetheless asymmetrical. Thus whilst rain 'is' Unitary Spirit, Unitary Spirit is not rain; whilst crocodiles 'are' a particular clan spirit, the clan spirit is not crocodiles; and whilst the various air-spirits 'are' Unitary Spirit, Unitary Spirit is not the various air-spirits.

In Evans-Pritchard's view, the Nuer situation casts considerable doubt on the validity of Lévy-Bruhl's thesis of the omnipresence of 'participations' in primitive world-views. First, a good many of the cases he examines are of metaphorical rather than substantial identity. Secondly, where an element of substantial identity does enter in, such identity is always asymmetrical. Since Lévy-Bruhlian 'participation' implies identity which is both substantial and symmetrical, it would appear to be absent from the Nuer scene.

In showing the subtlety and diversity of the logical relations involved, this work on identifications in Nuer religious thought has been a valuable stimulus to the study of traditional thought-systems generally. It has whetted the appetite of a number of scholars who might otherwise have been discouraged by the deceptively simple

---

[1] The discussion summarized in the next few paragraphs is to be found in NR, ch. 5: 'The problem of symbols'.

outward façade presented by many traditional cultures. It has also given rise to a lively debate which, while still largely confined to the ranks of the anthropologists, has related it to broader themes in the comparative study of thought-systems: as witness references in Lévi-Strauss's *LeTotemisme aujourd'hui*,[1] and a spate of articles and correspondence in *Man*.[2] For some, Evans-Pritchard has failed to disentangle the full intellectual ramifications that lie behind such statements as 'twins are birds.'[3] For others, he has overplayed the intellectual element and undervalued the emotional.[4] Indeed, the whole debate seems to be broadening out into a renewal of early twentieth-century discussions on the respective contributions of intellect and emotion to the life of ideas in society. Since, as Evans-Pritchard himself has pointed out,[5] the earlier discussions petered out more because fashions changed than because any satisfactory conclusions were reached, this renewal may well be a healthy development.

Before leaving this aspect of Evans-Pritchard's work, it seems worth pointing out that, in his use of Nuer data to cast doubt on the validity of Lévy-Bruhl's theory of 'participation', he is not entirely convincing. For to establish that all substantial identifications are also asymmetrical is not to dispose of Lévy-Bruhl's original problem of how, in certain situations, people can see a thing as at once itself and something other.

However, as Durkheim noticed, this is not a problem peculiar to 'primitive' societies. It crops up indeed at the heart of the sciences.[6] Thus, for the modern physicist, tables are at once their familiar solid selves, and segments of a vast, largely empty void, populated nonetheless with countless infinitesimal planetary systems. Lévy-Bruhl, as a strict positivist, was intellectually tortured by this problem when he

[1] Presses Universitaires de France, Paris, 1962, pp. 112–19.
[2] R. Firth 'Twins, birds and vegetables', *Man*, N.S., 1, 1, 1966, and correspondence in *Man*, N.S., 1, 4, 1966 and 2, 1, 1967; J. Buxton, 'Animal identity and human peril: some Mandari images', *Man*, N.S., 3, 1968; A. Hayley, 'Symbolic equations: the ox and the cucumber', *Man*, N.S., 3, 1968; and correspondence in *Man*, N.S., 3, 4, 1968; G. B. Milner, 'Siamese twins, birds and the double helix', *Man*, N.S., 4, 1969; and Richard Thorn, Roberto de Matta, 'Intuitional, emotional and intellectual explanation' (correspondence), *Man*, N.S., 4, 3, 1969.
[3] See Lévi-Strauss, op. cit., 1962.
[4] Firth, op. cit., 1966; Hayley, op. cit., 1968.
[5] SA, pp. 44–5; TPR, ch. 2: 'Psychological theories'.
[6] Durkheim, op. cit., 1957, pp. 234–9.

Introduction

encountered it in 'primitive' societies; but since he felt that the latter were an appropriate venue for the encounter, he dilated on the ubiquity of the problem in this context in a whole series of volumes. Many of the positivist philosophers of science were equally tortured when they saw the same problem at the heart of the sciences. In this case, since such an abomination had no place to be poking its ugly face out from the very centre of rational activity, they disposed of it by creating an unreal picture of the sciences in which there were only tables but no atoms. But this and other attempts to dispose of the problem created as many fresh puzzles as they solved. In the final analysis, it seems likely that we may simply have to accept certain Lévy-Bruhlian paradoxes even at the heart of the sciences; e.g. 'Where X is an explanandum, it is both X and not-X'.[1]

With respect to this problem, we look forward to seeing philosophers, phenomenologists and sociologists of science making the same use of *Nuer religion* as some of them have already made of *Witchcraft, oracles and magic*.

As a test report on Durkheimian theory, *Nuer religion* is mainly concerned with the thesis that the idea of God (or in this case, Spirit) is a product of the impact of society on the individual, and that it is nothing more or less than a symbol of society.[2]

At various points in the book, Evans-Pritchard argues fairly convincingly that Durkheim's thesis simply does not do justice to the facts. In the Nuer case, indeed, he makes us feel closest to the heart of the religion when we are dealing with its personal rather than its collective aspect. And when pressed to explain the importance of the idea of spirit in Nuer life, he seems to imply that such an explanation requires the theological premiss of God's existence and of his ability to make himself directly known to individual men. This, at any rate, is surely the message of the last page of the book.

But if we have to invoke theology to account for the presence of the essential features of the idea of Spirit, Durkheimian sociology has much to tell us about its more accidental features. As Evans-Pritchard

---

[1] On this, see R. Horton, 'Lévy-Bruhl among the scientists', *Second Order*, 2, 1, 1973.
[2] Although the exegesis of Durkheim's sociology of religion in NR scarcely does justice to the subtlety of the original, it certainly represents the orthodox social-anthropological view of what Durkheim was about.

45

puts it, the idea of Spirit is 'broken up by the refracting surfaces of nature, of society, of culture, and of historical experience'.[1]

Whilst we may question whether it is legitimate, in a study as opposed to an advocacy of a particular religious system, to mark off a preserve of theology and allow sociology free play only outside that preserve, we are nonetheless compelled to admire such use of sociology as has been made; and in what follows it is certain aspects of Evans-Pritchard's neo-Durkheimian approach upon which we shall concentrate.

Perhaps the outstanding contribution of *Nuer religion* as a phenomenological-cum-sociological study is its demonstration that there is neither contradiction nor incoherence in the co-presence, within a single world-view, of a supreme being and a multitude of lesser spirits. Up until the time of writing of this monograph, ideas of a supreme being and ideas of lesser spirits appeared to most comparative religionists either as downright incompatible or as mutually irrelevant. Thus, whenever a given religious system was found with both sets of ideas, it seemed natural to assume that one must be on the way out and the other on the way in. Not surprisingly, there was much debate as to which of the two sets enjoyed historical priority. In the absence of adequate sources, the debate was a futile one; but this did not detract from its appeal.

Nuer religion shows that further debate on this issue is unnecessary, for the categories of supreme being and lesser spirits emerge as complementary aspects of a single cosmological system. The concept of the supreme being comes into play when a person is considering his problems in relation to the total human community or to the world as a whole. Concepts of lesser spirits come into play when a person is considering his problems in relation to more limited social groups or to more restricted areas of experience. As Evans-Pritchard puts it: 'It is a question of the level, or situation, of thought rather than of exclusive types of thought.'[2]

Following Evans-Pritchard's lead, Lienhardt has made a similar analysis of the relation between supreme being and lesser spirits in his *Divinity and experience* (an analysis of the religion of the Dinka, also of the southern Sudan).[3] He adds a significant extra dimension. Like

---

[1] NR, p. 121.
[2] NR, p. 316.
[3] Lienhardt, op. cit., 1961.

46

Introduction

Evans-Pritchard, he shows how the total human community and the world as a whole are seen as underpinned by the supreme being, whilst more limited areas of social relations and experience are seen as underpinned by various lesser spirits. But he goes on to point out an interesting corollary: for Dinka, any marked increase in the importance of the wider world must be associated with a marked increase in emphasis on the supreme being. For example, the great Dinka prophet Arianhdit, who established an area of order which transcended the boundaries of Dinkaland, is thought of by the Dinka as being directly inspired by the supreme being. Similar emphasis on the supreme being has also been recorded elsewhere in a context of claimed spiritual sovereignty over a number of small independent polities each emphasizing a number of lesser spirits—for example the dominance of the Aro-Chukwu oracle in pre-colonial Iboland in West Africa.[1]

Such moves toward greater emphasis on the supreme being, occurring in situations either prior to or outside the range of Muslim and Christian proselytizing, open up fascinating possibilities for an understanding of the so-called 'conversion' of pagan peoples to these two great monotheistic religions. 'Conversion' has long been a puzzle for historians, for anthropologists, and, most of all, for missiologists. In the light of the analyses by Evans-Pritchard and his associates and of the instances of movement toward the supreme being before direct influence by Islam and Christianity, it becomes less mysterious. The move toward a more monotheistic religion can be seen as an inherent possibility of the pre-existing system, actualizable in specific social and political circumstances. Islam and Christianity are catalysts, hastening reactions all of whose necessary ingredients were already 'in the air'. Indeed, the horde of scholars now concerning themselves with the impact of the world religions on Africa and elsewhere might do well to start their reflections, not with the Koran and the Bible, but with *Nuer religion* and *Divinity and experience*; not with Ibn Yasin and Bishop Crowther, but with Arianhdit and the Aro Chukwu oracle operators.

Several essays in this book draw their inspiration from the vivid confrontation of theory with monographic description which gives both

[1] C. K. Meek, *Law and authority in a Nigerian tribe*, Oxford University Press, London, 1937, esp. p. 20 and chap. 2 generally. See also D. Forde and G. I. Jones, *The Ibo and Ibibio-speaking peoples of south-eastern Nigeria*, International African Institute, London, 1962, and unpublished work by Felicia Ekejiuba.

Introduction

Witchcraft, oracles and magic and *Nuer religion* their bite. This is particularly true of the essays which deal with the question of continuity between the 'mystical' and the 'empirical-scientific'.

The theoretical base-line of these essays varies from writer to writer; but the influence of Lévy-Bruhl and Durkheim is much in evidence. Horton argues that Lévy-Bruhl's emphasis on contrast has received far too much attention, whilst Durkheim's stress on continuity, which foreshadows some of the most striking new developments in the history of ideas and the philosophy of science, has suffered an astonishing neglect. Both Barnes and Lukes also draw attention to this strand of Durkheim's thought. Like Horton, Barnes puts the neglect down to the near-illiteracy of many anthropologists and sociologists when it comes to questions concerning the nature of the scientific outlook. As against these neo-Durkheimians, Tambiah implicitly follows Lévy-Bruhl in stressing the radical incommensurability of the 'mystical' and the 'empirical-scientific'.

Both parties to the debate draw with equal enthusiasm upon the ethnographic riches of *Witchcraft, oracles and magic*. Close inspection, however, shows that they draw on rather different selections of the data. Thus Barnes and Horton, in arguing the Durkheimian thesis of continuity, draw upon Evans-Pritchard's presentation of Zande ideas about supra-sensible entities—while Tambiah, in arguing the Lévy-Bruhlian thesis of radical incommensurability, draws upon his presentation of Zande ideas about magical formulae and symbols. Is there a clue here as to how the two parties may be reconciled? Perhaps with ideas about supra-sensible entities (religion), continuity really is more significant than contrast; whilst with the creative power of words and symbols (magic), contrast may be more significant than continuity. If this is true, the appropriate preliminary to a new synthesis must be an agreement to unscramble, at least for the time being, the unitary category of the 'mystical' or the 'magico-religious', and to see how far one can get by analysing its components separately.

In putting forward this view, we are in fact following Evans-Pritchard; for whereas the general tendency of recent theorizing on these matters has been to try to kill two birds with one stone,[1] he has

---

[1] For two recent examples, see J. Beattie, *Other cultures*, Cohen and West, London, 1964, chs. 12 and 13; Douglas, op. cit., 1966, ch. 5.

several times made quiet suggestions to the effect that the birds might be more easily picked off one at a time.[1]

Two essays, those by Gellner and Barnes, take as their starting point Evans-Pritchard's remarks on 'closure' and 'openness' in *Witchcraft, oracles and magic*, and Horton's attempt to develop them further. Both writers accept much of Evans-Pritchard's characterization of the 'closed' predicament. Both accept that there are important differences between the general predicament of the thinker in a 'closed', tradition-oriented culture and that of his counterpart in an 'open', science-oriented culture. Both, however, are critical of the stress upon development of an awareness of alternative explanatory possibilities as crucial to the transition from the 'closed' to the 'open' —Gellner because he is able to cite various social situations in which awareness of explanatory alternatives does not give rise to 'open', critical, or science-oriented thinking; Barnes because he holds that features likely to promote such awareness are not typically part of the environment in which scientists work.

Both writers, in their search for other possible concomitants of the rise of the scientific outlook, have turned to a variable which greatly interested Durkheim—'division of labour' or, in more contemporary language, role specialization and the institutional differentiation which is its concomitant. In his famous book on the subject, Durkheim touches briefly on the connection between increasing role specialization and changes in the realm of thought and belief.[2] It is true that he soon passes on to other things, and that, in his later works on the sociology of thought and belief, he gives very little further consideration to these connections.[3] Gellner and Barnes, however, show that Durkheim's half-developed suggestion can be pushed a good deal further.

---

[1] For more or less explicit remarks on this subject, see NR, pp. viii, 176; TPR, pp. 3, 33, 113.

[2] E. Durkheim, *The division of labour*, trans. George Simpson, Free Press, Glencoe, Illinois, 1960, pp. 168–73, 283–303. For Durkheim, the relation between the change from mechanical to organic solidarity and the 'weakening of the common conscience' seems to have been rather complex. Thus in the earlier part of the book, he talks of the 'weakening of the common conscience' as an *effect* of declining mechanical solidarity; whereas in the later part of the book, he talks about it as a contributory *cause* of growing organic solidarity.

[3] He says almost nothing about the relation of social to ideational change in *Elementary forms of the religious life*.

Introduction

Gellner sees a direct connection between increasing role specialization and the development of 'open', science-oriented thinking. He points out that, as particular roles and institutions become more closely associated with particular ends, the idea gains ground that activity devoted to one end, if it is to achieve its purposes with any degree of efficiency, must not be allowed to be diverted to the service of other ends. From here, it is a short step to the idea that activity devoted to the end of explanation can only be successful if it is kept insulated from other ends and desires. To put it in a nutshell, increasing role specialization gives birth to the ideal of efficiency, and the ideal of efficiency leads inevitably to the ideal of objectivity.

Barnes sees increasing role specialization and institutional differentiation as having multiple effects upon readiness to abandon established beliefs. Thus, to take one example, people have only partial identification with the more specialized roles, and hence only partial involvement in their associated beliefs. Again, during the course of role specialization, particular roles get associated with particular tracts of belief; hence, as specialization advances, the belief-system gets more and more fragmented. In these circumstances, abandonment of one fragment has few if any implications for the remainder; and pressures for the maintenance of the explanatory status quo are therefore relatively light.

These suggestions, however, need not necessarily imply outright rejection of Evans-Pritchard's intuition as to the importance of the development of an awareness of explanatory alternatives in the transition from the 'closed' to the 'open' predicament. Indeed, one factor which may contribute to 'open' thinking through the inculcation of awareness of explanatory alternatives is that very role specialization which so intrigues Gellner and Barnes. Where such specialization is strongly developed, each role is associated with a particular area of 'expert' knowledge and belief. At the same time, the player of the role is influenced by this knowledge and belief in his construction of a theory of the world as a whole. Hence different members of a single society come to hold, and to be aware of each other as holding, a series of only partially overlapping world-views. That we all recognize this situation is shown by our use of such phrases as 'a gardener's view of the world', 'an engineer's view of the world', or 'an accountant's view of the world'. Once more, the result is a tendency toward relativism and scepticism.

Introduction

Finally, when considering Barnes's view that awareness of explanatory alternatives is not a significant factor in the intellectual environment of the scientist, we should see this in the context of his explicit commitment to the views of Thomas Kuhn.[1] Kuhn has captured the imagination of the wider Western intellectual public in a way that no philosopher/sociologist/historian of science has succeeded in doing for several decades, but his views are also being strongly challenged by other philosophically qualified colleagues who share his knowledge of the recent history of the natural sciences. Lakatos and Feyerabend,[2] for example, claim that he has made a mistake in characterizing the history of the natural sciences as a one-at-a-time succession of monolithic 'paradigms'.

Proliferation [of theories] does not start with a revolution; it precedes it. A little imagination and a little more historical research then shows that proliferation not only immediately precedes revolutions, but that it is there all the time. Science as we know it is not a temporal succession of normal periods and of periods of proliferation; it is their juxtaposition.[3]

The debate, then, is still very much open; and a great deal more 'fieldwork' on science and scientists will have to be done before any worthwhile conclusion is reached. Such 'fieldwork' will need all the modern social scientist's determination to record both the ideal and the actual, and to cut through the first to get at the second. For, as Gellner shows in his essay, the actual practice of science is surrounded by myths which, though they bear virtually no relation to what actually goes on, nevertheless wax exceeding strong because they serve to defend science and scientists against the still-present threat from pre-scientific attitudes and interests.[4]

---

[1] Kuhn, op. cit., 1962 and 'The function of dogma in scientific research', in A. Crombie (ed.), *Scientific change*, Heinemann, London, 1963.

[2] I. Lakatos, 'Falsification and the methodology of scientific research programmes', and P. Feyerabend, 'Consolations for the specialist', both in I. Lakatos and A. Musgrave (eds.), *Criticism and the growth of knowledge*, University Press, Cambridge, 1970.

[3] Feyerabend, op. cit., p. 212.

[4] In the context of the present collection, it is interesting that he singles out for special mention the 'empiricist' (or positivist) myth which both Barnes and Horton indict as a major source of confusion in the sociology of ideas.

Introduction

(D) THE STUDY OF THOUGHT AND MEANING
THROUGH ORAL LITERATURE

Evans-Pritchard's early interest in the world-views of African cultures led him, fairly naturally, to an interest in the oral literatures of these cultures. In this respect, he was, for some time at any rate, curiously alone amongst his anthropological colleagues. Indeed, during the heyday of British anthropological enterprise in Africa (say from the 1930s to the 1960s), the massive output of detailed fieldwork monographs included very little information indeed on oral literature and its background. The reason seems to have been the difficulty of integrating literature into the structural-functional framework of the times. The over-riding interest of those who adhered to this framework was in the contribution that various cultural phenomena made to the harmony and integration of society. Apart from a few obvious 'mythical charters', oral literary phenomena ranked rather low on this scale of evaluation, and excited correspondingly little interest.[1] Given this background, Evans-Pritchard's position becomes less puzzling. Since he soon came to stand aloof from the structural-functional establishment, stressing 'meaning' as opposed to 'social function', the low contribution of oral literary phenomena to the harmonious running of society was no deterrent to his interest. Rather, since such phenomena were at least as meaningful as any other aspects of culture, and since they were clearly adjuncts of those world-views and modes of thought which interested him so deeply, they were obviously high on the list of research priorities.

Evans-Pritchard has contributed to the revival of interest in African oral literature at several levels. Thus, he has taken a leading part in launching the Oxford Library of African Literature—a series that has already done much to transform the outside world's conception of the scope and richness of Africa's oral prose, poetry and song. Again, in his own department at Oxford, he has sponsored a considerable body of research in this field. Finally, he has published his own specific contribution with *The Zande trickster*—a collection of Azande stories about a trickster named Ture.[2]

---

[1] On this, see R. Finnegan, *Oral literature in Africa*, Clarendon Press, Oxford, 1970, chs. 2 and 12.

[2] E. E. Evans-Pritchard, *The Zande trickster*, Clarendon Press, Oxford, 1967 (abbreviated as ZT).

Introduction

In the introduction to this book, Evans-Pritchard puts forward his interpretative suggestions in a nonchalant, almost lighthearted way. He poses a large number of questions about the trickster tales, answers some, and leaves others open. His questions and answers, though they relate to Zande material, should be of interest to scholars of oral literature generally.

The first question concerns the reality-status of Ture and his tales. Evans-Pritchard finds this one difficult to answer in an entirely clear-cut fashion. On the one hand, Azande often talk about Ture as a being who lived in their country a long time ago and who, having been abducted by the white men, showed them how to make their machines. Again, since these stories are first told to children at an age when they tend not to keep fact and fancy apart, their grip on the adult imagination consequently tends to be very strong. On the other hand, Azande are obviously not very serious about the reality claims they make for Ture, and consideration of the context in which his tales are told makes it clear that he is an essentially fictional character. He may perhaps be compared with those heroes of European fiction who gain a grip on the imagination of a whole society, like Sherlock Holmes (or, in our own times, James Bond).

In his discussion of Ture's reality-status, Evans-Pritchard warns his readers against attributing cosmological or 'mythical' significance to those of the tales which describe Ture's introduction of items of culture to mankind. He points out that, if we look at these tales in context, they turn out to be associated with the same attitudes as those associated with more obviously lighthearted tales, whilst 'introduction of culture' turns out to be just one stock plot among many.

This warning is a timely one for students of 'traditional' thought generally. Of recent years, there has been a tendency, for instance, to take all African narratives relating to creation or introduction of culture as 'creation myths', and to draw ponderous conclusions from them about the nature of African cosmological thought. Our own experience in other parts of Africa agrees with Evans-Pritchard's conclusion that, given a rudimentary knowledge of context, many such 'creation myths' turn out to have a much slighter significance.[1]

---

[1] Thus, amongst the Limba of Sierra Leone, narratives featuring the supreme being and various aspects of his creation differ little in their significance from lighthearted stories featuring animals and men (R. Finnegan, *Limba stories and*

Introduction

Evans-Pritchard also has some interesting things to say on the subject of whether Azande see Ture, whose name means Spider, as an animal or as a person. He says that considerations of gender and context indicate that they see him as thinking and acting like a person. As for his animal guise, he has a passage which may be pondered by students of this kind of tale all over the world:

> The animals act and talk like persons because people are animals behind the masks social convention makes them wear. What Ture does is the opposite of all that is moral; and it is all of us who are Ture. He is really ourselves. Behind the image convention bids us present, in desire, in feeling, in imagination, and beneath the layer of consciousness we act as Ture does.[1]

Though tantalizingly brief, the introduction to *The Zande trickster* suggests how rewarding a really context-conscious study of African oral literature could be. This would be a welcome counterweight to continental structuralism, which appears to rely very largely on internal as opposed to contextual criteria in assessing the 'meaning' or 'message' of oral narrative.

Two essays in the present collection are devoted to the topic of oral literature: one by Finnegan and one by Colby and Cole.

Finnegan's essay is very much in the spirit of the Oxford Library of African Literature: a plea for recognition that a lack of the written word does not mean a lack of literature. She discusses various differences in the artist-audience relationship as between oral and written contexts, but maintains that such differences are not as important as the many continuities between oral and written literature in terms of subtlety, scope for insight and individual creativity. She concludes that the development of literacy probably does not have the fundamental effects on broad patterns of thinking that it is often claimed to have.[2]

---

story-telling, Clarendon Press, Oxford, 1967, pp. 34–6). Amongst the Kalabari of Nigeria, there is a fairly clear distinction between *pakaye* ('history') and *oloko* ('stories'), but although narrative relating to the ancestors and to the hero gods and goddesses is almost invariably classified as *pakaye*, narrative relating to the supreme being is most usually classified as *oloko*. (Horton, unpublished field notes.) See also Finnegan, op. cit., 1970, pp. 361 ff.

[1] ZT, p. 30.

[2] As for instance, by Jack Goody and Ian Watt in their 'The consequences of literacy', *Comparative Studies in Society and History*, 5, 3, 1963.

54

Introduction

The essay by Colby and Cole bears, on the face of it, little relationship to that by Finnegan. The authors report the results of psychological experiments, and focus on differences rather than on continuities. Yet their essay is an excellent example of what can be achieved by following the thorough exploration of context so often insisted on by Finnegan.[1] Indeed, it suggests that plodding Anglo-Saxon empiricism, though it may seem dull by comparison with the pyrotechnic displays of Gallic structuralism, may nonetheless sometimes take us nearer the heart of things.

Colby and Cole report pioneering work in the cross-cultural study of memory mechanisms. Preliminary indications are that modes of recall differ as between oral and literate cultures, and that the differences may well be the result of adaptation of brain and behaviour to the difference in the nature of the material that has to be memorized in the two situations. They further suggest that, in oral cultures, adaptation to the need for recall of long tracts of narrative has given rise to special mechanisms which manifest themselves in an elaborate patterning of the material.

The relevance of this suggestion to an evaluation of structuralism is not far to seek. The average Anglo-Saxon who is out to 'make sense of' or 'understand' a myth comes away from Lévi-Strauss's analyses both frustrated and mystified. There is a pointlessness and a triviality about the results that makes him want to shout: 'So what?'[2] If he is the self-critical type, he is likely to remind himself that he may be dealing with cultural difference in what counts as a satisfying explanation, and to retire into a state of suspended judgement. We believe, however, that there is perhaps something more to the seeming inanity of the whole exercise than the limitations of the Anglo-Saxon imagination.

Now if the complex structural arrangements which Lévi-Strauss discerns in preliterate narrative are simply manifestations of mnemonic devices, the mystery of the 'so what?' reaction diminishes. For if this is all they are, they obviously bear little relation to the motives and intentions which underlie the continuing production and development

[1] Op. cit., 1967, 1970.
[2] This reaction came out clearly at a conference on recent anthropological studies of myth and totemism under the auspices of the Association of Social Anthropologists of the Commonwealth in 1964, summed up in E. Leach (ed.), *The structural study of myth and totemism*, Tavistock, London, 1967 (see Leach, p. xvii, and Mary Douglas's 'The meaning of myth', especially pp. 62–5).

of narrative. The scholar comes away from Lévi-Strauss saying 'So what?' for the good reason that Lévi-Strauss takes him nowhere near these underlying motives and intentions, hence nowhere near the 'meaning' or the 'message'.

Again, as is becoming clear that to those with some respect for the 'meanings' of those they study, 'structuralism', far from providing a short cut to understanding, may even distort rather than illuminate. A recent experiment in which texts were subjected to analysis by a series of structuralist experts, followed by a response by the anthropologist field-worker, was finally accepted by most of the participants as a fruitless exercise unless and until the necessary contextual material was available.[1] Even in structural terms, the provision of context in studying oral literature (as advocated by Evans-Pritchard and his pupil, Finnegan) can be seen as an essential, if unflamboyant, prerequisite to analysis.

These are just two examples of the way in which the more plodding, context-conscious approach to oral narrative and meaning advocated by Evans-Pritchard may help not only to clear some of the exotic-scented mists which currently swirl about the edifice of structuralism and its analysis of 'primitive' (and other) thought, but also to cut down to its proper size and put in perspective whatever lies hidden within the mists.

(e) CAN THERE BE A COMPARATIVE SOCIOLOGY OF IDEAS?

Evans-Pritchard has always insisted strongly on the kinship between social anthropology and history, and, in a seminal essay on the subject,[2] he has indicated how the two disciplines can learn from one another. Amongst other things, he points out that the experience of anthropologists in contemporary small-scale, non-industrial societies may be of considerable relevance for historians concerned with modes of thought in earlier Europe.

An anthropological training, including fieldwork, would be especially valuable in the investigation of earlier periods of history in which institutions and modes of thought resemble in many respects those of the simpler peoples we study. For such periods

---

[1] 'An experiment: suggestions and queries from the desk with a reply from the ethnographer' (A. Dundes, E. R. Leach, P. Maranda and D. Maybury-Lewis) in P. and E. K. Maranda (eds.), *Structural analysis of oral tradition*, University of Pennsylvania Press, Philadelphia, 1971.

[2] 'Anthropology and history', in ESA.

Introduction

the historian struggles to determine a people's mentality from a few texts, and anthropologists cannot help wondering whether the conclusions he draws from them truly represent their thought. Their wonder turns to astonishment when they find that the thought of the ancient Greeks and Hebrews is presented by excellent historians as far more uncritical, naïve, yes, even childish, than that of savages on a much lower technological and cultural level. And though we may know something about what the poets of Charlemagne's court wrote, can we know equally what they thought or even what their writings meant; and how, I must ask, can an Oxford don work himself into the mind of a serf of Louis the Pious? I hope, though not very optimistically, to see the day when a course of social anthropology, including some field research, regarded not so much as an end in itself as a means, will be regarded as a valuable part of a historian's training.[1]

In studying the thought-patterns of such periods, historians can benefit from the insights and experiences of anthropological research in two ways. First, they can learn a great deal about the interpretative benefits that come from looking at thought-patterns in the context of the total social, cultural and economic background of the times. They can also profit from a host of suggestions as to how particular modes of thinking are linked to particular socio-cultural contexts. Secondly, where they are involved with periods for which data on both thought-patterns and context are scanty, they can draw upon the interpretative suggestions of anthropologists who have experienced apparently similar thought-patterns as aspects of living, functioning societies.

A certain amount of work on these lines is already taking place. Particularly for the history of European thought from A.D. 200 onwards, the calibre and status of historians interested in this approach[2] seems likely to ensure a growing awareness of the comparative relevance of anthropological research (and in particular Evans-Pritchard's intuitions) with consequent influence on the historical approach itself. Somewhat less work seems to have been

---

[1] ESA, p. 58.
[2] See, e.g., K. Thomas, 'History and anthropology', *Past and Present*, 24, 1963, and *Religion and the decline of magic*, Weidenfeld and Nicolson, London, 1971 (on cosmological ideas in sixteenth- and seventeenth-century England, drawing largely on ideas in *Witchcraft, oracles and magic*); and the essays by A. Macfarlane, P. Brown and K. Thomas in M. Douglas (ed.), *Witchcraft confessions and accusations*, Tavistock, London, 1970 (a volume dedicated to Evans-Pritchard).

carried out on the relevance of recent anthropological research for the thought of the earlier classical period in Western civilization. There are, however, some signs of awakening interest here on both the anthropological[1] and the classical side,[2] so we may yet see Evans-Pritchard's exhortations applied to this ancient but perhaps most formative phase of Western thought.

None of the essays in the present collection is explicitly concerned with the methodology of inference from contemporary small-scale, non-industrial societies to earlier phases of Western society. Several contributors, however, exhibit more or less overt assumptions about the legitimacy of such inference. Thus, Barnes, Gellner and Horton assume the existence of a syndrome of 'traditional' thought which is present alike in contemporary small-scale non-industrial societies and in earlier phases of Western society. They also appear to take the view that findings in, say, contemporary Africa could be a valuable source of insights into the nature and determinants of earlier European thought. Other contributors, for instance Wolfram, could probably be registered as sceptics on both these counts.

It is perhaps no coincidence that those contributors who seem to take for granted the applicability of anthropological insights in the study of early Western thought are also those who appear most sanguine about the possibility of a generalizing sociology of ideas. For it may be that the kind of inferences which Evans-Pritchard would like to see, from living cultures to those of the long-distant past, can only reliably be made with the help of a body of well-established, broad generalizations—i.e., with the counterpart of the principles of vertebrate zoology as used by the palaeontologists. This conclusion could be challenged but, if true, it might be something of a disappointment to Evans-Pritchard. For one of his aims in trying to bring anthropology nearer to history has been that of separating it from the natural sciences and putting an end to its preoccupation with 'general laws'.[3]

Meanwhile, the sociology of ideas is still far from being able to lay claim to any such body of broad generalizations. As to whether or

[1] J. Argyle, 'Oedipus in Central Africa', University College, London, Seminar Paper, 1966 (unpublished); Goody and Watt, op. cit., 1963.
[2] G. E. R. Lloyd, *Polarity and analogy: two types of argumentation in early Greek thought*, University Press, Cambridge, 1966; G. S. Kirk, *Myth: its meaning and functions*, University Press, Cambridge, 1970.
[3] ESA, pp. 18–20, 47–8.

not it will ever be able to do so, it is probably too early to say. Perhaps a start might be made if we begin to get real evidence of broadly similar developmental sequences occurring under similar social, cultural and economic conditions but at widely different times and places.

In this context, it may be worth referring to the essays by Nagashima and Ita.

Nagashima is concerned, among other things, to throw light on the 'Japanese miracle'—the enormously creative response of the Japanese to modern Western technology and science. He demystifies the miracle by pointing out that, in fact, the Japanese had been modernizing themselves at the expense of the Chinese for a thousand years previously, and had made an adjustment in which the psychic stresses caused by reliance on foreign inspiration in certain key sectors of cultural development were palliated by the elaboration of a counter-culture which embodied a set of values diametrically opposed to those of Chinese-derived modernity, but which at the same time implicitly recognized the latter's right to coexist with it on Japanese soil. Hence Western technology and science found in the Japanese a people who were already used to accepting external aid and inspiration in their efforts to modernize, and had already made the complex psychological adjustment prerequisite to doing this in an enthusiastic rather than a grudging manner.

At the beginning of his essay, Nagashima notes in passing the parallels between the old-fashioned Japanese counter-culture and the modern francophone African philosophy of 'Négritude'. He does this fairly lightheartedly, and passes on to other things without elaborating. Yet, if we compare this with Ita's analysis of 'Négritude' and its socio-political background, the parallels are striking. Thus, on the one hand, there is the stress on intuition, feeling, symbolism and oblique statement, and the scepticism as to the value of direct, literal communication and of 'reason' generally. On the other hand, there is the insistent identification of the counter-culture and its values with the original indigenous culture—an identification belied by evidence that, whatever its relation to indigenous values, it developed first and foremost as a reaction against the over-weening claims of a foreign-inspired modernism.[1]

---

[1] Though Nagashima does not make this point explicitly, it emerges clearly enough in his essay if one compares his dating of the florescence of specifically 'Japanese' forms of thought with his dating of Chinese influence.

Introduction

These two essays are, of course, no more than two straws in the wind. Yet if we see many more such straws blowing by, should we not be tempted to start dreaming of a more unashamedly generalizing sociology of ideas? Or are comparative perspectives rather than general laws all we can or should aim for in the analysis of modes of thought?

(F) EVANS-PRITCHARD'S ACHIEVEMENT

We have tried to review some of the many lines of enquiry opened up by Evans-Pritchard's work on the phenomenology and sociology of thought and belief, and to show how the various essays in our collection relate to them. It is not easy to give a quick summing-up of Evans-Pritchard's work in this sphere. On a superficial reading, he would seem to be concerned almost entirely with meticulous descriptions of particular African world-views. Even his recent *Theories of primitive religion* is full of awful warnings as to the perils of generalization and grand theory. On a deeper reading, however, one finds all manner of highly generalizable interpretative suggestions scattered through his ethnographic monographs and essays. Indeed, we have spent much of this section in showing how much he has thrown out for others to develop and argue over.

Anyone who has drawn inspiration from Evans-Pritchard's work will feel bound to ask why he has refrained from developing his own interpretative suggestions more systematically, and why, indeed, he has tended to tuck them away between long passages of ethnographic description, often so cunningly that those who could benefit most from them do not even recognize their presence. Perhaps he is more than ordinarily afflicted by the sense, which overcomes most of us at times, of the *hubris* involved in large generalizations about human beings. More certainly, he has a strong distaste for the aspiration toward 'social engineering' which frequently accompanies the attachment to large generalizations. Finally, perhaps, he gets a certain mischievous delight in throwing out a fundamental sociological insight in a couple of sentences, hiding it carefully in a thicket of ethnography, then watching to see who will come along, sniff it out, and either inflate it solemnly into thousands of words, or disagree with it equally solemnly and at even greater length. If so, some of the contributions to the present volume should at least give him cause for a quiet chuckle!

Introduction

In the light of what we have just said, it is clear that, in spelling out Evans-Pritchard's suggestions in explicit form, and in arguing about them at a high level of generality, we and certain of the contributors are to some extent running counter to the spirit of his work. This, however, is a liberty we feel is worth taking.

As we have shown in this section, his work has undoubtedly stirred up a new ferment of enquiry amongst small groups of scholars in philosophy, history, and the sociology of science. Nevertheless, had he presented his interpretative suggestions more explicitly and more systematically in the first place, they would perhaps have enjoyed a very much wider acclaim. Think, for instance, how much richer Popper's discussions of 'closure' and 'openness' would have been had he drawn upon the insights in *Witchcraft, oracles and magic*.[1] Think, too, of all the scholars who write under the fashionable banner of Phenomenology, and who have much to say about the religions of small-scale, pre-industrial societies. Evans-Pritchard, of all people, has pioneered the phenomenological study of such religions. Yet in how many of these people's indexes does his name feature?[2] It is such considerations that make us feel justified in dragging the more general implications of his work into the limelight.

In trying to summarize Evans-Pritchard's achievement with a brevity which he would approve, let us simply say that, by his example, he has led us toward a conception of 'Sociology of Ideas' in which both terms of the phrase are accorded equal dignity.

III. Conclusion

Considered as a body, the essays included here show more dissension than agreement. However, one can at least point to certain questions and themes around which these dissensions have tended to focus

---

[1] Neither his *The open society and its enemies* (Routledge, London, 1945) nor his *Conjectures and refutations* (Routledge, London, 1963) contains any reference to Evans-Pritchard.

[2] The lack of reference to Evans-Pritchard is particularly noteworthy in the work of Peter Berger, a very fashionable 'sociologist of knowledge', who not only writes in the phenomenological tradition, but propounds much the same view of 'closure' and 'openness' as that adumbrated in *Witchcraft, oracles and magic* some thirty years ago. (See P. Berger and T. Luckmann, *The social construction of reality*, Allen Lane, The Penguin Press, London, 1967; P. Berger, *The social reality of religion*, Faber, London, 1969.)

(mainly discussed in the first part of this introduction), and to the way that questions like these have proved fruitful ones to enquirers from many backgrounds, Evans-Pritchard among them.

Perhaps the only definite conclusion that can be drawn from the discussions in this volume is that the essays have, in a number of ways, made it even clearer to us where we must doubt and where we must enquire further. The more one reflects on the kinds of questions raised here, the more, like Socrates, one becomes aware of one's ignorance—or, at least, of the many areas which are problematical and controversial. Certainly some interesting agreements and convergences do appear (mainly discussed in the second part of this introduction), but even here the questions sometimes seem more significant than the answers.

This awareness of areas of ignorance and uncertainty perhaps explains why so many of the essays in this volume have turned out to have so markedly an abstract rather than empirical leaning. The resulting balance of the volume is thus in favour of the essays involving relatively abstract analysis rather than those which (like Colby and Cole's for instance) report empirical findings. At first sight this emphasis may seem—to some—a disappointment. Others may feel equally disappointed that the volume has not resulted in clear-cut and agreed conclusions about, say, 'primitive thought' or the exact status of the sociology of ideas. Yet this very lack of definite conclusions or of verified hypotheses is in itself a significant feature of the volume. For many contributors have obviously felt the need for careful discussion of the various possible implications and interpretations of the central question before going on to analyse the empirical data that might pertain to the different possible strands that could be followed up. In this sense the essays here can make a contribution to further work around the same central question.

What we hope has been achieved in this volume, therefore, is a clarification of where some of the problems and controversies lie in the simple-sounding question from which this volume started—a clarification which may make it possible for others to pursue these problems further, whether through abstract analysis, empirical investigation, or, best of all, through following Evans-Pritchard's emphasis on a combination of both.

Culture, Memory and Narrative

Benjamin Colby and Michael Cole[1]

In the context of the contemporary social sciences this symposium's topic represents something of an intellectual anomaly. The term 'modes of thought', which can be found in any psychological treatise on cognitive activity, does not appear in the indexes of contemporary social anthropological, sociological, or historical texts. Yet the contributors to this volume come from these fields. This is not a new situation. If one reviews man's past attempts to understand intellectual differences among cultural groups it becomes clear that, with the exception of clinical psychology, anthropologists and those of allied disciplines have not been influenced by psychological contributions to the study of cognition. Conversely anthropological inquiry on the subject has been virtually ignored by psychologists. One may even say that scholars in the two fields are scarcely concerned with the same topics, even though both groups profess to study cultural differences in modes of thinking.

An example of the problems involved occurred when an anthropologist responded to a report on some cross-cultural experimental research on thought processes by Gay and Cole.[2] He said,

> The reasoning and thinking processes of different people in different cultures don't differ . . . just their values, beliefs, and ways of classifying things differ.

Implicit in this statement is a definition of thinking that excludes a great deal of what psychologists have traditionally included under

[1] The authors gratefully acknowledge research support from the National Science Foundation for grants GS-2306 to N. B. Colby and GS-1221 to M. Cole.
[2] J. Gay and M. Cole, *The new mathematics and an old culture*, Holt, Rinehart and Winston, New York, 1967.

that term. Implicit too is a distinction between what people think and how they think, the 'static' and 'dynamic' aspects of cognitive behaviour.

Some hints concerning the origin of the large differences between anthropological and psychological approaches to the study of cultural differences in cognitive processes can be gained from a brief look at the two fields toward the end of the last century when there was a high degree of interest in the topic.

The founding leaders of anthropology shared two general views about thinking. First of all, thinking was closely identified with formal logical processes. So common was this nineteenth-century intellectual view (handed down from Aristotle) that the mathematician George Boole could write a treatise on logic entitled *The laws of thought*. Examples of 'illogical beliefs' were the standard evidence of cultural differences in thinking.

Secondly, there was almost universal acceptance of the idea that Western, industrialized society had produced (or been produced by) men of higher intellectual power than their 'primitive' brethren. There is no need to quote Spencer, Darwin, Morgan and Tylor here; their belief in the evolution of intellectual functions, whether culturally or racially mediated, is too standard a whipping boy to require documentation.

The evidence which these men used to reach conclusions about cultural differences in thinking consisted for the most part of anecdotes reported by missionaries and travellers and, later, the observations of field anthropologists. Our point is not that the observer (especially the untrained observer) was biased in what he reported, but that what he reported was in large part *beliefs*: beliefs in spirits, totemic ancestors, etc. The differences in logical processes (and therefore thought processes) were thus inferences from verbally stated beliefs.

In late nineteenth-century psychology, we find that there was little the anthropologist could hope to learn from psychologists about thought processes. Men who identified themselves as psychologists were occupied almost entirely with the study of elements of sensation, using highly trained introspecters as subjects. In addition to the difficulties of getting a Bantu cowherder to introspect in the prescribed manner, there was the obvious absurdity involved in extrapolating such introspective reports concerning simple sensations into a theory of thinking.

64

Culture, Memory and Narrative

Around the turn of the century psychologists themselves became dissatisfied with the introspective approach. From both the behaviourists and the gestaltists came studies of concrete problem-solving situations. Since that period, 'thinking' has come to be identified with 'problem solving' or 'concept formation' by psychologists. For them, native beliefs were not sufficient evidence for the study of thought processes. In fact, beliefs would probably not be considered a relevant category in the study of thinking, which refers to hypothetical processes underlying successful problem-solving behaviour.

Thus scholars in two disciplines could claim 'thinking' as a proper subject for study, yet fail to interact (not to say co-operate) with each other in a common intellectual quest. To some extent this might have been the result of an implicit awareness that the quest was not so common as it seemed. Disciplinary parochialism, however, must bear some of the blame and it is to a *rapprochement* of anthropological, linguistic and psychological approaches to the study of thinking that we should like to turn our attention.

In our own work, we have found it useful to make the distinction between the *content* of cognitive activity and its *processes*. At the very least, one would agree that Eskimos and Bushmen often think *about* different things simply because of their radically different ecologies. General agreement can also be easily reached on the proposition that Bushmen and Eskimos 'think differently' about some things which they experience in common. For instance, both groups think about their families, but might classify family members differently, have different beliefs and values relating to kinsmen, etc. These examples characterize the kind of cultural differences in thinking that most anthropologists, including the one quoted earlier, would accept.

When one turns to a consideration of *how* people think, agreement comes less easily. When the immediate contexts of a problem-solving activity are the same, do people operate differently within these contexts if they have different cultural or experiential backgrounds?

It is the belief in such dynamic differences in thought processes that characterizes Lévy-Bruhl's much-scorned hypothesis that preliterates generally possess pre-logical mentalities. (Although, whatever one's evaluation of Lévy-Bruhl's ideas, he did carefully make the distinction between beliefs (collective representations) and the connections among beliefs, believing that cultural differences exist at both levels.)[1]

[1] L. Lévy-Bruhl, *Primitive mentality*, Beacon Press, New York, 1966.

Culture, Memory and Narrative

It is on the connection between beliefs that Horton's evidence about the many common elements shared by preliterate and literate thought processes rests.[1] The gist of Horton's argument is that in important respects relating to both function and structure the examples of primitive thought marshalled by Lévy-Bruhl and others are quite consistent with analogous belief-systems of Western man. The anthropologist should not be seduced by the seemingly bizarre beliefs of some primitive peoples into thinking that they do not share his thought *processes*. At the same time, however, we must also avoid the mistake of equating belief with culture, and equating processes with some kind of (non-existent) culturally independent thought. It would thus be more meaningful to ask whether there is a difference between primitive and modern *cultures* with respect to particular processes rather than primitive and modern *mentalities*. We contend there is a circularity in defining primitive and modern man (a definition usually given in terms of culture) and then looking for 'mental' differences between them which are culturally mediated. Because of their ignorance of (or indifference to) the dominating cultural component in 'mental' differences, most writers on the subject have been unaware of this apparent circularity. The problem greatly diminishes, however, when we move to a more concrete level of analysis and speak of comparing different aspects or domains of culture with each other, such as the political or technological with some narrowly specified intellectual sphere.

It is clear that there is a sequence of functional prerequisites in technological and political matters that usually occur in an 'upward' cultural development. For example, existence of social segments larger than the family must precede a supra-provincial organization, but usually follows the development of formal political leadership. A code of laws usually does not occur until after three or more levels of territorial administration and an administrative hierarchy have developed. More trivially, cities do not occur until towns and villages have. These and other cultural traits as they occur in specific societies can be arranged in a Guttman scale of progressive complexity[2] which provides clues to cumulative cultural development from preliterate to

---

[1] R. Horton, 'African traditional thought and Western science: I. From tradition to science; II. The "closed" and "open" predicaments', *Africa*, 37, 1967.
[2] R. L. Carneiro, 'Ascertaining, testing and interpreting sequences of cultural development', *Southwestern Journal of Anthropology*, 24, 4, 1968.

literate and pre-technological to technological if not certain types of broad evolutionary sequences—though great caution must be used in any such historical interpretation without collateral information.

What about the intellectual differences among cultures and, specifically, the idea of intellectual evolution? Since the early part of this century little scientific work has been attempted in this area except peripherally, in linguistics. Language, of course, is a cultural phenomenon which is intimately connected with thought, although the exact nature of the relationship is still a matter for study. The original notions of Humbolt, Dilthey, Sapir, Whorf and others in this regard are now being supplanted and modified by the less grandiose generalities of hard experimental data.[1]

Evolutionary ideas are not new to linguistics. In the nineteenth century Schleicher postulated a development toward increasingly complex word structure, but he has long since been disproven. A reverse process suggested by Jesperson[2] was limited to Indo-European languages and did not consider complexities in the relationships between efficiency (or information) and redundancy in different aspects of the sentence-producing process. After these earlier works, there has been a hiatus in evolutionary thinking until quite recently. For the most part linguistic and anthropological writings during the last half century have been espousing egalitarian ideology. Lay opinions (in the writings of Ernst Cassirer and others) that primitive peoples speak intellectually deficient languages were justly criticized. Some of these armchair philosophers maintained that primitive peoples spoke languages which were overly concrete. Others held the opposite, that instead of being concrete (they would say, precise) the words had meanings which were too loose and too vague (which in a less derogatory view would be called abstract). The actual data, along with current work in ethnographic semantics, which maps out different levels of contrast in a variety of vocabulary domains, render such questions naïve (though they still remain alive in French intellectual circles, viz the efforts of Lévi-Strauss in *The savage mind*).

Recently serious investigators have begun to re-examine the

---

[1] See J. A. Fishman, 'A systematization of the Whorfian hypothesis', *Behavioral Science*, 5, 1960; M. Cole, J. Gay, J. Glick and D. Sharp, 'Linguistic structure and transposition', *Science*, 164, 1969.

[2] O. Jesperson, 'Mankind, nation and individual', in *A linguistic point of view*, Oslo and Cambridge, 1925.

question of language evolution. Swadesh[1] and Hymes[2] have reopened the question, while Berlin and Kay[3] have advanced a case for the evolution of colour terms, and Berlin[4] argues for an evolutionary sequence in ethnobotanical nomenclature.

Except for language and semantics, however, the question of developmental sequences and functional prerequisites in intellectual spheres of cultural systems has hardly been considered; and, aside from semantic descriptions of ethnoscience domains, few anthropologists and psychologists have described cognitive processes that are culturally distinct. One example of such a description is an article by Gladwin,[5] who describes Trukese strategies involved in one of the most demanding intellectual activities for the Truk Islanders, navigation. The special logical processes employed, which are described as quite different from European navigation, may have dictated the direction of a general cognitive style among the Trukese. These processes do not, understandably enough, map into I.Q. tests designed in terms of European cognitive style. Another anthropologist interested in characterizing both the intellectual content and processes of a cultural-using group is Gregory Bateson.[6] Bateson's ideas were new to anthropology and he had to introduce new terms such as *eidos* (the intellectual aspects of culture) as opposed to *ethos* (the effective aspects) and *deutero-learning* (learning how to learn). Yet these anthropologists are notable exceptions to the general trend and Bateson's terms have not been picked up in the profession because anthropologists have not directed their attention to the phenomena they referred to. Neither Gladwin nor Bateson has followed up their intuitive characterizations with the kind of ethnographic and experimental study that their own work calls for.

[1] M. Swadesh, 'Origén y evolucion del lenguaje humano,' *Anales de Antropología Universidad Nacional Autónoma de Mexico*, 2, 1965.
[2] D. H. Hymes, 'Functions of speech: an evolutionary approach', in F. C. Gruber (ed.), *Anthropology and education*, University of Pennsylvania Press, 1961.
[3] B. Berlin and P. Kay, *Basic color terms: their universality and evolution*, University of California Press, Berkeley, 1969. [See also the paper by Whiteley in the present volume pp. 145–61, especially p. 161. Eds.]
[4] B. Berlin, 'Speculations on the growth of ethnobotanical nomenclature', *Cognition*, 1, 1971.
[5] T. Gladwin, 'Cultural and logical process', in Ward H. Goodenough (ed.), *Explorations in cultural anthropology*, McGraw-Hill, New York, 1964.
[6] G. Bateson, 'Social planning and the concept of deutero-learning', *Symp. Sci. Phil. Relig.*, 2, 1942.

Culture, Memory and Narrative

During the past decade, however, anthropologists have developed a new subfield, variously termed cognitive anthropology, or ethnoscience. This subfield has been devoted primarily to the way in which different culture-using groups label their environment, to how these labels are organized into taxonomic structures, and to the kinds of semantic component which might go into their definitions. At first there was much talk of 'psychological' or 'cultural' reality. It was felt, for instance, that the components of a kinship terminology (such as sex, generation and lineality) represented some sort of psychological reality in the same way that the phonemes of a language had psychological reality. Consequently many of these componential analyses were proclaimed as being 'emic' studies.[1] But then analysts began to come up with alternative componential analyses of the same terminology systems and, as informant validation techniques were worked out, different componential models for the same system emerged. Anthropologists are beginning to realize that it is quite possible not only for different individuals in the same culture-using group to have different semantic structures in their heads, but that the *same* individual can have different semantic structures for the same terminology set and that the usage of these different structures depends upon the context of situation.

* * *

For the past thirty years or more cross-cultural psychological research relating to differences in cognitive structures has been concentrated in the area of I.Q. testing. Only recently has interest branched out into a general study of cultural differences in cognitive processes. A major impetus for this research has been the resurgence of theory in the area of cognitive development. Two of the major psychological theoreticians of recent years, Jean Piaget[2] and Jerome Bruner,[3] have advocated the use of cross-cultural research design for the solution of general theoretical problems. Although they differ in the details of their theoretical constructs, both Piaget and Bruner believe that human thinking must be described in terms of complex cognitive structures

---

[1] A. Wallace and J. Atkins, 'The meaning of kinship terms', *American Anthropologist*, 62, 1960.

[2] J. Piaget, 'Nécessité et signification des recherches comparatives en psychologie génétique', *International Journal of Psychology*, 1, 1, 1966.

[3] J. S. Bruner, 'The course of cognitive growth', *American Psychologist*, 19, 1964.

and skills which are acquired during the development of the child. The use of cross-cultural research designs is motivated by interest in whether or not the sequence in which children acquire the hypothesized structures and skills is universal and whether or not the rate at which they are acquired is affected by cultural and environmental factors.

The ideas underlying this cross-cultural developmental research coincide with the ideas put forth by Bateson[1] because psychologists generally believe that learning how to learn (deutero-learning) is a ubiquitous and powerful factor in children's increasing ability to solve various kinds of problems.

The work of Piaget, Bruner and Bateson suggests a new form in which to raise the question of intellectual evolution—is there a recognizable *cultural* sequence in the power and variety of cognitive skills acquired by users of different cultures? For instance, Greenfield and Bruner[2] hypothesize that, without the benefits of classroom experience, adult Wolofs do not attain the final level of cognitive functioning which, according to Piaget's theory, is reached in early adolescence. In a similar vein, Price-Williams[3] has found that, within a particular Mexican town, the level of cognitive development of different children as measured by standard Piagetian tasks is a function of certain early experiences connected with family occupation.

Although the evidence that can be brought together on cultural differences in problem solving and other cognitive activities may be grounds for speculation on possible developmental or even evolutionary sequences, the state of the art today is such that we cannot even be sure what the relevant cultural *differences* are, let alone the *sequences of these differences*. Before such theorizing can be anything more than speculative, a thorough, experimentally based programme of studies on cultural differences in cognitive skills is absolutely necessary.

Unfortunately, research programmes relating to developmental theories and research programmes using cross-cultural designs for the study of the relation between cultural and cognition are only in their infancy. However, in some cases, results which seem to have general theoretical importance have been collected. As an example of the kind

---

[1] Op. cit.

[2] P. M. Greenfield and J. S. Bruner, 'Culture and cognitive growth', *International Journal of Psychology*, 1, 1966.

[3] Personal communication.

Culture, Memory and Narrative

of experimental research relevant to the question of culture and cognition which can be done, we will relate research recently completed by Cole and his colleagues[1] on the question of cultural differences in memory processes.

In recent years studies of memory have become a rich testing ground for theories of cognition. Since the study of verbal learning processes had for many years been a stronghold of stimulus/response theories of learning and memory, such a development might seem surprising. This changing orientation in the study of memory began with the publication, in 1953, of a paper by Bousfield.[2] He introduced a technique for studying how subjects meaningfully organize the material to be learned consonant with what is known about the semantic organization of those materials. Bousfield and his associates[3] demonstrated that, when the items to be remembered came from easily identifiable semantic categories, recall tended to be 'clustered'. That is, items from a given semantic category were commonly recalled together. More recently Tulving[4] has used another index of organization, which measures the consistency between successive attempts by one subject to recall the same list. This index does not impose the experimenter-defined categories on the data. Although there are many questions of fact and theory remaining to be clarified, it is clear from the work of Bousfield, Tulving and other investigators that North American high school and college students show a strong predilection toward reorganizing material presented for memorization and that the success of recall is related to the degree of organization.[5]

The standard results with American college and high school students contrast strongly with anecdotal evidence collected by anthropologists over many decades. For example, Riesman[6] quotes

[1] M. Cole, J. Gay, J. Glick and D. Sharp, *The cultural context of learning and thinking*, Basic Books, New York, 1971.

[2] W. A. Bousfield, 'The occurrence of clustering in the recall of randomly arranged associates', *Journal of General Psychology*, 49, 1953.

[3] Bousfield, op. cit.; B. Cohen, 'Recall of categorized word lists', *Journal of Experimental Psychology*, 66, 1963.

[4] E. Tulving, 'Subjective organization in free recall of "unrelated" words', *Psychological Review*, 69, 1962.

[5] See the summary in E. Tulving, 'Theoretical issues in free recall', in T. R. Dixon and D. L. Horton (eds.), *Verbal learning and general behavior theory*, Prentice-Hall, Englewood Cliffs, 1968.

[6] D. Riesman, *The oral tradition, the written word and the screen image*, Antioch Press, Yellow Springs, 1956, p. 9.

71

the report of an anthropological colleague that, among a remote people in the Philippines, 'messages are conveyed orally . . . with an accuracy which is fabulous to us.' The same point is made by Elenore Bowen[1] who recounts the displeasure and consternation of her Nigerian hosts at her inability to remember the names of local plants which every six-year-old in the village had long since committed to memory. Similar evidence is provided by Bartlett[2] in a memory test of a Swazi cowherder who one year earlier had been tangentially involved in a series of cattle transactions. The herder was able to recall identifying marks as well as the price paid for each cow in pounds, shillings and pence with almost no errors. Both Bowen and Bartlett attribute the memory feats of their informants to the great interest the subjects to be remembered had for those people. The cowherder's feat of memory seems outstanding because what is socially important to him is irrelevant to the Western observer who, therefore, finds a good memory for cows and prices unusual. We might, according to this theory, expect a Swazi herder to be equally astounded should he happen to encounter a Los Angeles ten-year-old trading baseball cards with a friend. The intricate recall of players, teams, batting averages and relative standing that the successful card-trader requires would seem virtually impossible to the Swazi cowherder to whom all baseball players look alike!

Differences in 'interest' or in 'social relevance' are not the only causes which have been offered for cultural differences in memory. For instance, Bartlett himself, when comparing the Swazi to the Westerner, suggests that culture determines a difference in the *way* things are recalled. He hypothesizes that rote memory is the preferred memory technique of non-literate peoples and defines rote memory as serial memorizing. He concludes:

> According to the general theory of remembering which has been put forward, there is a low level type of recall which comes as nearly as possible to what is often called rote recapitulation. It is characteristic of a mental life having relatively few interests all somewhat concrete in character and no one of which is dominant.[3]

Bartlett's characterization of the preliterate as a rote memorizer

[1] E. S. Bowen, *Return to laughter*, Doubleday, New York, 1964.
[2] F. C. Bartlett, *Remembering*, Cambridge University Press, London, 1932.
[3] Ibid., p. 264.

certainly coincides with the interpretations ordinarily proffered by anthropologists, although such explanations are usually a by-product of some other discussion. Returning to Bateson's concept of deutero-learning, the rote memorizing of the preliterate, should it be shown to exist, could be viewed as a generalized technique for learning which is a part of preliterate society. Various anthropological explanations for such a difference immediately suggest themselves. The most potent explanation contrasts preliterate and literate society in terms of the way in which information must be passed from one generation to the next. However, the philological-historical evidence collected by Parry, Lord and others (which we will discuss in some detail later in the paper) indicates that oral traditions go beyond the use of special mnemonic devices to that of a complex generative narrative grammar. Thus it seems reasonable to suppose that a child growing up in a pre-literate traditional society will have learned different ways of memorizing things than a child brought up with books and television sets. The problem then becomes one of trying to measure the differences in these deutero-learning processes using some technique which has cross-cultural relevance.

Whether or not reliable culture difference can be shown to exist in properly controlled experiments remains an untested question. In order to investigate this question, we must choose an experimental tool or set of tools which would be appropriate to the study of memory processes across cultures. This tool should both permit rote learning to 'occur' and yield evidence of non-rote organization processes where they occur.

The free recall experiment which was the original tool by Bousfield for the study of organizational processes seems an excellent candidate. First, it is extremely easy to administer. A subject is presented with a series of items, one at a time, and is told that he must try to learn them so that he can recall them at a later time. After the last item is presented, a fixed period is given for recall. The list can then be repeated as many times as the experimenter wishes.

Secondly, the subject is free to remember in any manner he chooses. The way in which he orders the to-be-learned lists when recalling them in this unconstrained fashion gives important insight into the organizational mechanisms of memory.

As a starting point for the research, sets of items familiar to our subjects, the Kpelle of Liberia, were constructed using standard anthropological eliciting techniques. The Kpelle are a large (250,000) tribe living in north-central Liberia and neighbouring areas of Guinea. The people live in small towns of between 20 and 300 huts with between 50 and 1,500 inhabitants. A few larger towns are located at strategic points along the all-weather highway which cuts through Kpelle-land on its way from the Liberian capital of Monrovia to the Sierra Leone and Guinea borders. The people are largely agricultural, with the bulk of their activities devoted to growing sufficient rice to feed their families.

Table 1

Stimulus Material for Recall Experiments

CLUSTERABLE LIST (in four clusters)	NON-CLUSTERABLE LIST
orange	rope
banana	cotton
onion	book
potato	candle
coconut	stone
	grass
pot	horn
calabash	battery
cup	mat
plate	cigarette
pan	nickel
	bottle
hoe	feather
file	nail
knife	stick
cutlass	orange
hammer	pot
	knife
headtie [i.e. headscarf]	shirt
singlet	box
trousers	
hat	
shirt	

Table 1 contains two lists of items derived by elicitation. The first list will be termed 'clusterable' because of the obvious division into easily identifiable semantic categories; the second will be termed 'non-clusterable' because it was constructed so as to provide minimal groupings into semantic categories.

The items listed in Table 1 were then used in a series of experiments to determine the major features of recall among the Kpelle.

The experimental attack focused on the types of persons, verbal instructions and material conditions which could reasonably be expected to affect the rate of learning and degree of clustering in the free recall of the experiment. The first variation involved the nature of the stimulus materials. One point upon which many observers of African language seem to agree is the presumed 'concreteness' of African thought. For instance, Cryns, who has no use for I.Q. tests as ordinarily applied, maintained that the 'empirical evidence suggesting the prevalence of a concrete way of thinking in the African . . . is too substantial to be refuted.'[1] Perhaps then, if we showed the objects named by each of our stimulus words to our subjects, instead of reading them aloud, we would observe greatly augmented recall and clustering. Several studies with Americans have shown increased recall using pictures rather than verbal stimuli. Thus, if African mentality is more 'concrete' than that of Americans, we should expect not only augmentation, but proportionally greater augmentation than is ordinarily observed with Americans.

A second variation involved the clusterability of the lists themselves. American evidence[2] indicates that clusterable lists are easier to learn, in general, than lists chosen so that their components belong to disparate classes. If the Kpelle rely on rote memory rather than the clusterability of the list, then they ought to recall equally well on both lists.

Another variable which has been found to affect clustering and recall is the arrangement of items in a clusterable list. If the items are *not* randomly arranged, as in our original experiment, but rather are

---

[1] A. G. J. Cryns, 'African intelligence: a critical survey of cross-cultural intelligence research in Africa south of the Sahara', *Journal of Social Psychology*, 57, 1962, p. 296.

[2] C. N. Cofer, 'Does conceptual organization influence the amount retained in immediate free recall?', in B. Kleinmuntz (ed.), *Concepts and the structure of memory*, Wiley, New York, 1967.

presented in a clustered fashion, clustering and recall are enhanced for American college students.[1]

Kpelle subjects of different ages and educational levels were studied because it was thought that these variables might influence clustering and recall. In order to make cross-cultural comparisons, data was collected from children in southern California.[2]

The first two variables we consider are education and the clusterability of the lists. In Table 2 we see that the clusterable list was more easily learned than the non-clusterable list and that the school children were superior to their illiterate counterparts. For American school children the clusterable list was more easily learned also, though the difference between clusterable and unclusterable lists was not so great. Unlike the Kpelle, the American school children showed considerable increases in recall and clustering scores with each new trial while the improvement across trials for the Kpelle was very small in magnitude.

Table 2

Free Recall Experiment

AFRICAN

Recall	TRIAL				
	1	2	3	4	5
Educated	8·0	9·0	9·0	9·4	9·8
Illiterate	6·2	7·2	7·6	7·7	8·0
Clusterable	7·6	8·6	9·0	9·2	9·6
Non-clusterable	6·6	6·8	6·6	7·8	8·2
Clustering score*	−0·17	−0·14	−0·23	−0·03	−0·08
Position Correlation	−0·05	+0·04	+0·02	0·00	−0·09

[1] C. N. Cofer, D. R. Bruce and G. M. Reicher, 'Clustering in free recall as a function of certain methodological variations', *Journal of Experimental Psychology*, 71, 1966.

[2] Of necessity these data are presented in extremely abbreviated form. For a full explication see Cole *et al.*, *The cultural context of learning and thinking*.

AMERICAN

Recall	TRIAL				
	1	2	3	4	5
1st grade	4·8	6·8	6·8	8·0	8·4
4th grade	7·4	9·2	9·8	10·8	11·2
6th grade	8·6	11·0	11·6	12·8	13·4
9th grade	8·8	11·6	13·1	14·6	14·9
Clusterable	7·6	10·8	11·8	12·2	12·4
Non-clusterable	7·0	9·1	9·9	10·9	11·6
Clustering score*					
1st grade	−0·69	−0·36	0·15	0·34	0·75
4th grade	−0·35	0·48	0·16	0·43	1·32
6th grade	0·49	1·17	0·89	1·71	1·40
9th grade	0·46	0·83	1·30	2·04	1·98
Position Correlation	+0·22	−0·17	−0·31	−0·25	−0·20

NOTE: A CLUSTERING SCORE of 0·0 is the level expected by chance. Positive scores indicate the presence of semantic clusters. Negative scores indicate below-chance clustering.

To find out whether the Kpelle showed less clustering because of a possible greater emphasis on rote learning, we studied the order in which words were recalled and compared them with the word positions in the original list given to them. The 'position correlation' measure in Table 2 shows that the Kpelle subjects are *not* rote learning while the Americans show a good deal of rote learning on the first trial but not subsequently.

Another difference is that Americans learned items best if they were toward the end of the list given them to learn, next best at the beginning and least best in the middle. This is a typical serial position curve.[1] The African data, however, are relatively undifferentiated with respect to serial position. How, then, can we interpet these differences? Are

[1] J. Deese, 'Serial organization in the recall of disconnected items', *Psychological Reports*, 3, 1957.

they a result of trivial effects such as differences in item familiarity or could they, for instance, reflect the difference between typical daily activities in pre-industrial or pre-scientific societies and industrial or scientific ones? Let us examine some further experiments.

We found that when words were presented in a blocked fashion, that is, when all the items from a given category occurred together, significant clustering appeared both for the Kpelle and American subjects. In terms of the average magnitude of the effects, the Kpelle children performed very much like American first-graders who were 4.8 years younger on the average. Thus, while Kpelle and American subjects are affected in a similar manner by some standard experimental manipulations, the Kpelle performance remains inferior in quantity recalled, and the pattern of responding under different circumstances is quite different. In particular, the Americans seem to take much greater advantage of such presumed aids to learning as organization according to semantic category, physical presence and privileged position in listing the materials. Even when we tried to motivate the Kpelle further by offering monetary reward for performance, the results were no different in significance.

Then we tried another tack. We cued some of the subjects on the way the objects could be clustered by holding each object over one of four chairs representing the four categories the words could be clustered in. For the second group of Kpelle subjects items were assigned at random to the four chairs with the assignment remaining the same for each trial. For the third group the items were all held over a single chair, the other three chairs not being used. As predicted, those who were cued clustered more, with an average clustering score of 2·27, while those with only one chair had a score of −0·27 and those who were deliberately confused by random assignments to the four chairs had a score of −0·59. Interestingly enough, while organization improved by cuing, there was no difference among the three groups on recall.

We then tried an experiment with verbal rather than physical cues, using a variation on a technique described by Tulving and Pearlstone.[1] Subjects were read the standard clusterable list and recall was measured under five conditions. For the groups cued when the list was introduced on each trial, the experimenter said, 'I am going to tell

[1] E. Tulving and Z. Pearlstone, 'Availability versus accessibility of information and memory for words', *Journal of Verbal Learning and Verbal Behavior*, 5, 1966.

you about several things. *These things will be clothing, tools, food and utensils.* When I tell you these things, listen carefully.' The list was then presented in the standard, oral fashion. For groups cued at the time of recall, the list of categories was repeated. If no cuing occurred, the italicized sentence was omitted. The possibilities of cuing or not cuing, prior to presentation (input) or prior to recall (output), resulted in four experimental conditions. In addition, a group of subjects was run for four trials with no cuing at input, but highly constrained cuing at the time of recall. After the list of items was presented to the subjects in this group, they were asked to recall the items by category. For instance, the experimenter would say, 'Tell me all the clothing you remember.' After the subject had named all the clothing items he could remember, the experimenter would repeat the procedure with each of the other categories. On the fifth trial no cuing was given at all, and these subjects were told simply to remember as many of the items as they could.

Comparison of the first four groups indicated that our unconstrained cuing manipulations had little effect on recall or clustering. There were no significant differences between groups on either measure and performance measures were comparable to those obtained in the standard, oral presentation situation.

The results from the fifth groups were quite different from those of the four unconstrained groups. Recall for the first four trials was extremely high, averaging approximately 17 items per trial. Moreover, recall remained high on trial five, when 15·2 items were recalled. Clustering was forced to be perfect for the first four trials with this group; but on trial five clustering remained high, 2·23, a score comparable to that achieved with the chairs and comparable to the performance of American school children. It appears that good performance at memory and organization can be induced through sufficiently explicit verbal instruction and training.

The demonstration that there are ways of presenting material in the free recall experiment which greatly enhance the Kpelle person's ability to remember items in our standard task fits in well with the distinctions that Mandler,[1] Tulving[2] and others have made between

[1] G. Mandler, 'Organization and memory', in K. W. Spence and J. T. Spence (eds.), *The psychology of learning and motivation*, Academic Press, New York, 1966.
[2] E. Tulving, 'Theoretical issues in free recall', in Dixon and Horton (eds.), op. cit., 1968.

storage and retrieval mechanisms, or between availability and accessibility. In such terms, the difficulty our Kpelle subjects experience is a difficulty in making material accessible (or, alternatively, in retrieving material that is stored). It could be said that the constrained recall made stored material accessible and in the process taught the subject retrieval habits that carried over to the unconstrained recall trial.

One would speculate, then, that the observed difference between American and Kpelle children is that the experimental tasks of memory and organization resemble tasks in American society (which might be characterized as 'industrial' or 'scientific'?) which are of sufficient importance to internalize as part of the cultural system used by Americans, while these tasks have not been of sufficient frequency and importance in Kpelle society (pre-industrial or pre-scientific?) to have brought about an internalized cultural system which facilitates the tasks. They thus require external cuing such as the one we used in our experiment. Though we have now speculated on the relation between our findings and a general technological level of development, such speculation goes rather further than we would like; and we feel much safer simply in suggesting that there is something as yet undetermined about these two societies and the cultures they use which causes the observed differences.

A logical next step is to search for an experimentally accessible but natural situation in which efficient retrieval processes would routinely be used by Kpelle subjects. Our strategy was to provide a continuum of story contexts in which to present the 20 basic clusterable items from Table 1 used in most of the previous studies. These contexts varied from no context at all (our basic oral-presentation procedure) through a highly constrained story context in which each item is meaningfully linked to the neighbouring item within the story.

The first story, for example, presented a list of objects which a chief showed to a travelling man as a test of his memory prior to either marrying the chief's daughter or being killed, depending on the outcome of the memory test. In the second story four suitors brought different groups of gifts to a chief's daughter. In the third story a clever man conned a foolish man into giving him a series of objects, each with a stated purpose. Finally, in the fourth story a girl being abducted by a bogeyman laid out a series of objects with a variety of symbolic meanings which revealed the route of the bogeyman to the girl's rescuers.

Stories three and four, which present items in a meaningful and sequentially organized story, produce high correlations between the order in which the items are presented and the order in which they are recalled (r's = 0·56 and 0·51 respectively). These figures are far higher than we have seen under any other circumstances in any of our work. The correlations for the other story groups average about 0·15 and for the control group (who were given lists to recall without the story context) about 0·21. Recall of the second story was extremely poor because the subjects tended to recall only one of the four groups of gifts brought, perhaps because there was such a strong predisposition for the listener, encouraged by the instructions, to choose only one suitor and forget everything, including the gifts brought, about the others. Thus, while recall was very good for one of the four groups, and clustering consequently was also good, total recall was poor. The results of the responses to the first story were similar to the control group and the findings of the previous experiments already described. For story three and story four, we know that serial organization, which works counter to clustering, is dominating recall.

While the results of story one showed that a bare story context is not sufficient to affect recall, the results of story two responses show how an emphasis on disputation (which suitor should be permitted to have the girl?) tends to decrease overall recall. The performance of those who were given stories three and four, however, showed that many subjects implicitly were 'retelling' the story when asked for recall and there was a close correspondence between adequacy in retelling the story (which they were asked to record on tape) and recall adequacy.

Considering the story experiment, one is struck both by the fact that for the first time one observes the high degree of organization that is characteristic of the recall of typical American subjects, and by the fact that, so strong is the role of the story context in mediating recall, it can actually lead to impaired performance when a culturally unexpected recall task for that story (i.e., the experimental task) is given.

*　　　*　　　*

Given the obvious importance of the narrative in recall, we next turn our attention to an exploration of narrative structure and its role in preliterate society. As we have seen, serial organization and clustering become immensely complicated phenomena when considered in the context of folktales, myths and other cultural productions that result from integrative mechanisms built up and passed on for many generations.

It seems quite clear that folk narratives, like their constituent sentence strings, are organized in a variety of different kinds of cognitive 'chunks' which have certain 'valences' for particular kinds of structures. Recently, developments in eidochronic analysis (from the Greek *eidos*, image or form, and *chronikos*, concerning time and sequence) indicate that folktales in at least some cultures show a sequential pattern of a special kind of 'chunk', an eidochronic narrative element, shortened to *eidon* for convenience, which can be discovered and tested by distributional analysis.[1] An eidon is an abstract narrative event consisting of a class of event varieties that typically occur in a particular sequential order predetermined by rules of narrative syntax.

An example can be given in the study of myths of the Ixil, a Maya people living in the north-west Guatemalan highlands. The Ixil number some 50,000 people in an isolated area of 2,314 square kilometres. They live in three small towns with populations ranging from 3,600 to 5,200 inhabitants and in smaller villages and hamlets in the surrounding countryside. They are a maize-growing people; but land scarcity requires the importation of maize and the seasonal exportation of labour. The Ixil constitute 92 per cent of the total population of the area, the remaining 8 per cent being *Ladinos*, non-Indians who use the dominant Guatemalan hispanic culture.

Two myths, 'The Fish Merchant' and the 'Marcao' myth, will illustrate a number of eidochronic elements. In the first myth the eidon *Capture* takes the form of the hero's being swallowed by a large animal, whereas in the second myth the eidon is represented by the hero's being wounded and gathered up.[2] The eidon *Transport* in the 'Fish Merchant' is the moving of the animal (with the fish merchant inside) to heaven while in the Marcao myth it is the bringing of the wounded bird (the form the protagonist has assumed) into the house

---

[1] B. N. Colby, 'A partial grammar of Eskimo folktales', *American Anthropologist*, 75, 1973.

[2] Though these examples are given eidon designations, they should be regarded as only provisionally identified pending the collection of a larger sample of myths which a finished eidochronic analysis requires.

of the girl being courted. The *Task* eidon has three varieties in the two stories. In one version of 'The Fish Merchant' the protagonist is given the job of dispensing rain and lightning (which he bungles) and the performing of an anal operation on some immortals who desire the orifice in order to eat, which changes them to mortals, and they die. In the Marcao myth the task is to build a house. In both stories the tasks are immediately followed by a departure and a return to the dwelling place of the protagonist. In the first story the fish merchant is magically transported to his home canton. In the second the protagonist enters his home in the sky. In both cases *Capture* occurs before *Transport* which occurs before *Task* which immediately precedes *Return*. These eidons for 'The Fish Merchant' are shown at level five in Figure 1. In this figure the transportation eidon is singled out for further expansion at lower levels. For example, of the two eidon varieties already mentioned where the protagonist is carried to the land of the gods (shown as $Trans_1$ in the diagram of the story in Figure 1) and he is carried into a house (which occurs in the second story, not shown in the diagram, and which would be designated as $Trans_2$), we follow the first alternative down through a synopsis at level seven to the actual verbatim account at level eight.

A complete eidochronic analysis is a lengthy and complex procedure,[1] but it is the single most important part, the warp, of a structural analysis of narrative. With this as a basic skeleton, a good teller of tales can use a variety of poetic and stylistic devices, themselves organized into cognitive 'chunks', which produce a finished story.

Bartlett's well-known experiments,[2] in which a story is told to one individual who then tells it to another and so on through a long chain, demonstrate the inaccuracy of recall and how new elements intrude themselves according to the various cognitive sets of the purveyors of the story. Although certain gross tendencies, such as increasing simplification across successive repetitions, could be discerned, the precise delineation of how these distortions occur was not possible. Each person brought his own past experiences and memory habits to bear in dealing with the story and there was no *a priori* way to know

---

[1] See V. Propp, *Morphology of the folktale*, trans. L. Scott, Pub. 10, Indiana University Research Center in Anthropology, Folklore and Linguistics, Bloomington, 1958; and Colby, op. cit.
[2] F. C. Bartlett, *Remembering*.

Figure 1

Diagram for Ixil myths and folktales exemplified by 'The Fish Merchant' with special focus on the Transportation eidon

Level

1   Folktale

2   Initial Situation   Plot   Terminal Situation

3   Injury   Restitution

4   Motivation   Consequences   Appeal   Answer

5   Setting   Absence   Court-ship   Rejec-tion   Capture   Transpor-tation   Encoun-ter   Identifi-cation   Task   Revela-tion   Return   Villainy   Marriage avenged

6   Trans₁—Protagonist is carried to land of the gods

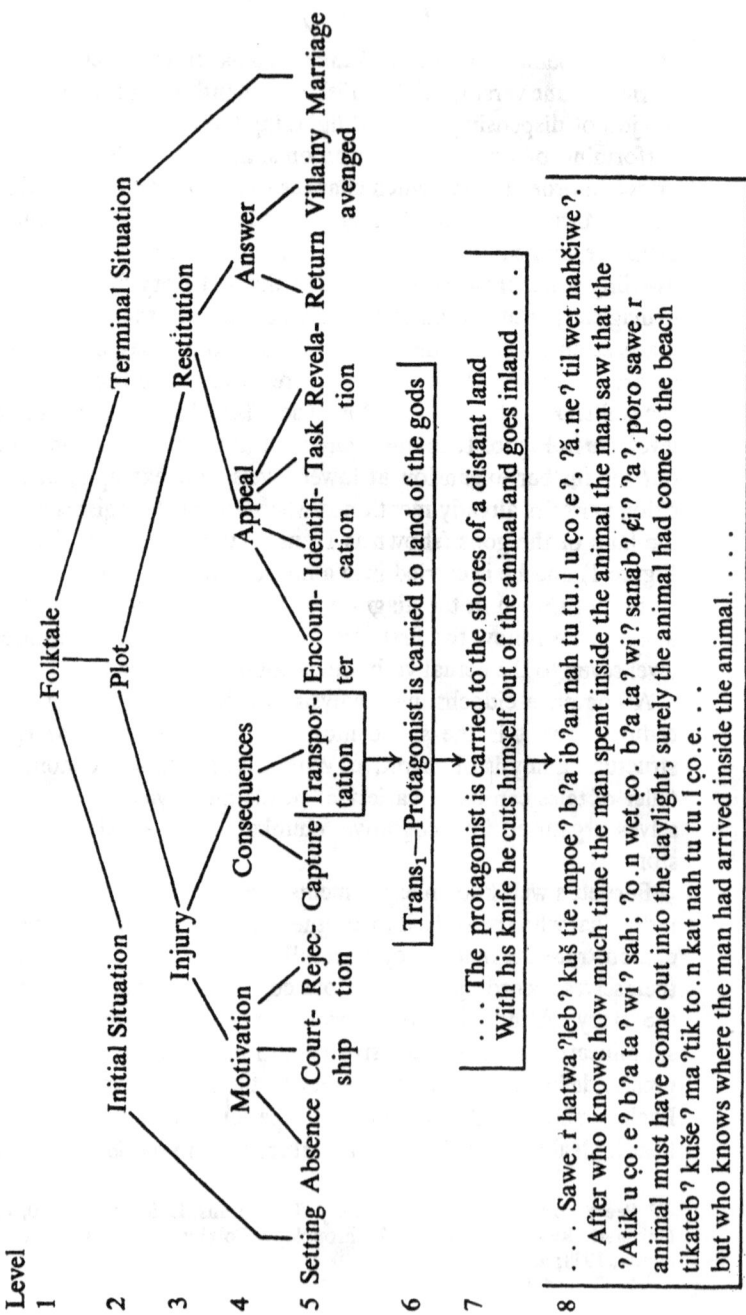

7   . . . The protagonist is carried to the shores of a distant land
With his knife he cuts himself out of the animal and goes inland . . .

8   . . . Sawe. r̂ hatwa ʔleb ʔ kuš tie. mpoe ʔ b ʔa ib ʔan nah tu tu. l u ço. e ʔ, ʔă. ne ʔ til wet nahč̆iwe ʔ.
After who knows how much time the man spent inside the animal the man saw that the
ʔAtik u ço. e ʔ b ʔa ta ʔ wi ʔ sah; ʔo. n wet ço. b ʔa ta ʔ wi ʔ sanab ʔ ¢i ʔ ʔa ʔ, poro sawe. r
animal must have come out into the daylight; surely the animal had come to the beach
tikateb ʔ kuše ʔ ma ʔtik to. n kat nah tu tu. l ço. e. . .
but who knows where the man had arrived inside the animal. . . .

what these individual differences were. If instead we had chosen some area of concern where several people brought virtually the same system of associations and habits to bear on the problem, then we might be able to learn about the nature of this system through the regularities and patterns of the verbal output of the subjects, just as we can learn about grammatical structure from a study of sentence strings produced by people who use grammar, or semantic structure through clustering in free recall. In other words, if we assume that each person possesses a series of generative-learning and other systems, it might be better research strategy to work in some area where the systems are similar enough from one person to the next (as in language or eidochronic syntax) to permit us to map them out and study processes through the recurrence of regular patterns, rather than to work with more idiosyncratic systems. An important task in this direction is the writing of narrative grammars.

A narrative grammar is a description of the narrator-hearer ability to communicate. If this grammar is explicit in all details and does not require a subliminal 'filling in' by the reader, it can be called a generative narrative grammar in a manner similar to Chomsky's definition of a generative grammar of language.[1] A narrative grammar should encompass all the basic regularities of a narrative above the level of the actual language itself (level eight in Figure 1). An eidochronic analysis, on the other hand, is but one part (though a very fundamental part) of a narrative grammar.

Another part which may come under the heading of poetics has been closely studied in Yugoslavia by Milman Parry and Albert Lord. By recording South Slavic epic songs from the best performing artists available and by attending to the circumstances and history of such performances, Parry and Lord have made a truly outstanding contribution to the study of narrative recall and narrative production. The singers they found would often say they sang their songs exactly as they had heard them from other singers when in fact their songs were greatly changed. The singer-poet would compose as he performed. His songs, which were topically and metrically determined by tradition, reflected not only the tradition, but also the singer's own personality, skill and interests. Further, his songs reflected the mood of his audience and the occasion of the performance.

[1] N. Chomsky, *Aspects of the theory of syntax*, M.I.T. Press, Cambridge, Mass., 1965.

Culture, Memory and Narrative

What a singer means when he says that he sings a song exactly as he has heard it is understandable, given his twofold definition of song. The illiterate (and all the singers interviewed by Parry and Lord were illiterate) consider either the particular performance of a song or the song expressed in all performances to *be* the song. There was no concept of a fixed and sacred 'original', of which each rendition was more or less an imitation. Here is where the preliterate conceptualization can affect not only the style of learning a narrative but also the way in which the analyst is likely to view the process. The literate bias of the analyst makes the skill of an epic singer, who can sing, for example, a different song all night through for each of the forty nights of Ramadan, all the more astounding. Also, when we present non-Western subjects with word lists and request exact recall, we may be introducing a task which is several orders of magnitude more alien than we had expected.

According to Lord, the singer's idea of the stability of song, 'to which he is deeply devoted, does not include the wording, which to him has never been fixed, nor the unessential parts of the story. He builds his performance, or song in our sense, on the stable skeleton of narrative, which is the song in his sense.'[1] It is possible that the singer, unencumbered with the concept of word as we know it, is able to devote his learning to other, different kinds of patterns. Certainly the rapidity with which the master composes while he performs cannot be explained by word-for-word memorization of the vast number of songs in his repertoire. He does not attempt it.

The young learner of epic songs goes through three stages of narrative song competence: (1) listening and absorbing, (2) application, and (3) singing before a critical audience. In the application stage, he probably memorizes themes and formulas exactly as he heard them. But later he leaves this imitative stage with an increase in repertory and competence. With increasing ability, he learns how to expand and ornament any song he hears with enough thematic material to lengthen, or shorten, or perhaps create a new song. 'The singer never stops in the process of accumulating, recombining, and remodelling formulas and themes, thus perfecting his singing and enriching his art.'[2]

[1] A. B. Lord, *The singer of tales*, Atheneum, New York, 1965, p. 99.
[2] Ibid., p. 26.

The process of elaboration, enrichment and ornamentation was dramatically illustrated when Parry had an exceptional singer, Avdo Medodovic, listen to a previously unheard song rendered by a performer of lesser ability, Mumin Vlahovljak. Without forewarning Parry then asked Avdo to repeat the song. In doing so, Avdo lengthened the song many times, adding similes, finer characterization, a greater depth of feeling and further ornamentation. One example of the different treatment of the same theme by the two men was the arrival of a messenger in the assembly:

> Mumin simply said that the door creaked and a messenger entered. Avdo described how Mustajbey looked out the window and saw a cloud of dust from which emerged a rider bearing a message on a branch.[1]

Another time Avdo expanded a published song of 2,200 lines to one of 12,000 lines. What makes such an astounding feat possible? Lord and Parry attribute it to patterns and combinations of formulas and themes, particularly the formulas which are groups of words regularly used under the same metrical conditions to express given essential ideas. These involve melodic, metric, syntactic and acoustic patterns.

Through the use of these metrical patterns, which the singer associates with specific segments of his tale, systems of substitution are set up. For instance, the following phrases (all with the same metric value in Serbo-Croatian) are representative of one formula used by many singers.

> By Allah, he said, he mounted the white horse
> By Allah, he said, he mounted the animal
> By Allah, he said, he mounted the brown horse
> And he said this, he mounted the brown horse
> And he said this, he mounted the animal

Thus the singer does not have to learn a vast array of separate formulas but rather patterns where various elements of the patterns can be changed and substituted for. Although the singer does remember and use phrases he has previously heard from another singer, when he does not remember the phrase verbatim he forms one according to the internalized patterns of the appropriate formula; and, in so doing, the singer is a true creator.

---

[1] Ibid., p. 81.

Coinciding with our emphasis on eidochronic action, Lord offers evidence which gives more psychological importance to the action than to the characters of the story.

> The fact that the same song occurs attached to different heroes would seem to indicate that the story is more important than the historical hero to which it is attached. There is a close relationship between hero and tale, but with some tales at least the *type* of hero is more significant than the specific hero. It is convenient to group songs according to their story content, or thematic configurations, because songs seem to continue in spite of the particular historical hero; they are not connected irrevocably to any single hero.[1]

In speaking of the various actions, or what we have called eidons, Lord singles out the return song as of special interest. The sequence goes like this:

1. How the hero was captured.
2. Shouting of the hero in prison after a long period of years.
3. Release with stipulation of return to prison.
4. Flashback of how hero was captured (or introduction).
5. Return home of hero.
6. Return of the hero to the enemy prison.
7. Rescue of someone else from that prison.

There is another group of songs that begins with the same themes but ends with a different sequence of different themes. These appear to be typical characteristics of the eidochronic phenomenon.

It is obvious from the scholarly studies of Lord and Parry that in the recall of vast quantities of data, such as a song which sometimes must be sung for an entire night, rote memory is not sufficient. It is necessary to learn a complete generative system or grammar which is capable of handling all aspects of such a complicated cultural production as a narrative—from the plot structure and gross constituent elements all the way down to the poetic subtleties of rhyme and metre. Such generative systems are built up over the centuries and learned in ways that are probably similar to the learning of a language at an earlier age. (Lord notes that the best singers usually learn before the age of 14, which is also about the upper limit for learning second languages with a minimum of linguistic interference.)

[1] Ibid., p. 121.

Culture, Memory and Narrative

Some sub-systems of a culture, such as those which are utilized in the production of an epic song, appear in many respects to be fairly self-contained in the same way that language is. We thus often speak of language as being distinct from all other aspects of culture. At other times, as in the case of the Ixil myths, there seems to be a more comprehensive series of linkages with other aspects of social life, such as divination, curing and religion in general. Thus level four in Figure 1, with its *Motivation, Consequences, Appeal* and *Answer*, may also, we suspect, apply to curing and religious ritual as well as Ixil myth. Similarly the Eskimo eidochronic structure[1] with its emphasis on abduction and power struggle has close correlates with actual life situations.

If we return to a consideration of language, however, we find that we speak of these same kinds of relationships the minute we begin to discuss meaning. The conventional distinction between semantics and syntax is based on this empirical situation. As we get into the analysis of narratives and other cultural productions and thought processes, we also find it useful to distinguish between a kind of semantics and syntax. In myth for instance, the eidochronic structure is clearly a syntactic system. It is thus no surprise that we find the notation of transformational generative grammar useful in describing the generation of a folktale. The story of the Fish Merchant, for example, can be represented diagrammatically:

THE FISH MERCHANT

1. Ixil Folktale → Initial Situation + Plot + Terminal Situation
2. Plot ⟶ Injury + Restitution
3. Injury ⟶ Motivation + Consequences
4. Restitution ⟶ Appeal + Answer
5. Motivation ⟶ Absence + Courtship + Rejection
6. Consequences → Capture + Transportation
7. Appeal ⟶ Encounter + Identification + Task
   + Revelation
8. Answer ⟶ Return + Villainy Avenged

*   *   *

[1] B. N. Colby, 'A partial grammar of Eskimo folktales', *American Anthropologist*, 75, 1973.

Culture, Memory and Narrative

The study of thought processes, memory and narrative requires a great deal of cross-cultural study and we are only just beginning. We must exercise close control in the kinds of experiments described here as well as seek out 'natural' cultural regularities which provide us with another kind of control. In the beginning of this paper we have criticized traditional anthropological approaches to the study of cultural differences in cognitive processes. We also raised the possibility that in a manner analogous to the development of social organization it might be possible to discern developmental sequences in the power and variety of cognitive systems available to users of different cultures. Clearly we have sampled an insignificantly small fraction of the 'generative systems' that are manifested in the daily cognitive life of different peoples. However, our purpose was not to attempt an exhaustive analysis of all possible cognitive systems. Rather, we wanted to show that an analysis of the intellectual behaviour of peoples living in different cultures, in terms of the cognitive skills characteristic of those cultures, can be a useful approach to the cross-cultural study of thought processes. Moreover, we would submit that such analysis is a necessary first step for any enterprise claiming as its end point a theory of intellectual development; for what has been lacking in all previous attempts in this area is agreement concerning the significant elements, the structure of which could be said to be evolving. Certainly in biological evolution, and in the examples of social organization and language which we summarized in the introduction to this paper, an enquiry into the evolution of the system must be preceded by agreement on what constitute the important structural elements that are said to evolve. At the moment we are nowhere near the identification of evolutionary sequences; what we are nearing is a way in which we can specify the important kinds of cognitive structures and skills that different peoples possess and use.

In continuing work on the problem of culture differences in thought processes, it is important, when speaking of individuals or groups, to speak of culture users rather than cultures. One is *not* a *member* of a culture, nor does one '*participate*' in a culture. One *uses* the culture. We know that language is not coterminous with a community of people for whom it is a mother tongue. If we look upon culture as a congeries of systems, of which language is one, it is immediately evident that these systems can be passed along piecemeal to people of other social groups as well as to children being socialized in the same group.

By speaking of culture user and culture use we avoid the trap of reification represented by the famous superorganic position of Kroeber, now long since rejected, but which still creeps up in various guises in even the most modern of anthropological writings.

Of greatest importance to our present concern is the fact that we are not speaking of differences in primitive and modern mentalities but rather of differences in primitive and modern cultures, conceived in all their complexity as combinations of subsystems which enable one to perform better the intellectual tasks at hand. From the experimental work described here we would say that when dealing with short-term memory tasks American school children have more of these subsystems, which are more flexibly interrelated than the cultural subsystems available to the Kpelle and other peoples who have been socialized into less technologically advanced social groups. On the other hand, both the experimental work and the description of epic narrative suggest that few, if any, of the systems developed by the average American adult are as highly tuned to specific dominating tasks (such as the performance of an epic song) as is true of some Yugoslavs. This raises the important problem of the distribution of skills *within* each of the cultures considered. Clearly not every Yugoslav is an epic poet, nor can all Americans remember the batting averages of all the New York Yankees in 1960. We have also seen that rote memory is not necessarily a concomitant of less technologically advanced peoples.

Given the many complexities of the enquiry and the primitive state of our knowledge of the basic elements involved, we can only conclude that an understanding of the relation between cultural processes and the development of special and general cognitive skills is *possible*, but such understanding is a long way off.

A Reversed World: Or Is It?

THE JAPANESE WAY OF COMMUNICATION
AND THEIR ATTITUDES TOWARDS ALIEN CULTURES

Nobuhiro Nagashima

From the Yayoi Era (200 B.C. to A.D. 300) up to the present time, alien cultures and technologies have never ceased to flow into Japan. It was in that era, for instance, that the basic technologies for rice cultivation and the manufacture of bronze and iron tools were introduced mainly from southern Korea and southern China, and established in the main parts of Japan,[1] although political unification was achieved only later by the Yamato Court around the middle of the fourth century. At no time in Japanese history has there existed any monolithic totality of culture. Seen within the framework of Japanese history, therefore, there have always been heterogeneous elements in culture and values, or alternatives in terms of the world-view, but from a comparative point of view there appear to have been certain features which are distinctively Japanese.

In this paper,[2] I shall consider two sets of values from a historical

[1] E. Ishida, 'Minzoku bunka no keisei' (The formation of the folk culture) in K. Ishida (ed.), *Nihon bunkashi gairon* (An introduction to the history of Japanese culture), Yoshikawa-Kobunkan, Tokyo, 1968, p. 65. Apart from these new technologies the Yayoi culture itself may have largely been based on the preceding Jomon culture (12,000 B.C.–300 B.C.) of hunting and gathering economy.

[2] Unfortunately, or fortunately, as I was engaged in fieldwork in Uganda at the time of writing this paper, I had to rely on only a few books for the information regarding Japanese history. Apart from this shortage of references, it is a reckless attempt for an anthropologist, who has never read Japanese history as a discipline, to discuss anything concerning Japanese history. My only excuse to do so is that as a Japanese citizen I ought to be entitled to participate in a national game of discussing, intellectually or otherwise, the differences between the West and the East.

A Reversed World: Or Is It?

perspective, instead of discussing directly the modernization in Japan in the light of traditional culture and values, as first suggested by the editors. The first set of values to be discussed will be called a 'Minimum Message Complex' which is directly concerned with the differences in modes of thought between the West and Japan; while the second concerns Japanese attitudes towards foreign culture and technology.

* * *

Most Japanese appear to believe that the Western way of thinking is radically different from their own. How the Japanese perhaps see the differences is illustrated by the table on page 94.

This table may appear to be full of either ethnocentric or xenophilic non-senses, and yet it contains certain features of analytical interest. First, it can be seen as an example of the tendency among various peoples to regard other cultures as a reversed world to their own in terms of their value system. The Japanese image of the West is thus a mixture of Utopia and the world of witches, or of monsters of excessive rationality—a Western version may be the opposing notions of 'noble' and 'beastly' savages. If we replace 'West' by 'China' as the heading in the table, it is still, in many respects, valid, while in view of what has been advocated by the 'Négritude' movement, 'Japan' could be replaced by 'Africa' as opposed to 'West'.

Second, most of these opposing values could be summed up as the difference in communication, namely, logical/scientific versus instinctive/subjective ways of communication. I shall call these two types of communication 'Maximum Message Communication' and 'Minimum Message Communication' respectively. The definitions of terms to be used for the following discussions are as follows:

Sender: A person who sends a message.
Receiver: A person who receives the message.
Message: Oral or written form of information.
Information: An entity which the sender wants to communicate.

My thanks should go respectively to Mrs. L. V. Bennett and Mr. M. Wakabayashi of Soroti, Uganda, for correcting my English (except for this Note), and for offering me accommodation so that I could concentrate on this paper.

[1] This table is made out of my memory of what I have heard and read. I came across similar contrasts made by Nigel Gosling between the styles of da Vinci and of Flemish masters, such as van Eyck and Memling ('On the drawings of L. da Vinci', *The Observer Review*, 1-6-1969).

A Reversed World: Or Is It?

Table 3

Pairs of opposing values (the West and Japan)

WEST	JAPAN	WEST	JAPAN
Objective	Subjective	Intellectual	Emotional
Analytical	Synthetic	Cold-hearted	Warm-hearted
Logical	Non-logical	Argumentative	Harmonious
Consistent	Inconsistent	Insensitive	Considerate
Definite	Vague	Rigid	Flexible
Impersonal	Personal	Mechanical	Humane
Far-sighted	Short-sighted	Revengeful	Forgiving
Public-minded	Factional	Distant	Intimate
Preferring Contract	Obscure Agreement	Ruthless	Permissive
Respectful of Privacy	Intrusive upon Privacy	Egocentric	Conformist
Pastoral (in origin)	Agrarian	Conquest-minded	Peaceful
Meat Eaters	Grain Eaters	Cruel	Merciful
Monotheistic	Animistic	Intolerant	Tolerant
Absolute	Relative	Competitive	Co-operative
Dualistic	Less categorical	Exclusive	Inclusive

Maximum Message Communication. The sender first analyses the information, orders it, and then transforms it into the message, which should be as exact, clear and logically consistent as possible. The length of the message is immaterial so long as it represents the information completely.

The success of communication depends almost entirely upon the sender's ability to compose a logically consistent message, the receiver being only required to understand the language used. The relationship between the sender and the receiver can, therefore, be distant and impersonal. Objective kinds of information are suitable for this type of communication, but even information of a very subjective nature attains objectivity, in that the receiver has little to guess.

94

A Reversed World: Or Is It?

Minimum Message Communication. The sender first abstracts the essential feature of the information and expresses it in a few selected words. The message must be charged with highly evocative power, so that it leads to, as it were, an explosion of the total information in the mind of the receiver.

The success depends not only upon the quality of the message, but also upon the receiver's instinctual understanding of it. The more common the experience shared between the sender and the receiver, the easier becomes the communication. The relationship between them must, therefore, be intimate and personal. Subjective kinds of information are suitable for this type, but even objective ones are bound to become subjective because of the vagueness of the message.

In any society, these two types of communication exist—prosaic and poetic expressions, for instance—and daily communication may contain both elements in various degrees. It appears, however, that the maximum message type has radically developed in the West probably in accordance with the development of science, while in Japan the minimum message communication has shown its particular development, which is, I think, deeply connected with the Japanese way of non-rational and instinctual approaches to the world. In the following sections, social and cultural aspects of the minimum message communication in Japan will be considered.

* * *

Owing to the obscurity of messages, the probability of failure in communication is structurally much higher for the minimum message type than for the maximum message type. Certain Japanese social values could be interpreted either as efforts to increase the probability of success in communication, or as results of frequent failures in it.

A common way in which to increase efficiency in communication is, in any society, to have as many opportunities as possible for getting to know each other. Because of the weighty dependence on the receiver for successful communication, the Japanese case in this respect is on the radical side by any standard. Thus among any social group based on common interests, it is an obligation rather than an entertainment to drink together—especially among unequals. The word *tsukiai*, meaning literally 'social intercourse' but more particularly 'drinking together', has compulsory effects, especially in the business world, in which *tsukiai* is regarded as a duty at an off-duty time, and as an important prerequisite for any serious business talk.

A Reversed World: Or Is It?

An extreme form of the minimum message communication is expressed by the words *ishin-denshin* (first used in *Zen* Buddhism) which means a 'direct communication from mind to mind' without using words—communication without message. This can be achieved only, so it is said, between those who understand each other perfectly. Whether or not this is possible, Japanese belief in it is a collective representation, comparable to the belief in telepathy among Australian Aborigines and to the Christian theory of Revelation.

Another extreme is to give up communication totally, or, more properly, to make oneself both the sender and the receiver; the only form in which a perfect communication is possible. Keeping a diary (a national habit), seeking solitude in the wilderness (many recluses in Japanese history),[1] running away from home (a modern habit among youth), and the 'I am not understood' type of suicide (fairly frequent) seem to be related to this desire for discommunication, or for perfect communication.

If a communication fails, the receiver, not the sender, is apt to be accused of lack of comprehension. On the other hand, the sender may be accused of sending too clear a message, for it implies disrespect to the receiver's sensibility. To argue with logical consistency is thus discouraged, and if one does so continuously one may not only be resented but also be regarded as immature. This attitude might account for the poor development of logic, or lack of logic, in Japanese history. Too much dependence on the receiver's ability to appreciate obscure messages may also be responsible for the self-indulgent attitudes of the Japanese in expecting others to understand their wishes, without making enough effort to let them be known.

This minimum message communication demands a considerable amount of experience and sentiment to be shared between the sender and the receiver. It also, ironically, creates a nation-wide experience in the form of failed communication, which appears to be one of the main foundations of Japanese sentimentalism. Thus, unlike the Greek

---

[1] The contribution made by various kinds of recluses or hermits in the history of Japanese literature is very remarkable. Those outstanding are Priest Saigyô (*waka* poet, †1190), Kamo Chômei (essayist, †1213), Yoshida Kenkô (essayist, †1350), Shinkei (*renga* poet, Muromachi Era), Sôgi (*renga* poet, †1502), Matsuo Bashô (*haiku* poet, †1694) and Priest Ryôkan (*waka* poet, †1831). Diaries written by ladies during the Heian and Kamakura Eras are also significant as literature. As these recluses cut themselves off physically from their own communities, so did the lady writers mentally.

tragedies in which Fate plays a vital role, the Japanese cause for tragedies expressed in literature, drama and popular music is often that of not being properly understood.

These social aspects of the minimum message communication are as prominent as ever in contemporary Japanese society, but for its cultural aspects it is necessary to refer to early Japanese history.

* * *

In this and the following sections, two features of the minimum message complex in Japanese culture will be discussed, namely, the development of short poems and certain Buddhist theologies and practices.

Table 4

Chronological division of Japanese history adopted in this paper[1]

AGE	DATE	ERA
Primeval	Up to A.D. 537	
Ancient	538–794 794–1185	Asuka-Nara Heian
Medieval	1185–1334 1334–1573	Kamakura Muromachi
Pre-Modern	1573–1600 1600–1867	Azuchi-Momoyama Edo (Tokugawa)
Modern	1868–	

First, short poems: the development of the *waka*, *renga* and *haiku*. The form of a definite number of verses had probably been established during the latter half of the seventh century under the influence of Chinese poetry. *Manyo-Shû* ('A collection of ten thousand leaves',

---

[1] K. Ishida, 'Bunkashigaku to Nihon bunkashi' (Culturology and the history of Japanese culture), in K. Ishida (ed.), *Nihon bunkashi gairon*, p. 11.

possibly completed by 777) was the first anthology of waka[1] or Japanese poems, comprising 4,505 poems. In style the *Manyo* poems are on the whole realistic, straightforward and virile, and few Chinese influences are found in the themes,[2] which range from natural beauty and love affairs to a complaint about tax. Its contributors were of various social backgrounds, ranging from emperors to anonymous peasants.

There are two main forms of poem in the anthology, that is, long (of continuous 5–7 rhythm[3]) and short (comprising 31 sounds grouped in units of 5,7,5–7,7), the short form being the development of the concluding verse of the long poem. Suggestively short poems of a later period show a slight change in style, becoming subtler and more emotional.

During the later Heian Era, there were significant changes in the style and social background of *waka*. First, long poems had almost completely disappeared and the word *waka* came to mean specifically the short poem of 31 letters. Second, *waka* had attained the utmost significance among the various arts considered necessary for the literate class. Third, it had become an essential means of social intercourse. Few love affairs could be developed without sending and replying in *waka*. Much of the daily conversation and correspondence was replaced or reinforced by *waka*. Thus the exchange of *waka* was practised not only between lovers-to-be but also between families, friends and even between enemies. An old warrior, for instance, expressed his disappointment with his overdue promotion in *waka*, and his promotion followed as a result of his poetic complaint. Many meetings for *waka* competitions were held and various games based on *waka* became popular.[4] In short, *waka* was established not only as an important art but also as a common means of communication, and became a way of life in aristocratic society.

It was against this background that *Kokin-Shû* was edited in 905

---

[1] *Waka* literally means 'Japanese songs', as opposed to the word *kanshi*, 'Chinese poems'.

[2] S. Ienaga, 'Kodai kokka no shûkyô, shisô, bungei' (Religion, thought and literature in the ancient Japanese state), in K. Ishida (ed.), *Nihon bunkashi gairon*, p. 118.

[3] The figures 5 and 7 stand for the number of semi-syllabic letters used, which form a unit in any poem.

[4] A. Tsujimura, *Nihon bunka to communication* (Japanese culture and communication), N. H. K., Tokyo, 1968, pp. 42–55.

A Reversed World: Or Is It?

as the first of twenty-one Royal anthologies of *waka*—hitherto Royal anthologies had been confined to Chinese-style poems. The prevailing aesthetic notion of this period was expressed by the Japanese word *awarè*, a state of mind which was deeply moved by beauty in nature, in rituals or in human affairs. Harmony and refinement were much valued and various adjectives came into use in order to distinguish different kinds of beauty. The style of *Kokin-Shû* was generally static and sensuous.[1]

According to the editor of *Kokin-Shû*, a *waka* should be a perfect representation of one's aesthetically moved state of mind, neither more nor less. If we call this view a 'concord theory' of mind and poem, or of the information and the message, the notion of *yu-gen* advocated by Fujiwara Shunzei three hundred years later is structurally different. According to him, one should not express fully one's mind in *waka*, so that the imaginative world created by the poem could obtain a perspective and have deeper and more profound after-effects on the mind of the receiver. The word *yu-gen*, originally Chinese, means 'remote and faint, or obscure' and those *waka* influenced by yugenism are mostly found in *Shin-Kokin-Shû* (1205, the eighth Royal anthology). Their aesthetic world is remote, quiet, vague and meditative, as represented by the word 'autumn dusk' which is frequently used in *Shin-Kokin*.

It would not be too much of an exaggeration to say that in *Manyo*, *Kokin* and *Shin-Kokin*, three outstanding anthologies in classical Japanese poetry, the process of change from the maximum message communication to the minimum message communication can be found; from long poems to short poems, from a realistic and objective world to a subtler and more emotional one, from the rising sun (*Manyo*) to the setting sun (*Shin-Kokin*), and the increased degree of participation by the receiver, as suggested by the theory of *yu-gen*.

This view might be supported by the two forms of short poems later developed, *renga* and *haiku*. *Renga* is a serialized form of *waka* composed by a few contributors, each of whom develops either the main theme given at the beginning or in the opening verse, or a particular theme in the verse composed by the preceding contributor. There are two features of analytical interest in *renga*. First, the receiver, who has in the world of *waka* been in a passive position of appreciating a

---

[1] Y. Nishio, 'Kyûtei seikatsu no shisô to bungei' (Thought and literature of private life in the royal court), in K. Ishida (ed.), *Nihon bunkashi gairon*.

given *waka* in his own way, is now allowed to participate fully in creating a poetic world, assimilating in himself the roles both of sender and receiver. Second, in *renga* the more radically different the images of one verse are from those of the verse on which it is developed, the more highly esteemed it is aesthetically. 'Bridging by scent' is a technical term to explain this procedure, scent being the vaguest possible form of message.

Renga was fashionable throughout the Muromachi Era of the Medieval Age and in the early Pre-Modern Age, when it ended in the shortest form of poem in the world called *haiku*, comprising 17 letters of 5,7,5 rhythm, the opening verse of *renga* having become independent.

It should be noted that the composers of short poems were not professional in the true sense of the word, and their social backgrounds became wider in accordance with the increase in literacy. Founders and most followers of *haiku* in the Pre-Modern Age, for example, were of the merchant class, which was, under the feudal regime of Tokugawa, officially ranked as the lowest of four classes, Warriors, Peasants, Craftsmen and Merchants. In the case of *waka*, it was first confined to aristocrats, but during the Medieval Age it was established among warriors of non-aristocratic origin. Later, a person of any social significance became expected, at the time of his death, to leave his last *waka* expressing how he had seen his life and death—a remarkable contrast to the Western custom of leaving a will. At the present time, there are thousands of *waka* and *haiku* groups of ordinary citizens and an astronomical number of verses is published every year, although exchanging *waka* for communication purposes has become very rare.

*   *   *

Of the three main traditional religions and philosophies, Shintoism, Confucianism and Buddhism, Buddhism appears to have been most responsible for the formation of the minimum message complex in Japanese culture. Although it is far beyond my ability to discuss theologies developed among various Buddhist sects, very roughly speaking there were three main views regarding the relationship between Buddha and human beings.[1]

---

[1] Not that between Creator and Creature in any sect; hence no creation myths.

A Reversed World: Or Is It?

First, in early Buddhism in the Ancient Age, human beings are an impurified part of Buddha. In order to restore the purity, they have to acquire theological knowledge, to observe various precepts, and undergo severe ascetic exercises.[1] In emphasizing the significance of systematic learning, early Buddhism in Japan was mainly for literates and closer to the maximum message communication.

Second, according to Jôdo and its related sects, men are not a part of Buddha but helpless beings living in this filthy world. The only way to be admitted into the world of Buddha (Jôdo) is by purifying one's mind through the incessant practice of *nen-butsu*, a very short invocation to Amida Buddha of usually seven letters. Thus in Jôdo Buddhism the communication between Buddha and men became the minimum message type. The practice of *nen-butsu* was first advocated by Kôya (†972) and followed by Ryô-nin (†1132), both of whom combined it with simple dances and succeeded in popularizing Buddhism among non-literate people. During the Kamakura Era, *nen-butsu* was firmly established among common people through the efforts of Hônen, Shinran, Ippen and their followers.[2]

Third, according to *Zen* Buddhism, which was introduced by two Japanese Buddhists from Sung China in the early Kamakura Era and became popular during the Muromachi Era, Buddha exists only in one's mind, and the object is to attain the perception of the ultimate oneness of Buddha and one's mind. Once having attained this perception, one begins to see this world as does Buddha, or, to put it another way, this world becomes that of Buddha. From this point of view, all things and beings in this world lose their objective basis of existence, as they exist only in one's mind. The notion of subjectivity, too, loses its ground, because to identify oneself with Buddha is to lose one's Ego, the very basis of subjectivity, and the distinction between subjectivity and objectivity does not exist in Buddha.[3]

---

[1] K. Haga, 'Zen no shisô to Muromachi bunka no seishin' (The *Zen* philosophy and the spirit of Muromachi culture), in K. Ishida (ed.), *Nihon shisôshi gairon* (An introduction to the history of Japanese thought), Yoshikawa-Kobunkan, Tokyo, 1963; and K. Ishida, 'Zen no shisô to bungei bijutsu' (*Zen* philosophy and literature and fine arts), in K. Ishida (ed.), *Nihon bunkashi gairon*.

[2] S. Ienaga, 'Kodai kokka no shûkyô . . .', pp. 110–14.

[3] K. Furuta, 'Shin bukkyô no seiritsu' (The establishment of new Buddhism), in K. Ishida (ed.), *Nihon bunkashi gairon*, and K. Ishida, 'Zen no shisô to bungei bijutsu' (*Zen* philosophy and literature and fine arts), in K. Ishida (ed.), *Nihon bunkashi gairon*.

A Reversed World: Or Is It?

It is logical, therefore, for *Zen* Buddhists, for whom the world is indefinite and inconstant, to reject establishing and established categories with which the objective world is classified, and the search for orders and regularities with which it is explained. In this sense, *Zen* Buddhism is one of the most non-rational, or non-scientific, approaches to the universe.

Zen Buddhism also rejects, in principle, writing as a means of conveying the state of mind which has attained the ultimate perception, although symbolic poems in Chinese were frequently used for this purpose during the Muromachi Era.[1] Pupils are expected to learn through their own experiences in ascetic exercises of mainly sitting and meditating, and instruction, if given at all, is either through deliberately illogically arranged words, or by simple objects or limited gestures. In short, communication in *Zen* is based on short, simple and symbolic messages.

Zen philosophy and its particular way of communication has had a profound influence on both Japanese culture and values in general, and also on the formation and development of *Noh* and *Kyôgen* theatre, the tea ceremony, flower arrangements, black-and-white paintings, and *renga* in particular. *Zen* Buddhism had integrated the existing non-rational elements in both literate and non-literate sections of Japanese society[2] with the newly developed cultural features just mentioned, into what I have called the 'Minimum Message Complex'. In the case of *Noh* theatre, for instance, Zeami Motokiyo integrated yugenism and *Zen* philosophy in his theorization of the drama. He argues in *Kaden-Sho*[3] that 'if you conceal the flower, it remains as the flower, but if you reveal it, it is no longer the flower.' This proposition was later taken up by Yamamoto Tsunetomo who claimed in his *Hagakure*[4] that 'the only proper way for warriors is to die', without expressing their inner struggles caused by the prospect of death. He also referred to love affairs, stating that the only genuine form of love was a concealed love.

---

[1] K. Haga, 'Zen no shisô to Muromachi bunka no seishin' (The *Zen* philosophy and the spirit of Muromachi culture), in K. Ishida (ed.), *Nihon shisôshi gairon*, p. 141.

[2] M. Yamaguchi, 'Ushinawareta sekai no fukken ('For the restoration of the lost world'), Mikai to bunmei, Gendaijin no Shisô, 15, Heibon-Sha, Tokyo, 1968, p. 11.

[3] 'A book on conveying the flower', 1402. The word 'flower' might be translated as 'ultimate reality', or in the context of this paper as 'information'.

[4] 'Hiding behind leaves', 1716, on the philosophy of warriors.

102

A Reversed World: Or Is It?

It might appear that both Zeami and Yamamoto advocated total discommunication, but their ultimate concern was, if I understand them rightly, with how to solve the eternal dilemma between the virtual impossibility of perfect communication and the burning desire of human beings to communicate. Their solutions to this problem were either to minimize the message, relying much on the instinctual, not intellectual, understanding of the receiver, as indicated by the very restricted movements of actors and the simple but refined stage and settings in *Noh* theatre, or to be content with retaining the purity of information by not sending any message at all.

Learning by one's own efforts and experience through the attentive observation of what one's master does without being given much instruction from him, is another feature of this cultural complex. This form was most explicit in the fields of various military arts and handicrafts, but was found in every field of traditional education.[1]

*　　*　　*

If the Muromachi Era can be regarded as the era of development and florescence of the minimum message complex, it was also in the last thirty years of this era that the first contact with the West began to take place. In this section, however, I shall first consider Japanese attitudes towards Chinese and Korean influences shown in the Ancient Age so as to obtain a better understanding of what happened later.

Situated at the eastern end of East Asia adjacent to the old civilizations of China and India, Japan had long been in the position of a 'secondary civilization'. It is also significant that Japan had not experienced military occupation by a foreign force. These two factors might account for the open attitudes and enthusiasm with which Japanese have looked for new things from overseas, and which on many occasions attained the characteristics of a cult.

To be more precise, open attitudes towards foreign elements could be classified in two ways according to two different criteria: first whether *Active* or *Passive* in obtaining foreign things, and second, whether *Positive* or *Negative* in reproducing them domestically. By permuting these two sets of criteria, we have four conventional categories for placing different degrees of open attitudes to foreign elements, from *Passive-Negative* to *Active-Positive*, the most radical form of openness. To draw a conclusion first, Japanese attitudes

---

[1] A. Tsujimura, *Nihon bunka to communication*, p. 76.

undoubtedly belong to the *Active–Positive* category throughout history, with consistent watchfulness of what is going on in other, usually regarded as higher, civilizations.

From the middle of the fourth century until 668,[1] Japan had been deeply involved in Korean affairs both politically and militarily. During this period, many skilled craftsmen, men of administrative and clerical knowledge and a few scholars, were invited, mainly from Korea but some directly from China, and naturalized. With them, Chinese ideograms, Confucianism, Buddhism, the lunar calendar, astronomy in the form of astrology, and various advanced technologies in weaving, pottery using the wheel, and salt manufacturing were brought into Japan.[2]

From the turn of the seventh century, the Royal Court's attitudes became more active. Prince Shôtoku, the regent, sent two missions of students and priests to the Chinese capital (Sui Dynasty) in 607 and 614 in order to learn Chinese culture directly. This was followed, after the fall of the Sui Dynasty, by more than ten missions sent to the Tang Dynasty over two hundred years, ending in 836.

Influences of the Tang culture covered a very wide range. In politics, the centralized bureaucratic government on the Chinese model was founded. In education, Chinese history and theories in Confucianism formed the main parts of the syllabus at colleges founded for bureaucrats. In economy, the production of coins started, though it did not last long. In literature, Chinese essays and poems were widely read among aristocrats, who themselves left many essays and poems written in Chinese. Buddhism was established as the state religion and many temples were built as state enterprises.[3]

In the process of adopting these foreign elements, three different stages could be distinguished. First, the stage of simple reproduction or copying, second, that of adjustment or modification and, third, the stage of refinement or final Japanization. At the end of the final stage,

---

[1] In 668, Japan abandoned all political claims in the Korean Peninsula, owing to the defeat inflicted by the Chinese forces. (M. Inoue, *Nihon kodai kokka no kenkyu* (The study of the ancient Japanese state), Iwanami-Shoten, Tokyo, 1965, p. 485).

[2] M. Inoue, *Shinwa kara rekishi he* (From myth to history), History of Japan, Series 1, Chuôkôron-Sha, Tokyo, 1965, pp. 411–27.

[3] S. Ienaga, 'Kokka no keisei to tairiku bunka' (The formation of the nation and the continental culture), in K. Ishida (ed.), *Nihon bunkashi gairon*, pp. 104–106.

A Reversed World: Or Is It?

the product may not resemble the original form. To take the development of scripts as an example, Chinese ideograms were first used by naturalized clerks of Chinese/Korean origin and then learnt by Japanese officials (copying stage). In due course, some of these characters began to be used for representing sounds instead of meaning, so as to make it possible to write in Japanese (adjustment stage); *Kojiki*, which will be discussed later, and *Manyo-Shû* were written in this style. During the ninth century, syllabic letters were developed from abbreviated forms of Chinese letters (final Japanization). The completion of the syllabic letters (about fifty in number) called *kana* led to the remarkable improvement of Japanese literature in the tenth century in the form of diaries, fiction and *waka*.

This process from copying to the refinement stage was also noticeable in handicrafts, architecture and fine arts.

The introduction of so many foreign cultures and values did not, however, necessarily suppress indigenous elements. The process of Japanization of one foreign element was often accompanied by a parallel development of a corresponding indigenous element. The development of Japanese poems represented by *Manyo-Shû* was one example. Another was the expansion of Shintoism, an ancient religion based on ancestral cults, at the height of enthusiasm for Buddhism during the seventh and eighth centuries. Architecturally, Shinto shrines were of an entirely traditional Japanese style as opposed to the Continental style of Buddhist temples. The Royal Court's support of both Buddhism and Shintoism was partly political, for while Buddhism provided a unifying factor, Shinto was the ideological basis of sovereign power.[1]

The emphasis on Shintoism was also due to the realization of the fundamental difference regarding the nature of the sovereign between China and Japan, namely, the Chinese notion of Heaven's Decree as a basis of authority to rule, as opposed to the hereditary principle of the Japanese monarchy.[2] To demonstrate this difference was one of the main purposes of editing, under Royal order, two Japanese histories, *Kojiki* and *Nihon-Shoki*, both of which took nearly half a century to complete (in 712 and 720 respectively).

Kojiki ('Records of ancient affairs', 3 volumes) and *Nihon-Shoki* ('History of Japan', 30 volumes) form the oldest remaining literature;

[1] Ibid.
[2] S. Ienaga, 'Kodai kokka no shûkyô . . .', p. 116.

105

they are based on two preceding books, 'The genealogy of the Royal Family' and 'Ancient stories'[1]—both of which were lost. Differences between these two are, however, suggestive of Japanese attitudes in this period towards foreign and domestic elements.

Kojiki is written in much-Japanized Chinese and edited by an official, mainly on the basis of the orally transmitted contents of the two previous books. Its quality as literature is highly valued. Thus Motoori Norinaga (†1801), an outstanding scholar of Japanese classics in the Pre-Modern Age, claimed that in *Kojiki* the naturalistic and anthropocentric attitudes of the ancient Japanese, unaffected by foreign ideologies of Confucianism and Buddhism, were fully expressed—which he regarded as an ideal way of life.[2] In contrast with *Kojiki*, *Nihon-Shoki* is written in Chinese and was edited at the Department of History which was specially founded for this purpose. It is based on various written sources, and modelled on the style of Chinese historical books.

Thus we have indications that at this time writing in Chinese was considered more official and given greater prestige than writing in Japanese. This higher prestige value attached to foreign things is clearly seen in the way in which *kana*, Japanese syllabic letters, were named and used. The word *kana* means 'spurious letters', while Chinese letters were called *mana*, 'genuine letters'. *Kana* letters were first mainly used by ladies in the Heian Era in the form of diaries, stories, essays and *waka*, freely mixed with Chinese letters, while official documents, Buddhist theologies and serious essays were written by men in *mana*. Associated values attached to *mana* and *kana* could be suggested as follows:

Mana	*Kana*
Foreign	Domestic
Masculine	Feminine
Public	Private
Hard	Soft
Superior	Inferior

[1] M. Inoue, *Shinwa kara rekishi he*, p. 14.
[2] T. Itô, 'Nihon kenkyû to seiyô gakujutsu no juyô' (Japanese studies and the acceptance of Western disciplines), in K. Ishida (ed.), *Nihon bunkashi gairon*, pp. 393–4.

A Reversed World: Or Is It?

Thus, the Introduction of *Kokin-Shu*, which was the first literature written mainly in *kana* and which advocated the restoration of the traditional Japanese mind by means of *waka*, was written in both *mana* and *kana*, perhaps in order to make the anthology appear more respectable. Ki Tsurayuki, one of the editors of *Kokin-Shu*, assumed the personality of a lady when he used *kana* for writing *Tosa nikki* (935, a diary of his journey).

Japanese reactions to Chinese influences in the Ancient Age may be summed up as follows. First, the Japanese were very active in adopting things Chinese both on state and individual levels. Second, positive efforts were made to reproduce those alien elements locally, usually resulting in the complete Japanization of them. Third, stimulated by new ideas, certain indigenous elements had shown remarkable development. Fourth, in spite of this, much higher prestige value was attached to things foreign. Fifth, partly as a reaction to this over-valuation of foreign culture, and partly as a result of realizing differences in modes of thought and feeling between Chinese and Japanese, nationalistic movements, which invariably advocated a return to Shintoism, recurrently emerged.

There is, in fact, little change in these patterns in later Japanese history from the Medieval Age up to the present, as far as Japanese attitudes towards foreign cultures and technologies are concerned.[1] After the fall of the Tang Dynasty, new knowledge continued to flow into Japan from the four successive Chinese Dynasties, Sung, Yüan, Ming and Chi'ng, and later from the West.

* * *

The first contact between the West and Japan took place in 1543, when crews of a wrecked Portuguese ship took refuge at a tiny island south of Kyûshû; the first firearm was brought into Japan on this occasion. This was followed by the arrival of Francisco Xavier of the Jesuits at Kyûshû island in 1549, and Christianity then expanded rapidly in western Japan until it was officially prohibited by the newly established feudal regime of Tokugawa in 1613. Meanwhile, trading relations were established with Portugal, Spain (1584), Holland (1609) and England (1613), which, however, soon came to an end (except for that with Holland) owing to the policy of seclusionism adopted by the regime.

[1] Y. Masuda, *Junsui bunka no jôken* (Conditions for a homogenous culture), Kodan-Sha, Tokyo, 1967.

107

A Reversed World: Or Is It?

During this brief period of contact, advanced technologies and scientific knowledge of various kinds had been introduced, together with systematic school education,[1] and these were willingly accepted and earnestly learnt by Japanese of various backgrounds, including peasants and merchants.

The production of firearms by the Japanese may be a good example with which to illustrate the positive attitudes shown in the technological field. Within less than two decades from the first arrival of firearms, more than one hundred thousand guns were locally produced by mostly illiterate blacksmiths, helped a great deal by the increasing demand created by continuous civil wars. This is, however, a phenomenon not found, so far as I know, in other non-Western societies in which demands for firearms were as great as those in Japan; these demands were met by trade, an 'active' but 'negative' attitude towards foreign technologies.

In spite of the policy of seclusionism of Tokugawa, Western knowledge continued to come into Japan through the Dutch establishment at Nagasaki, the only permitted channel to Europe. By distinguishing Christianity and sciences, and from pragmatic necessities, the feudal regime did not much discourage Western studies. Thus various sciences began to be established during the later Tokugawa Era, in the order of medicine, botany, astronomy, mathematics, geology, chemistry, physics and military science.[2] The development of these autonomous cognitive disciplines owed much to individual efforts rather than to the government, which eventually returned to the ancient policy of sending students overseas, this time to Holland, in 1862, only six years before the final downfall of the feudal regime itself.

In political studies, Neo-Confucianism, established as a state discipline in Ming and Chi'ng China, also became dominant in Japan.[3] In literature, especially in classical studies, a significant nationalistic movement started at about the same time as Western natural sciences were established. This movement, spearheaded by Motoori Norinaga, ideologically aimed at restoring the optimistic

[1] There were about 200 primarios, two seminarios and one collegio in Western Japan in 1580 (A. Ebisawa, 'Kirishitan-shû no shinkô to shisô' (The belief and thought of Christianity), in K. Ishida (ed.), *Nihon shisôshi gairon*, p. 168).
[2] T. Itô, 'Nihon kenkyû to seiyô gakujutsu no juyô', pp. 396–400.
[3] M. Bitô, 'Hôken shakai to Jugaku' (The feudal society and Confucianism), in K Ishida (ed.), *Nihon bunkashi gairon*.

A Reversed World: Or Is It?

and naturalistic ancient Japanese mind expressed in Shintoism, reject-ing both Confucianism and Buddhism as pessimistic philosophies which had suppressed human nature. This in practice led to empirical studies of Japanese classics, many of which were reprinted at this time, and thus to the establishment of Japanese studies.[1] Motoori contrasted the Chinese and Japanese minds, for instance, in terms of impersonal and personal approaches to the world. This contrast was later rephrased as 'the Japanese mind and Western technology', an indication that Japanese ethnocentrism seldom assumed overall superiority in every field, as did the ancient (and modern?) Chinese and Victorian British.[2]

At the dawn of the Modern Age, Japan was thus equipped with various sciences, fairly advanced technologies combined with small industries, humanities with a keen awareness of the differences between the West and Japan, widespread literacy,[3] many publications, a long tradition of monetary economy, and, above all, a number of determined individuals who were ready to take up any new ideas and technologies, urged both by the sense of national crisis and by the traditional enthusiasm and curiosity for things foreign.

*　　*　　*

It appears that the Japanese people have long taken for granted their desire to absorb seemingly advanced foreign culture and technology, to the extent that it has become one of the favourite national subjects for self-ridicule. Recently, however, as the problem of modernizing many non-Western nations has become one of the serious world issues, the Japanese have become aware that active and positive

---

[1] T. Itô, 'Nihon kenkyû . . .' pp. 393–400.

[2] G. Lienhardt, *Social anthropology*, Oxford University Press, London, 1964, ch. 1.

[3] According to R. P. Dore, *Education in Tokugawa Japan*, Routledge, London, 1965, about 50 per cent of adult males and 15 per cent of adult females had had some sort of school education at this time.

Japanese writing usually comprises both Chinese ideographic and Japanese syllabic letters. Ideographic letters are not as difficult to learn and read as sug-gested by J. Goody and I. Watt ('The consequences of literacy', in J. Goody (ed.), *Literacy in traditional societies*, Cambridge University Press, 1968), and they did not prevent literacy from being widespread either in China (K. Gough, 'Implica-tions of literacy in traditional China and India', in J. Goody (ed.), op. cit.) or in Japan. The greatest disadvantage of them is of course the difficulty in international communications.

attitudes to alien elements are not so universal, and that it is embarrassing to answer the question of 'How have you done it?', implying 'within so short a time', as the Japanese 'take-off' in this respect took place so long ago. It might be suggested, however ethnocentric it may sound, that considering the favourable conditions obtaining in Japan at the dawn of the Modern Age, what has happened since then would not offer an easy model to follow for those societies which are lacking in some of the conditions.

There could be various answers to another related question as to why Japan has been able to retain her traditional culture and values in the course of modernization, but the shortest answer may be 'Why not?' It is possible to overthrow a political regime overnight, but it is not easy to destroy a culture in a hundred years or so, even if it is considered desirable to do so at all. As discussed in the case of Japan, and also illustrated by the co-existence of Christianity and science in the West, it is an entirely misleading and irrational assumption, often asserted by very rational people, that the existence of non-rational elements in a society would deter certain rationalizing social institutions, that these elements should, therefore, first be got rid of, and that modernization (Chinesation, Westernization, Americanization or whatever it is) must be achieved at the cost of the indigenous (non-Western) culture. Yamaguchi argues that one of the priorities of modern times is to restore a proper place for non-rational elements within a culture, so that the complementary opposition between rationality and non-rationality could result in a healthier society.[1]

The contrast between modernization and traditional culture in Japan has certainly been exaggerated, perhaps because traditional elements appear so exotic and hence remarkable to Western eyes, or perhaps because of the recent economic expansion of Japan. From a Japanese point of view, however, it is simply the process of incorporating both domestic and foreign elements, however mutually contradictory they may be, in order to improve the standard of living in the true meaning of the word, not necessarily in terms of materialism.

* * *

If there is anything in common between the two sets of values discussed in this paper, it is the emphasis on being a good receiver of information.

---

[1] M. Yamaguchi, 'Bunka to kyoki' (Culture and delirium), *Chuô-Kôron*, Tokyo, Jan. 1969, p. 354.

The corollary of this is that the Japanese are very poor, or passive and negative, as the senders of information in both personal and international communications. Thus, in the long history of East Asia, Japanese influence on other, neighbouring civilizations has virtually been nil. Certain traditional Japanese cultures now valued in the West were often first, as it were, discovered by Europeans themselves. The number of Western books translated into Japanese may have reached one million or more, while the number of Japanese books translated into Western languages might be less than one hundred— I do not know of any Japanese book translated into Chinese.

In discussing the two types of communication as the main source of difference in modes of thought between the West and Japan, I may have exaggerated the differences a little too much. There is, however, at least one difference between the two worlds: the very rigid distinction between modes of thought and structures of sentiment, between rationality and non-rationality, or between logos and pathos, is typically of the West. In the Japanese word *omoi* both elements are integrated, or indistinguishable, as it simply means works of the faculty of the human mind. The minimum message communication, or a non-rational way of thinking, was developed in Japan through the Ancient and Medieval Ages among the literate section of society, although it had also been deeply rooted in the non-literate folk society. This means that literacy itself does not necessarily lead to a scientific way of thinking, as it is often assumed.

Literacy versus Non-literacy: The Great Divide?

SOME COMMENTS ON THE SIGNIFICANCE OF 'LITERATURE' IN NON-LITERATE CULTURES

Ruth Finnegan

When people wish to make a basic distinction between different societies or historical periods, one of the commonly invoked criteria is literacy. In particular those who wish to avoid the connotations of 'primitive', 'uncivilized', 'aboriginal' tend to turn to a description in terms of 'non-literate' or 'pre-literate'. Certainly, other characteristics are also employed (particularly that of technology) but that of the absence or presence of literacy is increasingly stressed.

If literacy is to be regarded as a fundamental mark of distinction between two basically different types of society, it is relevant to examine it further. How far is it significant for the main question of this symposium? Does non-literacy have consequences for modes of thinking? Do non-literates *ipso facto* think differently from literates? If so, how significant are these differences? In view of the constant use of the differentiating criterion of literacy, this is a question that needs to be faced more directly than it usually is.[1]

One common answer that is often implied is that the presence or absence of literacy is of absolutely crucial significance for the quality of thought in a given culture. Thus in the view of the Director-General

---

[1] Relatively little solid work has been done to tackle this question directly; see, however, the essays in J. Goody (ed.), *Literacy in traditional societies*, University Press, Cambridge, 1968 (especially those by Goody and Watt and by Gough); also R. Finnegan, 'Attitudes to speech and language among the Limba of Sierra Leone', *Odu*, n.s., 2. 1969.

Literacy Versus Non-literacy: The Great Divide?

of UNESCO, René Maheu, mankind can be divided into two main groups, the difference between them being apparently directly attributable to literacy: 'those who master nature, share out the world's riches among themselves, and set out for the stars', and 'those who remain fettered in their inescapable poverty and the darkness of ignorance'.[1] It is only with the establishment of mass literacy that 'the liberation and advancement of man' is possible, and the ending of 'darkness in the minds of men'.[2] Again, a recent book by Talcott Parsons represents writing as a 'watershed' in social evolution, 'the focus of the fateful development out of primitiveness',[3] and it is almost a commonplace to speak of the 'revolution' brought about by the invention or adoption of writing.

This kind of approach is strengthened by the apparent association between non-literacy and illiteracy. We tend to associate the latter with an individual or group that has failed to master the generally accepted skills of the culture and is thus cut off from the cultural heritage of contemporaries without having anything of his or their own to put in its place. It is easy to assume that a similar kind of picture must apply to *non*-literate cultures where all or most of the community are without written modes of communication. Further, we all only too easily slip into the habit of mind, which assumes that those apparently very different from ourselves necessarily have less wisdom, less sensitivity to the beauties or tragedies of life than we have ourselves—and to this extent at least must perforce be said to think differently. This kind of feeling too makes us ready to embrace a view which sets non-literate societies and their inhabitants on the far side of a great chasm separating them from more familiar cultures which rely on the written word.

An important factor which tends to underlie this view is one apparent consequence of non-literacy: lack of literature. *Prima facie* it seems obvious that individuals and societies which are without writing also lack literature with all that that implies. In other words, they have no access to that part of culture which we would normally

---

[1] René Maheu in UNESCO, *World congress of ministers of education on the eradication of illiteracy, Teheran 1965. Speeches and messages*, UNESCO, 1966, p. 29.

[2] Ibid., pp. 40, 82.

[3] T. Parsons, *Societies. Evolutionary and comparative perspectives*, Prentice-Hall, Englewood Cliffs, 1966, p. 26.

8   113

regard as among the most valuable parts of our intellectual heritage and perhaps the main medium through which we can express and deepen mankind's intellectual and artistic insight. If in 'primitive' societies access to this medium and its riches is truly lacking, then it is hard not to conclude, with Maheu, that there is indeed a basic divide between them and 'civilized' communities and that this is therefore a fact to be taken account of in any consideration of differing modes of thinking.

In this essay I intend to examine this view about the apparent lack of literature, and its consequences for thought in non-literate cultures. Is it true that the label 'non-literate' necessarily implies 'without literature'? or even if *some*, rudimentary, analogue to literature can be found there, is it perhaps 'literature' of a fundamentally different kind from written literature? Does it follow that societies can be divided into two radically different types so far as their intellectual and aesthetic development goes—the gulf between them being that of literacy and its corollary, literature? What are the implications for some of the more intangible aspects of thinking like self-awareness, detachment or intellectual probing?

There are of course a number of other possible consequences of literacy which could be discussed.[1] However, the existence of a (written) literature is one of the first to spring to mind and is the only one I intend to discuss here. Unlike the possible connections of literacy with, say, banking, administration or bureaucracy, its implications for literature are of direct relevance for the whole question of 'modes of thought'—in the context, at least, of our common view of literature as both the expression and the moulder of thought.

* * *

Is it in fact only in literate societies that we find 'literature'? Must literature, in other words, be *written*? Those who have been brought up in a society which, like the contemporary Western world, assumes a strong association between literacy and literature will feel inclined to answer in the affirmative. We naturally have a bias in favour of the associations and forms that we know—especially if this is combined with ignorance of those of other peoples.

It is worth however considering both the many periods of history and the many recent and contemporary societies which have existed

---

[1] See especially Goody and Watt in Goody (ed.), op. cit.

Literacy Versus Non-literacy: The Great Divide?

largely or completely without making use of the written word. The period and area in which writing is taken for granted as the main mode of artistic or intellectual communication is relatively small. When one looks beyond our own immediate horizons, it is clear that there are many other possibilities. Some groups are, or have been, completely without writing—like, say, the Australian aborigines, the Eskimos, the Polynesian islanders (so famed for the riches of their verbal art), and some of the American Indian and African peoples. Others again, basically non-literate themselves, have lived at least on the margins of literate cultures and have been to some extent influenced by them: one could instance parts of the West African savannah areas, where Arabic literacy and culture were known (in some areas well known) even though the great mass of the community remained themselves non-literate, or the areas of Asia touched but not pervaded by the influence of China and of India. Other peoples—as in early Ireland, Ethiopia, parts of contemporary North Africa or medieval Europe—have possessed a definite literate and literary class whose compositions were transmitted largely by oral means to the non-literate masses. This shades into the kind of situation of classical Greece, traditional India and China or, indeed, the not so remote past in Europe where written literature was accepted as the highest form, but for many people access to it could still only be through the spoken or enacted word. Here and elsewhere we may find that the established and respected tradition is that of literacy, but oral litera-ture is still a living art and there is constant interplay between oral and written forms.[1] When we survey these many different possibilities, it helps to bring home how very limited is the world's experience of printed literature and mass literacy—the situations we tend to take for granted as the natural form to which all others must tend.

By now, few who have considered these and similar cases would deny that such cultures possess at least the parallel to what we term literature. Their forms are unwritten,[2] it is true, but in many other

---

[1] E.g. medieval Europe, the nineteenth-century western Sudan or modern Thailand and Yugoslavia. (See H. J. Chaytor, *From script to print*, Heffer, Cambridge, 1945, esp. ch. 6; R. Finnegan, *Oral literature in Africa*, Clarendon Press, Oxford, 1970, pp. 49 ff; Tambiah in Goody, op. cit., p. 116; A. B. Lord, *The singer of tales*, Harvard University Press, Cambridge, Mass., 1960, esp. pp. 23 ff.)

[2] Or, in some cases, are written at some point but transmitted and 'published' by oral means.

respects appear comparable to what we know as literature. Non-literate communities have, for instance, what have been described as lyrics, panegyric poetry, religious poetry, love songs, prose narratives, or drama.

The sort of forms that are possible in these oral cultures can best be illustrated by a few examples. Here, for instance, is the opening of a 450-line praise-poem to Shaka, the great nineteenth-century Zulu king and warrior. The figurative and evocative diction makes it obscure to English readers, but something of its tone comes across even in translation.

> Dlungwana[1] son of Ndaba!
> Ferocious one of the Mbelebele brigade,
> Who raged among the large kraals,
> So that until dawn the huts were being turned upside-down.
> He who is famous as he sits,[2] son of Menzi,
> He who beats but is not beaten, unlike water,[3]
> Axe that surpasses other axes in sharpness;
> Shaka, I fear to say he is Shaka,
> Shaka, he is the chief of the Mashobas,
> He of the shrill whistle, the lion;
> He who armed in the forest, who is like a madman,
> The madman who is in full view of the men.
> He who trudged wearily the plain going to Mfene;
> The voracious one of Senzangakhona,
> Spear that is red even on the handle[4] . . .

Again, there is the Yukagir girl's song from northern Siberia,

> When our camps separated
> I looked after him
> He is tall like a mountain ash
> His hair covered his shoulders
> Like black squirrels' tails.
> When he disappeared
> I lay down in the tent.
> Oh, how long is a spring day?
> But the evening came

---

[1] A praise-name meaning the rager or ferocious one.

[2] Shaka's famous praise-name sometimes translated 'He who is famous without effort'.

[3] Water can be beaten, but to no effect; Shaka cannot be beaten at all.

[4] T. Cope, *Izibongo. Zulu praise-poems*, Clarendon Press, Oxford, 1968, p. 88.

Literacy Versus Non-literacy: The Great Divide?

> And through a hole in the tent cover
> I saw my love coming
> When he came in
> And looked at me
> My heart melted
> Like snow in the sun[1]

or the modern Gaelic lament for a hunter in the Western Isles of Scotland

> I am along on the wave-girt island and the birds remain on the shore. Well they may and forever, I have lost the gun-equipped hunter who would leave the brown stag lying, and take the grey seal from the wave mouth.[2]

It is tempting to continue endlessly with similar instances of unwritten 'literature'. There are the dirges of the Sea Dyaks of North Borneo, the profoundly meaningful myths of the American Winnebago, Mozambique satirical songs, Somali love poetry, or 'the finest epic poetry of modern times. . . from the Kara Kirghiz, tent-dwelling shepherds of the Tien Shan mountains'.[3] But perhaps enough has been said to show that we must approach, as at least analogous to our literature, the unwritten forms of millions of people throughout the world, now and earlier, who do not employ writing.

*   *   *

It could be argued however that these analogues to literature in nonliterate (and even perhaps semi-literate) societies are analogues only in certain respects and are not essentially 'literature' in our own sense

---

[1] W. R. Trask, *The unwritten song. Poetry of the primitive and traditional peoples of the world*, Jonathan Cape, London, 1969, vol. 2, p. 125 (quoted from W. Jochelson, *Peoples of Asiatic Russia*, American Museum of Natural History, 1928, p. 224).

[2] J. Ross, 'Formulaic composition in Gaelic oral literature', *Modern Philology*, 57, 1, 1959, p. 7.

[3] N. K. Chadwick, 'The distribution of oral literature in the Old World. A preliminary survey', *Journal of the Royal Anthropological Institute*, 69, 1939, p. 89. For further examples see the various works cited in the present essay and, in particular, H. M. and N. K. Chadwick, *The growth of literature*, University Press, Cambridge, 3 vols., 1936–40; W. R. Trask, *The unwritten song. Poetry of the primitive and traditional peoples of the world*, Jonathan Cape, London, 2 vols., 1969; C. M. Bowra, *Heroic poetry*, Macmillan, London, 1952, and *Primitive song*, Weidenfeld and Nicolson, London, 1962; R. Finnegan, *Oral literature in Africa*, Clarendon Press, Oxford, 1970; P. Radin, *Primitive man as philosopher*, Dover Publications, New York, revised edn., 1957.

of the term. The differences may be as important as the similarities. It is therefore worth discussing a little further the kinds of expectations we have of literature and whether these apply in non-literate societies. The whole area of 'What is literature?' is of course a controversial and unending one which clearly cannot be covered here even in summary fashion. It is relevant, however, to point to some obvious and common-sense points which would occur to most people considering the subject.

One obvious function that we tend to associate with literature is that of intellectual expression. Indeed for some this seems to be its essence. Literature conveys some truth perceived by the poet,[1] and expressed in terms intelligible to his audience—not necessarily, it goes without saying, a factually accurate description of something which can be grasped in simple terms, but a form of expression which can be recognized as having its own profound or inner truth. As Aristotle put it, in terms which still influence our attitudes to literature today, it is a representation of reality, it expresses what is in a sense universal.

This may, certainly, not be all we demand of literature—but it is one common expectation of it. If so, it is easy to see how any assumption that non-literate peoples do not have literature in our sense must lead to the view that their thinking is to that extent limited. Connected with this is the old picture of 'primitives' as emotional, close to nature, incapable of standing back and seeing things intellectually. And indeed, if there is no literary medium through which they can express and communicate their insight into the nature of the world and of human beings, this must profoundly affect their whole mode of thought.

In fact an examination of what has been termed the 'oral literature' of non-literate groups shows that this assumption is far from justified. When one reads—or, better, hears—some of the oral literary forms in such contexts one cannot help but admit that expression of insight and understanding by no means necessarily depends on writing. The Homeric epics—to take a well-known example first—would be accepted by all (including Aristotle) as illuminating our knowledge of man and the universe through a literary medium; and yet it is now widely accepted that these poems were composed *orally* and not

---

[1] I am using 'poets' here and later to include creators of prose as well as of verse.

primarily in writing.[1] Or take the insight into the problem of poetic composition conveyed, through the image of fishing, in a short Eskimo poem.

I wonder why
My song-to-be that I wish to use,
My song-to-be that I wish to put together,
I wonder why it will not come to me.
At Sioraq it was at a fishing hole in the ice,
I could feel a little trout on the line,
And then it was gone.
I stood jigging.
But why is it so difficult, I wonder?
When summer came and the waters opened,
It was then that catching became so hard.
I am not good at hunting.[2]

Again an Ewe poet on the West African coast tells of a man who has lost his relatives through death. But in bewailing his fate he also expresses his underlying fortitude and his comment on the human condition.

Last remaining, last to go:
A border mark I stand.
Were I a boundary post
On the farm's edge,
I'd heave myself
Aside and free me.
What can't be cursed must be endured,
Some folk unwisely fret
Under ills they can't prevent.
You who mock my loss of kin,
Know you the will of Fate?[3]

There is a further problem about regarding oral literature as a form of intellectual expression. This involves the question of artistic 'distance'. One aspect of literary expression is surely the sense of detachment that it somehow involves, so that even when the poet and

[1] See for instance the various essays in G. S. Kirk (ed.), *The language and background of Homer*, Heffer, Cambridge, 1964.
[2] K. Rasmussen, *The Netsilik Eskimos. Social life and spiritual culture*, Gyldendalske Boghandel, Copenhagen, 1931, p. 517 (quoted in Bowra, op. cit., 1962, pp. 45–6).
[3] G. Adali-Mortty in U. Beier (ed.), *Introduction to African literature*, Longmans, London, 1967, p. 4.

his public are emotionally engaged, there is also a feeling of standing back, as it were, of universalizing a particular topic or problem, of conveying some kind of detached comment. It could be argued that this kind of detachment and perspective may not so readily be achieved in oral literature when the poet is merely one of his own audience: when, for instance, an African story-teller produces his narrative to a group with whom he has already spent the day and who are predominantly his close neighbours and relatives. There can be no masking of the author from close familiarity, no interposition of the written word between poet and public.

There are however various ways in which, in non-literate contexts, the same function of 'distancing' can be achieved that is performed elsewhere through the written page. In the first place the village story-teller situation is not the only or even the most common type of oral literature. There are many cases, in totally non-literate as well as in semi-literate groups, where we encounter professional poets and raconteurs. Many wander from place to place to perform before unfamiliar audiences, like, for instance, the modern Moorish trouba-dours,[1] the northern Nigerian Hausa praise-singers,[2] the professional minstrels and saga-tellers among the Tatars of the far Asian steppes,[3] or the early Irish poets.[4] Others again stand apart through having some particular position or recognized poetic skill which sets them at one remove from their audiences. There are the official bards of Zulu kings,[5] the Polynesian *tohunga* priest-poets,[6] or the highly trained intellectual élite of Ruanda.[7] Even in the absence of such experts, there may be devices which enhance the detached effect of literary forms. It has often been remarked how many African stories clothe their characters in animal form rather than speaking directly about, say, the quirks or the virtues of everyday people, and this clearly has

---

[1] See, e.g., H. T. Norris, *Shinqīṭī folk literature and song*, Clarendon Press, Oxford, 1968, pp. 51 ff., 65.

[2] M. G. Smith, 'The social functions and meaning of Hausa praise-singing', *Africa*, 27, 1957, pp. 38–9.

[3] H. M. and N. K. Chadwick, op. cit., vol. 3, esp. pp. 174 ff.

[4] E. Knott, *Irish classical poetry*, Colm Ó Lochlainn, Dublin, 1957, p. 8; R. Finnegan, 'Early Irish kingship', unpub. B.Litt. thesis, University of Oxford, 1960, pp. 184 ff.

[5] Cope, op. cit. pp. 27 ff.; Finnegan, 1970, op. cit., pp. 83–4.

[6] H. M. and N. K. Chadwick, op. cit., vol. 3, pp. 443 ff.

[7] A. Kagame, *La poésie dynastique au Rwanda*, Institut Royal Colonial Belge, Brussels, 1951, pp. 21 ff.

the effect of putting the narrative at one remove from reality by its very setting. As Evans-Pritchard writes of spider tales among the Sudanese Azande, 'the animal forms might be compared to the masks in Greek or in mediaeval drama.'[1] A somewhat similar point could be made about the element of fantasy that often enters into the stories, or the musical embellishments that sometimes accompany them. Again, the stress on authority—'we learnt this from the ancestors'—can be taken not so much as a literal attribution of origin but as another means of raising the composition above the ordinary level of communication. It was not only the ancient Greeks, furthermore, who used masks to enact their plays before largely non-literate audiences: the same custom of masking the actors and thus adding an extra dimension of distance between them and their audience also occurs in the dramatic performances of a number of non-literate peoples. In the water-spirit masquerades of the Kalabari fishermen of south-eastern Nigeria, for instance, the masks serve to disguise the individual actors and, with the religious associations of the plays, help to bring about 'psychical distance'.[2]

In these cases the audience is still a face-to-face one, it is true. But it is easy to forget that it is only in a relatively short period of history that dissemination through the written word has been the accepted vehicle for literary communication. In both the classical and the medieval world, oral delivery (even of previously written forms) was the accepted medium—and this does not lead us to assume that the verbal art conveyed through this means was therefore lacking in the artistic detachment of 'literature'. There is then no reason to presuppose that this is a *necessary* consequence of oral delivery in totally non-literate societies either. In all these cases the special nature of literary as distinct from everyday communication is made clear to its hearers by the recognized conventions—whether these are to do with the position, appearance or dress of the poet, the verbal formulae, a special poetic language,[3] or the embellishment in language and music.

[1] E. E. Evans-Pritchard, *The Zande trickster*, Clarendon Press, Oxford, 1967, pp. 25–6.
[2] R. Horton, 'The Kalabari *Ekine* society: a borderland of religion and art', *Africa*, 33, 1963, esp. pp. 103 ff. This article has suggested several of the points discussed here.
[3] E.g. the use of Mandingo as the conventional language for minstrels throughout a wide area of West Africa (including among non-Mandingo speakers) (see Finnegan, 1970, op. cit., p. 96 and references given there), or the special language of early Irish poets (Finnegan, 1960, op. cit., p. 187).

Literacy Versus Non-literacy: The Great Divide?

The very expression of some sentiment in an accepted literary form in itself implies a kind of detachment. Take, for instance, the ironical dance song of the Tikopian islander in the western Pacific, a comment on self-righteous converts. The poet stands back from the immediate situation to comment ironically

> My dwelling is evil,
> I dwell in darkness;
> My mind is dark
> Why don't I abandon it?
>
> It is good that I should die
> Die with the mind
> Of one who dwells in darkness.
>
> Stupid practices to which I have clung;
> Let them be pulled down and caused to slip away.[1]

It is clear that for something to be locally accepted as literature (and the *local* appreciation is what is relevant here) there is no need to rely solely on the particular convention of the printed page.

If then we think of literature as a condition for the flowering of intellectual and perceptive thought it is hard to see any great divide between those societies which happen to use *writing* for literary expression and those which do not. In the use of literature as communication of insight, there is nothing radically 'other' about non-literate societies—just as there is nothing magic about writing. In this respect writing is just like oral media in that both can be used in a variety of ways—for literature and non-literature, to illuminate and to obscure. Whether we are dealing with literate, semi-literate or totally non-literate societies, there is the opportunity for their literature both to mould and reflect the culture which forms and follows it.

The consequence for the basic question of this symposium is clearly an important one. Far from non-literate societies being radically different in that they lack any medium of thought comparable to our literature, they in fact seem in no essentials different from us in this respect. True, their literature may—sometimes—be less specialist, less fixed to the verbal invariability of the written word, more tied to specific occasions. But these are all matters of degree, and do not

[1] R. Firth, *We the Tikopia: a sociological study of kinship in primitive Polynesia*, Allen and Unwin, London, 1936, p. 44.

Literacy Versus Non-literacy: The Great Divide?

necessarily affect the functions of literature as expression of thought. Individuals in non-literate as in literate societies grow up in an atmosphere in which literary forms are there to mould their thoughts, heighten their awareness and provide a form through which they can convey their own insight and philosophy. In some cases there is provision for specialist education in the composition and delivery of oral literature—the Maori 'school of learning',[1] for instance, the Ruanda training in poetry,[2] the professional training and public examination of Uzbek epic singers,[3] the Druidic schools of Caesar's Gaul,[4] or the later Irish bardic schools.[5] But even individuals in societies without such formal institutions are not without an opportunity for literary education in the broader sense. The Akan child in the West African forest areas grows up hearing spoken, sung and intoned poetry, as well as the special verbal poetry for horns and drums and the constantly recurring imagery of proverbs,[6] while a little further east the Yoruba are exposed from birth to 'tonal, metaphor-saturated language which in its ordinary prose form is never far from music in the aural impression it gives and which has produced an extensive variety of spoken art characteristic of the people'.[7] In Yugoslavia the future singer imbibes from childhood the complex oral artistry of their epic song: 'the fact of narrative song is around him from birth: the technique of it is the possession of his elders and he falls heir to it.'[8] And even in quite recent times in the Gaelic-speaking parts of western Ireland there has been the oral intellectual fare of their famous 'fireside literary circles' which has given intellectual enjoyment to those without access to written literature in their own language.[9]

[1] E. Best, *The Maori school of learning*, Dominion Museum monograph 6, Wellington, 1923 (cf. H. M. and N. K. Chadwick, op. cit., vol. 3, pp. 459 ff.).
[2] Kagame, op. cit., p. 24.
[3] N. K. Chadwick and V. Zhirmunsky, *Oral epics of Central Asia*, University Press, Cambridge, 1969, pp. 330 ff.
[4] Caesar, *De bello gallico*, 6, 14.
[5] Knott, op. cit., p. 43; M. Dillon, *Early Irish literature*, Chicago University Press, Chicago, 1948, pp. 73, 149. For further discussion of training see Bowra, op. cit., 1952, pp. 427 ff.
[6] See K. Nketia, 'Akan poetry', *Black Orpheus*, 3, 1958.
[7] S. A. Babalǫla, *The content and form of Yoruba ijala*, Clarendon Press, Oxford, 1966, p.v.
[8] Lord, op. cit., p. 32.
[9] See J. H. Delargy, 'The Gaelic story-teller', *Proceedings of the British Academy*, 31, 1945, p. 192.

Literacy Versus Non-literacy: The Great Divide?

It is no longer possible, therefore, to accept the old picture of 'the primitive' (or the non-literate) as unselfconscious and unaware, incapable of contemplating the world with intellectual detachment, a picture conveyed to us through our (perhaps unconscious) association of these attributes with lack of literacy and hence, we imagine, of literature. In some respects one might even argue that individuals in many non-literate societies are liable to grow up with even more acquaintance with literature than those in modern Western societies. As Phillpotts put it in her book on Icelandic literature,

> Printing so obviously makes knowledge accessible to all that we are inclined to forget that it also makes knowledge very easy to avoid. . . . A shepherd in an Icelandic homestead, on the other hand, could not avoid spending his evenings in listening to the kind of literature which interested the farmer. The result was a degree of really national culture such as no nation of today has been able to achieve.[1]

Similarly a peasant in an African village or an islander in the remote Pacific—or a medieval courtier for that matter—cannot escape the experience of hearing lyrics, or stories, or sagas throughout his life. The impact of this literature, we must assume, will influence his outlook on life and his perception of the social, natural and human world around him.

*   *   *

There is a further point that may still make one want to question the underlying similarity of written and oral literature. This is the awareness of another facet of literature about which I have as yet said little: what might be called its function of expression—aesthetic expression in general and the individual's vision and urge to create in particular. If 'oral literature' cannot also be shown to have some relevance in this sphere—unclear though it is—then we may well feel that, for all its contribution to more intellectual concerns, it must be basically only a limited medium and lacking in what some would regard as the most valued aspect of literature.

There are several popular notions about the nature of non-literate and of 'primitive' culture which might seem to support this view of their 'literature'. Though few or none of those assumptions would be

[1] B. Phillpotts, *Edda and saga*, Thornton Butterworth, London, 1931, pp. 162–3 (quoted in Goody, 1968, op. cit., p. 60).

accepted by most scholars now—at least in their extreme form—they still tend to linger at the backs of our minds. In order to assess the aesthetic significance of oral art it is necessary to discuss them directly.

First, there is the idea that *oral* literature, just through being oral, is handed down word for word over the generations. Now there are a few cases where—it seems—this is indeed done[1] (though more likely over the years than over generations), but by and large the most striking characteristic of oral as opposed to written literature is precisely its variability. There is little concept of the verbal accuracy typical of cultures which depend on the written, particularly the printed, word. By its very nature oral literature is changeable: it cannot be checked by reference back to a written standard, and the performer/composer is aware of the need to speak in accordance with the demands of his audience rather than some authenticated but remote prototype. This facet of oral literature comes out, for instance, in a recent description of story-telling in Kenya.

> Each person will tell the same story differently, since he has to make it personal and not simply a mechanical repetition of what he has heard or narrated before. He becomes not only a 'repeater' but also a 'creative' originator of each story . . . The plot of the story and the sequence of its main parts remain the same, but the narrator has to supply meat to this skeleton. This he will do in the choice of words, the speed of reciting, the imagery he uses, the varying of his voice, the gestures he makes with his face and hands, and the manner in which he will sing or merely recite the poetical portions . . . The narrator puts his personality into the story, thus making it uniquely his own creation.[2]

A similar account can be found in Lord's well-known discussion of the process of composition among Yugoslav poets.[3] These singers create long and colourful epics through completely oral composition and dissemination. The formulae and sequences may draw on conventional forms, it is true, but each poem as actually performed on a particular occasion is unique—the product of its particular singer. Passages like the following are filled both with traditional motifs and at the same time with the poet's individual treatment.

---

[1] For some instances see Trask, op. cit., vol. 2, pp. xxix–xxx, Chadwick, 1939, op. cit., p. 78.

[2] J. S. Mbiti, *Akamba stories*, Clarendon Press, Oxford, 1966, pp. 26–7.

[3] A. B. Lord, *The singer of tales*, Harvard University Press, Cambridge, Mass., 1960. (The material is also discussed by Colby and Cole above, pp. 85–8.)

The bey prepared himself in his white tower,
And girded on his belt and arms,
And prepared his broad-backed chestnut stallion,
He put on him his arms and trappings,
With a cry to Allah he mounted his beast,
And he drove him across the level plain,
Like a rabbit he crossed the plain,
Like a wolf he ranged along the mountains. . . .[1]

Then he summoned the youths:
'Bring me writing table and paper!
I must now send out letters,
To gather the well-dight wedding guests.'
Ever since the world began,
Youth has ever obeyed its elder.
They brought writing table and paper.
See the old man! He began to write letters.
He sent the first to Mustajbey
To the broad Lika and Ribnik,
And thus he spoke to the bey. . . .[2]

Such passages and the much longer poems in which they occur are not unchanging. As Lord puts it,

Any particular song is different in the mouth of each of its singers. If we consider it in the thought of a single singer during the years in which he sings it, we find that it is different at different stages in his career. . . . The larger themes and the song are alike. Their outward form and their specific content are ever changing.[3]

The same kind of description is given by Radlov of composition among the Kara Kirghiz of the Asian steppes. Here again the minstrel improvises his song according to the inspiration of the moment. He draws on well-tried motifs (or 'formative elements'), it is true, but impresses his own personality on these and never recites a song in exactly the same form.

The procedure of the improvising minstrel is exactly like that of the pianist. As the latter puts together into a harmonious form different runs which are known to him, transitions and motifs

[1] Ibid., p. 59 and discussion pp. 58–60.
[2] Ibid., p. 86.
[3] Ibid., p. 100.

Literacy Versus Non-literacy: The Great Divide?

according to the inspiration of the moment, and thus makes up the new from the old which is familiar to him, so also does the minstrel of epic poems. . . . The minstrel can utilise in his singing all the formative elements. . . . in very different ways. He knows how to represent one and the same picture in a few short strokes. He can depict it more fully, or he can go into a very detailed description with epic fullness. . . . The amount of the formative elements and the skill in putting them together is the measure of the skill of the minstrel.[1]

In oral literature there is thus no requirement that the poet should reproduce word-perfect 'traditional' versions. In non-literate and semi-literate cultures we encounter the same blend, familiar from written literature, between what is conventional (or 'traditional') and the personal inspiration of the individual poet.

It is easy to slip from this into the opposing idea that, if oral literature is not handed down word for word, then it is haphazard, spontaneous, perhaps short and crude, and certainly without deliberate and studied artistry—'mere improvisation'. If so, this verbal art is presumably very different from what we regard as literature. In fact, many of those who have made close studies of oral literature have commented on its use of style and complex techniques. It is easy to mention the well-known cases of the Homeric hexameter and Homeric epithets, or the forms and formulae of Anglo-Saxon and early English poetry—all, it appears, orally developed.[2] There are also innumerable lesser-known examples: the complicated rhythmic patterns which, together with elaborate tonal techniques, give form to non-metrical Yoruba poetry in West Africa,[3] the lengthy praise-poems of the Zulu with their studied use of parallelism and alliteration and their richly figurative style,[4] the subtle tonal requirements of Efik poetry[5] or the careful art of the long oral epics of twentieth-century Yugoslavia.[6]

---

[1] V. V. Radlov, *Proben der Volkslitteratur der türkischen Stämme und der dsungarischen Steppe*, St. Petersburg, 1866–1904, vol. 5, pp. xvi ff. (quoted from English translation in N. K. Chadwick and V. Zhirmunsky, *Oral epics of Central Asia*, University Press, Cambridge, 1969, pp. 222–3).

[2] For references on these oral formulaic techniques see below, p. 136.

[3] See S. A. Babalola, *The content and form of Yoruba ijala*, Clarendon Press, Oxford, 1966, especially Appendix A, pp. 344–91, and references given there.

[4] Cope, op. cit., pp. 38 ff.; cf. Finnegan, 1970, op. cit., ch. 5.

[5] D. C. Simmons, 'Tonal rhyme in Efik poetry', *Anthropological Linguistics*, 2, 6, 1960.

[6] Lord, op. cit.

Again, there are the exacting formal conventions of Somali poetry. Here alliteration is the most striking feature—the rule that in each hemistich of the poem at least one word has to begin with a chosen consonant or vowel.

> The rules of alliteration are very rigid in the sense that only identical initial consonants are regarded as alliterative . . . and no substitution by similar sounds is admissible. All initial vowels count as alliterative with each other and again this principle is most strictly observed.
>
> The same alliteration is maintained throughout the whole poem. If, for example, the alliterative sound of a poem is the consonant *g*, in every hemistich there is one word beginning with *g*. A poem of one hundred lines (two hundred hemistichs) will therefore contain two hundred words beginning with *g*. . . .
>
> While [some] poets find the restrictions of alliteration an unsurmountable obstacle, men with real talent dazzle their audience with their powers of expression, undiminished by the rigidity of the form.[1]

On the other side of the world too, in the western isles of the south Pacific, we find in the poems of the Gilbert islanders 'clear-cut gems of diction, polished and repolished with loving care, according to the canons of a technique as exacting as it is beautiful'.[2] This technique is a conscious one, employed by poets who

> sincerely convinced of beauty, enlisted every artifice of balance, form and rhythm to express it worthily. The island poet thrills as subtly as our own to the exquisite values of words, labouring as patiently after the perfect epithet.[3]

It is thus not only in written literature that we find an interest in form and style as one aspect of literary expression. The fact that oral literature is unwritten does not *ipso facto* absolve the poet from adhering to locally accepted canons of aesthetic form (which may be very complex) nor prevent him from delighting in the elaboration of beauty in words and music for its own sake.

[1] B. W. Andrzejewski and I. M. Lewis, *Somali poetry: an introduction*, Clarendon Press, Oxford, 1964, pp. 42–3.

[2] A Grimble, *Return to the islands*, Murray, London, 1957, p. 200.

[3] Loc. cit.

Literacy Versus Non-literacy: The Great Divide?

There is little to be said, either, for the related idea that non-written literature is somehow 'communally' rather than 'individually' created. This notion is associated with a certain era of the romantic movement and few who know anything of oral literature at first hand would accept it now in its extreme form. There is of course a grain of truth in the idea. While every poet is to some extent influenced by expectations of his public's reaction, the *oral* composer experiences this most directly. Each piece of oral literature is realized in its actual performance and—the relevant point here—before a particular audience. It is directly influenced, and thus moulded, by the audience as well as by the composer. The listeners may even take a direct part in the performance, and altogether make a more obvious contribution than with written literature. But here again this is a matter of degree. The public to which a piece is directed always has some influence and it is never true to think of a poet as an island to himself, unaffected by the society in which he lives.

There is a great deal of evidence to show how important the *individual* composer can be in non-literate as in literate societies. In both cases he is to some extent conditioned by conventional patterns but this can of course give scope as well as limits to his genius. In respect of actually communicating his words, the oral performer has even more opportunity for individual expression than one who must commit his imagination to the written page. He can enhance and point his words by his mode of utterance, embellish them with music, movement and even on occasion dance, bring out the intended humour or pathos or irony of his vision by his expression or tone.

Among many descriptions of the art of the individual oral performer and its contribution to the effectiveness of the actual composition, one can quote Ó Murchú's account of hearing an Irish storyteller:

> His piercing eyes are on my face, his limbs are trembling, as, immersed in the story, and forgetful of all else, he puts his very soul into the telling. Obviously much affected by his narrative, he uses a great deal of gesticulation, and by the movement of his body, hands, and head, tries to convey hate and anger, fear and humour, like an actor in a play.[1]

In his choice of words and subject too, the individual oral poet has

[1] Quoted in Delargy, op. cit., p. 190.

many opportunities. In any community, of course, one can find derivative as well as creative practitioners. But there is no reason to suppose that only the first occur in cultures which happen not to use writing as a vehicle for their thought. Among the Limba peasants of the West African savannah, for instance, I have had the opportunity of comparing a gifted and a merely adequate story-teller working on the same basic plot. The second gave us a competent narrative, enjoyable and perfectly satisfying. But the first—we ended up with a new insight into the ways of human beings: we had joined in his affectionate mockery of a virile young chief's boastful arrogance, his humorous comment on a girl's subtle efforts to attract the youth's attention, and his delight in the beauty of words and music. The imprint of his individual personality, and his personal perception of the world and its artistic potentialities, were too striking to be forgotten.[1]

A similar description has been given of story-tellers among the American Indians.

> That far-reaching variants in the manner . . . of telling a tale exist we all know, but a relatively small number of investigators have ever taken the trouble to inquire just wherein the full implication of the variation lay . . . With this object in view, I obtained different versions of the same myth from three individuals. Two of them were brothers and had learned the myth from their father. The differences between these versions were remarkable, but *the significance of the differences lay in the fact that they could be explained in terms of the temperament, literary ability, and interests of the story-teller.*[2]

Or take the Alaskan Eskimo term for poetic concentration, *qarrtsiluni*, lit. waiting for something to break. This is not spontaneous communal creation, but a deliberate and personal concentration on poetic composition. The poets must wait in deep stillness and darkness while, as an Eskimo put it, they 'endeavour to think only beautiful thoughts. Then they take shape in the minds of men and rise up like bubbles from the depths of the sea, bubbles that seek the air to burst in the

---

[1] For a discussion of differences between individual Limba story-tellers, see R. Finnegan, *Limba stories and story-telling*, Clarendon Press, Oxford, 1967, pp. 70 ff., 93 ff.

[2] Radin, 1957, op. cit., pp. 53–4. (My italics, R. F.)

light!'[1] Again there are the Gilbertese island poets of the southern Pacific of whose poetic compositions Grimble has given so vivid a description.

> It is only when the poet feels the divine spark of inspiration once more stirring within him that he deviates from the ordinary course of village life. . . . He removes himself to some lonely spot, there to avoid all contact with man or woman . . . This is his 'house of song,' wherein he will sit in travail with the poem that is yet unborn. All the next night he squats there, bolt upright, facing east, while the song quickens within him.

The next morning he performs the prescribed ritual for a poet, then goes to the village for five friends whom he brings back with him to his 'house of song'. Together they work on his 'rough draft'.

> It is the business of his friends to interrupt, criticize, interject suggestions, applaud, or howl down, according to their taste . . . They will remain without food or drink under the pitiless sun until night falls, searching for the right word, the balance, the music that will convert it into a finished work of art.

When all their wit and wisdom has been poured out upon him, they depart. He remains alone again—probably for several days— to reflect upon their advice, accept, reject, accommodate, improve, as his genius dictates. The responsibility for the completed song will be entirely his.[2]

It is of course notoriously difficult to appreciate the art of foreign cultures but, even so, it is hard to deny the individual inspiration of such a lyric, created by one of these Gilbertese poets, as

> Even in a little thing
> (A leaf, a child's hand, a star's flicker)
> I shall find a song worth singing
> If my eyes are wide, and sleep not.

> Even in a laughable thing
> (Oh, hark! The children are laughing!)
> There is that which fills the heart to over-flowing,
> And makes dreams wistful.

---

[1] P. Freuchen, *Book of the Eskimos*, Arthur Barker Ltd., London, 1962, p. 281.
[2] A. Grimble, *Return to the islands*, Murray, London, 1957, pp. 204–5. For some further accounts of similarly deliberate poetic composition in oral contexts, see Finnegan, 1970, op. cit., pp. 268 ff. and references given there.

Literacy Versus Non-literacy: The Great Divide?

Small is the life of a man
(Not too sad, not too happy):
I shall find my songs in a man's small life. Behold them soaring!
Very low on earth are the frigate-birds hatched,
Yet they soar as high as the sun.[1]

The same applies to the many love poems which have been so widely recorded for non-literate (and thus supposedly 'communally' dominated) peoples like the Maori:

Love does not torment forever
It came on me like the fire
Which rages sometimes at Hukanui.
If this beloved one is near to me,
Do not suppose, O Kiri, that my sleep is sweet.
I lie awake the livelong night,
For love to prey on me in secret.
It shall never be confessed lest it be heard by all.
The only evidence shall be seen on my cheeks.
The plain which extends to Tauwhare:
The path I trod that I might enter
The house of Rawhirawhi.
Don't be angry with me, O madam; I am only a stranger.
For you there is the body of your husband,
For me there remains only the shadow of desire[2]

or the North American Tewa:

My little breath, under the willow by the water side we used to sit
And there the yellow cottonwood bird came and sang.
That I remember and therefore I weep.
Under the growing corn we used to sit,
And there the leaf bird came and sang.
That I remember and therefore I weep.
There on the meadow of yellow flowers we used to walk
Oh, my little breath! Oh, my little heart!
There on the meadow of blue flowers we used to walk.
Alas! how long ago that we two walked in that pleasant way.
Then everything was happy, but, alas! how long ago.

[1] Grimble, op. cit., pp. 207–8.
[2] Radin, 1957, op. cit., pp. 118–19.

Literacy Versus Non-literacy: The Great Divide?

There on the meadow of crimson flowers we used to walk.
Oh, my little breath, now I go there alone in sorrow.[1]

To be sure, there is often little interest among non-literate and
semi-literate peoples in the individual personality of the author,
particularly of the romantic and intense kind characteristic of a
certain period of Western literature or Western capitalism. Nor is
there often an idea of copyright: in societies without the tradition of
a printed and fixed version, literary proprietorship is not really
relevant.[2] But to deny the effect of individual inspiration and creativity
in oral literature for this reason is to ignore the empirical evidence.
From the early English ballad singers[3] or recent Yugoslav epic poets[4]
to modern American narrators[5] or gifted tellers of myths among the
Winnebago,[6] we hear of the skill and inspiration of the individual
artist.

What about the 'functions' of this literature? It has often been
assumed that oral literature, because it is embedded in 'primitive
society', must somehow have essentially different aims from that of
literate cultures. Most often these aims are thought of as in some way
practical. Perhaps the literature has a magical or religious purpose?
or is in some way tied up with fertility? or satisfies some deep psychological need in mythic terms? Among other writers it has been fashionable to represent its function as very specifically 'social': perhaps with
a conscious social purpose like education or moralizing, perhaps an
unconscious function such as upholding the social structure. This
kind of pragmatism is often contrasted with the idea of 'art for art's

[1] H. J. Spinden, *Songs of the Tewa: preceded by an essay on American Indian
poetry*, The Exposition of Indian Tribal Arts, Inc., New York, 1933, p. 73 (quoted
in Trask, op. cit., vol. 2, p. 257).
[2] On this see Chadwick, 1939, op. cit., p. 78. There are however some instances
in which songs are 'owned' by individuals, e.g. the Dobuan islanders of the
western Pacific (R. F. Fortune, *Sorcerers of Dobu*, Routledge and Kegan Paul,
London, 1932, p. 251).
[3] L. Pound, *Poetic origins and the ballad*, Macmillan, New York, 1921,
especially ch. 1; W. J. Entwhistle, *European balladry*, Clarendon Press, Oxford,
1939, ch. 6: MacE. Leach (ed.), *The ballad book*, Yoseloff, London, 1955, esp. pp.
29 ff.
[4] Lord, op. cit.
[5] R. M. Dorson, 'Oral styles of American folk narrators', in T. A. Sebeok
(ed.), *Style in language*, John Wiley and Sons, New York, 1960.
[6] P. Radin, *The trickster. A study in American Indian mythology*, Routledge and
Kegan Paul, London, 1956, p. 122.

sake' supposed to characterize 'civilized' cultures. But too often what is given is an over-simplified and over-generalized picture—as if the literary achievements of even one society at one period of history could be reduced neatly to a single aim or a single function. Certainly it is true that there are some special opportunities open to the oral composer. Oral literature can, in principle, be employed in almost any circumstances in which there is an audience, and the practical power of oral poets to eulogize or satirize, and to gain profit thereby, is constantly being mentioned.[1] Similarly certain types of oral literature —some kinds of songs, for instance, and proverbial formulations— can be turned to account in almost any situation. Among the Maori, for instance, sung poems are used for many purposes.

> If a woman was accused of indolence, or some other fault, by her husband, she would in many cases retaliate, or ease her mind, by composing and singing a song pertaining to the subject. In the event of a person being insulted or slighted in any way, he was likely to act in a similar way. Songs were composed for the purpose of greeting visitors, of imparting information, of asking for assistance in war, and many other purposes of an unusual nature from our point of view. Singing entered largely into the social and ceremonial life of the people, and in making a speech the Maori breaks readily into song.[2]

Such uses are not in the same way open to the creator of written forms. On the other hand a writer has *other* opportunities, which he can choose to exploit if he wishes, whether for propaganda, moralizing, satire, or whatever. Beyond certain once-fashionable assumptions, there is no real reason to suppose that there is necessarily and universally a more practical aim in oral than in written literature. Certainly artistic conventions vary from place to place and time to time: it is hard to appreciate those of others, and thus tempting to explain them away in some such simple terms. But in *all* societies literature is likely to have many different aims in different contexts—to delight, propagandize, moralize, shock, cajole, entrance, eulogize, inform—and we

---

[1] E.g. the Hausa praise poets of Northern Nigeria or the 'griots' of Senegambia (see Finnegan, 1970, op. cit., pp. 96 ff.), the early Irish poets (see especially F. N. Robinson, 'Satirists and enchanters in early Irish literature', in *Studies in the history of religion presented to C. H. Toy*, Macmillan, New York, 1912) or the Icelandic poets (see S. Einarsson, *A history of Icelandic literature*, Johns Hopkins Press, New York, 1957, ch. 3 on skaldic poetry).
[2] E. Best, *The Maori as he was*, Dominion Museum, Wellington, 1934, p. 147.

can take no such short cut to their analysis as to suggest that these differences coincide exactly with the differences between literate and non-literate. Certainly as far as the appreciation of aesthetic and personal expressiveness goes there seems little to choose between the literatures of oral and of literate cultures.

Thus when we consider what are usually assumed to be the basic characteristics of literature (disputed though these are in detail) it is difficult to maintain any clear-cut and radical distinction between those cultures which employ the written word and those which do not. Such differences as there are do not neatly correspond with the presence or absence of literacy, and in both contexts it seems absolutely justifiable to speak of 'literature'. When we reflect how profoundly we expect the possession of literature to colour our own modes of thought we can see that the fact that, after all, it exists in non-literate societies also must greatly affect our estimate of their modes of thought too. We can no longer keep to the old picture of non-literates as without deliberate intellectual probing or aesthetic insight, submerged, as it were, in an unmoving and communal quagmire. In using literature to convey and form their artistic and intellectual awareness they are, at root, not dissimilar from those who live in contexts where writing is prevalent.

* * *

There are also a number of differences between literature in literate and in non-literate contexts which it is interesting to go on to consider. For, however similar in fundamentals, literature in non-literate communities does have the special characteristics of an *oral* literature. Can these special qualities also shed light on our general problem?

One crucial difference as between oral and written literature is the important factor of its dissemination. In literate communities this is primarily through the written word, whereas in non-literate or semi-literate groups it must be orally delivered for its communication as literature. In the oral context, that means, the literature comes across as *performance* as well as a sequence of words. The actual *enactment* of the literary piece is necessarily a vital part of its impact and this fact can be exploited in many ways by the oral poet. His audience, furthermore, sees as well as hears him and the skilful composer/ performer takes advantage of this fact. Characterization, for instance, need not be expressed directly in *words* when it can be as clearly and as subtly portrayed through the performer's face and

135

gestures; conversations too can be lavishly introduced, a sure technique for the performer to convey personification and drama—points that have been made for recited literature as different otherwise as medieval narratives or contemporary African tales.[1] Similarly, the styles of these pieces may be related to their form of delivery. Repetition may be particularly marked, and also the use of various well-known formulaic phrases and runs,[2] or the highlighting of particular dramatic episodes or detailed descriptions in a way not altogether in keeping with the unity of the whole when *read*. In medieval literature, 'the whole technique of *chanson de geste*, *roman d'aventure*, and lyric poem presupposed . . . a hearing, not a reading public'[3]—and the same point can be made of orally delivered literature generally.

This is something which it is essential for us to bear in mind when we attempt to *read* publications of literature originally designed for oral delivery. When one misses the interplay of ear and eye, of audience and performer, which is an essential part of oral literature, it is hard for it not to seem pale and uninteresting. 'The vivacity is lost: the tone of voice, the singsong of the chants, and the gestures and mimicry which give emphasis to what is being said and are sometimes a good part of its meaning.'[4] We similarly miss something by following the modern habit of reading classical Greek and Roman literature silently, through the eye only; it too was expected to be read aloud and it was a common practice in antiquity to publish a work by recitation before an audience. Medieval literature too was commonly

---

[1] H. J. Chaytor, *From script to print. An introduction to mediaeval vernacular literature*, Heffer, Cambridge, 1945, pp. 3, 12, 55: Finnegan, 1967, op. cit., pp. 52, 83 ff.

[2] There is a large and increasing literature on this topic, ranging from treatments of Homeric epic to Gaelic songs in the Western Isles of Scotland. The main references include: Lord, op. cit.; Kirk, op. cit.; F. P. Magoun, 'Oral-formulaic character of Anglo-Saxon poetry', *Speculum*, 28, 1953; R. A. Waldron, 'Oral-formulaic technique and Middle English alliterative poetry', *Speculum*, 32, 1957; J. Ross, 'Formulaic composition in Gaelic oral poetry', *Modern Philology*, 57, 1, 1959; J. H. Jones, 'Commonplace and memorization in the oral tradition of English and Scottish popular ballads', *Journal of American Folklore*, 74, 1961; L. D. Benson, 'The literary character of Anglo-Saxon formulaic poetry', *Publications of the Modern Language Association*, 81, 1966; B. A. Rosenberg, 'The formulaic quality of spontaneous sermons', *Journal of American Folklore*, 83, 1970. On larger units see also V. Propp, *Morphology of the folktale* (trans. L. Scott), Indiana University, Bloomington, 1958, on 'functions', and R. Benedict, *Zuni mythology*, Columbia University, New York, 2 vols., 1935, on 'incidents'.

[3] Chaytor, op. cit., p. 13.

[4] Evans-Pritchard on Zande stories (Evans-Pritchard, op. cit., p. 19).

chanted to a musical instrument and is 'filled with expressions which indicate the author's intention that his work shall be read aloud, shall be heard'.[1]

This stress on literary impact through the *spoken* rather than the written word, sometimes further enhanced by the visual element, should not in fact seem so strange to contemporary European culture. With the spread of radio and television we are beginning to capture something of the same effect. To some this is a matter of regret. It is interpreted as a threat to the more scholastic form of education and outlook which had been so much admired earlier. Maheu speaks with alarm of the danger arising from the new media of mass communication:

> Unless we take care, we shall have a form of communication . . . based purely on images, visual and sound, which will develop, parallel but independent, alongside instruction based on writing. This dualism endangers the spiritual unity of civilization because of the deep psychological differences that separate the two processes of mental training, one of which—that based on the image—appeals mainly to feeling, emotion and reflex response, while the other—based on writing—is, on the contrary, essentially an exercise in critical thought.[2]

Others will think that these 'deep psychological differences' are exaggerated and that this kind of assessment arises more from one particular cultural background in a particular period than from a dispassionate assessment of the available facts; and the suggestion that the use of non-written media necessarily leads to 'conditioning as opposed to education',[3] may seem an extreme one. But the relevant point to stress here is that, even if one does accept such a view, this in fact tends to undermine the assumption that any great divide between cultures (and their thought) coincides with that between modern Western peoples on the one hand and those of the rest of the world on the other. For if more reliance on non-written media involves —as some have suggested[4]—a 'revolution' in communication and

[1] R. Crosby, 'Oral delivery in the Middle Ages', *Speculum*, 11, 1936, p. 98 and, for references to classical recitations, pp. 88–9.
[2] UNESCO, *World Congress of ministers of education on the eradication of illiteracy, Teheran, 1965. Speeches and messages*, UNESCO, 1966, p. 32.
[3] Ibid., p. 33.
[4] See in particular the widely acclaimed writing of M. McLuhan, especially *Understanding media, the extensions of man*, Routledge and Kegan Paul, London, 1964.

hence perhaps in thinking, then it is the highly industrialized nations that are moving fastest towards this—and moving, it would seem, in the direction of something taken for granted in societies which already make use of auditory means in the transmission of literature. Again, we find that the simple view of two basically different types of society, characterized by radically different communication media, just does not accord with the facts. There are differences *and* similarities between non-literate and television-influenced societies just as there is clearly neither a sharp break nor complete continuity between recent periods in European countries characterized, respectively, by the presence and absence of electrical media of communication.

A further factor in the actualization and transmission of oral literature is the audience. In a non-literate context an audience is in practice essential[1]—there is no written form in which it can be expressed otherwise than in front of those to whom it is directed. This contrasts with a written literature: even when his ultimate public is clearly in the writer's mind, his essential task is to get his composition on *paper* rather than directly to his audience. It is different too from the mass media of television and radio. Here an audience is, certainly, implied; but it is not face to face and has no direct and immediate impact on the poet. In the more direct oral context of non-literate cultures, however, the audience's reaction is an integral and continuing part of the whole artistic situation. It contributes not only to the mode of delivery but to the actual words used, by its overt reactions and additions, even by its passivity or at times evident boredom. Radlov has given a vivid description of this role of the audience in his account of the Kara Kirghiz poets of nineteenth-century Asia.

> Since the minstrel wants to obtain the sympathy of the crowd, by which he is to gain not only fame, but also other advantages, he tries to colour his song according to the listeners who are surrounding him. . . . By a most subtle art, and allusions to the most distinguished persons in the circle of listeners, he knows how to enlist the sympathy of his audience. . . . The sympathy of the hearers always spurs the minstrel to new efforts of strength, and it is by this sympathy that he knows how to adapt the song exactly to the temper of his circle of listeners. . . .

[1] Songs and poems are sometimes chanted by individuals while alone, so oral literature is conceivable without an audience. But in practice the normal situation involves an audience.

138

Literacy Versus Non-literacy: The Great Divide?

The minstrel, however, understands very well when he is to desist from his song. If the slightest signs of weariness show themselves, he tries once more to arouse attention by a struggle after the loftiest effects, and then, after calling forth a storm of applause, suddenly to break off his poem. It is marvellous how the minstrel knows his public. I have myself witnessed how one of the sultans, during a song, sprang up suddenly and tore his silk overcoat from his shoulders, and flung it, cheering as he did so, as a present to the minstrel.[1]

The audience is thus more involved, more imbued with literary creativity than is possible when communication is through the more remote medium of writing. This may have certain consequences for the nature of literary activity in such societies. It is likely, in many cases at least, to be somewhat less specialist and remote than it has—sometimes—been in societies where the interposition of writing can create an extra barrier between the creator and his audience. But there are obvious exceptions to this, in the many non- and semi-literate societies where it is possible to speak of an intellectual class: the Polynesian *tohunga*,[2] for instance, the Mandingo 'jellemen' of West Africa, or the poetic order of early Ireland or modern Ruanda. But even in these cases the very fact of delivery before an audience must have kept the compositions of such poets from becoming too remote from their audiences. Again (the same point put in a different way) in non-literate societies individuals may be less likely in some respects to escape direct experience of the literary achievement of their local culture.

It is clear however that this whole question is a complex one and demands much further research. Obviously the significance of the audience as a direct factor in oral literature must be taken into consideration. But for the nature and impact of the literature it may be that the *kind* of audience or public to which it is directed and the functions expected of it by composer and public are equally important —and these seem to have varied as much *within* as between non-literate and literate communities.

A further obvious difference is in the degree of verbal flexibility. Variability seems generally to be the norm in oral cultures in contrast

---

[1] Quoted in Chadwick and Zhirmunsky, op. cit., pp. 225–6. On Kirghiz poets' use of standard themes and runs see ibid., pp. 221 ff.

[2] H. M. and N. K. Chadwick, op. cit., vol. 3, pp. 443 ff.

to the fixity of the written word with which we are more closely acquainted. Surprisingly to one brought up in a literate culture, those without writing tend to have little concept of verbal accuracy. There is no possibility of a written document to act as the yardstick of accuracy and the whole conjoint process of composition/extemporization in oral literature tends to get away from the idea of a fixed and correct archetype. By contrast, it is in literate cultures that we tend to find the magic of the written word and the concept of a text as the immutable and once-for-all authentic version. There have been plenty of examples in Western history of the reverence for the written word for its own sake, whether in a transmitted manuscript tradition or on the printed page. This is a sphere in which the difference between literate and non-literate culture can be profound, and perhaps one of the first prerequisites for an appreciation of the subtleties and individual inspiration of oral literature is to understand this difference.

It is so important, indeed, that it is tempting to regard it as a key to all other differences. But we cannot, alas, push this point too far. Even in literate cultures there are many differences of degree in the respect accorded to a fixed text. There seems to be somewhat less of this attitude in parts of Western Europe now, say, than in the last century; there are variations according to the type of text involved (sacred books like the Bible, Koran or—an oral example—the Rig-Veda, attract more reverence for word-perfectness than more popular writings); and even within a single community different groups will take, say, the immutability of a particular form of prayer or of a well-known textbook more, or less, seriously. It is possible indeed that we should regard *printing* rather than writing in itself as the most important factor here. This at any rate is the view of one authority on medieval literature.

> The invention of printing and the development of that art mark a turning point in the history of civilisation. . . . The breadth of the gulf which separates the age of the manuscript from the age of print is not always, nor fully, realised by those who begin to read and criticise mediaeval literature. . . . We bring unconsciously to its perusal those prejudices and prepossessions which years of association with printed matter have made habitual.[1]

The degree of verbal fixity is, then, one very important sphere of difference between the literature of oral and literate cultures and as

[1] Chaytor, op. cit., p. 1.

140

such must affect the outlook of the corresponding communities. But, like the other differences discussed, it does not produce a clear-cut and fundamental division between them, and, if there is a divide, perhaps it is between societies with and without printing rather than with and without writing.

There is not space to treat other possible differences that spring to mind[1] but one further point should be mentioned. This is the suggestion that non-literate societies as such necessarily have less comparative perspective—i.e., less awareness of other cultures, less realization that their own ways are not unique. This is probably true to some extent and as such must affect the general outlook in such societies. But again it is easy to exaggerate. The isolation of non-literate communities has for various reasons often been overestimated in the past. Ethnocentricism, furthermore, is by no means limited to 'primitive' societies. More important in the present context is the possibility that it may not necessarily be non-literacy itself which leads to such isolation as there is—various technological factors seem more relevant here—and its presence need not therefore of itself imply a limited outlook. Written literature, particularly the printed word, does indeed provide certain opportunities for wider communication. But so too can an *oral* literature. We can instance the travelling 'jellemen' of the great western savannah region of Africa who created a vast cultural area throughout many different kingdoms and linguistic groups by their arts of word and music,[2] the wandering *azmaris* of Ethiopia who helped to bring about the striking uniformity of Ethiopian poetry among the many groups of the area,[3] the unifying effects of their reverence for Homer among the disparate Greeks, or the early poets of Ireland who 'in the absence of towns or any centralized political system . . . were the only national institution'[4]—all performing the same kind of functions as the medieval jongleurs and minstrels of Western Europe or their counterparts in the Arab world. Here again

[1] In particular the question of historical perspective often said to be lacking to those without written literature. On this see the recent discussion in Goody, op. cit., especially the comments by Goody and Watt, pp 44 ff., and Gough (with whose sceptical approach on this question I am very much in agreement), pp. 74–6.

[2] See Finnegan, 1970, op. cit., p. 96.

[3] H. M. and N. K. Chadwick, op. cit., vol. 3, p. 525.

[4] D. Greene in M. Dillon (ed.), *Early Irish society*, Radio Éireann, Dublin, 1954, p. 85.

it turns out that the differences are not clear-cut and that the detailed forms and impact vary with the general nature and outlook of the society as much as or more than the question of whether or not that literature appears in writing.

This brings us to a final difference that should be mentioned here—though strictly it has not necessarily to do with the presence or absence of literacy. This is the difference in outlook and general development that exists between any two cultures unknown to each other. It is very hard to believe that people very different from us can really have anything approaching the depth of understanding or grace of expression that we know in our own society and its literature. This barrier cuts us off to some extent from all other cultures. But it often seems particularly insurmountable for those brought up in a largely literate culture contemplating the arts of non-literate groups—particularly (if irrationally) when these groups are very different from us in *material* development. How few Englishmen, for example, would have been prepared to recognize in the ragged Russian peasant, Yakushkov, one of the greatest composers and singers of the famous local epics?[1] Again, scholars have acquainted us with the rich and elaborate poetry of early and medieval Ireland; but from the point of view of their conquerors these Irish *literati* could be dismissed as 'rebels, vagabonds, rimers, Irish harpers, bards and other malefactors'.[2] It is not only the literate who are ethnocentric. It is salutary to remember the comment of a native of the Gilbert Islands—the Pacific group so imbued with their rich heritage of song—when he heard about aeroplanes and wireless.

'It is true the white man can fly; he can speak across the ocean; in works of the body he is indeed greater than we, but'—his voice rang with pride—'he has no songs like ours, no poets to equal the island singers.'[3]

The fact that an unfamiliar literature is not immediately pervious to a foreign observer need not therefore mean that it lacks its own depth and richness for those who practise it or that there is some fundamental mental difference between the two.

* * *

[1] N. Chadwick, op. cit., p. 79.
[2] Quoted in T. F. O'Rahilly, 'Irish poets, historians and judges', *Proceedings of the Royal Irish Academy*, 36, 1922, p. 86.
[3] Grimble, op. cit., p. 199.

Literacy Versus Non-literacy: The Great Divide?

What emerges is that there are indeed many differences between the literatures of literate and non-literate cultures, and that some of these may be relevant for their modes of thinking. But there are a number of difficulties about taking the sum total of these differences as marking a fundamental division between the two. It is perhaps worth summing these up at this point.

First, the implication that non-literate societies do not have 'literature' turns out to be without foundation. This literature, furthermore, can achieve the same range of things we expect from written literature, with all that this means for the mode of thinking in such contexts. It is true that, as with most foreign literatures, it is not always easy for us to appreciate that of cultures very different from our own. It is also true that much research remains to be done on the different psychological and social effects of reliance on oral as opposed to visual media, as well as on the differences both between direct and indirect (or mass) oral media, and the psychological processes involved in visual communication through written *words* on the one hand and non-verbal visual images on the other. But these problems merely show that the subject is a complex one—much more complicated than the clear-cut chasm between 'oral' and 'visual' (or non-literate and literate) cultures which some people assume. Questions for further thought do not invalidate the main point being made in this essay: the presence of literature as a vehicle for intellectual and aesthetic expression in non-literate as in literate societies.

The final point to make is that, though there are indeed interesting differences between the literary media in non-literate and in literate groups, these seem to be no more fundamental than differences *within* each of these. To take just one relatively short period of Western European history and the many vicissitudes that have affected literature there: we have experienced the change-over from script to print, then the expansion of the range of print with increasing literacy, the move from a reliance on the Greek and Roman 'classics' as the eternal standard to more local and contemporaneous writing, the recent paperback 'revolution', and the expanding influence of radio and television. Thus to take as our yardstick the present circumstances of literature in Western Europe—or rather perhaps those of a generation or so ago—and assume that this is the standard by which we estimate all other literatures is to show a profound lack of historical and comparative perspective. There is no reason to suppose that our

143

peculiar circumstances are the 'natural' ones towards which all literature is somehow striving to develop or by which it must everywhere be measured. In particular there is no reason to hold that it is only through the written—far less printed—page that man achieves literary and artistic development and that we can ignore as wholly other the literary expression of thought and artistry in other forms. As Levin put it in his preface to Lord's analysis of Homeric and Yugoslav sung epics, 'We live at a time when literacy itself has become so diluted that it can scarcely be invoked as an esthetic criterion. The word as spoken or sung, together with a visual image of the speaker or singer, has meanwhile been regaining its hold through electrical engineering. A culture based upon the printed book, which has prevailed from the Renaissance until lately, has bequeathed to us—along with its immeasurable riches—snobberies which ought to be cast aside.'[1]

This essay has perforce skated over many highly controversial questions and has not ended up with any clear definition of either 'literature' or 'thinking'—or of the exact relation between these. The subject tackled is a huge one and all I have tried to do is to make a few obvious (if sometimes ignored) points about it. What I hope I have established is that it *is* a huge and complicated subject—far too complex to be reduced to trite classifications or the categorization implied when we facilely define certain groups as 'non-literate' and unthinkingly go on to assume consequences from this for the nature of their thought. Much work clearly remains to be done on these questions, including careful comparisons among different non-literate cultures themselves. But despite the scattered nature of the illustrations given here it does seem at least clear that one cannot assume as necessarily so, that individuals in non-literate (or largely non-literate) cultures are *ipso facto* less creative, thoughtful, self-aware or individually sensitive than people in literate cultures, and therefore fundamentally different in their modes of thought. Non-literacy itself is unclear and relative enough as a characterization; but the further assumption that non-literate cultures and individuals necessarily lack the insight and inspiration—the modes of thought—that we associate with literature seems on the basis of present evidence an unjustified conclusion.

---

[1] Lord. op., cit, p. xiii.

Colour-words and Colour-values:
The Evidence from Gusii

W. H. Whiteley

'All thinking involves classification and every classification involves judgements to the effect that one or more objects possess, or lack, one or more characteristics.' S. KÖRNER.

The tradition that different 'modes of thought' are *ipso facto* inferior modes of thought, still persists, and nowhere more insidiously than in attitudes to non-Western societies, despite the erosions on it by modern psychology and social anthropology. What plausibility such comparisons may possess derives largely from ignorance of the patterns of thinking in such societies, and the present essay represents a modest attempt to document one area of thinking—that of colour-classification—in an East African rural community. It is, I believe, only by building up detailed accounts of particular aspects of thinking in specific societies that one can acquire the necessary foundation for answering the broader comparative question in more realistic terms.

* * *

In recent years interest in colour has come from at least three different quarters. Firstly, there is the group of social anthropologists for whom colour is one aspect of the more general study of symbolism: the work of Beidelman and Needham on laterality[1] and of Turner on colour among the Ndembu of Zambia[2] are among the most sophisticated and

[1] T. O. Beidelman, 'Right and left hand among the Kaguru: a note on symbolic classification', *Africa*, 31, 1961; R. Needham, 'The left hand of the Mugwe: an analytical note on the structure of Meru symbolism', *Africa*, 30, 1960.

[2] In particular, V. Turner, *Chihamba the white spirit. A ritual drama of the Ndembu*, Rhodes-Livingstone Papers, 33, University Press, Manchester, 1962; 'Three symbols of *passage* in Ndembu circumcision ritual: an interpretation', in M. Gluckman (ed.), *Essays on the ritual of social relations*, University Press, Manchester, 1962; 'Colour classification in Ndembu ritual' in M. Banton (ed.), *Anthropological approaches to the study of religion*, A.S.A. Monographs 3, Tavistock, London, 1966.

detailed examples of this. Secondly, there is the interest which derives
from the wider study of folk taxonomies, which seeks, by enquiry and
discussion, to exhaust the range of distinctions made by a particular
speech community within a particular field, e.g. colour, disease,
plants etc. This interest has produced such classic studies as those of
Conklin and Frake.[1] Finally, there are the social psychologists, who
are interested in how different people perceive colour.[2] Each has
developed specialized techniques which have been largely unexplored
by the others. In part this is inevitable: the symbolists have been
concerned with colour as an immanent quality, round which accrue
sets of values which can be examined only in context; the folk taxono-
mists have been interested in how classification is established in terms
of lexical sets, for which non-contextual study may initially be
adequate. The separation is to be regretted, and in the present brief
essay I want to suggest that a set of values symbolized in colour terms
may co-exist with a different set associated with the occurrence of
colour-words in a range of lexical sets.

Both Beidelman and Turner deal in concepts which tend to polarize
experience in terms of symbolic antitheses. Thus, Beidelman in writing
of sexual symbolism among the Ngulu[3] finds patterns of physical
qualities, of colour or light, of spatial orientation, with such pairs as
fluid/solid, unstable/stable, red/white, low/high, left/right. These
patterns are abstracted from various ritual contexts and Beidelman
is careful to point out when referring to some of his polarity sets that
'. . . some of the items entered are only implied by Ngulu and not
directly presented in a ceremonial act. The reader must judge how
appropriate my selection may be.'[4] Two points may be made: firstly,
it is not clear to what extent, or in what manner, the concepts are
formulated by Ngulu themselves, and to what extent they represent
the abstractions of the anthropologist; secondly, it is unclear to what
extent they pervade daily life beyond the rituals from which they were

[1] H. C. Conklin, 'Hanunóo color categories', *Southwestern Journal of Anthropology*, 11, 1955; C. O. Frake, 'The diagnosis of disease among the Subanum of
Mindanao', *American Anthropologist*, 63, 1961.

[2] For example, R. W. Brown and E. H. Lenneburg, 'A study in language and
cognition', *Journal of Abnormal and Social Psychology*, 49, 1954; and B. Berlin
and P. Kay, *Basic color terms: their universality and evolution*, University of
California Press, Berkeley, 1969.

[3] T. O. Beidelman, 'Pig (Guluwe): an essay on Ngulu sexual symbolism and
ceremony', *Southwestern Journal of Anthropology*, 20, 1964.

[4] Ibid., p. 374, fn. 14.

taken. Is one to understand that pairs like behind/ahead, fluid/solid etc. are imbued in other aspects of daily life with a symbolic flavour? This seems to be so from Beidelman's concluding remarks, 'It is possible now to see how these basic sensory and spatial attributes previously cited are utilized to give more "reality" to moral or social categories. They are associated with values; they are rated in some manner. Similarly, simple physiological acts or states, such as hunting, sexual congress, striking, eating, becoming hot, becoming wet, may be used to express more abstract social actions or moral states. . .'[1]

The same two points are raised by Turner's work on Ndembu colour concepts, again deriving from ritual contexts, where the red/black/white triad symbolizes three 'principles of being' which, Turner comments, '. . . are held by Ndembu to be scattered throughout nature in objects of these colours, such as trees with red or white gum, bark, or roots, others with white or black fruit, white kaolin clay or red oxidized earth . . .'[2] From an examination of texts written by Ndembu informants on what they had learned of the significance of colours in different rituals, there seemed to be agreement that certain 'white things' stood for 'whiteness' which in turn was equated with such qualities as goodness, health, life, huntsmanship, to laugh, to sweep clean, etc. Though these symbolic equations are established within specific ritual contexts, it is again not clear to what extent they are predicated as occurring more generally, though Turner, like Beidelman, seems to suggest this: thus, 'Whiteness not only has the note of social cohesion and continuity . . . Behind the symbolism of whiteness, then, lie the notions of harmony, continuity, purity, the manifest, the public, the appropriate and the legitimate' and, finally, 'The point I am trying to make here is that the three colours white-red-black for the simpler societies are not merely differences in the visual perception of parts of the spectrum: they are abridgements or condensations of whole realms of psychobiological experience involving the reason and all the senses and concerned with primary group relationships.'[3]

Much of the discussion is concerned with the intrinsic colour of certain key objects which figure in the ritual context, e.g. the *mudyi* and *muyombu* trees, and their symbolic significance in those contexts.

---

[1] Ibid., p. 388.
[2] Turner, 1966, op. cit., p. 58.
[3] Ibid., pp. 66, 82–3.

Colour-words and Colour-values: The Evidence from Gusii

The meaning of such objects is established at three levels: that of the interpretation given by informants, that of usage in context, and that of relationship to other objects within the same complex. In all this, however, rather little reference is made to words for members of the colour triad themselves, i.e. white, red and black.

In what follows I take a complementary view and look first at the distribution of 'colour-words' in a number of non-ritual contexts among the Bantu-speaking Gusii of Kenya.[1] Subsequently I consider the evidence to suggest that there co-exists a set of values related to colour deriving, as in Ndembu, from certain objects in ritual contexts. The meaning of the 'colour-words' will be shown to be derived partly from the number of terms comprising the set under consideration, and partly from the nature of the referent. Thus, to quote a familiar example, if the universe of colour is divided into four parts, each will have a smaller range than in a language where the division is into three parts. Equally, while members of the set may have a predominantly chromatic significance in relation to the field of 'clothing', it may be friability which is the important characteristic for members of the set referring to 'soil types'.

* * *

The Gusii, numbering perhaps three quarters of a million, live in well-watered highlands in the western part of Kenya. Their neighbours on three sides are the non-Bantu Luo, Masai and Kipsigis respectively, while to the south, on the fourth side, the related Kuria straddle the Kenya-Tanzania border. Their fertile homeland supports a density of around 600 persons per square mile and permits the growth of cash crops such as coffee, tea and pyrethrum and the grain staples of maize and millet. Gusii are also pastoralists, though it is evident that with the increase of population and consequently of cultivated land, herds are smaller than formerly. The Catholics and Seventh Day Adventists have been active for more than half a century and more recently they have been joined by the Church of God, the Pentecostal Assemblies of East Africa and the Swedish Lutherans. Their impact on Gusii has

[1] An anthropological study of the Gusii was made by Philip Mayer in the late 1940s: among his publications are *Gusii bridewealth law and custom*, Rhodes-Livingstone Papers, 18, Oxford University Press, Cape Town, 1950; *The lineage principle in Gusii society*, Oxford University Press, London, 1949; 'Gusii initiation ceremonies', *Journal of the Royal Anthropological Institute*, 83, 1953. There is little reference to colour in these studies.

148

Colour-words and Colour-values: The Evidence from Gusii

been considerable, and it is not unusual to find families with three generations of Christians, though two is the more common in the area of Getutu where I did my fieldwork.

In considering my own material on colour I am conscious that the same charges can be levelled against me that I have levelled at others, namely that I have not made any systematic attempt to establish for what types of people my data is valid, though I can say that the families in Sengera where I have done most of my fieldwork comprise members of both sexes, all generations, educated and uneducated, Christian and non-Christian.[1]

Like the Ndembu the Gusii have three primary words, cognate with the verbs, *-ráb-*, Be bright, shining, clean; *-mwám-*, Be dark, dirty, cluttered; *-bariir-*, Ripen and change colour, redden. In the appropriate contexts they may be translated as white, black and red respectively. Other colour-words are derivative, thus:

-nyaronyansi[2] Blue-green	Cog. *-nyansi* 14/6 Grass (general term) *-nyaronyansi*, 9/10, Non-poisonous grass snake
-ikɔndɔ Yellow	Cog. *-kɔndɔ* 7/8 Species of monkey, Blue-faced Vervet(?) *-kɔndɔ* 3/4 Species of trailing vine with highly poisonous fruit
-monuuri Yellow	Cog. *-nuuri* 3/4 Yellow Ochre
-sosera Bright green	Cog. *-sosera* 9/10 Species of pond weed, slippery deposit found on stones in ponds, rivers etc.
-matobu Brick red	Cog. *-tobu* Ripe
-bárááti Orange	Cog. *-bárááti* 7/8 Species of bush fruit(?)

[1] I am particularly grateful to the families of Mr. Erasto Abuuga and Mr. Cornelius Oseebe and their friends for their help and patience over the years from 1954–8 in the first instance and again during 1968–9.

[2] In Bantu languages adjectives are characterized by a prefix appropriate to the referent noun. Nouns are grouped into Classes according to the shape of their prefixes which commonly mark singularity and plurality. These Classes are numbered thus: 1/2, 3/4 etc. All examples are given in their stem or root form, i.e. without prefixes. Gusii is a 7-vowel language, with 'ɛ' and 'ɔ' as open varieties of 'e' and 'o'. Long vowels are doubled. The acute accent represents a high tone; the circumflex a falling tone.

149

The three primary terms, like those of the Hanunóo described by Conklin, are associated with a number of non-chromatic connotations of which the following are the most important:

(a) Along a cleanness/dirtiness scale. With clothing as the referent the three terms occur in the following series:

-rábu, Clean
-mwámu, Dirty
-bariiri, Muddy. Not accepted by all informants.

It is thus perfectly acceptable to say:

ésaati yané éndábú nêmwámu, My white shirt is dirty, and also, but less commonly, My clean shirt is (a) black (one)

ésaati yané émwámu nêndábu, My black shirt is clean, and also, but again less commonly, My dirty shirt is (a) white (one)

(b) Along both the cleanness/dirtiness scale and that of clarity/opacity. With water as referent the primary words appear in the following series:

-ya, Clean, clear
-rábu, Clean, clear. Less common than the foregoing
-be, Dirty, stale. Used of water that has stood for a long time
-mwámu, Dark, still—of deep pools. Used as the foregoing but less commonly
-bariiri, Muddy.   It happens that the dominant soil colour in that part of the highlands is red, but the important point is its unfitness for use.

Another dimension is that of heat, thus:

-rero, Hot
-kendu, Cold

(c) Along a lightness/darkness scale. With clouds as the referent two of the words occur in the following series:

-rábu, of a bright cloud, one on which the sun is shining
-ikɔndɔ, of the dark, under-surface of a cumulus cloud
-mware, of a developing cumulus cloud
-mwámu, of a heavy, dark rain cloud
-monuuri, of the yellowish quality of certain stratus clouds.

Colour-words and Colour-values: The Evidence from Gusii

Where human beings are the referent all three of the words occur:

-*rábu*, Light-complexioned
-*mwámu*, Dark-complexioned
-*bariiri*, Medium-complexioned
-*séru*, Medium-complexioned. Difficult to distinguish from the foregoing.

These distinctions, of course, operate for Gusii themselves and their neighbours, and are not used to differentiate Gusii from Europeans for whom there are a number of special words which appear to require no qualification.

(d) Where the referent is a locality only two of the words have been noted and only one is at all common, thus:

-*rábu*, Unoccupied, empty. *ás(e) aariá n'óborábu*, This place is empty, is free of trees, suitable for grazing. The archaic phrase *m'bórábú ngócia*, I'm going to the hills, related to a time when these were unpopulated but probably, as a matter of fact, forested

-*mwámu*, Cluttered up, without room to move.

The longest series in which the three primary words occur are those relating to food-crops and to domestic animals, but it is clear that the classification is only partly by colour, and in some cases this is only of minor importance. I consider first the food-crops.

A. FOOD-CROPS
(i) -*ri* 14/6 *Bulrush-millet*
All the three colour-words occur in this series, designating grain which varies from light yellow (-*rábu*) through reddish brown (-*bariiri*) to very dark brown (*mwámu*), but as the women were quick to point out, colour as such is less important than knowing how hard the grain is, how heavily the variety bears, how early or late it matures, and how much or how little rain it requires. For this reason the colour-words as such are less commonly used than others like the following:

-*marɛgɛ*, a variety which ripens early and dislikes too much rain. The grain is light in colour and grinds and chews easily
-*kundi* 7/8[1] a variety whose grain head has the appearance of a fist. Cog. -*kundi* 9/10 Fist

[1] This and the fourth word in this series seem to be sufficiently well established to be able to occur without their referent in the speech of some informants.

151

nyakóŋaanyi, a variety which bears heavily but dislikes too much
rain. The grain is light in colour
nyaikoro 9 A quick-ripening variety, easily damaged by rain.
Grain reddish in colour. Derived from the town of
Nakuru from which it was introduced in Colonial
times.

(ii) *-ɲɛnde* 9/10 *Beans*
While the remarks about millet made above also apply here, beans
fall rather more neatly into those which are grouped by colour and
patterning, and those grouped by habit or origin. Thus in the first
group we find the three primary terms plus, among others:

-marɛ́gwa, Greyish blue, spotted[1]
-mamɛ́ka, Blackish, blotched
-nyakumúmuri, Reddish, spotted
-ámaikanse, Blackish, with whitish lines in whorls
-makarabê, Reddish black
-nyaikɔndɔ, Yellowish, small in size

and in the second group:

-nyabaruuri, a variety introduced by Europeans. Cog. *-ruuri* 1/2 A
European
-nyabagúnde, a climbing, large-seeded variety introduced by the
Arabs (?) Cog. *-gúnde* 1/2 Arab (?)
-nyamanoa, a tall, climbing variety, recently introduced
-nyabaragoori, a quick-growing variety with a very small reddish
bean, very popular. Cog. *-ragoori* 1/2 A Logoli
(another Bantu group of western Kenya). Other
names for this include *-ɔnyɔ́ɔ́ró* and *-muyááre*.

Other series occur for Maize and Cassava, but they are shorter and
exemplify the same kind of pattern.

B. DOMESTIC ANIMALS
(i) *-(n)gɔ́kɔ* 9/10 Hen. May include chickens and cocks though there
is a special term for the latter and a short series of terms applied to it.

---

[1] The glosses here and subsequently are imprecise, and constitute no more than
rough identifications. They should ideally be accompanied by slides in colour.

Colour-words and Colour-values: The Evidence from Gusii

This series is relatively short, and colour and patterning appear to be the main criteria:

-*mwámu*, Black
-*bariiri*, Rich, chestnut brown
-*rábu*, White
-*kánga*, Black and white, spotted. Cog. -*kánga* 9/10 The Guinea-
fowl
-*mware*, Streaked, reddish brown. Cf. series for clouds
-*monyinga*, Deep chestnut, darker than 2. Cog. -*nyinga* 6 Blood
-*kánga nyakerongo*, Spotted (the spots being of different sizes),
black and white. Cog. -*rongo* Porcupine 7/8.

(ii) -*mbóri* 9/10 Goat. Here the series is longer and includes terms relating to the hair of the goat and to its horns, as well as to the patterning and colour of the hide:

-*nyandábu* OR -*rábu*, White
-*nyamwámu*, Black
-*bariiri*, Brown, reddish brown
-*nyankororo*, Blotched, especially on the underside. Cog. -(*n*)*kororo*
9/10 Small predator, species of Serval Cat (?)
-*nyankánga*, Blotched, spotted. Cog. -*kánga* 9/10 Guinea-fowl
-*nyanseetwa*, A beast with fawn on the body but different head
markings. Cog. -(*n*)*seetwa* 9/10 Species of forest
bird, a Touraco (?)
-*nyamóngoro*, Very dark red-brown. Cog. -*ngóra* 3/4 Species of
Bulrush Millet whose grain is often eaten raw after
drying in the sun and being cleaned. The goat is
here likened to the smooth, even colouring of the
grain
-*nyamonyinga*, Less dark red-brown. Cog. -*nyinga* 6 Blood
-*nyamonúngú*, Hornless. Cog. *monúngú*, Something left unfinished,
half grown, immature
-*nyaiŋo*, Pale yellowish colour. Cog. -*ŋó* 5/6 Species of buck, long
since driven from the area
-*nyameera*, Charcoal-grey
-*nyaságáti*, A beast with blotches on neck or shoulders; colour not
important.

153

(iii) -*ŋɔmbɛ* 9/10 Cow

The importance to Gusii of their cattle is considerable, and was certainly greater in the past,[1] when herds were larger and a man's wealth and status depended on them. Gusii oral tradition is rich in references to exploits concerning cattle.

Cattle are classified by the colour and pattern of their hide, and the terms by which they are identified are in most cases compounds of the element -*nya*- and[2] a referent to which the beast is likened by analogy, thus:

> -*nyaiŋaaya*, A cow with a large patch on it of any colour. Cog. -*ŋaaya* 9/10 Variety of large shield

Whether this is of any relevance for historical purposes must be left to another occasion. While a majority of these analogues are living creatures, this is not by any means true of all cases. Nevertheless the pattern seems closer to that described by Evans-Pritchard for the Ngok Dinka, than to that more recently presented for the Karimojong by Dyson-Hudson.[3]

The three primary words occur in this series but serve only to provide general reference; as one man remarked, 'you only use them if you don't know the proper term.' Amongst the younger generation few were familiar with more than a dozen of the commoner terms and mistakes in identification were often made. It seems likely that a full series would comprise about forty terms, but I have only about thirty and many of these were difficult to identify with certainty because such beasts were scarce. As the specialists in grain were all women, so the specialists here were all men and all of middle age or older.

> -*nyabárááti*, Reddish brown, deep biscuit. Cog. -*bárááti* 7/8 Bush-fruit (?)
> -*nyaiŋo*, Pale yellowish. Cog. -*ŋó* 5/6 Species of buck long since driven from the area

---

[1] See Mayer, 1950, op. cit.

[2] In contrast to their southern neighbours the Kuria, Gusii do not alternate this element with -*ke*- for bulls. It may be preceded by the usual prefix or it may not.

[3] E. E. Evans-Pritchard, 'Imagery in Ngok Dinka cattle-names', *Bulletin of the School of Oriental (and African) Studies*, 7, 1934; N. Dyson-Hudson, *Karimojong politics*, Clarendon Press, Oxford, 1966, pp. 96–9.

-nyamónyinga, Dark red-brown. Cog. *-nyinga* 6 Blood
-nyaseru, Dark fawn. See series on human beings
-nyamotika, Light biscuit all over
-nyaikɔndɔ, White with black flecking. Cog. *-kɔndɔ* 7/8 Species of monkey. Blue-faced Vervet (?)
-nyaiŋaaya, Marked with a large patch of any colour. Cog. *-ŋaaya* 9/10 Variety of large shield
-nyacɛngɛ́, Spotted, mainly below, e.g. chest and belly. Cog. *-cɛngɛ* 9/10 Species of wasp which makes a nest of small nodules of earth and stick, species of Hornet (?)
-nyangubo, Grey. Cog. *-(n)gubó* 9/10 Hippopotamus
-nyasanako, Blotched, usually black and white[1]
-nyangonco, Brown animal with a white face. Cog. *-(n)gonco* 9/10 The White-browed Robin-Chat which has a characteristic white eye-stripe
-matɛɛgɛ́, Brown animal with a different colour on belly and round udders
-nyaitɔɔsi, Grey with blotching. Cog. *-tɔɔsi* 5/6 Species of inedible fungus
-nyaimisɔ, Yellowish brown. Cog. *-misɔ* 3/4 Species of tree with a sap which dries to this colour
-nyabisɛmbɛ, Blotched on the under-surfaces. Cog. *-sɛmbɛ* 7/8 Indelible mark on anything
-nyaibumburia, Pepper-and-salt colouring. Cog. *-bumburia* 5/6 Species of small predator, Genet (?)
mogúmó, Hornless. Cog. *mogúmó*, Without identification, used nowadays of an unsigned letter
-nyasaamó, Fawn in colour with fine white flecking. Cog. *-nyasáámo* 7/8 Species of small fieldmouse
-nyaikobe, Large patch on the body. Cog. *-ikobe* 5/6 Something of a different colour to that on which it is superimposed, e.g. a patch
-nyamecege, Of different colours, esp. browns and whites. Cog. *mecege*, Of different colours
-nyamatɔtɔntɔ, Of more than two colours. Cog. *-matɔntɔ*, Multi-coloured

[1] It is interesting to note that this term occurs also among the Cushitic Iraqw, who live some 200 miles to the south in Tanzania. Their set of cattle terms includes a number of terms relating to the provenance of the animals.

-nyakenɔ́ci, Animal with a white end to the tail. Cog. *-nɔ́ci* 7/8
    Something round which is of a different colour to
    its environment, e.g. a light-coloured bangle in a
    group of dark-coloured ones, rings on an animal's
    tail

-nyamasie, Pure white. Cog. *-sie* 14/6 Flour

-nyagetambaa, Pure white. Cog. *-tambaa* 7/8 Piece of cloth. Derived
    from Swahili

-nyabosie OR *-nyabosio*, Animal with white forehead. Cog. *-sio* 14
    Forehead

-nyaŋera, Wholly black. Cog. *-ŋera* 9/10 Buffalo

-nyagesanko, Animal with different coloured spots. Cog. *-sanko* 7/8
    Species of tree with flecked sap

-nyamonge, Animal with white stripe along the backbone

Some of the terms may also occur in combination with others, thus:

-nyabárááti nyaitɔɔsi, Black or reddish blotches all over.

        *   *   *

A consideration of this material suggests that objects in the real world, whose socially significant attributes are variable, require a set of qualifiers to mark this fact. Some of these may designate colour. They derive their meaning both from the nature of the referent, and from the length of the series in which they occur, indeed the length of the series itself is in direct proportion to the polygenous character of the referent. In the Ndembu material Turner was dealing both with objects whose colour was intrinsic, for which no colour terminology was necessary; and also with values relating to those colours. One might suggest that a colour terminology is concomitant with the social recognition of colour as extrinsic to a series of referents; colour values, by contrast, are concomitant with the social recognition of colour as intrinsic to a series of objects/events, and with the social importance associated with them. It may be that non-ritual contexts favour the former, while the latter are characteristic of ritual contexts.[1]

---

[1] The distinction made by Ardener (Introductory Essay to E. W. Ardener (ed.), *Social anthropology and language*, Tavistock, London, 1971, p. xliii) between 'linguistic signs' and 'ritual' is, I believe, corroborated by the Gusii evidence though, as it stands, it is plainly inadequate to carry the argument much further forward.

Colour-words and Colour-values: The Evidence from Gusii

Ideally one should now turn to Gusii ritual, but unfortunately data are lacking: firstly this was not my main interest while I was in the field, but also many important ceremonies, especially the crucial *rites de passage*, now occur only in a highly attenuated form. Nevertheless there is some vestigial evidence to suggest that a set of colour values exists, and that where such polygenous referents as cows, goats or chickens participate in a ritual context such concepts become operative.[1] Pure white cows, for example, are favoured for sacrifice, as white is held to be a lucky colour in the sense that it is associated with the protection of the homestead against pollution. Outside this context, however, pure white cows are not viewed with favour since, it is claimed, they are prone to skin disease and are bad breeders: they are not therefore picked for the marriage settlement. Curiously enough pure black cows are popular, not only because they too are associated with good luck, but because they are held to be resistant to disease. In non-ritual contexts cows like the tenth, thirteenth and eighteenth in the above list[2] are unpopular for various reasons, while the third, fifth and twenty-fifth are especially popular.

The material I have been able to collect as evidence for the co-existence of a set of colour values is patently fragmentary but is probably adequate to establish its existence. From discussions with Gusii over a long period I infer that though at least two systems co-exist they do not merge: language behaviour in secular situations is not, it appears, imbued with the values that are generated in ritual situations. Evidence derives from the following contexts:

(a) A man who has killed a lion (or, formerly, an enemy) has a live white ram placed on his shoulders; this is then killed by his father or father's brother and the heart removed and given to the warrior to eat, in order to strengthen and bless him. He may also be anointed with the fat of a pure white cow.

(b) A white chicken is sacrificed in order to expiate guilt. The story is told that following a particularly famous murder, some years ago, the murderers when caught were found to be wearing feathers of a sacrificed white chicken to ensure that blame for the crime should not be attached to them.

---

[1] It is interesting to note here that where this occurs the non-ritual name is commonly discarded.

[2] Pp. 154–6 above.

(c) Following the circumcision ceremony for boys, the youngsters remain in seclusion for several weeks, during which time they clean their bodies with ashes, which have both a whitish appearance and whitish connotation.[1] On the day when the boys are due to come out of seclusion they are anointed with *ébundo* or *éngoso*, a whitish clay. Later in the day this is washed off and they then anoint themselves with fat and hematite (*étaago*) and acquire—with the redness—a clean and manly appearance. Mayer reports that the girls too, on their 'coming out', anoint their skin-aprons with hematite, and he includes songs which refer to being anointed with 'red ochre' and to 'red vaginas'.[2]

(d) Should one kill a man, either in a brawl, or in self-defence against a thief or intruder, a black chicken or goat should be sacrificed to remove the pollution. The subsequent sacrifice of a white goat or chicken re-establishes ritual cleanliness. Such a sacrifice may also be made following the death of a close relative to ensure that there will be no repetition.

(e) At the dances held during the marriage ceremony (*ényangi*), there were traditionally a number of wrestling contests (*ómweleko*) between the two kin groups. The contestants were usually anointed with hematite. At other dances, too, notably at the *riibína*, a women's dance after the harvest, the dancers were anointed with hematite, especially on the head, face and hands.

During inter-group warfare a man who killed another had the right side of his face anointed with hematite and the left with a greyish substance.

By contrast, during the funeral ceremonies participants were anointed with kaolinite.

Traditionally shields were decorated with all three primary colours, and where a fourth was added this would be yellow.

(f) Prior to setting out on a journey (or following a nightmare), a man would grind some millet, *ékeramókya*, 7/8, a variety with a very

---

[1] The 'whiteness' appears to be given a depreciatory connotation in P. Mayer's account: 'Gusii initiation ceremonies', *Journal of the Royal Anthropological Institute*, 83, 1953, p. 24.

[2] Mayer's account makes it clear that the initiation ceremonies are highly charged symbolically, but his account is avowedly descriptive, and there is little that one can infer from the description as to the use of colour concepts.

light-coloured grain, place it in a basket, mix it with water, then anoint himself on the forehead, throat, abdomen, knees, elbows and feet. The remainder would then be mixed with a species of grass, *óboncanancera* (literally: waving-about-on-the-path), and splashed round the homestead.

It is not uncommon nowadays to find a piece of soapstone (kaolinite) near the doorway of a house which can be used for the same purpose. There appears to be no sanction on a child using this as a plaything, or indeed making something with it: none of its 'luck', in any case, is held to rub off on the child. 'How could this be so', commented a parent when asked, 'when it is simply a plaything?'

(g) After leaving the homestead to go on a journey it is extremely inauspicious if the path is crossed from right to left by one of the following creatures, most of which are dark-coloured, and a return is advocated:

(i) A black dog
(ii) One of the following snakes:

-*rubi*, 5/6, Spitting Cobra
-*ŋére*, 5/6, Puff-Adder
-*basweti*, 9/10, Python. This last requires purification with a black sheep if seen.

While the first two are still fairly common, there are a number of black snakes which do not carry such 'bad luck' and are equally common.

(iii) A Rhinoceros, -*úbíírya*, 7/8. This has completely disappeared from the area I was working in, and probably from elsewhere in the Gusii highlands.
(iv) A species of buck, -*cúúre*, 7/8, which has also completely disappeared from the area.
(v) One of the following birds:

-*nyamunyonge*, 7/8, Jackson's Widow Bird (?)
-*(n)témabobe*, 9/10, possibly a Flycatcher or Puff-Back Shrike
-*kóru*, 5/6, Species of Eagle, possibly the Black-Chested Eagle
-*nyamúceera*, 9/10, Fiscal Shrike.

Again, there are a number of black birds of which this is not true, e.g. the Fork-Tailed Drongo.

Colour-words and Colour-values: The Evidence from Gusii

An important point here, especially in the case of the last two, is whether the birds have their back to one or not—it is more generally speaking an insult to have someone turn his back on one. Should they appear facing one and coming from the left side, this is regarded as an extremely auspicious sign.

In none of the above cases does the aura of ill luck carry over to other situations: people do not seem to mind having black dogs around, and while there is a general, and understandable, dislike of Puff-Adders etc. there is, so far as I can tell, no special association of them with ill luck. What appears to be important is the conjunction of a number of factors, of which colour is only one.

From this evidence one can discern patterns which would sustain a belief in the existence for Gusii of a colour triad similar to that reported for Ndembu. The connotations of white listed by Turner, e.g. goodness, making strong or healthy, purity, to lack bad luck etc., could be inferred from the Gusii examples, and the reference to blackness, as lacking luck or purity, accords well with the material. While evidence on redness is particularly exiguous the Ndembu belief that 'red is peculiarly the colour of blood or flesh, the carnal colour' might well be sustained if the data on the initiation ceremonies were fuller. Further research is now required to establish the extent to which the colour terminology and the colour values operate independently of one another.

* * *

The Gusii data suggest that two processes are operating, which may be termed qualification and evaluation. The former has been exemplified by examining the 'primary' words A, B and C in a number of series in which they occur, noting that in some cases they have an achromatic, in some a partially chromatic and in others a wholly chromatic connotation. Taken in isolation, however, the words could not be said to have any meaning, but are simply neutral. In evaluation, the significance and efficacy of certain items for particular events may be attributed, among other things, to their inherent colour. In my own rather superficial investigation I did not find Gusii to be as articulate as Ndembu appear to be, but this is not perhaps very surprising since evaluation is rather similar to other processes of abstraction, like those for establishing the grammatical rules in a language, which are accessible to, but not utilized by, most members of the community, who leave such exercises to specialists and foreigners. If I understand Turner rightly he suggests that values, which are held to inhere in certain concepts deriving from ritual situations, will spill over into areas of non-ritual activity. What I have suggested here is that just as terms like A, B and C lack meaning without a referent, so also do the values lack substance without the ritual matrix—just as the associations of whiteness in the ceremonial Lily do not influence the house-decorator.

Implicit in the use of the term 'process' above is the idea of change. The lexical sets in which the terms A, B and C occur respond, in general, to changes in social life, and not the other way round as Whorf would have us believe. If the set for cattle terminology is shrinking rapidly among the younger generation, as the importance of cattle diminishes, so new sets are being created from referents which are currently of greater moment, such as clothing, cash crops etc. One would also expect this to be happening in the realm of colour concepts, and one might agree in general with the conclusions reached by Berlin and Kay that the elaboration of a colour lexicon is an evolutionary process, accompanying and perhaps reflecting technological and cultural change,[1] yet take issue with them over what seems to me a rather simplistic view that the colour lexicon can be treated as a single system. At any given moment in the community, indeed, we would expect to find evidence of terminologies and concepts which are obsolescent for some groups, alongside others which are still developing. It is thus an over-simplification to suggest, as I did at the outset of the paper, that we are dealing only with the co-existence of two sets of variables: reality is considerably more complex.

[1] Berlin and Kay, *Basic color terms*, e.g. pp. 16, 104.

The Savage and the Modern Mind

Ernest Gellner

What makes Modernity?—and what makes the Savage? Each of these questions has a strong popular appeal. We gaze in the mirror and hope to catch an innocent glimpse, and see ourselves as we truly are. We also long for the *frisson* of seeing, of seizing conceptually, the wholly Other, the savage. There is an unmistakable element of voyeurism both in anthropology and philosophy. We hope to see what is normally obscured by the decencies, and to find out some truth about ourselves in the process.

The problem of modernity is not exclusively, or even predominantly, a concern of the academic philosophers. Theories of modernity in terms of industrialization, bureaucracy or the division of labour, are not the stock in trade of the conventional philosopher. This is rather a mistake on his part, but, for better or worse, it is so. The philosophers take an interest only when modernity is defined in the sphere of cognition. They are not averse to trying their hand at defining rationality, but they feel really at home when it comes to defining science. Hence, by a little extension, it is easy to extract from their work a theory of scientific mentality. So, if science is a crucial element of modernity, the philosophers are unwittingly of some help in giving an account of it.

Of course, it would be mistaken to suppose that the Savage and the Modern mind jointly exhaust the world, that everyone must needs be one or the other. Clearly, this is not so. Many schemata of the Evolution of the Human mind interpose a middle stage, between, say, the religious and the positive mentality, or between magic and science. The modern mind, that's *us*; and the savage mind is very distant and exotic, a titivating Other; but between the two, much of human

162

history is taken up by civilizations whose privileged and literate classes, at least, were not savage, though they were not like the citizens of modern, technological society either. One must allow for this middle ground. It covers, perhaps, the most interesting part of human history.

Nevertheless, for analytic purposes, it may be worth while to think away this enormous middle ground. It is probably as well to do it knowingly, rather than conjure it away by definition or stylistic sleight of hand. Likewise, it is probably as well to be clear about another tacit assumption which underlies this kind of reasoning: it is only an assumption, not an established truth, that there is one homogeneous kind of modernity and one homogeneous kind of savagery. It is certainly not self-evident.

Lévi-Strauss, for instance, explicitly adheres to this general approach. He argues that it is essential for us 'to understand how [neolithic or early historical man] could have come to a halt and how several thousand years of stagnation have intervened between the neolithic revolution and modern science *like a level plain between two ascents*'.[1] Just as evolutionism came naturally, almost inevitably, to nineteenth-century thinkers, so the pattern which most naturally leaps to our own minds is that of a *flat plain* between the neolithic revolution and modern science. Those who lived on that plain often found it rugged, though.

Despite Lévi-Strauss's partial disclaimer,[2] his own account of the one Great Divide which remains when we think away the intervening plain is strikingly reminiscent of Frazer's. Like Frazer, he sees primitive man as seeking intelligible connections. According to Frazer, the primitive assumption was that the connections had to make a kind of sense (be 'sympathetic'); according to Lévi-Strauss, on the other hand, they were formulated at the level of 'perception and the imagination', in other words in concrete terms close to what is seized by the senses, as opposed to the abstraction of science.[3] The difference between the two thinkers is not very great: in fact, it could be argued that each of the characterizations implies the other. A 'sympathetic' connection, at least, presupposes the possibility of concrete imagery. There is more difference in the positive characterization of the other

---

[1] C. Lévi-Strauss, *The savage mind*, Eng. trans., Weidenfeld and Nicolson, London, 1966, p. 15. (Italics mine. E.G.)
[2] Ibid., p. 13.
[3] Cf. Edmund Leach, *Lévi-Strauss*, Fontana, London, 1970, pp. 49, 84.

pole, science, by each of the two thinkers. For Frazer, science is primarily distinguished by experimentation, as opposed to *a priori* 'sympathetic' plausibility. Lévi-Strauss cannot use this criterion (nor does he wish to do so), for he believes primitive man to be a systematic experimentalist too. So he invokes, instead, *abstraction*, in the sense of the formulation of generalizations in terms far removed from sensory perception.

Such, then, are the rules of the present game: one kind of savage mentality is seen as confronting one kind of modern mind, and the intermediate ground is ignored as irrelevant. These are but interim conventions, not dogma. They do however enable us to look, experimentally, at what the anthropologists have to say about the Savage Mind, and what the philosophers say about the Delimitation of Science, as obverses of each other. This may prove illuminating.

* * *

A striking recent effort to pursue this kind of strategy is Mr. Robin Horton's 'African traditional thought and Western Science'.[1] The present attempt overlaps with and diverges from Horton's at a variety of points. Horton lists a number of ways in which traditional African thought resembles science and its theory, and other ways in which the two styles of thought stand contrasted. If this were all, his argument would merely present a kind of shopping list or check-list of traits. But Horton goes much further. He singles out one differentia as crucial, in that the others flow from it: '. . . in traditional cultures there is no developed awareness of alternatives to the established body of theoretical tenets; whereas in scientifically oriented cultures, such an awareness is highly developed.'[2] Horton goes on to call this the contrast between the Closed and the Open, acknowledging an affinity to Sir Karl Popper, but explicitly narrowing down his own version of the opposition, in contrast to Popper's. Where Popper includes individualism and achievement-orientation in his notion of 'openness', Horton restricts his own use of the term exclusively to a sense-of-theoretical-alternative.

It is interesting to note that Horton's bibliography includes the name of Thomas Kuhn, whose *The structure of scientific revolutions*[3]

[1] *Africa*, 37, 1967.
[2] Ibid., p. 155.
[3] Chicago University Press, Chicago, 1962 (revised edn. 1970).

is enjoying a great vogue and has had an enormous impact on contemporary thought. This is slightly surprising, in so far as Kuhn's central point, when formulated in this kind of language, amounts to a claim that science is not nearly as open as had been popularly thought. Scientific inquiry does not range freely amongst boundless alternatives, as the popular image suggests, but, at any given time, is constrained by the currently dominant 'paradigm', whose hold only weakens at the time of major scientific revolutions. The only people whose minds are truly 'open', who lack a paradigm, are people like social scientists—but the reason is not that they are freer, but, alas, that their poor disciplines are in a pre-scientific stage. For all these reasons, one should expect that an awareness of Kuhn's work, unless it is simply rejected as unsound, would make it harder to find the essence of science and modernity in 'openness'. Horton does not, in fact, dismiss Kuhn as unsound (though perhaps from his own viewpoint he ought to do so), but he overcomes the difficulty in somewhat cavalier manner: [the scientist's] pushing of a theory and his reluctance to scrap it are not due to any chilling intuition that, if his theory fails him, chaos is at hand. Rather, they are due to the very knowledge that the theory is not something timeless and absolute.[1]

In the end, Horton's account of scientific conduct is quite unlike Kuhn's: 'The scientist is, as it were, always keeping account, balancing the successes of a theory against its failures. And when the failures start coming in thick and fast, defence of the theory switches inexorably to attack on it.'[2]

So, in the end, the traditional picture, which allows the scientist to deal directly with an External Reality and to dismiss theories if they sin against reality too much, is upheld. In Kuhn's own disturbing scheme, on the other hand, there is no room for any such direct intercourse with Objective Reality: the scientist is only capable of checking little theories against the socially imposed Paradigm, and there seems to be no way of checking these paradigms themselves against reality, for science cannot do without *some* paradigm. (This explains some of Kuhn's popularity. He provides an easy way to attack or to uphold 'paradigms'—to dismiss anyone else's position, however well based, and to uphold one's own, however arbitrary. Kuhn certainly cannot be blamed for this popular use of his ideas.)

[1] Horton, op. cit., p. 168.
[2] Ibid., p. 168.

It was worth noticing this: despite Horton's complimentary mention of Kuhn, he does not really use Kuhn's conclusion, and on the contrary presupposes its falsity. Horton assumes the existence and observability of an external reality other than the social perceptions of it, such that styles of thought can be classified in terms of their stance vis-à-vis that external reality. Horton also assumes that this reality is such as to render the 'open' outlook sounder, or at least cognitively more effective, than the closed visions. All these assumptions seem to me most laudable, but it is worth spelling them out, if only so as to be aware of having made them.

Horton's identification of the key property of primitive or traditional mentality seems to me mistaken, partly because some modern men *also* experience the greatest difficulty in even conceiving an alternative to their own favoured world-vision, and because many members of traditional, pre-scientific societies *do* possess this capacity of multiple vision. Horton invokes Evans-Pritchard's classic work on the Azande:

> In this web of belief every strand depends upon every other strand, and a Zande cannot get out of its meshes because it is the only world he knows. The web is not an external structure in which he is enclosed. It is the texture of his thought and he cannot think that his thought is wrong.[1]

No doubt, situations of this kind—conceptual loyalty without any option—do occur. But consider the implications of accepting this as a general criterion of traditional mentality: it means that in traditional society there can be no syncretism, no doctrinal pluralism, no deep treason, no dramatic conversion or doctrinal oscillation, no holding of alternative belief-systems up one's sleeve, ready for the opportune moment of betrayal. Frankly, I do not believe this. Some savages may live in a unique, optionless world. Many do not. Yet they do transcend their condition not by reaching out to science, but simply through syncretism, through the cohabitation of incompatible belief-systems, or doctrinal opportunism. If, for instance, Dr. Edmund Leach[2] is right in his account of the tribesmen of highland Burma, and some of

---

[1] E. E. Evans-Pritchard, *Witchcraft, oracles and magic among the Azande*, Clarendon Press, Oxford, 1937, pp. 194–5.

[2] *Political systems of highland Burma*, London School of Economics and Political Science, London, 1954.

the tribesmen oscillate between two quite incompatible visions of their own society, it would seem to follow, by Horton's criterion, that this very oscillation would promptly propel them out of the traditional realm into the scientific one. Such a conclusion seems paradoxical. One can think of many other examples, many of them not contingent on daring anthropological interpretation. In brief, not all plural situations are *ipso facto* modern or scientific. The existence of plurality, and the sense of choice it engenders, may perhaps be a necessary condition of the modern outlook; but it is certainly not a sufficient condition. Even Mr. Horton's use of quotations from Evans-Pritchard's work on the Azande, partly reproduced above, is somewhat selective. Horton invokes those passages which suggest that a Zande cannot escape his own system of thought: '. . . he cannot think that his [own] thought is wrong.' But Horton omits to quote the sentence which *immediately* follows on the passage quoted:

> Nevertheless, [Zande] beliefs are not absolutely set but are variable and fluctuating to allow for different situations and to permit empirical observations and even doubts.[1]

Speaking of the ordinary, non-royal Azande, Evans-Pritchard also tells us

> . . . they adapt themselves without undue difficulty to new conditions of life and are always ready to copy the behaviour of those they regard as their superiors in culture and to borrow new modes of dress, new weapons and utensils, new words, and even new ideas and habits . . .[2]

Apparently it is, or was, only the royal class who were 'more proud and conservative'. So, as far as the lower orders were concerned, even the Azande faced a plural, and hence 'open', situation. Did they consequently exemplify the scientific spirit? I suspect they did not. Nor could such a claim be made for all those numerous populations which are familiar with conceptual alternatives through living in frontier areas between diverse cultures, and which often have no difficulty in switching from one 'language' to another, in a deep rather than superficial sense of 'language'.

It is considerations such as these which make me reluctant to accept Horton's key criterion as it stands. The sense of alternatives like

[1] Evans-Pritchard, op. cit., p. 195.
[2] Ibid., p. 13.

patriotism is not enough. The criterion of a 'developed sense of alternatives' does not, in fact, help separate the sheep from the goats in an acceptable manner. Yet one may well feel reluctant to reject his touchstone outright. The underlying intuition seems too valuable. Can it be reformulated and saved?

*　　*　　*

One defect in Horton's formulation of his own position (a surprising one in an anthropologist) is its *individualism*. The 'awareness of alternatives' seems credited to individuals. This is most regrettable. One consequence is that individual scientists who happen to be unimaginative, dogmatic, over-confident, ignorant of the history of their own subject, and without a nose for new ideas, promptly become excluded from the community of those sharing the scientific spirit. Are there no such scientists—vegetables? They may not be particularly good, inspiring, creative scientists, and one may prefer not to converse with them or to see students indoctrinated by them; but to exclude them from science altogether seems not only harsh but arbitrary. And similarly, not every opportunist guru or dervish who can switch from one cosmology to another, if his pursuit of a powerful patron or clientèle requires it, can thereby become a worthy exemplar for textbooks of sound scientific method.

Thus the first emendation I should propose for Horton's scheme is that Horton's crucial differentia be credited not to individuals, nor even groups, but to systems of thought. If applied to individuals, or even to 'cultures', it becomes untenable, for the reasons indicated. This emendation does admittedly have an obvious disadvantage: systems of thought, unlike individuals or groups, are abstractions. They can be observed only as incarnated in the verbal and other behaviour of individuals or groups, and their isolation from the continuum of behaviour may well be question-begging. The observer may isolate one or more such 'systems' which then illustrate his point, whilst a rival observer may choose to isolate quite other units. How could one choose between the claims of such rivals? There are two principal methods normally employed for identifying, isolating a 'belief-system': one uses the observer's own sense of coherence, and the other invokes written sources and documents. The possibility of bias or arbitrariness inherent in the first method is obvious. But the danger is clearly not absent from the second method either. The fact that a corpus of writings exists, recording the beliefs and prescriptions of a given social tradition, in no way excludes possibilities such as, for instance, syncretism within that corpus, or, on the other hand, selection and bowdlerization. In many cultural contexts, the scribes are but one of a number of groups disputing the cultural heritage and authority within it. What the scribes put down is one version of the system, not necessarily the 'correct' one. On the contrary, it tends to be one biased towards the set of values normally associated with literacy.

Despite these difficulties inherent in using the notion of a 'system of belief' instead of the individual or group credited with holding it—difficulties for which there may be no formal solution—I nevertheless think it essential that the great Dividing Line be drawn in some such terms.

*　　*　　*

But this is not the only emendation which is proposed. Horton clearly supposes that this one trait is crucial, a 'key difference', and that the other differentiae 'flow from it'. It seems to me, on the contrary, that we are faced with two opposed syndromes, and that, within each, there is not one but a number of crucial traits. Each of these tends to have a natural affinity with the others in its own group, and one could perhaps slant the characterization of either group in such a way that it seems to 'flow' from one trait. But this would be arbitrary and misleading. I shall sketch the opposition, as it 'really' seems to me to be. Apart from diverging from Horton's in the ways already indicated, and perhaps in some others, it also overlaps with his at many points.

There seems to me to be not one, but about four crucial distinctions between the Savage and the Scientific Mind. First of all, it might be useful to give them names. The Savage Mind displays:

1. The use of idiosyncratic norms.
2. A low cognitive division of labour, accompanied, at the same time, by a proliferation of roles.
3. The entrenched clauses of its intellectual constitution, so to speak, are very diffused and pervasive.
4. The lack of diplomatic immunity for cognition.

These four traits are not independent of each other. But they can usefully be characterized separately.

169

The Savage and the Modern Mind

The use of idiosyncratic norms

A traditional belief-system contains at least one general vision of 'what is normal'. The normal differs from the abnormal in that it either requires no explanation at all, or only requires explanation of a kind radically different from that which is required by the abnormal. The normal, if explained at all, is explained wholesale, by the general myth. No specific explanation is required on individual occasions.

This normality is both cognitive (in the sense of having these implications for explanatory strategy), and moral. It defines a social order as well as a natural one. In consequence, it is 'meaningful'— truth and social order support each other—and rather untidy. It has, so to speak, jagged edges. Normality is very specific and concrete. The language of cognition must be rich enough for all moral nuances. Explanation does not fall on the just and the unjust indifferently.

By contrast, the crucial feature of scientific thought-systems is that the notion of normality is not conspicuously present in them. They do, admittedly, distinguish between what does and what does not require explanation, and this might be held to be an equivalent of 'normality'. But the base-line for explanation, so to speak, is very different from the 'normality' of traditional belief-systems. It is relative, temporary and problem-bound rather than socially entrenched. It is also tidy, symmetrical and has fairly straight rather than jagged edges, so to speak. It is not incarnated in details of life. Above all, it can generally be specified only in terms of the formal properties of explanation, rather than in terms of concrete properties of the thing explained. The most widely favoured baseline of this kind is what is popularly conceived as mechanism or materialism: the existence of a structure, built of publicly available materials with no unsymmetrical, locally idiosyncratically defined properties, and repeatable in accordance with a publicly stateable and socially neutral recipe or formula, such that the behaviour to be explained follows from the properties of that structure.[1] (The materialism is in fact irrelevant: as long as the

---

[1] The importance of the absence of unsymmetrical elements in explanation is noted by Mr. Steven Lukes in 'Some problems about rationality', *European Journal of Sociology*, 8, 2, 1967, p. 259. Lukes lists no fewer than ten senses of rationality, and this one is given the fourth place on the list. His own characterization of this type of irrationality is that beliefs are irrational in this way if 'they are situationally specific or *ad hoc*, i.e.: not universalised because bound to particular occasions'. Lukes rightly hints at the affinity between this kind of cognitive rationality and ethical theories formulated in terms of 'universalization'.

170

criterion of publicity and repeatability is satisfied, it matters little whether the structure invoked is built of tangible materials, or remains abstract.) It follows that such cognitive base-lines are *not*, at the same time, the delineation of a moral or social order. On the contrary: the formal criteria they must satisfy, at the same time make them singularly ill suited for the underpinning of moral expectations, of a status- and value-system. They tend to be 'meaningless' and 'morally blind'.

Another way of making this point is to say that an important distinguishing mark of science is the mechanistic outlook. (The well-advertised allegedly non-mechanical features of some parts of modern science are in no way in conflict with this contention.) It is interesting, however, that the best-known and probably the most influential tradition in the philosophy of science has *not* adopted this kind of criterion as an answer to the *Abgrenzungsproblem* (the problem of the delimitation of science). Instead, it has chosen to delimit science, not in terms of the type of *explanation* it tolerates, but in terms of its sources of *information*. It insists, in its most famous formulations, on the availability, in principle or in fact, of verification, or of falsification. It leads one to look to the *data*—to whether data of a certain kind (such as would verify, or falsify, the explanatory theory) are or could be available.

This is not the place to argue this difficult point, but my belief is that, in so far as the verificationist or falsificationist criteria actually succeed in drawing any boundaries, and in segregating the scientific sheep from the goats, they do it by covertly employing the kind of mechanistic criterion indicated above. One advantage of that particular criterion (an advantage which, on its own, is admittedly by no means conclusive) can be stressed: it high-lights an important link

---

He fails, however, to comment on the connection between this kind of rationality and his rationality no. 1, which is defined in terms of avoiding inconsistency, self-contradiction or invalid inference. In so far as a society tolerates unsymmetrical, context-bound concepts, it can, if it is concerned with its own façade, always *appear* to avoid inconsistency and thus satisfy rationality 1, simply by means of hiding all inconsistency under irrationality 4. Asymmetry can easily be built *into* the local concepts, and thus camouflaged. In brief, what really matters is the type of criterion a society applies to distinguish acceptable from unacceptable concepts. If asymmetry within concepts is condoned, the society has little to fear from any requirement of *formal* consistency. (It can easily pay lip-service to it.) If, on the other hand, it is *not* condoned, formal consistency is already presupposed.

between the sociological problem of delimiting social 'modernity', and the philosophical problem of delimiting 'science'. An important tradition in sociology sees the crucial feature of modernity as 'bureaucratization'. The central idea in the notion of bureaucratic conduct is the orderly treatment of cases in accordance with fixed rules—the ethic of rules as opposed to the ethic of loyalty. The mechanistic world-picture is, in this sense, simply the bureaucratization of nature. This deep underlying affinity is of great importance.

Something should perhaps be said of the way in which philosophers have treated this bureaucratization of nature. Philosophers have not, of course, talked of it under this name: their own names for it have tended to be 'the principle of causality', or the 'regularity of nature', etc. In the main, they were interested in it not for the purpose of delimiting science, but of *vindicating* it. The classical assumption was that something of this kind needed to be proved in order to justify scientific extrapolation at all.

This matter needs to be looked at in a realistic, sociological way. The science-using society has two frontiers: one with Chaos, and the other with traditional society, with its idiosyncratic norms, miracles, meaningful world-picture, etc. The great philosophers of science have, in the main, manned the frontier with Chaos. They saw their job as somehow proving that Chaos, a nature not amenable to bureaucratization, was not possible. But, alas, this frontier is quite indefensible. Happily, there also happens to be no enemy on the other side of it. If Chaos were to obtain, no proof, found in any justification of scientific inference, from Kant to Lord Keynes or Sir Roy Harrod, would help us—any more than any pre-Kantian proof of the immortality of the soul will help us when we die. There is something very comic about all these defensive preparations along a totally indefensible frontier.

Comic, but not useless. The other side of this frontier is, it is true, completely uninhabited. No society has succeeded in devising a style of life based on the assumption of Chaos. But: the *other* frontier, the one with traditional society, is not uninhabited. There *are* numerous rival societies on the other side of it, with world-pictures and thought-styles which are a socially adapted compromise between some order and a socially meretricious Chaos, the bending of the regularity-expectation in the interest of the local status-system, and so forth.

So, all the noisy defensive preparations by the philosophers, along the indefensible but uninhabited frontier with pure Chaos, were not at all useless. They make so much noise, their weapons are so big and so terrifying, that they are quite visible from the other frontier, where there is a real live enemy and a genuine alternative. No society can live on the assumption of Chaos, but every society can choose between the mechanical-orderly and the meaningful-cosy pictures. The preparations against Chaos have done an enormous amount to fortify resolution along the border with the Meaningful Worlds. All those proofs of causality or regularity will never avert Chaos—should it befall us—but they have done much to destroy the claims of Miracles.

The Division of Labour

Philosophers do not generally consider the division of labour to be their special concern. This is a mistake. The most characteristic form of modern philosophy—the form in which it also makes the greatest impact on the general public—is as a set of doctrines concerning the intellectual or cognitive division of labour. Typically, it consists of a classification and characterization of broad types of knowledge (or uses of language). These types are generally defined in terms of the criteria of validity employed within each of them. Thus, in one of the best-known forms of this kind of theory, propositions are classified into those which stand or fall in virtue of factual checking, those which stand or fall in virtue of formal calculation, those which stand or fall in virtue of consonance with the speaker's feelings, and those which have no basis or anchorage at all.

What requires note is this: these theories make a really important impact not so much through their specific detail, through the manner in which they define their categories of knowledge or discourse, as through the general point and approach which is shared by all of them —the assumption of specificity of function. By habituating people to the idea that there is a single, simple criterion and function, governing the evaluation of any one given cognitive or verbal act, they profoundly modify their outlook. What these theories really inculcate is just this specificity of function. It is not denied that, in life as it is actually lived or language as it is actually used, various purposes or functions are conflated and confused. But this is dismissed as accident or shorthand, a compromise with the hurry and untidiness of daily life.

173

The various functions are seen as 'really' distinct. In fact, of course, this is a covert value judgement of the utmost importance. What is presented as an analytic, neutral requirement, in fact prejudges the question of the distinction, and the relative merits, of the savage and the scientific mind. It is of the essence of the savage mind, as of savage institutions, that there is a lower degree of functional specificity. The tacit but persistent propaganda by modern philosophy, in quite a broad sense, on behalf of functional specificity, introduced 'innocently', as a neutral analytic device, in fact favours the mechanistic, disenchanted vision of the world as against magical enchantment. The enchanted vision works through the systematic conflation of descriptive, evaluative, identificatory, status-conferring etc. roles of language. A sense of the separability and fundamental distinctness of the various functions is the surest way to the disenchantment of the world.

On this point, the present argument is in complete harmony with Horton's. Horton puts the same point as follows:

> One theory is judged better than another with explicit reference to its efficacy in explanation and prediction. And as these ends become more clearly defined, it gets increasingly evident that no other ends are compatible with them. People come to see that if ideas are to be used as efficient tools of explanation and prediction, they must not be allowed to be tools of anything else.[1]

All one needs to add here is that this consequence does not follow specifically and exclusively from the pursuit of the two special ends singled out by Horton (explanation and prediction): it follows from the clear specification of *any* ends or criteria. The world is not so conveniently arranged that one can generally serve two or more criteria at once. It is not only God and Mammon who cannot be served jointly. And philosophers have been in error when they supposed that what mattered most in their arguments was the particular way in which they defined the various ends or criteria of types of knowledge or language. Those scholastic details are often too abstruse to be remembered or to have much real effect on habits of thought. The part of the lesson which *is* retained (and which some of the philosophers, quite mistakenly, supposed to be merely part of their preliminary scaffolding) was the requirement that the various criteria be clearly

[1] Horton, op. cit., p. 164.

distinguished and separated. (Descartes, unlike many contemporary philosophers, was not guilty of this misunderstanding.) And part of the reason why this lesson could be learnt so effectively and retained was of course its consonance with other aspects of modern life, which also display, in contrast with intimate traditional society, a tendency toward orderly division of labour and specificity of function.

This brings us to a further mistake of the philosophers and, in this case, of empiricist philosophers in particular. Here, once again, the mistake arises from ignoring the social context of their own reasoning. Empiricists are generally concerned with drawing and stressing the distinction between what is empirically testable and what is not so testable. So far so good. They go on to presuppose a certain picture of the co-existence of the empirical and the transcendent in the minds of those who do not observe or respect their key distinction. This tacitly presupposed picture might be called the Accretion Picture, and it could be summed up as follows: there is an inner circle of the positively observable or scientifically testable. This is shared ground, as it were, for the empiricist and the metaphysician. But the metaphysician sees not merely this charmed circle (the Island of Truth, as Kant called it in one of his more lyrical moments), but also, impelled by a religious, aesthetic or other need, *adds* to it further and wider circles of transcendent, untestable Being. The empiricist then averts his gaze with embarrassment from such uncritical cognitive self-indulgence and expansionism. He knows, at any rate, that these wider areas must either be ignored and eschewed altogether, or, if like other addicts you cannot suppress your yearning, they must at least not be taken seriously.

The trouble with this picture is its total lack of sociological realism. An individual or society already capable of distinguishing clearly between the inner circle of the testable, and the outer circle of un-testable accretions to it, is already more than nine-tenths of the way towards the acceptance of the empiricist ideal. It is precisely in this way that the severely transcendentalist adherents of a pure and hidden God, scornful of divine conjuring tricks and of day-to-day interference in the details of His creation, prepared the ground for an orderly and secularized vision of the world. But a society which is truly immersed in the transcendent does not see or recognize such orderly lines of demarcation. Quite the contrary.

In such a society, the really important feature of the behaviour of concepts is that they habitually and constantly dart across this boundary, and that the boundary itself is barely perceived. It would be idle, in such a society, to ask to have concepts separated into two camps, those which have an empirically operational role, and those whose reference is transcendent. There may perhaps be a few specimens of such pure types; but the interesting and characteristic examples are concepts that are, so to speak, semi-operational, which have both empirical and transcendent reference, invoked according to a locally recognized sliding scale, the working of which dovetails neatly into the rest of local life and its ends.

The really important job done by three centuries or so of empiricist propaganda has not been the proscribing or the discouragement of the transcendent: it has been the systematic inculcation of a sensitivity to the existence of the boundary between that which is testable and that which is not, and above all the consequent inhibition of such boundary-hopping. It matters little whether this boundary can always be traced convincingly on the tortuous ground of our actual conceptual and scientific world (often it cannot). It matters little whether or not that which is beyond the boundary is proscribed, or whether some items which seem to lie beyond it are tolerated because they prove that they are indispensable—emotionally, socially, or for the services they perform for concepts lying on the right side of the border. What does matter is that an increasingly touchy and insistent sensitivity to the existence of such a boundary discourages systematic conceptual boundary-hopping: it becomes increasingly difficult for a notion to be empirical when successful but something else when it is not, to have one status in the mouth of a priest and another in the mouth of a peasant, one significance on a weekday and another on sabbath day. Orderly and regular conduct is exacted from concepts, as it is from people. No unsymmetrical privileges, no sliding-scale status, are easily tolerated.

This (and not some circumscribing of the Island of Truth) is the real and effective achievement of empiricist propaganda. This explains how, appearances notwithstanding, this propaganda really served the cause of the mechanistic, disenchanted, orderly vision of the world, by insisting on orderly, sober, consistent conduct on the part of concepts. This is otherwise puzzling and paradoxical. The thinkers of the Enlightenment, it is true, tended to be both empiricists and materialists; but they could never show how these two favoured positions of theirs could be made consistent. It almost looked like an accidental, political affinity, rather than a genuine one: one could suspect that the two positions came together merely because both were opposed to religious orthodoxy, and followed the political and opportunist principle that any enemy of my enemy is my friend. This suspicion might be encouraged by the materialist-empiricist confrontation, by what might be called the Berkeley/Lenin debate, concerning whether we were ghosts with sensations, or whether on the contrary hard heavy stuff came first and was somehow echoed in consciousness. The ultimate rights and wrongs of this debate cannot be pursued here. What matters is that if we see empiricist epistemology in terms of inculcation of sensitivity to the division of labour applied to cognition, and the requirement of functional specificity, we also come to understand the affinity between it and the orderly 'mechanical' ideal of explanation, and the profound, non-accidental reasons which make empiricism and materialism such faithful companions.

The pervasiveness of entrenched clauses

The stock of ideas or beliefs available to a given individual or society can be divided into the 'entrenched constitutional clauses' and the Rest. The distinction is a simple one.

I can divide the stock of my ideas and convictions into those which can be denied or replaced without significantly disturbing my total picture and composure, and those which can only be budged at the cost of a wide dislocation and disturbance. If, for instance, I discover at the last moment that the train on which I had been relying to reach home is no longer running, this is a considerable inconvenience—but, without claiming any remarkable imperturbability, I can say that my general conceptual composure remains unaffected. If, on the other hand, a man one day becomes convinced that the identity of his parents is other than he had been brought up to believe; or that the political movement he had supported all his life is in fact criminal and immoral; or that the interpretation of recent history officially put forward by his nation is fraudulent—discoveries or conversions of this kind cannot leave him unmoved. So much else is implicated in these crucial, favoured, so to speak entrenched convictions, that if they go, much else will topple too.

It is an interesting and important sociological truth that there is no *a priori* way of delimiting the area in which these crucial, entrenched convictions are to be found. Of course, one can do it by means of a camouflaged tautology, which boils down to the assertion that what is important is what is important. But there is no non-question-begging way of doing so from the outside, so to speak. In other words, there is no special, privileged type of basket into which all societies place their most valuable eggs. You cannot say, for instance, that in any society the world-foundation story, or the rule of selecting political leaders, or theology, or the rules governing sexual behaviour, will be singled out for special reverence and cross-tied by so many firm links to all other institutions, that they cannot be shaken without everything being shaken. Some areas are, indeed, more plausible candidates for the location of the sacred than others; but no area is necessarily predetermined for it, and no area is excluded from it. The sacred may lurk in most unexpected quarters. The surprising quality of its choice of incarnation does indeed sometimes seem to be one of the devices for ensuring *impact*.

But there is a systematic difference in the distribution of the entrenched clauses, of the sacred, in this sense, as between savage and modern thought-systems. In a traditional thought-system, the sacred or the crucial is more extensive, more untidily dispersed, and much more pervasive. In a modern thought-system, it is tidier, narrower, as it were economical, based on some intelligible principle, and tends not to be diffused among the detailed aspects of life. Fewer hostages are given to fortune; or, looking at it from the other end, much less of the fabric of life and society benefits from reinforcement from the sacred and entrenched convictions. (It follows from this contention or definition that some thought-systems which are 'modern' in a chronological sense are not 'really' so. For instance, from a socio-logical viewpoint, a striking feature of the psycho-analytical system of ideas is the intimate dovetailing of an organization and a status-system with a doctrinal network, so that the two become closely dependent on each other.)

This important trait of traditional belief-systems is, of course, a kind of obverse of a trait cited earlier—the tendency to rely on a socially idiosyncratic notion of the normal, which determines what does and what does not require explanation.

Here, once again, we can observe the marked distance between the latent and the manifest meaning of much modern philosophy. Modern philosophy writes about knowledge in what purports to be the indicative mood: knowledge really 'is' this, that or the other. The picture which it presents of knowledge is in fact an idealized and simplified model of a belief-system in which the entrenched clauses have been reduced to a kind of formal minimum. Consider, for instance, the empiricist theory: it describes our view of the world as a kind of mosaic, in which all individual pieces are independent of each other and can be replaced without disturbing any of the rest. The only thing which is entrenched, which could really shake the theorist, is the so to speak formal fact of the existence and nature of the mosaic's framework itself. This vision is shared by classical empiricism and by doctrines such as 'logical atomism'. (It was, in fact, the convergence of the picture generated by the new notation of symbolic logic, with the older picture of empiricism, which stimulated the emergence of one of the most characteristic philosophical movements of the twentieth century.)

Once again, if we approach this with a modicum of sociological realism, we see that this picture is not at all a generally usable account of how belief-systems or visions of the world generally work (or, indeed, of how any of them work), but a simplified, overdrawn, stylized account of *one* feature of certain, i.e. 'modern', belief-systems. But the sustained propaganda for this feature, presented as a neutral, universal characterization articulated in the indicative mood, in fact greatly helped to establish it and hence one particular kind of world-picture—the kind which reduces and minimizes the extent of its own entrenched clauses.

Perhaps I should say that I do not in the least object either to this propaganda or its success. But it is useful to understand what has really been happening, rather than to be deceived by the manner in which it has been presented.

The diplomatic immunity of cognition

In a sense, this trait is the obverse of the preceding one. The important achievement of empiricist propaganda is the establishment of the Autonomy of Fact. The 'mosaic' model, however inaccurate as an account of how knowledge really functions, conveys above all the idea that the individual stones on the mosaic are independent of each other, and indeed of anything else. This means that their fate cannot

179

endanger whatever entrenched clauses may exist, covertly or openly. The converse of this is that they in turn are neither required nor excluded by any entrenched clauses. Greater and greater expanses of truth acquire an autonomy from the social, moral and political obligations and decencies of the society. This autonomy of truth is even more important than the philosophically better advertised autonomy of value—though the two are of course linked, and are jointly corollaries of the cognitive division of labour discussed above.

In a traditional belief-system, cognition, the discovery or the endorsement of beliefs, is an event *in* the world, and this means in the social and moral world. Hence they are subject to the same kinds of obligations and sanctions as are other kinds of conduct—indeed, when these ideas touch the entrenched clauses, they are quite specially subject to them. Man the knower is not alienated from the citizen and the moral being. At this point, it is hard not to suppose that in one sense the traditional outlooks are, ultimately, correct: we do not really believe that our cognitive activities are *really* extra-territorial, are qualitatively distinct from the rest of our lives. Nevertheless, as Kant pointed out, we assume (contrary to all consistency) that such extra-territoriality in fact obtains, and our attribution of 'objective validity' to our own thinking hinges on this odd assumption.

The social implications of the assumption are of course of the utmost importance. Here there is an interesting difference between Western liberal societies, where the officially endorsed entrenched clauses of the belief-system have an eroded status and importance (comparable roughly to the heraldic devices inherited from the Middle Ages), and thus facilitate the assumption of autonomy, and those other societies which possess entrenched clauses that are still taken with some degree of seriousness, such as Marxism. The consequence of this is of course that in such societies the autonomy of cognition is only partial, and in so far as it exists—as, inevitably, it does—it generates painful strain.

Some traditions in modern philosophy (in a very broad sense) had supposed that certain substantive pieces of science were destined to acquire an 'entrenched clause' status comparable to the key religious dogmas of the past. Newtonian physics, for instance, was revered by many thinkers as the very paradigm of well-established, permanent truth. It is interesting to note that when Newtonian physics was tumbled from this pedestal, virtually no tremors were noticed in the rest of the social fabric.

Other modern philosophers have noticed this relatively low capacity of the *content* of modern science to achieve such status, and have quite mistakenly inferred from this that science or its content is philosophically neutral. This does not follow at all. At the very least, the content of science cannot be neutral, in so far as it is frequently in conflict with the messy, over-exposed entrenched clauses of the *older* traditional belief-systems. There is of course a major contemporary intellectual industry which specializes in pruning, restating those older belief-systems in such a way as to minimize this exposure to conflict. Arguments of this kind are invariably spurious and hinge on presenting bowdlerized, travestied reformulations of the old faiths. They are given a double identity, each activated according to a sliding scale, which works in terms of whether or not they are under attack. This might be called differential sophistication.

As stated, the four traits selected as the crucial differentiae are not independent of each other. But, though they do feed and reinforce each other, it is also well worth specifying and characterizing them independently.

The Comparison of Belief-systems: Anomaly Versus Falsehood

Barry Barnes

Attempts to understand or explain preliterate systems of belief have frequently led anthropologists to compare them with ideal 'rational' models of thought or belief; in practice such comparison has been used to separate beliefs into those which are 'rationally' intelligible and hence natural and not in need of explanation, and those which deviate from this ideal and are consequently puzzling and in need of explanation. It is clear that the form of many anthropological theories has been partially determined by the ideal of rationality adopted and in practice this ideal has usually been presented as that which is normative in the modern natural sciences, that is to say modern anthropological theory has been profoundly influenced by its conception of ideal scientific practice.[1] This conception has, however, been derived less from familiarity with the natural sciences than from familiarity with the philosophy of science and the abstract discussions of 'scientific method' to be found therein. British anthropologists owe little to physics or biology but much to a philosophical position steeped in empiricism, and the accounts of induction, deduction, observation and experimentation it has generated.

Empiricist models of scientific rationality, or indeed any models which claim to describe readily available general procedures for discovering the 'truth about nature', focus curiosity upon the causes of error or apparent error within preliterate belief-systems; truth and

[1] See for instance J. Beattie, 'Ritual and social change', *Man*, N.S., 1, 1966, pp. 60 ff., and I. C. Jarvie and J. Agassi, 'The problem of the rationality of magic', *British Journal of Sociology*, 18, 1967, pp. 55 ff.

The Comparison of Belief-systems: Anomaly Versus Falsehood

error as defined by the anthropologist are all too often accounted for by different systems of explanation. J. D. Y. Peel has most effectively revealed the inadequacies of this approach.[1] In this paper I shall stand firmly upon Peel's contribution and assume that all belief-systems, scientific or preliterate, 'true' or 'erroneous', are most profitably compared and understood within a single framework;[2] work of this nature has been handicapped because many anthropologists have compared the preliterate beliefs they know from concrete experience with the misleading view of modern scientific thought provided by empiricism.

It is clearly impossible within this essay to develop a detailed criticism of the empiricist view of science. Instead I shall expound a conflicting view and point to implications of possible interest to anthropologists. In contrast to most empiricist positions I wish to make two assertions:

(a) Rather than being inductive, deductive, or otherwise logical, much scientific thought is analogical or metaphorical; indeed, scientific theories can in most instances be regarded as models providing a series of analogies between familiar understood phenomena and the problems the scientist is attempting to solve;[3] they increase our understanding by the metaphorical extension of our cultural resources. An examination of the creation and development of

---

[1] J. D. Y. Peel, 'Understanding alien belief systems', *British Journal of Sociology*, 20, 1969, pp. 69 ff. (For some reason the author appears to regard his well-detailed and fully justified argument as in some way anti-scientific.)

[2] I assume the validity and value of cross-cultural comparisons; there is, of course, a point of view which entirely rejects theories claiming relevance to the beliefs and actions of all societies. According to this position a society can be understood only in terms of the criteria of identity of the actors in that society, no further explanation by means of theoretical terms supplied by the investigator being allowable. (See for example Peter Winch, *The idea of a social science*, Routledge & Kegan Paul, London, 1958.) Unfortunately the arguments for this position proceed by description of the 'language', 'way of life', 'criteria of identity', 'beliefs' and 'actions' of the 'actors' in an alien 'society'. How can we be persuaded not to use our criteria of identity in the study of other human groups by an argument that does precisely this? The use of terms such as 'language' or 'belief' in this argument must involve tearing them from our total system of ideas, the only context in which they can make sense (cf. Winch, op. cit., p. 107). It is no use being semi-scrupulous: if there is Anthropology then there is Comparative Anthropology.

[3] See for example M. B. Hesse, *Models and analogies in science*, University of Notre Dame Press, Indiana, 1966.

183

scientific concepts suggests that this process can be understood in terms of a model of metaphorical development relevant to conceptual change in general.[1]

(b) Scientific thought is essentially presuppositionalist and as such entails an ineradicable element of commitment on the part of the scientist. Instead of never going beyond the 'facts', scientific thought has to be seen as always being beyond the facts; indeed one has to appreciate that what is called a fact is a variable between different theoretical frameworks in science.

The most interesting recent work describing the importance of presupposition and commitment in science is that of Thomas Kuhn;[2] it arises from a genuine attempt to describe and understand concrete scientific practice. According to Kuhn most effective scientific progress occurs when a group of scientists come to define themselves as a community investigating a field in the light of a common orientation provided by a paradigm:

> A paradigm is a fundamental scientific achievement, and one which includes both a theory and some exemplary applications to the results of experiment and observation. More important it is an open-ended achievement, one which leaves all sorts of research still to be done. And finally it is an accepted achievement in the sense that it is received by a group whose members no longer try to rival it or create alternatives for it.[3]

Such a community practises what Kuhn calls 'normal science' and to a large degree is concerned with developing and checking a set of expectations about the natural world indicated by the paradigm:

> (the scientist) struggles to articulate and concretise the known, designing much special purpose apparatus and many special purpose adaptations of theory for that task. From these puzzles of design and adaptation he gets his pleasure.[4]

---

[1] See for example Donald A. Schon, *Invention and the evolution of ideas*, Tavistock, London, 1967.

[2] See T. S. Kuhn, *The structure of scientific revolutions*, University of Chicago Press, Chicago, 2nd edn., 1970, for the fullest exposition of his views.

[3] T. S. Kuhn, 'The function of dogma in scientific research', in A. C. Crombie (ed.), *Scientific change*, Heinemann, London, 1963.

[4] Kuhn, 1963, op. cit.

The Comparison of Belief-systems: Anomaly Versus Falsehood

Rather than the paradigm being believed because nature, as it were, insists, the natural world is seen through the paradigm (in terms of atoms for instance, or fields) and its behaviour is interpreted to accord with this perception, with the use, where appropriate, of secondary assumptions and arguments. It is pointless to talk of paradigms such as the atomic theory, the Copernican cosmology, or evolution as limitations on the objectivity of science, for they are what constitutes science: without them scientific problems would cease to exist as distinct problems. To become a scientist generally involves the uncritical reception of a paradigm during a training period. Kuhn has described features of the process and their function: the dogmatic presentation of scientific texts, the erasure of historical aspects of theories and past controversies in the field, the failure to consider difficulties in theories, and the stress on paradigmatic problem-solving procedures. Like the basics of other belief-systems those of science are not acquired because of the force of 'rational' demonstration, they are passively received. 'Rational' demonstrations in so far as they can compel assent must be considered as operating in paradigmatic frameworks. Consider a chemist accepting a demonstration that the methane molecule is tetrahedral or an Azande that his 'benge' is faulty: both actors take a whole framework on trust, both see (or are expected to see) the significance of relationships and deductions within the framework, both know of legitimate grounds for scepticism they might employ. If rationality is relevant at all, then both actors should be considered as rational within different belief-systems.[1]

This element of commitment in 'normal science' is not stressed by Kuhn as a criticism. On the contrary, it is to be regarded as a vital element in the growth of scientific theories. In the early stages of a research tradition scientists may have to face powerful objections, later there will always be anomalies and failures to be taken into

[1] Belief and action are inextricably intertwined as Kuhn was well aware when he formulated his concept of a paradigm; there are difficulties in simply talking about belief-systems. But to talk of social institutions implies that the system of belief and action referred to is a distinct cluster of roles, which is not always the case when the system is distinguished as a set of connected beliefs. In a previous paper discussing similar topics I referred to 'social paradigms' (S. B. Barnes, 'Paradigms—scientific and social', *Man*, N.S., 4, 1969), but perhaps this makes too strong an analogy with Kuhn's work. I have reverted to talking of 'belief-systems' in this paper on the assumption that such entities are not found, as it were, floating freely.

185

account, and at any stage of any paradigm logical and conceptual difficulties abound and philosophical criticism often attacks the very heart of a theory; sufficient commitment to put these things aside and 'get on with it' seems to have been the most productive way of dealing with these situations. The theory of evolution, for instance, was criticized by Lord Kelvin, who demonstrated by a physical calculation that the sun could not have supplied heat for a period long enough to encompass the events that it claimed had occurred.[1] In terms of the physics of his day there was no answer to Kelvin; evolutionary biologists were obliged to ignore him. There is no shortage of supporting examples.[2]

Kuhn's work then provides explicit arguments in support of my second assertion; I would suggest in addition that it provides implicit support for my first. So many of Kuhn's examples—electricity considered as a fluid, light as corpuscles, light as waves, matter as particulate, and so on—illustrate the use of analogy, that the importance of this process is put above doubt. Indeed, whilst there is no reason to think that this is Kuhn's own view, a paradigm can be regarded as embodying the dominant metaphor guiding a scientific community.

*　　*　　*

The question now arises as to how we are to compare preliterate beliefs with modern scientific ones, in the light of a presuppositionalist analogical view of the latter. Many similarities are suggested which are not admitted by empiricist views. Once the notion of a direct route to truth is dispensed with, and the central role of authority, trust and commitment in the transmission of scientific beliefs is clearly recognized, there is less incentive to examine the mentality of the preliterate actor for signs of impairment or to explain his beliefs *solely* in terms of unconscious or hidden motives. Neither can scientific concepts be differentiated by their precision or the rigour of their usage; key concepts tend to defy definition and to vary in usage during the development of a field, as the history of such terms as 'gene', 'chemical bond' or 'energy' illustrates.

---

[1] Lord Kelvin had, of course, no notion of sub-atomic processes such as fusion or fission.

[2] Kuhn's work cites some such cases as does Michael Polanyi, *Personal knowledge*, University of Chicago Press, Chicago, 1958 (2nd edn., Harper Torchbook, New York, 1964).

The Comparison of Belief-systems: Anomaly Versus Falsehood

It is important to note that this picture is not altered by the importance of experimentation within many of the natural sciences. Experimentation never falsifies a theory although its extension or elaboration may be entailed. Evans-Pritchard's celebrated account of how Azande can always interpret the behaviour of their poison oracle within the framework of their particular belief-system[1] must not be regarded as an antithesis to good scientific practice; one way to become convinced of the value of secondary elaboration is to study the history of chemistry.

From the present viewpoint it does indeed become difficult to identify systematic formal differences between scientific and preliterate belief-systems. Contrasts based on claims that scientific concepts are abstract, relational or culture-free, as found for example in such dissimilar work as that of Lévi-Strauss and Beattie,[2] are unacceptable because they ignore the central role of models and analogies in science; Lévi-Strauss's description of the 'bricoleur' is not inappropriate to the natural scientist. Attempts to discern differences within the structures of argument used in the two kinds of belief-system have, again, stressed the role of precision and logic within science and ignored its analogical nature. One most interesting suggestion that does not do this, but is unsatisfactory for another reason, has been made by Robin Horton.[3] Horton suggests that, whereas modern science will normally ascribe one cause only to an event, within preliterate belief-systems events are always linked to several causes; hence the role of any single factor can never be checked. The trouble with this suggestion is that scientific theories only exhibit 'simple' causal structures when expressed formally in ways that can never fit with actual situations; that is, in terms of such concepts as 'perfect radiators' or 'point masses'. With regard to any conceivable concrete event modern science will produce a causal account rivalling in complexity, and just as difficult

---

[1] E. E. Evans-Pritchard, *Witchcraft, oracles and magic among the Azande*, Clarendon Press, Oxford, 1937; cf. Kuhn, 1962, op. cit., pp. 77 ff.

[2] C. Lévi-Strauss, *The savage mind*, Eng. trans., Weidenfeld and Nicolson, London, 1966, ch. 1; Beattie, op. cit.

[3] Robin Horton, 'African traditional thought and Western science', *Africa*, 37, 1967, pp. 169 ff. This invaluable paper derives much of its merit from the author's familiarity with concrete scientific practice. For convenience of exposition I have mentioned several differences between our two positions here; this should not obscure the many important areas of agreement or the debt I owe to Horton's work.

187

to check as, the story produced by a preliterate culture. Hence if any meaningful comparison on these grounds could be made it would necessitate making an attempt to appreciate preliterate belief-systems as formal structures. The spirit of British anthropological tradition is set strongly against this sort of approach and it would doubtless be difficult to obtain even vestigial evidence from within it to test the point. In summary, the only commonly proposed point of structural difference that remains clearly valid seems to be between the strongly impersonal conceptual structure and idioms of modern science and the more anthropocentric and personalized theoretical entities of many preliterate belief-systems.

*   *   *

Instead of making static comparisons of belief-systems the processes by which they change can be examined; what is negligible morphologically may play a crucial role aetiologically. This suggestion raises technical problems due to the lack of longitudinal studies of preliterate cultures and the corresponding absence of the time dimension from anthropological theory. Nonetheless, I hope to show that consideration of how beliefs change over time may still be valuable, and shall examine this process within science, where it has been documented in some detail. Once again Thomas Kuhn's work is particularly important and I shall briefly review his conception of paradigm change or 'revolutionary science'.[1]

All paradigms involve anomalies: some are just ignored, as for instance was the anomalous orbit of Mercury by Newtonian physicists; others are put down as exceptional or anomalous examples, as were 'strong electrolytes' with respect to Arrhenius's theory of electrolytic dissociation[2] (even though at the time more exceptions than conforming examples were known). The existence of anomaly is essentially a normal state of affairs—not that it isn't unsatisfactory and disturbing. But at revolutionary periods in a discipline it often appears that the research tradition has become centred upon a number of refractory anomalies which assume exceptional importance. Under these conditions an embryonic alternative paradigm may appear and become accepted over an (often protracted) period of time. The new paradigm will involve anomalies of its own, sometimes more daunting

---

[1] Kuhn, op. cit.
[2] Polanyi, op. cit.

The Comparison of Belief-systems: Anomaly Versus Falsehood

than those of its predecessor, and no simple model for its adoption during the revolutionary period will suffice. The following generalizations about the process of change can, however, be made:

(a) At no point is an existing paradigm 'refuted'. In the absence of an alternative scientists will continue to use the current paradigm, suggesting ways in which anomaly can be assimilated or eliminated.

(b) At any one time an individual scientist will believe one paradigm only and bend his efforts to support it and criticize alternative views. A change in belief will occur from one paradigm to another directly, without an intervening period of detachment; the scientist may have acquired a full and detailed familiarity with the new paradigm in his efforts to refute it.[1]

(c) The establishment of a new research tradition occurs faster than the beliefs of individual scientists are changed. Many scientists may have become deeply committed to the previous paradigm and adhere to it for the rest of their lives; Priestley never lost his belief in phlogiston nor did Einstein ever fully accept quantum theory. Throughout the history of science the number of 'scientists' has grown exponentially; a research tradition is able to become dominant by attracting the major share of new recruits.

(d) The fact that a new paradigm can offer the possibility of dealing with those particular anomalies that had become crucial in the old system is vital to its acceptance. Without that commitment to the old paradigm which defined the anomalies and their importance, the new paradigm would not have arisen.

This is in many ways an unsatisfactory and incomplete account of paradigm changes, but it does nonetheless offer some valuable suggestions. Paradigm change may be regarded as a possible response to anomaly. It seems a reasonable assumption that all belief-systems have perpetually to deal with anomaly; that is not to say that they are perpetually threatened with chaos or ruin but merely that their systems of classification and causality will never be sufficiently perfect to deal with all their experience, especially new experience. It seems

[1] My view would be that paradigm change involves replacement of the dominant metaphor guiding the work of a community of scientists. Again no explicit sanction for this view is provided by Kuhn (but see his postscript in his revised (1970) edition).

The Comparison of Belief-systems: Anomaly Versus Falsehood

reasonable also that anomaly is inherently disturbing and automatically generates pressure for its reduction.[1] Now there are a number of mechanisms available for the reduction or removal of anomaly. Sometimes the mere extension of a taxonomy will suffice, or secondary elaboration. Mary Douglas[2] has demonstrated the use of taboo in this respect, and perhaps Lévi-Strauss's[3] description of myth indicates yet another available mechanism. The conceptual reorientation of an entire system or sub-system of beliefs, exemplified by paradigm change, is but one possible response. *I suggest that the occurrence and treatment of anomaly within various systems of belief forms the best framework within which to attempt comparison of those systems.*

As I have already argued, belief-systems cannot be profitably contrasted in terms of the ways in which individual actors receive beliefs, or in terms of the 'mentality' of the individual actors; comparison of the static structure of belief-systems has, on the whole, produced little of value; attempts to compare belief-systems on the basis of their relationship with 'reality' have merely disguised prejudices in favour of one particular belief-system. Anomaly within a belief-system, however, springs from the particular categories and classifications of that system, and its occurrence and consequences can thus form an unbiased basis for the comparison of belief-systems and the societies embodying them. Work of this kind can be found within the anthropological literature.

Robin Horton[4] is taking essentially this approach when he lists differences between preliterate and modern scientific belief-systems connected with the 'presence or absence of anxiety about threats to the established body of theory'. In Horton's opinion the preliterate actor meets anomaly with essentially conservative responses such as taboo and avoidance because he cannot contemplate the breakdown of his category system as anything other than the creation of chaos. The scientist is not in this position; he is aware of the existence of

[1] This assumption is central to dissonance theory in psychology: see L. Festinger, *A theory of cognitive dissonance*, Stanford University Press, Stanford, Calif., 1957.

[2] Mary Douglas, *Purity and danger*, Routledge and Kegan Paul, London, 1966.

[3] See for example, C. Lévi-Strauss, 'The story of Asdiwal', printed with discussion in E. Leach (ed.), *The structural study of myth and totemism*, Tavistock, London, 1967.

[4] Horton, op. cit.

190

belief-systems alternative to his own, which diminishes the hold of his own beliefs upon him and enables him to make radical responses to anomaly, involving the abandonment of his current beliefs.

It seems to me that two criticisms can be made of this very interesting point of view. Firstly, given that paradigm change processes within science occur over periods ranging from a decade to a century, and that the anthropological literature is so weak in longitudinal studies, can we be so sure of the comparative conservatism of preliterate cultures? Secondly, and more significantly, can so much explanatory weight be attached to the openness of the individual scientist? Probably the first criticism should be waived since so much evidence of the conservative treatment of anomaly exists in functionalist studies; but the second point must be pressed, especially if the picture of the individual scientist found in Kuhn's work is accepted. My view is that if science is more prone to make radical responses to anomaly than other belief-systems, then the reason lies more in the social structure than the behaviour of the individual actor; where the latter is significant it should be regarded itself as a consequence of the former. I shall now cite a writer who has developed what amounts to such a view.

Mary Douglas has suggested that differentiation is the key concept in understanding differences between preliterate and modern belief-systems.[1] Basic to her work is the view that the categories and classifications of a culture generate anomaly and ambiguity. Any culture will have provisions for dealing with these experiences, and because systems of classification are embedded in social institutions and not readily altered these provisions will be defensive ones. This will be especially true in primitive cultures where the problem of conceptual order is the problem of social order, and solidarity cannot be maintained by a high interdependence of roles and the use of specialized agencies of social control, as in differentiated societies.

---

[1] Douglas, op. cit. In giving this causal role to differentiation (an ascription with which I fully agree) one raises the problem of the origin of differentiation itself. Douglas does not follow Durkheim on this question but seems to imply that technological evolution is basic here; this would also be my view. It is interesting to note that most of the classic criticisms of Marx's view that the 'foundation' of society determines its 'super-structure' do not apply to the view that changes in the 'superstructure' are determined by changes in the 'foundation'.

The Comparison of Belief-systems: Anomaly Versus Falsehood

Without forms filled in triplicate, without licences and passports and radio police-cars they must somehow create a society and commit men and women to its norms.[1]

The primitive culture must make its crucial social classifications strongly binding and emphasize distinctions; ideas of taboo, pollution and danger will settle about anomalies; moreover the crucial classifications are buttressed by symbolic linkages to other systems, which also become permeated with defensive responses. Unlike the fragmented, unsystematic ideas of pollution and avoidance within differentiated societies, those of primitive cultures are pervasive and interrelated. Changes in entire systems of belief are more likely in a differentiated social structure.

I hope to support Mary Douglas's main thesis, as it were, from the other side, by briefly considering science as a social institution. But first some comments on the presentation of that thesis must be made. Pollution and taboo are treated in *Purity and danger* within the functionalist paradigm, and the arguments are intended, among other things, as rebuttals of a Frazerian position: coupled with exquisite functional analysis is the frequent suggestion that it would be naïve to think of erroneous functional beliefs as being the real truth to primitive peoples. The discussion invites classic counter-arguments— for instance, the comment that for beliefs to be tools relevant to the maintenance of mechanical solidarity *they have to be believed*. I want to suggest that this traditional controversy dissolves when the empiricist paradigm of rationality is abandoned. The presence of 'error' in preliterate beliefs then ceases to be a *prima facie* indicator of foolishness or mental inadequacy since no obvious route to its elimination is taken for granted; hence functionalism is no longer needed to 'defend' preliterate beliefs. But this moral concern seems to be the real heart of the controversy.

Traditionally the question has been whether apparently erroneous primitive beliefs are genuinely held as true or are primarily held because they are 'functional'. This either/or formulation misses the point that there is nothing mutually exclusive about the two types of explanation. Given that beliefs in all societies are for the most part passively received it would be odd if the Frazerian position were not justified for large numbers of preliterate beliefs we ourselves regard

[1] Douglas, op. cit., p. 91.

192

The Comparison of Belief-systems: Anomaly Versus Falsehood

as incorrect. Why should we set the wisdom of preliterate peoples above that of the phlogiston chemists, those scientists who believed in the aether, the Ptolemaic astronomers—or Newton or Einstein for that matter? Certainly it may well be that specific peoples have mistakenly been held to believe in the efficacy of their rituals and so on, and doubtless anthropological specialists should be concerned to point to such mistakes; but the status of functionalist interpretation, whatever it be, does not depend upon whether the beliefs with which it deals can be shown not to be 'genuinely' held. If we ask why an individual believes 'X' the usual answer in all cultures will be that he was told or taught 'X' by a trusted knowledge source. We can then ask why belief 'X' is present in the culture, and that is where functionalism makes claims to provide explanation. Essentially traditional Frazerian positions have been concerned with how beliefs are adopted and in what ways actors hold them; functionalism is really concerned with the self-maintaining properties of cultures and their beliefs, properties that have become built in over very long periods. Of course, the inability of anthropological methodology to deal with time has resulted in a quite artificial elimination of time from anthropological theory, so that there are few explicit statements that functional relationships in present societies are the result of long historical processes.[1] Nonetheless, that is what has to be said. Why do preliterate actors perform actions apparently irrational in our eyes? Probably because they genuinely believe things we regard as erroneous. Why are those beliefs present in their culture? Possibly because of their functional place in the social structure and belief-system, established over a long period.

The controversy between functionalism and more recent views sometimes called 'neo-Frazerian' has a rather more interesting basis, but again seems to rest on the treatment of quite compatible explanations as mutually exclusive. Compare for instance Mary Douglas's view that natural classifications are symbolically related to social classifications and developed to reinforce them, with Robin Horton's

[1] But note the following (Douglas, op. cit., p. 39): '. . . anomalous events may be labelled dangerous (by a culture). Admittedly individuals sometimes feel anxiety if confronted by anomaly. But it would be a mistake to treat institutions as if they evolved in the same way as a person's spontaneous reactions. Such public beliefs are more likely to be produced in the course of reducing dissonance between individual and general interpretations.'

suggestion that personalized categories are used as theoretical entities with which to provide genuine explanations of nature; again there is an apparent contrast between 'intellectual' and 'functional' accounts. But any ordered system can be used, by metaphorical extension, in an attempt to order or explain another area of experience; such processes, where successful, give rise to two systems bearing obvious analogies, analogies which can be utilized and extended in the process of maintaining mechanical solidarity. To believe that ancestral spirits cause the occurrence of certain natural events may be shown to reinforce the moral order of a preliterate culture; this does not prove that the belief was not initially produced, as explanation, by metaphorical extension of concepts within that same moral order. Similarly to show a belief operating as genuine explanation does not preclude its having 'crystallized in the social institutions' according to Mary Douglas's account. Can it be suggested that in the absence of evaluative questions generated by empiricism 'intellectual' and 'functional' accounts can co-exist without controversy?

* * *

I now want to support Mary Douglas's stress on the importance of differentiation by examining science as a specialized institution within a highly differentiated society. Too strong a contrast must not be made; the change to organic solidarity is never complete; an examination of our own paradigmatic notions of human responsibility or sexuality is salutary. The differentiated society does however possess structural features favouring changes in belief-systems at certain points within it. The separate institutions of a differentiated society—clusters of roles that can profitably be considered as separate sub-systems—will consist in distinct patterns of action and belief; knowledge will be to an extent fragmented. Individuals will play a succession of roles within the structure, gaining access to different fragments of knowledge, but, we may assume, having different degrees of involvement or identification with the roles they play. Typically they will identify with a sub-culture embodying distinct beliefs and values. There will be no single perceived social or moral order. In the conflicts and compromises entailed in institutionalization and the modification of existing institutions it will be difficult to employ 'the social order' as a standard of evaluation. Communication has to become increasingly impersonal in idiom, and institutions, reflecting the basis of

194

limited co-operation on which they rest, find their objectives narrowed and purified.[1]

Considered in its modern institutional framework, science reveals many features conducive to change in paradigms. Its very esotericity is one such factor; belief changes become easier the smaller the community involved. Another factor is that science has become institutionalized in the educational system where nearly all the rights and obligations of scientists to their sources of economic support are defined in terms of the role of teacher; research activities can accordingly be largely decoupled from general social control. (It is interesting to note that the precursor of the modern academic scientist was the 'amateur' scientist, almost always a 'gentleman of leisure' also free of economic control.) More important than either of these factors, however, is the limited scope of scientific paradigm.

It may seem strange to refer to scientific paradigms as of limited scope when, for instance, physics deals with concepts such as length, mass and time, crucial in our everyday understanding of the world, and behaviourist psychology has immense implications for our view of social relationships. But, in practice, the paradigms of scientists are conceived mainly in terms of their research tradition, and although extension of changes into other areas of society may occur, they are never entailed and rarely specifically aimed at. Time and mass for the physicist are concepts which take their meaning from the concrete practices of his problem-solving tradition; when catching the bus home he will switch to conventional time, that which is normative through society at large. Although scientists may carefully demonstrate that use of either notion of time will give near enough the same result in everyday life, nonetheless the two times, esoteric and conventional, are conceptually different; a major revolution affecting esoteric time would entail nothing for conventional time. The physicist can see the sense of both times because he uses both; he may express an ontological preference between the two but in practice both are treated as real.[2]

Thus scientific paradigms may be considered as having limited

---

[1] Cf. Horton, op. cit., pp. 64–5.

[2] Perhaps this lays too much stress on the separateness of scientific concepts. The really important point is that during paradigm change or large-scale conceptual reorganization in science only esoteric scientific practice is immediately at issue, even though individual scientists may be concerned about general implications of the change.

scope for the individual actor. They structure a particular area of activity only and one in which there is sometimes only a limited emotional investment; moreover they structure activities only obliquely related to social relationships and hierarchies. Some belief-systems are so pervasive that the actor cannot modify all the actions that a change of them would involve, some relate to activities fundamentally tied to the interests of the actor; the limited scope of scientific paradigms minimizes such factors. In this sense it is easier for the individual actor to abandon, say, relativity theory than most forms of witchcraft belief or our own beliefs about responsible (blameworthy) and nonresponsible action.

In considering paradigm change it is vital to remember the highly differentiated nature of science itself. This is important in considering the sources of new paradigms. When a scientific community abandons its current paradigm it is invariably to replace it by a new one which is either available, as it were, ready made, or is created by the metaphorical extension of some ordered structure in use either within another area of science or elsewhere. Such changes are social processes greatly aided by the fact that science consists in a large number of relatively independent paradigm-sharing communities.

Ready-made replacement paradigms can be preserved within a discipline by a sub-group of scientists who have rejected the main stream and formed their own community, sometimes operating with a paradigm already rejected by the main group. Thus the wave theory of light was largely replaced by the corpuscular theory at the time of Newton but was still used by a small group of scientists; later it became dominant again, dealing effectively with anomalies thrown up by the corpuscular theory; later still a further inversion occurred. Where ready-made paradigms are taken over from other disciplines the usual situation is for existing paradigms not to be replaced but to co-exist in a condition of lowered importance. Thus many practitioners in the biological sciences have become what could be described as specialized chemists or physicists, whereas the traditional forms of taxonomic zoology and botany have very much declined in importance; they cannot however be replaced by the new studies.

Paradigms from other disciplines are frequently extended by analogy to provide models for a field: physics and chemistry have provided models for physiology, and information theory for psychology. When Dalton arrived at his atomic theory he had studied 'chemical' problems based on weighing techniques and transformations of the properties of solids, with a training and background based on the behaviour of gases and its associated problems; the 'atomic' concepts of the latter blended fruitfully with the quantitative relationships of the former. Earlier in the history of science common-sense analogies were fruitful sources of models for scientific disciplines; one thinks of the fluid theory of electricity or ball-and-hook theories of valency. But science during its development has produced enormous numbers of models so that increasingly today its creative growth is becoming an internal process.

In the changes of paradigm I have described, the social organization of science is crucial. A new candidate for paradigm status is not typically propounded by a single isolated individual; rather, he will have the backing of an existing scientific reference group within the discipline, or another discipline entirely to fall back upon if rebuffed. In some cases the role of the isolated individual is more central than this: Ben-David has described how 'market pressure' can force individuals trained in high-status disciplines to accept posts in disciplines of lower rank; such individuals may continue to adhere to the values of their former reference group and to apply, so far as possible, its methods and practices in the new discipline, thereby generating a new paradigm.[1] But this process described by Ben-David also reveals the importance of the differentiated structure of science.

The various features favouring belief changes in science never result in anything approaching permanent revolution, however. Even with the resources of modern technology, research traditions take a considerable time to produce recalcitrant anomalies; furthermore, change in belief-systems can never itself become an institutionalized social process. Reward in science, whether in terms of recognition, status or financial advancement, rests upon research performance as evaluated by criteria embedded in scientific paradigms. The paradigm is a source of social control and as such is sometimes maintained against threat, and strictly separated from other paradigms by stress on disciplinary boundaries. Max Planck spent years in the scientific wilderness and Louis de Broglie missed failing his doctorate by a hairsbreadth, both

---

[1] J. Ben-David and R. Collins, 'Social factors in the origins of a new science: the case of psychology', *American Sociological Review*, 31, 1966, pp. 451 ff.; and 'Roles and innovations in medicine', *American Journal of Sociology*, 65, 1960.

suffering for setting their work against current paradigms.[1] As an example of the maintenance of disciplinary boundaries chemistry can be considered: this discipline for a long period was dominated by groups unwilling to allow living creatures a role in the aetiology of such processes as fermentation, and which resisted such techniques as chromatography and analysis using enzymes because of their connection with biology. Similarly, workers on 'boundary areas' in the sciences have had to develop their own journals for reasons going beyond the lack of interest of mainstream groups. Even with systems at opposite ends of the continuum of differentiation comparisons cannot be made in terms of black and white.

*   *   *

I hope to have shown above that the differentiated structure of science, and the societies containing it as an institution, are of crucial importance in understanding how changes of entire systems of belief occur therein. This demonstration forms part of a larger design based upon a presuppositionalist analogical view of scientific thought. Acceptance of this view leads to the dichotomy between 'truth' and 'falsehood', central to so much anthropology and sociology, being discarded. The possibility is created of treating all beliefs, preliterate or scientific, apparently true or apparently false, within a single framework; and of relating them all, whether through the concept of anomaly or otherwise, to the social structures in which they occur.

[1] It should be clear from the earlier part of this essay that this, in itself, does not represent a criticism of science on any standards; automatic maintenance of paradigms plays an important positive role in science. Both pointless and profitable attacks on paradigms can be made and the two can be distinguished only *ex post facto.*

Form and Meaning of Magical Acts: A Point of View

S. J. Tambiah

Introduction

Like one of the proverbial blind men who probed different parts of the elephant's body, I shall investigate merely a fragmentary portion of the gigantic question: is there a basic difference in the modes of thought of 'traditional pre-scientific' and 'modern science-orientated' societies? This was implicitly the theme of Evans-Pritchard's justly famous 'dialogue' with Lévy-Bruhl. I shall attempt here only a mini-dialogue with Evans-Pritchard concerning the theoretical implications of his Zande data on magic.

My general thesis will be as follows. The *analogical* mode of thought has always been exploited by man generally. While both 'magic' and 'science' are characterized by analogical thought and action, they comprise differentiated varieties whose validity it would be inappropriate to measure and verify by the same standards. Magical acts, usually compounded of verbal utterance and object manipulation, constitute 'performative' acts by which a property is imperatively transferred to a recipient object or person on an analogical basis. Magical acts are ritual acts, and ritual acts are in turn performative acts whose positive and creative meaning is missed and whose persuasive validity is misjudged if they are subjected to that kind of empirical verification associated with scientific activity. Neither magic nor ritual constitutes applied science in the narrow sense.

In contrast, the exploitation of analogical thought in science consists in making the known or apprehended instance serve as a model for the incompletely known in the phenomenon to be explained.

199

Form and Meaning of Magical Acts: A Point of View

The model serves to generate a prediction concerning the *explicandum*, which is then subject to observation and verification tests to ascertain the prediction's truth value.

Now 'performative' acts of a persuasive kind are by no means confined to the primitive: modern industrial societies also have their rites and ceremonies which achieve their effects by virtue of conventional normative understandings. However, science (strictly defined) is an achievement perhaps only of certain complex and literate civilizations: in the West at least where it has attained its fullest development, science probably developed and differentiated out of certain forms of traditional and magical thought and activity, but this should not automatically serve as a universal linear scheme, nor should there be a retrospective and backward thrust by which the 'rationality' of magic is pitted against the 'rationality' of science, to the former's inevitable and foregone detriment. Indeed it is precisely because many Western anthropologists have approached the ritual performances of other societies from the perspective of their own historical experience and intellectual categories that they have misunderstood the semantic basis of magical acts.

I shall try to give flesh to these programmatic assertions by working through a body of concrete ethnographic data.

The observer's problem: the example of the Azande

Although Evans-Pritchard in his book on the Azande[1] and in an earlier article written in 1929[2] admitted that the spell was nearly always a part of and indeed essential to Zande magical rites, he emphasized over and over again (perhaps to drive home the difference between Zande and Trobriand magical systems) that it was 'medicines' which played the major part. Mystical power, producing the desired end, resided in the material substance used, whereas spells, having no specific virtue by themselves, were merely words of direction uttered to the 'medicines' linking them to the desired ends.

A major concern of Evans-Pritchard was to investigate the attributes and logic of selection of Zande 'medicines', and their role in

[1] E. E. Evans-Pritchard, *Witchcraft, oracles and magic among the Azande*, Clarendon Press, Oxford, 1937.
[2] Idem, 'The morphology and function of magic, a comparative study of Trobriand and Zande ritual and spells', *American Anthropologist*, 31, 1929.

effecting the end sought by the rite. It is my view that in most of Evans-Pritchard's discussion of the potency of Zande 'medicines' he was troubled by a theoretical framework whereby 'magic' stood for effects automatically ensuing from the ritual operations alone (particularly the manipulation of material substances), and also whereby the efficacy of the ritual acts was sought to be seen within an observer's empirical 'cause-effect' scheme.

At several points in the book[1] Evans-Pritchard tried to apply the observer's distinction *ritual* (or *mystical*) versus *empirical* to the rites he was examining and found them difficult to apply consistently. This question whether Zande medicines were mystical or empirical plagued him with recurring insistence in the final chapter of the book on 'Leechcraft'. It is instructive to summarize the findings of this chapter, for here at least where the subject matter was the aetiology and cure of disease and the efficacy of Zande 'drugs' and 'pharmacopoeia' we might expect the discussion to be more concrete than that pertaining to the more elusive magical rites and witchcraft attacks. Apropos his use of concepts which I have put in quotation marks above, Evans-Pritchard disarmingly states: 'We can later decide to what extent their leechcraft is magic, their leeches magicians, and their drugs mere *materia medica* of magical ritual.' I shall be concerned in this paper with the implications of that postponed decision.

In the chapter under discussion Evans-Pritchard makes the following seemingly contradictory points in the space of a few successive pages:

1a. The object or animal chosen as 'resembling' the disease may not only constitute the medicine but also the cause of the disease (e.g. fowl's excrement is the cause and cure of ringworm).[2]

1b. In seeming contradiction to the above, Evans-Pritchard, agreeing with De Graer, asserts that a Zande, if he feels the need to do so, will attribute sickness to 'some mystical entity like witchcraft or magic'. The thing or animal that appears in the name of the disease may be a participant in the genesis or a tool of magic, *but is never the object of therapeutic treatment*. The implication of

---

[1] Evans-Pritchard, *Witchcraft, oracles and magic* . . .

[2] *Ima* the prefix literally meaning 'bringing misfortune' is translated as 'disease'; the suffix is the name of the natural object or animal which resembles the disease, e.g. *imanzingini* (*ima* = sickness; *nzingini* = porcupine).

this assertion is that the cause of disease is a 'mystical' entity, that there is no direct 'causal' relationship between symptom and object resembling it. What then is the logic of using the object as a 'cure' in treatment?

2a. The Azande show discerning powers of observation and common-sense inference—as seen by their naming of diseases by symptoms, by their perceptive diagnosis and cure of some diseases by the 'logico-experimental' use of drugs, and by the employment in a few instances of 'empirical therapeutics',[1] e.g. treatment of head-ache, use of massage or emetics etc.

2b. But the true answer to the question whether Zande leechcraft 'is in any degree empirically sound, or is it pure magic?' is this: 'The enormous number of drugs which Azande employ and the variety of herbal products they bring to bear on a single disease at once demonstrate their lack of therapeutic value when we reflect what scientific pharmacology really implies.'[2] Evans-Pritchard's final verdict is unambiguous: 'In spite of . . . em-pirical elements in Zande treatment of minor ailments, my own experience has been that Zande remedies are of an almost com-pletely magical order.'[3] And Evans-Pritchard concludes that the 'drugs' of Zande leechcraft are no different in their preparation from the 'medicines' of Zande magic,[4] that most cases of prophy-lactic and therapeutic treatment have little or no objective value. The performances of leeches are similar to the magical perform-ances: 'drugs of leeches are boiled and spells are uttered over them in the same manner as medicines of magicians.'[5]

Evans-Pritchard's final attempt at sorting the data, in answer to the query: 'to what extent are Zande medical practices 'empirical' as opposed to 'ritual'? ran something like this. In acute and sudden illnesses the attribution of genesis may be to 'mystical' causes like sorcery and witchcraft alone; in chronic and prolonged illness recourse is to a theory of *dual causation* in that there is the disease itself *plus* witchcraft which conditions its occurrence and continuance.

[1] Ibid., p. 495.
[2] Ibid., p. 494.
[3] Ibid., p. 499.
[4] Ibid., p. 499.
[5] Ibid., p. 504.

Form and Meaning of Magical Acts: A Point of View

(We may note that this dual theory is paralleled by Evans-Pritchard's earlier elucidation of witchcraft, that while the Zande are aware of the physical circumstances of accidents and disease, witchcraft explains why a particular sufferer and no other was the victim: 'Witchcraft explains why events are harmful to man and not how they happen.')[1] In both these cases of acute and chronic illness, in which mystical forces are at play, the drugs used are appropriately thought to have 'mystical' efficacy, as seen in the notion of *mbisimo ngua*, 'the soul of medicine' (corresponding to the notion 'soul of witchcraft').

Mild illnesses, in contrast, bring to the fore, so Evans-Pritchard says, 'natural' or organic causation with the witchcraft allegation sinking into the background. But even here 'the treatment may be just as useless in a slight as in a serious illness.'[2] It is not surprising then that Evans-Pritchard admits with a touch of bafflement: 'There are many varieties of behaviour and opinion which defies rigid classification because they shade into one another in a complicated pattern of interconnexions.'[3]

Despite this confession, it is evident that Evans-Pritchard did sort things out after a fashion. With the benefit of hindsight it might seem that a greater attention to folk classification of disease and 'medicines' and the native exegesis about them might have provided additional clarification. My thesis is that this lack itself is the concomitant of a certain theoretical perspective. Evans-Pritchard had clear clues that much of Zande magic was based on analogical thought and action, but rather than investigate its semantics deeply, he, being at this stage of his thought unable to liberate himself from the influence of the observer's distinction between things empirical and things mystical (and the like), simply subjected Zande magic and leechcraft to the Westerner's criteria of induction and verification. The unstated assumption of such an intellectual exercise is that Zande practices had the same empirical purposes and objectives as those of Western science and that they, like science, were concerned with 'causal' relations. This essay is largely concerned with the consequences of (erroneously) submitting Zande analogical thought and action to Western scientific standards of induction and verification.

---

[1] Ibid., p. 72.
[2] Ibid., p. 505.
[3] Ibid., p. 506.

Form and Meaning of Magical Acts: A Point of View

The uses of analogy

Evans-Pritchard's originality could not, of course, be confined for long within the bounds of limiting frameworks. Consequently, fresh insights break through here and there in the Zande book. One such is contained in the passing phrase 'imitative symbolism', and another in the idea of 'homoeopathy', once again discussed briefly in two pages (pp. 449–50). Here we find the seeds of an approach to Zande magic (and indeed other magical systems) which I shall call 'analogical action'.

Apparently the Azande themselves recognized the analogical and metaphorical basis for the use of material substances in their rites— a revelation which is also embedded in Malinowski's account.[1] Evans-Pritchard writes:

> They (the Azande) say, 'We use such-and-such a plant because it is like such-and-such a thing,' naming the object towards which the rite is directed. Likewise they say, 'We do so-and-so in order that so-and-so may happen,' naming the action which they wish to follow. Often the simalirity between medicine and desired happening is indicated in the spell.[2]

Evans-Pritchard proceeds to give the example (which he also gave in 1929) of the tall *bingba* grass, which is profuse in growth and has featherlike branches, being used by verbal direction and by direct action to make the oil-bearing melon (*kpagu*) flourish.

There are many examples of analogical action in word and deed scattered throughout the book. A systematic assembling and examination of these examples may provide an alternative interpretation to the one proposed by Evans-Pritchard.

Scrutinize these preliminary examples with this objective in view:

(1) When the Azande prick the stalks of bananas with crocodiles' teeth they say 'Teeth of crocodile are you, I prick bananas with them, may bananas be prolific like crocodiles' teeth.'[3]

(2) Azande tie *gbaga* (the fruit of a palm tree) to their girdles as a medicine of masculinity and to secure sexual potency. When

---

[1] S. J. Tambiah, 'The magical power of words', *Man*, N.S., 3, 1968.
[2] Evans-Pritchard, *Witchcraft, oracles and magic among the Azande*, p. 449.
[3] Ibid., p. 450.

tying they say: 'You are *gbaga*. May I be very potent sexually. May I not become sexually weak . . .'[1]

(3) Here is an expressive example that could equally well come from Ceylon or Thailand: If a man is a victim of *menzere* (sorcery) medicine, he goes to a much-frequented cross-roads, kneels there and verbally disperses it: '. . . If it is *menzere* may it follow all paths and not return.'[2]

(4) Finally, there is the celebrated case of the stone placed in the fork of a tree to retard the sun: 'You stone, may the sun not be quick to fall today. You, stone, retard the sun on high so that I can arrive first at that homestead to which I journey, then the sun may set.'[3]

Note here that the Azande refer to the stone used as *ngua uru* which Evans-Pritchard translates as 'sun-medicine'.

It is my submission that, had Evans-Pritchard followed leads of this sort, he could have thrown more light on why within the range of plant life and arboreal substances (which form the major category of 'medicines') used by the Azande, certain woods or roots or leaves rather than others were chosen to represent specialized ideas. Furthermore, the utterances and spells are in fact, as we have seen in these examples, critical for telling us which feature of an object-symbol is the focus of attention on an analogical basis. A shift of theoretical interest from 'inherent potency' of medicines to 'analogical transfer of their qualities' might have made the botanical enumeration of Zande medicines not so tedious and unnecessary as Evans-Pritchard feared.

Here is a critical passage which we may take as the text for our discussion in that it encapsulates the 'closed' system of Zande thought, a central theme of the book (and grist for the Popperian mill):

I do not know whether more than a verbal analogy is implied in the Zande name for mumps (the affected parts are massaged with an unguent): *imawirianzoro*, sickness of the little (*wiri*) *anzoro* birds (finches) which have lumps on their necks. But it may well be so, for we know that in primitive patterns of thought objects which have a superficial resemblance are often linked up by nomenclature and ritual and are connected in mystical patterns of thought. In Zande therapeutics this mystical connexion is found

---

[1] Ibid., p. 455.
[2] Ibid., p. 394.
[3] Ibid., p. 469.

in notions about cause and cure. Ringworm resembles in appearance fowls' excrement, and fowls' excrement is at the same time both cause and cure of ringworm. Blepharoptosis resembles a hen's egg, and a hen's egg is its cure. Generally the logic of therapeutic treatment consists in the selection of the most prominent external symptoms, the naming of the disease after some object in nature which it resembles, and the utilization of the object as the principal ingredient in the drug administered to cure the disease. The circle may even be completed by belief that the symptoms not only yield to treatment by the object which resembles them but are caused by it as well.[1]

A number of words appear in this commentary that are worthy of 'practical criticism': 'superficial resemblance' can get its meaning only by unstated comparison with the notion of deeper identity from a scientific causal viewpoint; 'mystical connection' can only mean unobservable and unknown connection by comparison with empirically observable connection. The backdrop then is the standards of verification of science.

Now, a classicist exploring the use of analogy by early Greek philosophers and who consulted Evans-Pritchard on Zande magic infers certain principles from the extract quoted above. He writes:

This passage illustrates very clearly three quite distinct functions which an analogy may serve.

(1) First an object may be named or described by referring to another object which it resembles. (Here it *need* not be implied that there is a causal connection between the two objects, though it is often the case that some causal connection is, in fact, assumed to exist.)

(2) Secondly, the recognition of a resemblance between two objects may serve as the basis for an explanation of one of them, that is an account of its cause.

(3) Thirdly, the resemblances between things may be thought to form magical links between them and attempts may be made to control or influence certain objects by manipulating other objects which resemble them: the Azande hope to effect cures by using the natural object which resembles the particular disease, and such 'homoeopathic' magical practices are, of course, common in all parts of the world.[2]

---

[1] Ibid., pp. 486–7.
[2] G. E. R. Lloyd, *Polarity and analogy: two types of argumentation in early Greek thought*, University Press, Cambridge, 1966, p. 178.

Form and Meaning of Magical Acts: A Point of View

I consider the last inference the most important (it includes the other two as well), for it is the basis on which philosophers and historians of science see the similarity and difference between magic and science as well as the ground on which they postulate linear evolution from magic to science. Lloyd thus takes the next interpretative step:

> We can see from these examples how analogy fulfils two roles in what is now for us largely, though not exclusively, the province of science, namely to provide explanations, and to control reality. As regards the second function, the most important difference between science and magic may be simply their relative effectiveness. Magic fails in practice. Yet its general aim is similar to that of applied science, to control events, and one of the means whereby it hopes to achieve this is *using the links which it believes may be formed between things by their similarities.*[1]

Most historians of science begin with the Greeks, and one of the principles of thought attributed to early Greek natural philosophy is that 'like attracts like', which in its application meant 'that a relationship of similarity may sometimes constitute a magical bond between two things, so that what happens to one of them may influence what happens to the other . . .'[2] Thus Hesse[3] explains that one of the commonest analogies in 'primitive' Greek thought was 'the analogy of attraction': men apparently, having experienced sympathy and antipathy, attraction and repulsion, between themselves and other men, and between themselves and nature, therefore see these as forces which can produce effects in nature. Popular maxims based on ideas of attraction and repulsion provided, we are told, concepts of *motion* and *change*—thus 'like attracts like' was supplemented by other maxims such as 'like nourishes like', 'like affects like', 'like perceives like'. The doctrine of attraction explained why animals flock together with their kinds, seeds of different size seek each other when shaken in a sieve, and likewise pebbles on the seashore. In Plutarch apparently is found the example of treating jaundice with the yellow eye of a stone curlew.

For the historian and philosopher of science, the analogy of attraction is principally of interest because the early Greek philosophers

[1] Lloyd, op. cit., pp. 178–9 (my italics, S.J.T.).
[2] Ibid., p. 180.
[3] M. B. Hesse, *Forces and fields: the concept of action at a distance in the history of physics*, Nelson, London, 1961.

used it to explain the phenomenon of *action at a distance,* a perennial problem in scientific explanation. The Greek breakthrough from primitive analogy into 'scientific' thinking, we are told, began to occur when two things happened:

(1) When a firm distinction was made between the animate and inanimate, and in recognizing that phenomena of gravity and radiation were different in kind from the behaviour of animals.

(2) When thereby a certain amount of 'mechanization' of physics took place with Aristotle and with the atomists. Indeed 'action at a distance' became intellectually problematic only when this stage had been reached. 'Part of the history of the problem of action at a distance is therefore that of the growth of a mechanical conception of matter, and the use of mechanical analogies in explaining natural processes.'[1] Thus for example it was the 'atomists', we are told, who by virtue of their notion of atoms in motion introduced a purely mechanical theory of motion and change through contact.

Readers of the Azande book will have noticed that Evans-Pritchard was very concerned with this classical problem of 'action at a distance' which was spelt out in terms of 'mystical' ties, the 'soul' of witchcraft or of 'medicine' affecting a victim, and the like, all of which are adduced in an attempt to solve an 'intellectual' problem which is not necessarily the Azande's.

How relevant are classical Greek scholarship and the writings of historians of science for illuminating the thought patterns of the Azande, Trobrianders, and the like? I cannot go into this matter at length here, but let me sound a note of caution. From a comparative point of view it is useful to bear in mind that many Western philosophers are concerned with how early Greek thought led by stages to the development of scientific thought wedded to experimental verification. In other words, how Greek thought was transformed from so-called 'magic' to 'science', and how the seeds sown by the Greek philosophers ultimately flowered in the scientific revolution of the seventeenth century when 'the analogy of mechanism' alone was exploited with respect to events in nature and when nature's laws were sought in mechanical conceptions. Indeed when, later, Newton's theory of gravity was propounded, the Cartesians attacked him for

---

[1] Hsese, op. cit., p. 30.

Form and Meaning of Magical Acts: A Point of View
propounding a theory of 'attraction' in the occult idiom, i.e. action
at a distance without contact. The linear evolution and transformation
of Western thought from the sixth century B.C. to the present day in
the field of science should not be taken as an intellectual model when
investigating the societies anthropologists study unless at the same
time one is deeply conscious of the underlying intellectual interests of
the scholars who formulated it. Their interests were the foundations
of scientific thought and of formal logic in Greece and the unique(?)
development by which Greek analogical thought became subject to
empirical verification, falsification and deductive–inductive reasoning.
Must analogical thought of the Azande necessarily be examined and
its form and meaning unravelled in relation to these intellectual
preoccupations?

In order to answer this question, let us examine carefully the kinds
of analogies that exist and their uses. First of all what do we mean by
analogy? Basically analogy depends on the recognition of similarities
between the instances compared, and, as many philosophers have
recognized, analogy stands as a prototype of reasoning from experience. J. S. Mill's paradigm serves well as a definition: 'two things
resemble each other in one or more respects; a certain proposition is
true of the one; therefore it is true of the other.' Lloyd elucidating
Keynes's thinking on the subject (in *A treatise on probability*) remarks
that 'both Bacon's own inductive method, based on the use of
"exclusions and rejections", and Mill's Methods of Agreement and
Difference, aim at the determination of the resemblances and differences between particular instances, at the determination of what
Keynes called the Positive and Negative Analogies.'[1]

Hesse in an instructive essay,[2] on which I draw, lists four kinds of
analogies. For my purposes, I shall modify her examples, and elaborate in new directions fundamentally two types of analogy—the
scientific predictive and the *conventional persuasive*. First, let us bear
in mind that 'positive analogy' relates to properties shared or points
of similarity between the things compared, 'negative' analogy to their
points of difference or properties they do not share, and 'neutral
analogy' to properties of the things compared of which we do not yet
know whether they are of positive or negative character.

[1] Lloyd, *Polarity and analogy*, p. 173.
[2] M. B. Hesse, *Models and analogies in science*, Newman History and Philosophy and Science series, 14, Sheed and Ward, London, 1963.

Form and Meaning of Magical Acts: A Point of View

Of the two fundamentally different types of analogies that can be distinguished, one serves as a model in science generating hypotheses and comparisons which are then subject to verification inductively. In this use, the known or apprehended instance serves as the 'model' and the unknown or incompletely known is the *explicandum*, the phenomenon to be explained by means of a theory.

Let us take some examples of analogies that might be used in science:

	SIMILARITY RELATIONS	
	Properties of sound	*Properties of light*
CAUSAL RELATIONS	echoes	reflection
	loudness	brightness
	pitch	colour
	etc.	

In this analogy, following Hesse, I indicate two kinds of dyadic relations that should be recognized, the *horizontal* and *vertical* relations. If it is to serve as a material analogy in science, the pairs of horizontal terms (echoes: reflection, etc.) should be either identical or *similar*, and the vertical relations (between the properties of sound such as echoes, loudness, etc.) should be '*causal*', which term given a wide interpretation should mean at least a tendency to *co-occurrence*, in that certain properties are necessary or sufficient conditions for the occurrence of other properties.

In the second 'looser' example given opposite the horizontal relation may show similarities of *structure* or of *function*, and the vertical relation that of whole to its parts depending on some theory of inter-relation of parts, evolutionary or adaptive.

Now it is essential to note that analogies can usefully serve as theoretical models only if the horizontal dyadic relations are relations of similarity (i.e. judged by identities and differences), if the vertical relations of the model are *causal* in some scientifically acceptable sense and if those of the *explicandum* also promise relations of the same kind, and if the essential properties and causal relations of the model have not been shown to be part of the negative analogy between model and *explicandum*. If these conditions are satisfied then predictions can legitimately be made from any set of known, say three, terms

	SIMILARITIES	
CO-OCCURRENCE	*Bird*	*Fish*
	wing	fin
	lungs	gill
	feathers	scales

to an unknown fourth. For example, in the case of the sound and light analogies stated before, if we have established the similarity of 'echoes' to 'reflection', then from the known property of 'loudness' in sound we may expect to find the 'similar' property of 'brightness' in light. Or in the bird and fish analogy, one can predict from the known parts of the bird skeleton to a 'missing' part of the fish skeleton. To put it differently, the fun lies in extrapolating from the domain of positive analogy into the domain of neutral analogy as these were defined above. Ultimately of course these predictions should be capable of verification or falsification in terms of observation statements.

There is another kind of traditional analogy used widely in human discourse that does not owe its genesis and use to the pursuit of 'scientific' knowledge. It would therefore be ridiculous to weigh and measure its adequacy in terms of inductive verification. Consider the following analogy that may occur in political rhetoric: the employer is to his workers as a father is to his children.

$$\frac{father}{children} : \frac{employer}{workers}$$

Let us say that the purpose of this analogy is propagandist, that it is disseminated by employers in order to 'evoke' attitudes in workers rather than to 'predict' them.

Now, it should be noted that in this example the vertical relations are not specifically causal; nor is it necessary that if three terms occur, the fourth also must. Even more importantly, there is not in this example any horizontal relation of similarity between the terms, except in virtue of the fact that the two pairs are up to a point *related by the same vertical relation*. (There may be other persuasive analogies in which, in spite of horizontal similarities between terms, the critical relation is still the vertical one.)

How must this analogy work if it is to succeed as political rhetoric? The relation of father to children bears some relation of employer to workers (positive analogy) in the sense let us say that just as the father provides for the material needs of his children so does the employer provide work and wages for his workers. Let us next say that the relation of children to father (and vice versa) is much more than this dependence; children should love their father, obey and respect him and so on. These meanings are not necessarily implied in the employer-worker relation (negative analogy). It is precisely this expansion of meaning or the transfer of these additional values to the employer-worker relations that is sought by invoking the father–children analogy. Since in this case the ultimate aim is to make workers believe that they are like 'children', there is a sense in which we can say that the operation consists in 'transferring' (rather than 'predicting') from the postulated three terms, the value of 'children' to the fourth term, the 'workers'. It is for this reason that this analogy and its variants are labelled 'persuasive', 'rationalizing' or 'evocative'.

It is my thesis that in ritual operations by word and object manipulation, the analogical action conforms to the 'persuasive' rather than the 'scientific' model. I shall later illustrate the argument that in Zande rites (as well as those of many other societies) the operation rests on the explicit recognition of *both similarity* (positive analogy) *and difference* (negative analogy) *between the vertical relations of the paired terms*. And the rite consists in persuasively transferring the properties of the desired and desirable vertical relation to the other which is in an undesirable condition, or in attempting to convert a potential not-yet-achieved state into an actualized one. The manipulation is made operationally realistic by directing the transfer not only by word but, as in the Zande case, by bringing a material piece of the object in the desirable–desired analogy into contact with the object in need of the transfer. There are nuances in this basic manipulation

212

which are best illustrated when dealing with the concrete cases. Thus a vital difference exists between the use of 'analogy' in science and ritual. Barring a few instances, in most Zande magical rites (especially those considered important by the people concerned), the analogical relation or comparison and the wished-for effect is stated *verbally* simultaneously with or before the carrying out of the so-called 'homoeopathic' act (of influencing certain objects by manipulating other objects which resemble them). Why must the analogy of attraction be stated in word and deed for it to be effective? No classical philosopher or historian of science appears to have asked this when propounding that the principle of 'like attracts like' activated primitive thought and action. In a laboratory of today, the only time a scientist may be found to foretell and verbally explain his actions while simultaneously doing his experiment would be, for example, when he is teaching a class the procedure involved in conducting that experiment. (And of course he does not expect that his words will automatically make the experiment come out right, as we know from the failed experiments in science classes we have attended at school.) Outside some such situation, his sanity would be suspect if he gave instructions aloud to his apparatus to do his bidding.

Note also how extraordinary the magical operation must look in terms of the traditional explanation (of like attracts like) when placed in relation to the use of analogy made by a scientist. Supposing a scientist constructs an electronic brain-model to 'simulate' in some ways a human biochemically structured brain. The former is useful as a predictive model only in those areas where the material make-up of the analogue is not essential to the model (i.e. constitutes the innocuous negative analogy) but where the pattern of mutual relation of the parts and the behavioural relations expressed by it are the essential features. If, say, a man is weak in arithmetic the scientist does not bring a brain-model that can add and place it in contact with the head of the former so that his additions may be thus 'caused' to be correct. But this is precisely what we are told the primitive magician might attempt to do! (On the other hand the scientist may demonstrate the working of an adding machine to our hypothetical subject, and it is possible that after sufficient demonstration of its workings his abilities might increase. This is a technique of 'persuasion' through contact. Could it be that this is the logic of the magical operations as well . . .?)

213

Form and Meaning of Magical Acts: A Point of View

Some Zande analogies

We have already noted that for the first time, well towards the end of the Azande book, Evans-Pritchard broached the question of the analogical basis of magical rites as seen by the actors. It is however a pity that he did not compile a more thorough indigenous exegesis on why certain 'medicines' were used, and what properties or features of the substance used were singled out as 'similar' to those of the recipient of the rite. Hence in the examples he cryptically cites, the logic of their use is open to an alternative interpretation that is as plausible as Evans-Pritchard's own implicitly theory-dictated view that the medicines and drugs, chosen on the basis of superficial resemblances and to which is given mystical significance, are empirically ineffective and scientifically false, although used as if they had automatic effects. Let us look at some Zande cases:

(1) At a certain time of their growth the stems of the creeper *araka* lose their leaves. These are replaced by a double row of bands, joined to the stalks, which little by little dry, split, and fall in small pieces just as the extremities of the hands and feet disappear in '*la lèpre mutilante*'. This creeper is highly thought of as furnishing treatment for this kind of leprosy.[1]

	POSITIVE AND NEGATIVE ANALOGIES	
CO-OCCURRENCE	*araka creeper* falling leaves etc. ——————— growth	:	*human being* falling extremities ——————— disease (leprosy)

I suggest that the analogical reasoning in this example is more complex than is implied by a simplistic 'like attracts like' in that it brings to view both similarities and differences, positive and negative analogies, in the *vertical relations* of the terms. In the case of the

[1] Evans-Pritchard, *Witchcraft, oracles and magic . . .*, p. 450.

214

creeper, the falling of its extremities is a *phase of its growth cycle*, whereas in the case of human beings the decay of limbs through leprosy is a *disease that leads to degeneration and death*. Thus this comparison proceeds to use the *araka* creeper in the rite as a vehicle or agent of life, the message being: may the leprosy disappear and health appear, just as the shedding process in the creeper stimulates growth. The rite expresses the wish that one 'vertical' relation that is undesired be replaced by another desired one; it itself represents symbolic not causal action.

(2) Let us next take the celebrated example already cited of a man indulging 'in the action of placing a stone in the tree and relating by a few words this action to a desired end'. We should bear in mind that the man is on a journey and wishes to arrive home before sunset.[1]

We can plausibly say that here the initial comparison is between the sun 'travelling' towards sunset (in the sky) and a man travelling (on land) to his homestead. The sun and the man are therefore similar in their situations but their interests are not identical (the difference

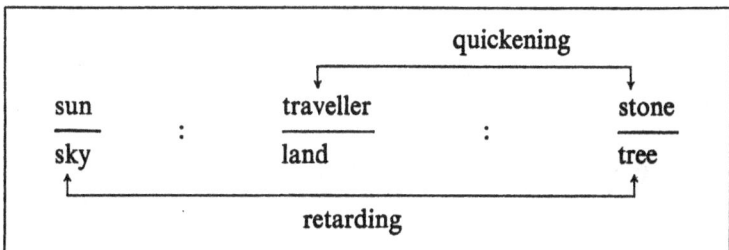

that constitutes the negative analogy). The man wishes to travel faster than the sun. It is in this context that we must view the operation of putting a stone in the fork of a tree and thus wedging it. It represents the desired positive effect of retarding the sun and the implicit counter effect (or negative analogy) of quickening his footsteps home, which in fact the traveller actually does by performing this rite.

(3) To examine now a case of 'homoeopathic' treatment of a disease. Ringworm in children is called *imanduruakondo* (*ima* = sickness, *nduruakondo* = fowl house).

[1] Ibid., pp. 468–9.

It is so called because the scabby patches of the disease resemble fowls' excrement: hence they appear to consider the disease due to the afflicted child having eaten food grown on a dung heap in the vicinity of a fowl house: hence also they consider the remedy to consist in fowls' excrement dried and reduced to ashes and mixed into a paste with a little palm-oil and applied to the ringworm.[1]

	SIMILARITY		
RELATION OF ELIMINATION	excrement / fowl	:	scabby skin / child	RELATION OF ADHERENCE

While the 'like attracts like' argument would say that the fowls' excrement is (falsely) used to attract the scabs on the skin which it (falsely) resembles, I am tempted to say that the analogy is interesting and is capable of being acted upon creatively because, once again, of the positive and negative features it exhibits. The relation of fowl to excrement is one of *elimination* of (unwanted) waste product, while that of scabby skin on child is one of (unwanted) *adherence* to body. Hence it is that the fowl's excrement can convey the desired idea of eliminating the scabs when applied to the body, because while in one sense similar to it, it is also essentially different.

(4) Epileptic fits (*imawirianya*; *wiri* = small, *nya* = animal) are associated with the red bush monkey which is thought to display certain movements resembling epileptic symptoms. Before sunrise this monkey seems to be in a torpor, but as he comes out of it under the warm rays of the sun, so does the epileptic slowly recover when placed in the warmth of a fire. One of the remedies for epilepsy is to eat ashes of the burnt skull of the red monkey.[2] Superficially considered it seems inconsistent and absurd that the ashes of the skull of the 'epileptic' monkey can cure an epileptic man. But in fact the

[1] Ibid., p. 485.
[2] Ibid., pp. 483–4.

Form and Meaning of Magical Acts: A Point of View

analogy moves in two steps, exploiting the fact that although the monkey's movements resemble epilepsy, yet it is a normal occurrence for the monkey to revive daily from its torpor under the warm rays of the sun, and the same recovery is desired in the patient. It is this capacity of the monkey to revive daily that is persuasively exploited by the rite of eating the ashes of the monkey's skull.

Enough Zande examples have been given to suggest how the analogical thought and action of the persuasive types are exploited. A well-known example such as the cure of elephantiasis by the use of ashes from a piece of burnt elephant's leg looks much less bizarre when subjected to similar analysis. Nor is this underlying logic peculiar to the Azande. Numerous cases were documented by Malinowski: one example that neatly illustrates analogical action is that in which the Trobrianders, having postulated an analogy (or homology) between the yam house with yams stored in it and the human belly with food inside it, act upon the former in order to influence the latter. 'The Trobriand logic is that the rite is really a metaphorical analogy urging the human belly to restrain its hunger and greed for food.'[1] The application of 'similarity and difference' analogically also serves to unravel the logic of some Trobriand food taboos.[2]

Closer to the Azande, a number of examples can be taken from Turner's voluminous and excellent documentation of the symbolism exploited by the Ndembu in their rites. For instance, take the Ndembu *Ntambu* cult which deals with the hunter's affliction of failure to kill animals. The mode of manifestation of the disease is that the afflicted hunter sees a lion in his dreams and the ritual consists of making an effigy of a lion on a mound and the miming of the lion's actions by the hunter and the practitioner.[3] Or again consider the simple persuasive analogy which exploits identity and difference between a Mujiwu tree which has many roots (empirically a true and desirable state of affairs) and a woman who wants to have many children (desired but not an empirically inevitable state of affairs). The Ndembu penchant for use of arboreal substances rests on such

[1] See S. J. Tambiah, 'The magical power of words', *Man*, N.S., 3, 1968, pp. 201–2.
[2] Ibid., p. 196.
[3] See V. Turner, *The drums of affliction: a study of religious processes among the Ndembu of Zambia*, Clarendon Press, Oxford, 1968, p. 301.

analogies and persuasive manipulations which are cultural equations. There is no intrinsic reason why the tree should be similar to a mother and the roots to children, but the analogy which says that roots are to the tree as children are to the mother make relational sense that can be used to 'transfer' effects.

Finally, take this fragment from Dobuan magic (close in form to the Trobriand system) which displays a persuasive analogical act. Fortune writes 'The woman magician next breathes a spell into two or three water gourds containing (sea) water, and pours the water over the heaped seed yams. . . . The spell breathed into the water gourds and continued while the water is being poured runs—

> murua octopus
> from its inner cave
> it thrusts a left arm out
> on the left side it lies, head inland,
> it thrusts a right arm out
> comes over and lies down . . . etc. . . .'[1]

The analogical pattern of this rite is crystal clear. Verbally a comparison is made between the octopus which has many tentacles and the yam which it is desired will sprout many roots and shoots (like an octopus). The sea water in which the octopus lives metonymically represents it, and it is realistically poured on the yam to transfer to it the desired properties of the octopus. This Dobuan example portrays equally well the underlying design of Trobriand analogical action.

How to understand ritual (which includes 'magic')?

I have perhaps so far only indicated negatively how 'magic' should not be viewed and not positively how it might be viewed in terms of a new perspective. I have argued that to view magic as an attempt at science that failed (or more crudely a 'bastard science' in the manner of Frazer, or more sophisticatedly as a 'closed' system of thought that allows for no verification and falsification of its principles *à la* Popper) is to assert that in their magic and ritual[2] the primitives tried to achieve results through 'causal' reasoning and failed. I have also

---

[1] R. F. Fortune, *Sorcerers of Dobu*, Routledge and Kegan Paul, London, 1932, p. 117.
[2] For me magic is embedded in ritual.

argued that while it is the case that much primitive magic is based on analogical thought and action as is Western science, the difference between them is that whereas in science the use of an analogy is closely linked to prediction and verification, and its adequacy judged in terms of inductive support, or of meeting standards of probability criteria, or standing up to tests of falsifiability and the like, the semantics of a magical rite are not necessarily to be judged in terms of such 'true/ false' criteria of science but on different standards and objectives. The corresponding objectives in (magical) ritual are 'persuasion', 'conceptualization', 'expansion of meaning' and the like, and the criteria of adequacy are better conveyed by notions such as 'validity', 'correctness', 'legitimacy', and 'felicity' of the ceremony performed.

It is this latter assertion that I wish to elucidate now. In my essay on 'The magical power of words'[1] I took some steps towards under-standing the form and meaning of ritual in terms of its inner semantic frame and outer pragmatic frame. My starting point with regard to the former was that most 'magical rites' (as indeed most rituals) combine word and deed and that the rite is devoted to an 'imperative transfer' of effects, which some might phrase as the 'telic' and others as the 'illocutionary' or 'performative' nature of the rite.[2] The semantics of the transfer itself, the logic of construction of the transfer, in the Trobriand case depends on (1) metaphorical and analogical transfers by word mediated by realistic contact transfer through objects used as 'transformers', and (2) on imperative verbal transfer of energy to a 'whole' through the metonymical naming of the parts. One of the points I made was that the same laws of association that apply to ordinary language apply to magical language—I reiterate this because one reader at least has managed to misunderstand my effort and thinks I tried to deal with the special character of 'magical' utterances,[3] thereby also not appreciating my critique of the theory of 'magical' language held by Ogden and Richards, Malinowski, and others. But fortunately, in compensation, Finnegan has led me to Austin,[4] whose ideas I shall exploit in an attempt to formulate a

---

[1] *Man*, N.S., 3, 1968.
[2] J. L. Austin, *How to do things with words*, Clarendon Press, Oxford, 1962; R. Finnegan, 'How to do things with words: performative utterances among the Limba of Sierra Leone', *Man*, N.S., 4, 1969.
[3] Finnegan, op. cit., p. 549.
[4] Austin, op. cit.

perspective, according to my own design, for viewing the form and meaning of ritual.

In Austin's *How to do things with words* the chief topic of elaboration is what he calls the 'performative' or 'illocutionary' act, in which the uttering of the sentence cannot merely be described as saying something, but is, or is a part of, the *doing of an action*. When in a marriage ceremony the man says 'I do take this woman to be my lawful wedded wife' (or some such formula), or the man says in a will 'I give and bequeath . . .', to utter these sentences in the appropriate circumstances 'is not to *describe* my doing of what I should be said in so uttering to be doing or to state I am doing it: it is to do it.'[1]

What ultimately I think Austin arrives at towards the end of his exercise is a classification of speech acts, 'the issuing of utterances in a speech situation', which makes any stating 'performing an act'. (This is close to Malinowski's approach of seeing speech as part of action.)[2] How many senses may there be in which to say something is to do something, or in saying something we do something, or even by saying something we do something? The following classification of speech acts may help to answer the question:

(1) to perform a *locutionary* act: to utter a sentence with a certain sense and reference (an assertion, a descriptive statement of fact) which is *true or false in a referential sense*.

(2) to perform an *illocutionary* act: this relates to an utterance which has a *certain conventional force*, a performative act *which does something* (as implied in promising, ordering, apologizing, warning etc.). Usually the explicit illocutionary utterance is reducible or analysable into a form with a verb in the first person singular present indicative active (i.e. the 'I', the 'active' and the 'present' seem appropriate).

[1] Ibid., p. 6.
[2] See Tambiah, op. cit., pp. 185 ff.

Form and Meaning of Magical Acts: A Point of View

These statements cannot be subject *to the true–false test*, but are *normatively judged* as 'happy'/'unhappy', valid/invalid, correct/defective etc.

(3) to perform a *perlocutionary* act:

this refers to what we bring about or achieve *by saying something* (as connoted by convincing, persuading, misleading etc.). It refers to both the intended and unintended *consequence* upon the hearer of words uttered by the speaker. (By saying it I convinced him . . .)

These three are analytically separate but in reality not exclusive categories: both locutionary and illocutionary acts can have consequences listed as perlocutionary; and an illocutionary act can have referring and predicating elements together with the performative.[1] We could perhaps say that an imperative illocutionary act attempts to get the world to conform to words, whereas 'true' when ascribed to illocutions attributes success in getting words to conform to the world.

Now adapting these ideas for our purposes, we can say that ritual acts and magical rites are of the 'illocutionary' or 'performative' sort, which simply by virtue of being enacted (under the appropriate conditions) achieve a change of state, or do something effective (e.g. an installation ceremony undergone by the candidate makes him a 'chief'). This performative aspect of the rite should be distinguished from its locutionary (referential, information-carrying) and perlocutionary (consequences for the participants) features.

It was quite evident to Austin that, while he focused on the role of speech in illocutionary acts, the utterance was not the sole thing

---

[1] It is for this reason that J. R. Searle prefers a different classification in terms of the elements of speech acts (*Speech acts, an essay in the philosophy of language*, University Press, Cambridge, 1969, ch. 2), although, and this is what is important for us, he too preserves the essential distinction between an *assertion* which is a very special kind of commitment to the *truth* of a proposition (usually in terms of empirical verification), and the *illocutionary* act (which contains Austin's performative verbs) and which in contrast is appropriately subject to judgements of success, defectiveness and felicity of performance. (Ibid., p. 54.)

necessary if the illocutionary act was to be deemed to have been performed, and also that *actions other than speech* whether physical or mental were entailed for the full realization of the performance. Indeed it is even possible at the other extreme to enact a performative act without uttering words at all—a hypothetical example would be the establishing of blood brotherhood by the physical exchange of blood (without an exchange of words).

The vast majority of ritual and magical acts combine word and deed. Hence it is appropriate to say that they use words in a performative or illocutionary manner, just as the action (the manipulation of objects and persons) is correspondingly performative.

I shall attempt to formalize in a few words the essentials of what I see as the form and meaning of magical ritual acts. The rite usually consists of a close interweaving of *speech* (in the form of utterances and spells) and *action* (consisting of the manipulation of objects). The *utterance* can be analysed with respect to its 'predicative' and 'illocutionary' frames. In terms of predication and reference the words exploit analogical associations, comparisons and transfers (through simile, metaphor, metonym etc.). The illocutionary force and power by which the deed is directed and enacted is achieved through use of words commanding, ordering, persuading and the like: 'Whistle, whistle, I send you after a thief . . .', so commands an Azande spell. And a Trobriand spell combines both metaphor and illocutionary force by urging the *taytu* yam to throw out foliage like the spider spinning its web:[1]

The spider covers up, the spider covers up . . .
The open space, the open space between thy branches, O taytu the
                                                           spider covers up,
. . . Shoot up, O head of my taytu
. . . Make mop upon mop of leaves, O head of my taytu . . .

The action can be similarly analysed. The objects manipulated are chosen analogically on the basis of similarity and difference to convey meaning. From the performative perspective, the action consists of an operation done on an object-symbol to make an imperative and realistic transfer of its properties to the recipient. Or to put it differently, two objects are seen as having resemblances and differences,

[1] B. Malinowski, *Coral gardens and their magic*, Indiana University Press, Bloomington, 1965, Vol. 1, p. 148.

and an attempt is made to transfer the desirable quality of one to the other which is in a defective state.

Now it is clear that the words and action closely combine to form an amalgam which is the magical or ritual *act*. The interrelation between the two media—speech and object manipulation—can take different forms.[1] What I want to emphasize here is that this way of looking at 'magical art' breaks through the Saussurean *langue/parole* distinction. On the one hand, the magical act bears predicative and referential *langue*-type meanings and on the other it is a performative act. Both frames are co-existent, and it is as a *performative* or 'illocutionary' act directed by analogical reasoning that magic gets its distinctiveness.

Now it is *inappropriate* to subject these performative rites to verification, to test whether they are true or false in a referential or assertive sense or whether the act has effected a result in terms of the logic of 'causation' as this is understood in science. Let me illustrate the point by considering the Thai rite of blessing a new house by Buddhist monks (so that evil spirits may be driven out and prosperity result) through the recitation of sacred verses and the performance of certain acts. Several conditions have to be satisfied if a performance of this rite is not, to use Austin's word, to become an 'infelicity': that there exists a conventional procedure properly enacted only by authorized persons, e.g. monks, householders etc.; that, in this particular instance, the monks who took part were entitled to conduct the ceremony, and that the actual ceremony was executed both correctly and completely.

Quite another set of conditions relates to the *bona fides* of the actors. For example, the rite is intended for beneficiaries who expect to conduct themselves in certain ways and who have the right intentions. In fulfilment of this, it is necessary that the participants, in the actual rite performed, satisfy these expectations and actually so conduct themselves subsequently.

---

[1] I cannot go into this question here, but it may be indicated that the relation between the media may be (1) equal and 'redundant', (2) 'unequal', one medium being dominant and the other subsidiary, (3) 'complementary', and 'linked', e.g. the words being 'metaphorical', and action 'metonymical', and, finally, (4) separate and discontinuous. These kinds of relation are not necessarily exclusive, and any complex rite may express all relations not only between these two media but between them and others as well, such as music, dancing, use of diagrams, food prestations, etc.

Form and Meaning of Magical Acts: A Point of View

Now suppose that after the performance of the rite it is found that one or more of these conditions were not fulfilled—the monks may have been bogus, the ceremony incorrectly performed, or the householder never intended to live in the house with his family but planned to use it for an illicit purpose—we cannot in these circumstances say that the rite itself was false or empirically ineffective in a causal sense. The ceremony *itself* cannot ever be said to have been proved to be false or untrue or ineffective; however, any particular enactment of it may be said to be void, unworthy or defective. A bigamist who on false pretences has gone through a second marriage ceremony, does not on that account make the institution of marriage false, wrong or ineffective; what can be said is that he has undergone the ceremony in bad faith and that he has not properly 'married' a second time.

The conclusions therefore are that (1) while to particular instances of ritual enactments of the illocutionary or performative type *normative* judgements of efficacy (legitimacy, defectiveness, propriety, etc.) may be applied, it is inappropriate to judge their efficacy in terms of *verification statements* and inductive rules, and (2) while ritual in general as an institution cannot be declared to be defective, particular instances of it may be so declared, if the proper conditions of performance were not met. It is at this point that I wish to join issue with Evans-Pritchard first and then Robin Horton afterwards.

Evans-Pritchard in his classic study of Zande witchcraft, oracles and magic, having elucidated the coherence and close linkage of these systems of belief, felt it necessary to ask how they fitted into the observer-imposed ritual/empirical categories and how they related to Zande 'practical' day-to-day activity. More pointedly, Evans-Pritchard, naturally interested in a 'European' intellectual problem, asked how magic, which was oriented to achieving effects, compared with Western empiricism based on canons of proof and experimentation. Evans-Pritchard gave various reasons why the Azande did not disbelieve in magic even when the expected or wished-for magical effect did not materialize. His answer was that although Azande may be sceptical about the skills and knowledge of particular witch doctors or their poor medicines or the correct performance of particular performances, and the like, their belief in the efficacy of the system itself was not thereby assailed. Now, whereas Evans-Pritchard gave this as evidence of why Zande magic cannot be empirically proven wrong, he did not perhaps fully appreciate that the answers he received

224

were appropriate to all conventional performative and illocutionary acts—particular performances may for various reasons be 'unhappy' or 'incorrect' and therefore inefficacious while the convention itself is unassailable.

Robin Horton compounds the 'error' in his challenging essays, suggestively entitled 'African traditional thought and Western science'.[1] On the one hand Horton argues that African traditional thought (with its supernatural entities couched in a personal idiom) and Western science (with its concepts couched in an impersonal idiom) are similar in that reference to theoretical entities is used to link events in the visible, tangible world (natural effects) to their antecedents in the same world (natural causes). On the other hand, however—and here is the sting—this same African thought-system whose aim is explanatory and predictive (just like science) refuses to subject itself (like good science) to falsifiability and other verification tests. Indeed African traditional thought (just as Evans-Pritchard elucidated it) is a 'closed system'; the believer cannot get outside the web of his thought, he cannot be agnostic, there is no vision of alternatives; furthermore it portrays unreflective thinking, i.e. traditional thought lacks logic and philosophy and reflection upon the rules of explanation. Evans-Pritchard's demonstration is driven home in traditional thought by a process of *secondary elaboration*; other current beliefs are utilized in such a way as to 'excuse' each failure as it occurs and thus the major theoretical assumptions are protected even in the face of negative evidence. By comparison the collective memory of the European scientific community is littered with the wreckage of discarded theories . . . true, but Horton's enthusiasm for Popper's idealizations may benefit from some of Kuhn's scepticism.

I think it is possible to differ from Horton on the basic assumptions of the comparisons between traditional and scientific thought. One does not deny that traditional societies reflect the patterns he enumerates. But I think it is fundamentally mistaken to say that African religion and ritual are concerned with the same intellectual tasks that science in Western society is concerned with: this is a case of analogy abused. The net result of such comparative pursuit is to land oneself where Frazer found himself—magical rituals are like science with the difference that they are mistaken and false.

[1] *Africa*, 37, 1967.

Form and Meaning of Magical Acts: A Point of View

My counter-argument is that to view most ritual and magical acts as if they were directed to the purposes of scientific activity—to discover natural causes, predict empirical consequences in terms of a theory of causation—is inappropriate and not productive of maximum understanding. Analogical thought of Western science and of primitive ritual have different implications. Like 'illocutionary' and 'performative' acts ritual acts have consequences, effect changes, structure situations not in the idiom of 'Western science' and 'rationality' but in terms of convention and normative judgement, and as solutions of existential problems and intellectual puzzles. These orders of thought and action after all are to be found in Western societies as well—they co-exist with science and thrive outside its field of action or relevance. (It would be interesting to know what Horton thinks is the relation between science and religion in Western society.)

But returning to the problem of magic itself: have I merely evaded answering what magic is by embedding it in ritual and seeing it as an analogical *cum* performative act? By and large I think this is a correct representation of it. But I must also go on to say that in so far as magical rites try to effect a transfer they are often geared to achieving practical results—such as cure of disease or production of a fine harvest, etc.—as much as they are geared to effecting social results. Although we should not judge their *raison d'être* in terms of applied science, we should however recognize that many (but not all) magical rites are elaborated and utilized precisely in those circumstances where non-Western man has not achieved that special kind of 'advanced' scientific knowledge which can control and act upon reality to an extent that reaches beyond the realm of his own practical knowledge. Let us not forget what Evans-Pritchard's conclusion was. Zande rites were most 'mystical' where the diseases they dealt with were the most acute and chronic. These rites then are on a different wave length from scientific technology; or at least in primitive societies it is better to assimilate witchcraft and magic to 'ritual' rather than to 'applied science'.

Let us also not forget one of Evans-Pritchard's most pregnant observations, that the Zande belief in witchcraft does not exclude 'empirical knowledge of cause and effect' but that it provides a social and cultural method of acting upon the world: 'In every case witchcraft is the socially relevant cause, since it is the only one which *allows*

Form and Meaning of Magical Acts: A Point of View

intervention and determines social behaviour'.[1] Thus through ritual man imposes meaning on the world, anticipates the future, retrospectively 'rationalizes' the past and effects results.

It is perhaps because magic and applied science are so to say on different wave lengths, yet may (partially) overlap over the ground they cover, that the results of the spread of modern science and technology in so-called 'traditional' societies are complex, inconsistent and non-linear. An effective pesticide may over time render a 'magical rite' for killing pests redundant and unnecessary. But a sacrifice which creates the cosmos persists because it 'creates' the world in a sense that is different from that known in the laboratory. How does one understand the Hindu theory of sacrifice which asserts claims vaster than the causal act itself? And in the new urban communities of developing societies, 'drugs' may replace traditional 'medicines', but scientific 'scepticism' and 'prediction' do not replace astrology, or consulting of oracles or of diviners, for the guidance of human actions and for providing meaning in perplexing situations.

But what may be true of non-Western societies may not be true of Western civilization in its recent past. And hereby possibly hangs a tale.

The relevance of European experience

In certain respects the history and experience of Western civilization are unique. There is the possibility that, perhaps because the Western anthropologist himself is so naturally grounded in his own civilization, he may at times project it as a potentially universal experience. Let me clarify. If Western anthropologists faced with certain ritual procedures of non-Western societies view them as 'magic' that is empirically false and doomed to concede to the claims of science, they are right as far as their own history is concerned, irrespective of the truth of the assertion elsewhere. There is no denying that in Europe there is some kind of developmental sequence by which out of more 'primitive' notions and 'magical' practices more 'scientific' notions and experimentation were born. The process was by no means linear but it is true that alchemy gave way to chemistry, astrology to astronomy, leechcraft to medicine, etc. It is also to be borne in mind that

[1] Evans-Pritchard, *Witchcraft, oracles and magic . . .*, p. 73 (my italics, S.J.T.).

old concepts from Greek natural philosophy (such as 'atoms', 'species', 'force', 'attraction') and from Greek medicine (especially the Hippocratic corpus) still persist (in form) although they have been transformed (in meaning) in the process. Somewhere in the middle of the transition it is very plausible that science differentiated out of magic, while magic itself was at the same time making 'empirical' claims. It may very well be that the Western experience is a *privileged* case of transition from 'magic' to 'science'.

It is further possible that the outlines of similar transitions and developments can also be discerned in other great literate civilizations like China and India. For example, the relation between early Vedic ritual and cosmological ideas and the concepts of classical Indian medicine of later times is comparable to the development in Europe, although the trend may not have gone as far. Filliozat who has examined the question with great scholarship (and who is interesting in that he thinks Indian medical ideas may have influenced the Greeks rather than vice versa) came to the conclusion that between the ideas of Vedic times and later periods of Indian developments in the field of medicine there were both discontinuities and continuities.

> Classical Indian medicine claims to explain by means of a coherent system the pathogeny and applies its therapeutics as a function of its theories; its design is entirely scientific, even though many of its doctrines are, in fact, erroneous. It cannot, therefore, have its bases in the pathology and the therapeutics of the Veda. It does not, however, follow that the classical medical texts are not rich in Vedic souvenirs. We have seen that a number of Vedic names of diseases are explained by naturally climbing back from their meaning in classical medicine to the sense possessed by them in the Veda. But in the Veda, we have not found the prefiguration of ulterior pathological doctrines.[1]

We should heed this warning in our comparative studies. By simply naming rituals of non-Western societies as 'magic', and the substances they use as 'medicines' and 'drugs', we cannot thereby attribute to the phenomena so named, by virtue of that naming, characteristics that may be peculiar to one's own contemporary civilization. It is only a short step from here to go on to measure these same ritual practices

---

[1] J. Filliozat, *The classical doctrine in Indian medicine. Its origin and Greek parallels*, Munshiram Manoharlal, Delhi, 1964, p. 137.

and ideas as equivalent to, but of course misguided and falling short of, empirical science. It is not that such a perspective is wrong but that it may hide from view the positive, persuasive and creative, though 'non-scientific', features of analogical thought and action expressed in magical rites. The dangers of excessive historical universalization should be kept in view. The rise of industry, capitalism and experimental science in Europe in recent centuries found its counterpart in sociological theorizing in Weber's doctrine of growing 'rationality' and 'rationalization' in Western civilization—an inevitable historical process towards efficiency of social forms like bureaucracy, towards pragmatic orientation whereby means were closely linked to ends, and towards the generation of context-free, neutral and universal constructs and principles. I am merely indicating that this is a particular historical experience which need not and should not be universalized if it entails automatic projections of how things traditional inevitably become things rational.

On the Social Determination of Truth[1]

Steven Lukes

'. . . I think that I gained some understanding of communist Russia by studying witchcraft among the Azande.'

E. E. EVANS-PRITCHARD[2]

The argument of the following paper may be stated abstractly as follows: (1) there are no good reasons for supposing that all criteria of truth and validity are (as many have been tempted to suppose) context-dependent and variable; (2) there are good reasons for maintaining that some are not, that these are universal and fundamental, and that those criteria which *are* context-dependent are parasitic upon them; (3) it is only by assuming such universal and fundamental criteria that a number of crucial sociological questions about beliefs can be asked, among them questions about differences between 'traditional' and 'modern' or 'pre-scientific' and 'scientific' modes of thought; and therefore (4) despite many possible difficulties and pitfalls, the sociologist or anthropologist need not prohibit, indeed he should be ready to make, cognitive and logical judgements (however provisional) with respect to the beliefs he studies.[3]

[1] I wish to thank Robin Horton, Martin Hollis, Jerry (G. A.) Cohen, Michael Inwood, Bill Newton-Smith and David Wood for their criticisms of an earlier draft of this paper.
[2] E. E. Evans-Pritchard, *Social anthropology*, Cohen and West, London, 1951, p. 129.
[3] The reader will see that my position is in a number of respects opposed to that adopted by Barry Barnes in his essay in this volume. I disagree radically with his Kuhnian claim that an appreciation of the role of analogy in scientific thought leads to 'the dichotomy between "truth" and "falsehood", central to so much anthropology and sociology, being discarded' (p. 198).

On the Social Determination of Truth

It will be seen that this argument has four distinct stages: critical, philosophical, sociological and prescriptive. None of these is conclusive in itself, but hopefully they are more effective in combination than any of them taken singly. I take them to apply quite generally to the sociology of belief, and to be as relevant (see the quotation above) to the study of primitive religion and magic as to the study of ideology in contemporary industrial societies.

1. Critical

A wide range of thinkers in various traditions of thought have been tempted by the view that criteria of truth, or logic, or both, arise out of different contexts and are themselves variable. The temptation consists in an urge to see the rules specifying what counts as true and/or what counts as valid reasoning as themselves relative to particular groups, cultures, or communities. (I shall leave aside purely philosophical attempts to establish relativism.)[1] Among those who have succumbed to the temptation in varying degrees have been a number of sociologists of knowledge (especially Mannheim), as well as philosophically minded social anthropologists and philosophers interested in the social sciences (from Lévy-Bruhl to Winch), linguists (most notably Whorf) and, most recently, historians and philosophers of science (notably Kuhn). Among those who have successfully resisted it are other sociologists of knowledge (including Durkheim), Marxist theorists (from Marx onwards), other social anthropologists (from Frazer and Tylor to Evans-Pritchard) and other philosophers of science (such as Popper). What forms has the temptation taken?

The various forms it has taken really amount to different ways of taking seriously Pascal's observation that what is truth on one side of the Pyrenees is error on the other.[2]

Thus Mannheim writes of revising 'the thesis that the genesis of a proposition is under all circumstances irrelevant to its truth'. For him

---

[1] They have been interestingly made, and combated, within the Polish philosophical tradition and subsequently among Polish Marxists (e.g. Schaff and Kolakowski). See H. Skolimowski, *Polish analytical philosophy*, Routledge, London, 1967, and Z. Jordan, *Philosophy and ideology*, Reidel, Dordrecht, 1963. Also relevant is the American pragmatist tradition, and, especially, the work of Quine.

[2] *Pensées*, V, 294, quoted in P. L. Berger and T. Luckmann, *The social construction of reality*, Anchor Books, New York, 1967, p. 5.

On the Social Determination of Truth

the sociology of knowledge is an attempt to analyse the 'perspectives' associated with different social positions, to study the 'orientation towards certain meanings and values which inheres in a given social position (the outlook and attitude conditioned by the collective purposes of a group), and the concrete reasons for the different perspectives which the same situation presents to the different positions in it . . .'. He holds that social or 'existential' factors are relevant 'not only to the genesis of ideas, but penetrate into their forms and content and . . . decisively determine [*sic*] the scope and intensity of our experience and observation . . .'. This, he claims, has decisive implications for epistemology:

> The next task of epistemology, in our opinion, is to overcome its partial nature by incorporating into itself the multiplicity of relationships between existence and validity as discovered by the sociology of knowledge; and to give attention to the types of knowledge operating in a region of being which is full of meaning and which affects the truth value of the assertions.

Yet he also writes, as though trying to resist temptation, that it 'is, of course, true that in the social sciences, as elsewhere, the ultimate criterion of truth or falsity is to be found in the investigation of the object, and the sociology of knowledge is no substitute for this.'[1]

Likewise, Lévy-Bruhl, who followed Durkheim in many respects, diverged from him in this, arguing that primitive thought violates 'our most deeply rooted mental habits, without which, it seems to us, we could no longer think': it is 'mystical, that is oriented at every moment towards occult forces . . . pre-logical, that is indifferent for most of the time to contradiction' and committed to a view of causality 'of a type other than that familiar to us . . .'. For Lévy-Bruhl (above all in his earlier writings), primitives literally 'live, think, feel, move and act in a world which at a number of points does not coincide with ours'[2] and 'the reality in which primitives move is itself mystical.'[3] Furthermore, he began from the hypothesis that societies with

---

[1] K. Mannheim, *Ideology and Utopia* (1936), Routledge, London, 1960, pp. 262–3, 255–6, 240, 264, 4.
[2] L. Lévy-Bruhl, *La mentalité primitive*, Alcan, Paris, 1922, pp. 48, 85, 47.
[3] L. Lévy-Bruhl, *Les fonctions mentales dans les sociétés inférieures*, Alcan, Paris, 1910, p. 30.

different structures had different logics:[1] what he came to call 'pre-logical' thinking might violate 'our' rules but it had its own 'structure', albeit 'strange and even hostile' to 'our conceptual and logical thought'.[2] But, in his latest writings, Lévy-Bruhl too struggled to resist the temptations of this position, acknowledging that the 'mystical mentality' only defined part of the primitives' world and that 'the logical structure of the mind is the same in all known human societies.'[3]

Winch gives a general philosophical rationale for giving in to temptation. For him 'our idea of what belongs to the realm of reality is given for us in the language that we use',[4] so that '[w]hat is real and what is unreal shows itself in the sense that language has. Further, both the distinction between the real and the unreal and the concept of agreement with reality themselves belong to our language.'[5] Similarly, '. . . criteria of logic . . . arise out of, and are only intelligible in the context of, ways of living or modes of social life': in fact, 'logical relations between propositions themselves depend on social relations between men.'[6] Indeed, for Winch, 'standards of rationality in different societies do not always coincide' and rationality itself comes down in the end to 'conformity to norms'.[7] Yet Winch too goes some way to qualifying this position, at least with respect to logic, when he speaks of 'certain [which?] formal requirements centering round the demand for consistency'—though he (mysteriously) thinks that these 'tell us nothing about what in particular is to *count* as consistency'.[8]

Whorf's linguistic relativity principle represents a relatively unqualified form of the view we are considering. For Whorf, 'all observers are not led by the same physical evidence to the same picture of the universe, unless their linguistic backgrounds are similar, or can in some way be calibrated.' We 'dissect nature along lines laid down by our native languages'; we 'cut up and organize the spread and flow of

---

[1] See *Les carnets de Lucien Lévy-Bruhl*, Presses Universitaires de France, Paris, 1949, p. 61.

[2] *La mentalité primitive*, p. 520.

[3] *Les carnets*, p. 62.

[4] P. Winch, *The idea of a social science and its relation to philosophy*, Routledge, London, 1958, p . 15.

[5] P. Winch, 'Understanding a primitive society', *American Philosophical Quarterly*, 1, 4, 1964, p. 309.

[6] P. Winch, *The idea of a social science*, pp. 100, 126.

[7] 'Understanding a primitive society', pp. 317, 318.

[8] Ibid., p. 318.

233

events as we do, largely because, through our mother tongue, we are parties to an agreement to do so, not because nature itself is segmented in exactly that way for all to see'. Whorf also speaks of 'possible new types of logic' and even claims that 'science CAN have a rational or logical basis even though it be a relativistic one', which 'may vary with each tongue'. Indeed,

> when anyone, as a natural logician, is talking about reason, logic, and the laws of correct thinking, he is apt to be simply marching in step with purely grammatical facts that have somewhat of a background character in his own language or family of languages but are by no means universal in all languages and in no sense a common substratum of reason.[1]

Finally, it is worth citing some of the statements of Kuhn who has been strongly tempted by this view in relation to scientific paradigms, whose 'incommensurability' he stresses:

> Examining the record of past research from the vantage of contemporary historiography, the historian of science may be tempted to exclaim that when paradigms change, the world itself changes with them . . . paradigm changes do cause scientists to see the world of their research-engagement differently. In so far as their only recourse to that world is through what they see and do, we may want to say that after a revolution scientists are responding to a different world.[2]

From wanting to say it, Kuhn gradually induces himself to say it. Thus he writes that at 'the very least, as a result of discovering oxygen, Lavoisier saw nature differently' and 'in the absence of some recourse to that hypothetical fixed nature that he "saw differently", the principle of economy will urge us to say that after discovering oxygen Lavoisier worked in a different world.'[3] Then, more boldly, he expresses his conviction that 'we must learn to make sense of statements

---

[1] *Language, thought and reality: selected writings of Benjamin Lee Whorf*, ed. with intro. by J. B. Carroll (1956), M.I.T. Press, Cambridge, Mass., paperback edition, 1964, pp. 214, 213, 240, 241, 239, 211.

[2] T. S. Kuhn, *The structure of scientific revolutions* (1962), University of Chicago Press, Chicago, Phoenix edition, 1964, p. 110. For Kuhn's more recent statements concerning these issues, see his postscript to the second edition (1970), and his contributions to I. Lakatos and A. Musgrove (eds.), *Criticism and the growth of knowledge*, Cambridge University Press, Cambridge, 1970.

[3] Ibid., p. 117. I owe to Jerry Cohen the observation that it is an odd principle of economy which favours a policy of multiplying entire worlds.

that at least resemble these'; and finally, he claims that in 'a sense that I am unable to explicate further, the proponents of competing paradigms practise their trades in different worlds.' Kuhn explicitly suggests that we may need to revise the traditional 'epistemological viewpoint that has most often guided Western philosophy for three centuries' as well as our conception of scientific progress; we may 'have to relinquish the notion, explicit or implicit, that changes of paradigm carry scientists and those who learn from them closer and closer to the truth'. In paradigm choice 'there is no standard higher than the assent of the relevant community'; in fact, the 'very existence of science depends upon vesting the power to choose between paradigms in the members of a special kind of community.'[1]

So far I have tried to show how a number of thinkers with an acute sense of the diversity of human thought (whether linked to social position, as in Mannheim; or culture, as in Lévy-Bruhl and Winch; or language, as in Winch and Whorf; or changing scientific paradigms, as in Kuhn) have allowed themselves to advance the further, crucial claim that truth and validity are similarly diverse. Do they advance any good arguments to support that claim?

Briefly, they appear, with varying degrees of explicitness, to offer two sorts of argument. The first is that since men's perception and understanding of the world is ineradicably theory-dependent, there is no theory-independent reference for terms like 'the world', 'nature', 'reality', etc.,[2] and therefore no theory-independent criterion of truth; and since theories differ, as between social positions, cultures, languages or scientific communities, standards of truth likewise differ. Similarly, since men's notion of what constitutes a valid move from p to q is theory-dependent, there is no theory-independent logic, and so, for parallel reasons, canons of validity are variable. The second sort of argument, found most explicitly in Mannheim, rests on a denial of the so-called genetic fallacy and asserts that identifying the social determinants of beliefs is not irrelevant to their truth and validity— on the ground that canons of truth and validity can thereby be shown to be socially variable.

---

[1] Ibid., pp. 120, 149, 125, 169, 93, 166.
[2] Thus, e.g., for Kuhn, paradigms are 'constitutive of nature' (ibid., p. 109) and for Winch 'there is no way of getting outside the concepts in terms of which we think of the world . . .' (*The idea of a social science*, p. 15).

On the Social Determination of Truth

The first argument is implausible for two reasons. In the first place, no reason is given for passing from the first step to the second. The influence, however deep, of theories upon men's perceptions and understanding is one thing; the claim that there are no theory-independent objects of perception and understanding is another. Similarly, the influence of theories upon what men may count as valid or consistent is one thing; the claim that validity and consistency are theory-dependent is another. In the second place, it does not follow from the diversity of theories, or indeed from the existence of different concepts or criteria of truth and validity in different contexts, that there may not be some such criteria which are invariable because universal and fundamental (see section 2 below).

As for the second argument, to assess it fully would require a detailed analysis of the possible interpretations of 'social', 'determination' and 'belief' (not to mention 'truth' and 'validity'). Let us, briefly, assume a range of definitions of 'social' extending from the purely material or morphological (e.g. physical size or spatial arrangement of groups) to the purely ideational or cultural.[1] Let us take 'determination' to mean any form of explanatory relation—whether causes; or reasons, motives, desires, purposes, aspirations or interests;[2] or structural identities or correspondences.[3] Let us take 'belief' to mean a proposition accepted as true. One can now ask: if beliefs are socially determined, are there any good reasons for seeing truth and validity as variable?

First, suppose a causal relation can be established between a social factor and a belief or set of beliefs: a certain social factor is shown to have a causal influence (whether weak or strong, partial or total) on the appearance or the adoption or the maintenance of a belief or set of beliefs or on their content or their form. This provides absolutely no ground for concluding that their truth or validity are relative—a point on which Marxists, maintaining that 'social being determines

---

[1] For an interesting discussion of different definitions of 'social', see W. L. Wallace, *Sociological theory*, Heinemann, London, 1969.

[2] I leave aside the controversial question of whether, or to what extent, this set of relations can be regarded as causal.

[3] The term 'structural identity' comes from Max Scheler. I have in mind a wide range of such relations, ranging from Durkheim's and Mauss's attempts to relate symbolic classification and social structure, on the one hand, to Sorokin's attempts to identify structural relations between particular ideas with a given *Weltanschauung*, on the other.

236

consciousness', have always been clear (since they count their own theories as non-relatively true). This is true even if all beliefs are causally determined—since some men may be lucky enough to be caused to believe what is true.[1] Causation may operate on both sides of the Pyrenees, but that does not commit us to French and Spanish truths and logics.

Secondly, it might be shown that a certain group of persons have certain good reasons or motives to adopt or adhere to certain beliefs because such beliefs accord with their desires, purposes, aspirations or interests: beliefs are imputed to them as expressing, whether in a transparent or distorted form, their aims or interests in a particular historical situation. They believe their beliefs because they have intelligible reasons for doing so, which can be explicated by an analysis of their situation. This might be shown for all beliefs, but still nothing would follow concerning the truth or consistency of what is believed by any particular category of persons (though, again, it might be shown, as Marx thought was the case, that a certain class of men had no good reason not to believe, and every good reason to believe, what is true).

Finally, the identification of structural identities or instances of conceptual fit between beliefs on the one hand and other social factors (including beliefs) on the other can show how these beliefs cohere with other beliefs and with other features of social life, but it will not in itself have any bearing on their truth or validity.

I conclude that, among the writers we have considered, no satisfactory reason has been given for supposing that there are no invariable and context-independent criteria of truth and valid reasoning.

2. Philosophical

Are there, then, any good reasons for supposing that there are such criteria? I have argued elsewhere that there are,[2] and will merely summarize those arguments here. Of course, any really hard-boiled relativist could just reject these arguments as themselves relative, but to do so he must realize the full implications of the pluralistic social

[1] This is evidently Lukács's view: see G. Lukács, *Histoire et conscience de classe* (1923) tr. into French by K. Axelos and J. Bois, Editions de Minuit, Paris, 1960, esp. pp. 189–256. (See also English translation by Rodney Livingstone, Merlin Press, London, 1971.)

[2] S. Lukes, 'Some problems about rationality', *European Journal of Sociology*, 8, 1967 (reprinted in B. R. Wilson (ed.), *Rationality*, Blackwell, Oxford, 1970).

solipsism his position entails: thus, he cannot speak, as Mannheim does, of 'perspectives' (on what?) or, as Whorf and Kuhn do, of different ways of dissecting nature and seeing the world. The consistent relativist must take the theory-dependence of his worlds seriously.

Let us suppose we are considering the beliefs of a group of persons G (which may be identified in any way—as occupying a particular social position, as sharing a culture or a language, as a scientific community, etc.). Are the truth of their beliefs and the validity of their reasoning simply up to them, a function of the norms to which they conform?

I maintain that the answer to this question is no—or at least that we could never know if it were yes; indeed, that we could not even conceive what it could *be* for it to be yes. For, in the first place, the existence of a common reality is a necessary precondition of our understanding G's language. Though we need not agree about all 'the facts', the members of G must have our distinction between truth and falsity as applied to a shared reality if we are to understand their language, for if, *per impossible*, they did not, we and they would be unable even to agree about the successful identification of public, spatio-temporally located objects. Moreover, any group which engages in successful prediction must presuppose a given reality, since there must be (independent) events to predict. Thus, if we can in principle learn G's language (and they ours) and we know that they engage in successful prediction, then we and they share a common and independent reality.

Secondly, G's language must have operable logical rules and not all of these can be pure matters of convention. Winch states that 'logical relations between propositions . . . depend on social relations between men.' Does this imply that the concept of negation and the laws of identity and non-contradiction need not operate in G's language? If so, then it must be mistaken, for if the members of G do not possess even these, how could we ever understand their thought, their inferences and their arguments? Could they even be credited with the possibility of inferring, arguing or even thinking? (Lévy-Bruhl came perilously near to maintaining this.)[1] If, for

---

[1] E.g.: '[primitive thought] is not oriented, like our thought, towards knowledge properly so-called. It does not know the joys and the usefulness of knowledge. Its collective representations are always in large part of an emotional nature. Its thought and language remain scarcely conceptual . . .' (*La mentalité primitive*, p. 50).

example, they were unable to see that the truth of p excludes the truth of its denial, how could they ever communicate truths to one another or reason from them to other truths?

I conclude that if G has a language in which it expresses its beliefs, it must, minimally, possess criteria of truth (as correspondence to a common and independent reality[1]) and logic—which are not and cannot be context-dependent. Suppose that G's language and belief-system operated according to quite different criteria. But then, if the members of G really did not have our criteria of truth and logic, we would have no adequate grounds for attributing to them a language expressing beliefs and would *a fortiori* be unable to make any statements about these.

The argument sketched here does not, however, entail that the members of G might not, against the background of what I claim are universal criteria of truth and logic, adhere systematically to beliefs which violate those criteria. This may happen unconsciously. Thus, according to Spiro, following Frazer and Roth, the Tully River Blacks 'are ignorant of physiological paternity, believing rather that conception is the result of four kinds of "magical" causation'.[2] Again, as Evans-Pritchard reports, Azande do not perceive contradictions in their beliefs, 'because they have no theoretical interest in the subject, and those situations in which they express their beliefs in witchcraft do not force the problem upon them'; indeed, 'it would involve the whole notion of witchcraft in contradiction' were they to pursue some arguments to their conclusions.[3] On the other hand, the violation of criteria of truth and logic may be quite conscious, as when contemporary theologians explain 'seeming' contradictions as mysteries. Again, it may be relatively harmless and socially insignificant, as when a religious sect engages in fantasy and inconsistency of thought; or it

---

[1] Cf. Russell's definition: 'when a sentence or belief is "true", it is so in virtue of some relation to one or more facts; but the relation is not always simple, and varies both according to the structure of the sentence concerned and according to the relation of what is asserted to experience.' (B. Russell, *My philosophical development*, Allen and Unwin, London, 1959, p. 189.)

[2] M. E. Spiro, 'Religion: problems of definition and explanation', in M. Banton (ed.), *Anthropological approaches to the study of religion*, Tavistock, London, 1966, p. 111. I do not see that E. Leach ('Virgin birth', *Proceedings of the Royal Anthopological Institute for 1966*, 1967) has in any way cast doubt on this interpretation.

[3] E. E. Evans-Pritchard, *Witchcraft, oracles and magic among the Azande*, Clarendon Press, Oxford, 1937, pp. 25, 24.

239

may be of the greatest social and political importance, as when the ideological controls over a society involve the systematic propagation of falsehoods and incompatible beliefs.

If, as I have claimed, there are universal criteria of truth and logic, why do I wish to call these criteria fundamental? I think it can be shown that they are fundamental in at least two senses. In the first place, they specify the ultimate constraints to which all thought is subject. Thus all societies, with languages expressing beliefs, must apply them in general (though they may violate them in particular); indeed, it could be argued that they represent basic adaptive mechanisms for any human society. But they are also, I think, fundamental in a second sense: namely, that it can probably be shown that those criteria of truth and validity which are at variance with them and *are* context-dependent are in fact parasitic upon them. That is, where there are second-order native beliefs about what counts as 'true' or 'valid' which are at odds with the basic criteria, those beliefs can only be rendered fully intelligible as operating against the background of such criteria.

For example, according to Franz Steiner,[1] the Chagga have a concept of 'truth' which is 'connected with the institution of the oath' and oath, vow and swearing are 'concerned in the formation of jural relationships and in legal procedure'. Steiner attempts to sketch 'an analysis of truth concepts and their relation to structural situations' among the Chagga. Their words *lohi* or *loi* mean 'a completely reliable statement'; *Ki lohi* means 'this is true' and *Kja lohi* means 'to speak true'. Witnesses, instead of acting as instruments of verification, are 'persons who, under oath, declare their solidarity with one of the parties and his statements'. The 'story to which they finally bind themselves is *lohi* and a 'witness in court merely agrees to the words of the party under oath. He speaks *lohi*.' But Steiner's analysis shows that among the Chagga certain structural situations require *alternative* ways of guaranteeing the reliability of statements than verification (which is the basic way): as he says, the witness 'helps to establish a "truth" because no "verification" is possible'.[2] Again, it is clearly a parasitic notion of truth which is presupposed by Stalin's favourite ideological slogan during the last two decades of his rule: that in the dialectical unity of theory and practice, theory guides practice, but

---

[1] F. Steiner, 'Chagga truth', *Africa*, 24, 1954.
[2] Ibid., pp. 364, 368, 366, 365, 368, 367, 364.

practice is the criterion of theoretical truth.[1] Here practice, as officially interpreted, served as a substitute for, and functional equivalent of, verification.

This last is, clearly, an empirical question. All I claim is that, while, as Steiner says, anthropologists (and sociologists) 'are interested in the social reality of "truth" rather than in its logical connexion with verification',[2] verification is likely to provide the basic paradigm against which other criteria of truth gain their sense.

3. Sociological

What consequences does the assumption of universal and fundamental criteria of truth and validity have for the sociology of belief? There are, I think, at least four sorts of questions which such an assumption opens up, and which denying it closes off.

In the first place, there are questions about the content and structure of a belief-system itself. A belief-system may consist in a number of ideas, theories and doctrines that are held to be plausible and naturally related partly because a number of distinctions have not been made or conclusions drawn. The good historian of ideas does not seek merely to reproduce a belief-system; he also aims to analyse it and thereby reveal its inner structure—a structure that may not have been perceptible to the believers. In order to do this, he must apply external and critical standards—not just the standards of his own culture or period, but the closest approximation he can make to standards of rational criticism.

Thus Lovejoy describes the first task of the historian of ideas as one of 'logical analysis—the discrimination *in* the texts, and the segregating *out* of the texts, of each of . . . the basic or germinal ideas, the identification of each of them so that it can be recognized wherever it appears, in differing contexts, under different labels or phrasings, and in diverse provinces of thought'. And his next task, according to Lovejoy, is 'to examine the relations between these ideas . . . logical, psychological and historical—and, especially, under the latter, genetic —relations'. By 'logical relations' Lovejoy says he means

---

[1] See D. Joravsky, 'Soviet ideology', *Soviet Studies*, 18, 1, 1966, pp. 2–19, esp. p. 10.

[2] Art. cit., p. 364.

relations of implication or opposition between categories, or tacit presuppositions, or express beliefs or doctrines. When he has ascertained the currency and influence of a given idea in his period, the historian does well to ask himself, what does this idea logically presuppose, what does it imply, and with what other ideas is it implicitly incompatible—whether or not these logical relations were recognised by those who embraced the idea. For if it should turn out that some of its implications were not recognised, this may become a highly important, though negative, historical fact. Negative facts are of much more significance for the intellectual historian than is usually appreciated. The things that a writer, given his premises, might be expected to say, but doesn't say—the consequences which legitimately and fairly evidently follow from his theses, but which he never sees, or persistently refuses to draw—these may be even more noteworthy than the things he does say or the consequences he does deduce. For they may throw light upon peculiarities of his mind, especially upon his biases and the non-rational elements in his thinking—may disclose to the historian specific points at which intellectual processes have been checked, or diverted, or perverted, by emotive factors. Negative facts of this kind are thus often indicia of positive but unexplicit or sub-conscious facts. So, again, the determination of not-immediately-obvious *in*compatibilities between ideas may lead to the recognition of the historically instructive fact that one or another writer, or a whole age, has held together, in closed compartments of the mind, contradictory preconceptions or beliefs. Such a fact—like the failure to see necessary positive implications of accepted premises—calls for psychological explanation, if possible; the historian must at least seek for a hypothesis to account for it.[1]

This leads directly to the second sort of question, intimately related to the first, that assuming non-context-dependent criteria makes possible—namely, why certain beliefs continue to be believed, or cases to be. It is only through the critical application of rational standards that one can identify the mechanisms that prevent men from perceiving the falsity or inconsistency of their beliefs, or the reasons which might lead some men at certain junctures to modify or reject accepted beliefs.

---

[1] A. O. Lovejoy, 'The meaning of romanticism for the historian of ideas', *Journal of the History of Ideas*, 2, 1941, pp. 262, 264–5.

On the Social Determination of Truth

Only thus can one ask, as Evans-Pritchard does, why it is that Azande 'do not perceive the futility of their magic', or how ideological consensus may be maintained in the face of disconfirming evidence and internal incoherence. Only thus, for instance, can one identify the whole network of 'secondary elaborations' which protect 'sacred' beliefs against predictive failure and falsification. Such procedures are quite obviously not confined to primitive magic and witchcraft; they are part of the stock-in-trade of the professional ideologist (and Kuhn's work suggests that they are not absent from the practice of 'normal science'): it is, for example, highly instructive to examine critically the precise ways in which the seeming closure and internal coherence of Soviet ideology is maintained, how *a priori* assertions are substituted for, and hence preclude, empirical inquiry, and incompatibilities between different assertions are concealed.[1] And, finally, change in, and rejection of, prevailing ideas cannot be entirely explicable in terms of context-dependent criteria, above all where the criteria themselves are questioned or rejected. Only by assuming rational criteria applicable to all contexts can one fully explain why men abandon religious or magical beliefs, or scientific paradigms in the face of intolerable anomalies (what makes an anomaly intolerable? The answer to this question cannot be internal to the paradigm), or why intellectuals come to reject official myths.

This, in turn, leads to the third set of questions that assuming non-context-dependent criteria makes possible—namely, questions about the social role of ideology and false consciousness. These arise wherever men's beliefs about their own or other societies can be characterized as to some degree distorted or false and where, in virtue of this feature, such beliefs have significant social consequences. It is only by assuming that one has a reliable, non-relative means of identifying a disjunction between social consciousness or collective representations on the one hand and social realities on the other that one can raise certain questions about the ways in which belief-systems prevent or promote social change.

Only such an assumption, for instance, can enable an anthropologist to distinguish between, say, the 'conscious model' of a tribe's

---

[1] See G. Wetter, *Soviet ideology today*, tr. P. Heath, Heinemann, London, 1966, and D. Bell, 'Soviet ideology', *Slavic Review*, 24, 1965; and the present writer's review article about the former in *New Society*, 16 June 1966.

On the Social Determination of Truth

marriage-system and its actual structure,[1] or between 'real Kachin society' and its 'ideal structure'.[2] Only such an assumption could enable Marx to relate the 'insipid illusions of the eighteenth century', picturing society as made up of abstracted, isolated and 'natural' individuals, to ' "bourgeois society", which had been in course of development since the sixteenth century and made gigantic strides towards development since the eighteenth':

> ...the period in which this view of the isolated individual becomes prevalent, is the very one in which the inter-relations of society (general from this point of view) have reached the highest state of development.[3]

Similarly, only such an assumption could enable Lukács to speak of the 'incapacity' of 'bourgeois thought' to 'understand its own social bases' and of 'unmasking' the 'illusion of the reified fixity' of social phenomena.[4] And only this assumption could enable Ossowski to explore the consequences of certain conceptions of social structure in the social consciousness. Thus, in considering the concept of non-egalitarian classlessness, he shows how

> the objective reality with which these ways of viewing are concerned may impose an interpretation which is very far from that which a classless society would require. But from the viewpoint of the interests of privileged and ruling groups the utility of presenting one's own society in terms of a non-egalitarian classless society is apparent. In the world of today, both in the *bourgeois* democracies and the people's democracies, such a presentation affords no bases for group solidarity amongst the underprivileged; it inclines them to endeavour to improve their fortunes, and to seek upward social mobility by means of personal effort and their own industry, and not by collective action.

It is on this assumption that Ossowski can observe (with truth) that 'Marxian methods—and in general all sociological methods that threaten stereotypes and social fictions—are rarely found suitable

[1] See, e.g., P. Rivière, *Marriage among the Trio*, Clarendon Press, Oxford, 1970.
[2] E. Leach, *Political systems of highland Burma*, L.S.E. and Bell, London, 1954, p. 106.
[3] K. Marx, *Introduction to the critique of political economy* (1857), in *A contribution to the critique of political economy*, tr. N. I. Stone, Kerr, Chicago, 1913, pp. 226–8.
[4] Op. cit. (French ed.), pp. 229, 253.

from the viewpoint of the ruling or privileged groups for the analysis of their own society.'[1] The central point here is that to speak (non-rhetorically) of 'illusions' and 'social fictions' whose social functions one seeks to explain involves the critical application of criteria that are not merely relative to a particular social position.

Thus a student of Soviet ideology has recently observed, pursuing an argument interestingly parallel to that advanced here, that

> The only way to prove which ideological beliefs have performed what functions in the social process is to study the beliefs and the social process from the vantage point of genuine knowledge. Consider, for example, this belief, which was mandatory in the thirties: The land belongs to the people, and therefore collective farmers hold their land rent free. This . . . presents a specific, verifiable statement as a logical consequence of a vague but stirring principle.

The appropriate model for the historian of ideology should, it is argued, be

> not Voltaire's brilliant mocking of religious illogic, but the anthropologist's strenuous effort to discover the social functions of various types of thought. As the student of primitive religion begins his analysis of rain-making ceremonies with the quiet assumption that they do not affect the weather, the student of Soviet ideology should begin his analysis with the observation that rent has existed in the Soviet Union, whether or not Soviet leaders have been aware of it.

Thus '[s]erious analysis begins when one asks how the systems of agricultural procurement have been distributing rent from the twenties to the present, and how beliefs and systems have been inter-acting and changing each other.' In this way one can examine the latent functions of the denial of rent in the context of forcible collectivization—for example, 'to reassure "realistic" leaders that an insoluble problem, the result of their own wild action, did not exist'.[2]

---

[1] S. Ossowski, *Class structure in the social consciousness*, tr. S. Patterson, Routledge, London, 1963, pp. 154, 116. Ossowski treated the 'official image of contemporary Soviet society' as in crucial ways at variance with social realities (he attempted the same for 'the American Creed') and he wrote optimistically of 'the Polish October of 1956' as leading to 'the destruction of the official myths which concealed our reality' (ibid., pp. 112, 193).

[2] Joravsky, art. cit., pp. 11, 13, 14. 'The outside observer', Joravsky writes, 'has easily identified an illogical argument and an unverified belief by reference to his own genuine knowledge of logic and economics' (ibid., p. 12).

On the Social Determination of Truth

Finally, the fourth set of questions which non-relative criteria open up relates to the differences between traditional or 'pre-scientific' and modern or 'science-oriented' modes of thought. Among the most central of such questions is: what factors have made possible the immensely superior cognitive powers of the latter? Another is: in what spheres are the former cognitively weak, or strong, and why? To see the matter in this way is not necessarily to make ethnocentric assumptions about 'the stupidity of savages'.[1] On the contrary, it is to acknowledge the underlying unity between pre-scientific and scientific world-views.

As Durkheim said, in criticism of Lévy-Bruhl,

> We believe . . . that these two forms of human mentality, however different they are, far from deriving from different sources, are born one from the other and are two moments of a single evolution.[2]

Both seek, among other things, to explain the natural and social world—so as 'not to leave the mind enslaved to visible appearances, but to induce it to master them and to connect what the senses separate'. Thus:

> The explanations of contemporary science are surer of being objective because they are more methodical and because they rest on more rigorously controlled observations, but they do not differ in nature from those which satisfy primitive thought. Today, as formerly, to explain is to show how one thing participates in one or several others. It has been said that the participations postulated by mythologies violate the principle of contradiction and are, for that reason, opposed to those implied by scientific explanations. Is not the statement that a man is a kangaroo, or that the sun is a bird, equal to identifying the two with each other? But our mode of thinking is no different when we characterize heat as movement, or light as a vibration of the ether, etc. Whenever we unite heterogeneous terms by an internal bond, we

---

[1] E. Leach, 'Virgin birth', *Proceedings of the Royal Anthropological Institute for 1966* (published 1967), p. 46. This article constitutes something of a credo for the opposite view to that which I am advancing. For a splendid defence and application of the latter, see R. Horton, 'African traditional thought and Western Science', *Africa*, 37, 1967 (and his earlier papers referred to therein).

[2] E. Durkheim, Review of Lévy-Bruhl, *Les fonctions mentales . . .*, and his own *Formes élémentaires de la vie religieuse*, *Année Sociologique*, 12 (1909–1912), publ. 1913, p. 35.

necessarily identify contraries. Of course the terms we unite in this way are not those which the Australian aborigine connects together; we select them according to other criteria and for other reasons; but there is no essential difference in the process by which the mind relates them.[1]

From this standpoint, while conscious of the infinitely rich and various symbolic and expressive features of primitive and traditional thought and ritual (as Durkheim evidently was), one will be under no temptation to explain away false or inadequate attempts at explaining the world and reasoning about it as 'really' emotive, or expressive, or symbolic utterances, and thereby removed from the sphere of application of non-context-dependent criteria of truth and logic.

4. Prescriptive

The final section of this paper can be brief, since it merely draws the practical moral of the previous three. The sociology of belief need not prohibit a critical cognitive and logical stance vis-à-vis the beliefs it studies; indeed, such a prohibition precludes its raising a whole range of problems which are, on the face of it, both genuine and important. On the other hand, there is a real danger involved in adopting such a stance which needs to be appreciated.

The danger lies in confusing the *current content* of Western beliefs with universal and fundamental criteria of truth and validity and in then proceeding to use this current content as a yardstick for classifying other people's beliefs. The English 'intellectualist' school so castigated by Lévy-Bruhl—above all Frazer and Tylor—certainly erred in this direction. Thus Tylor could speak confidently of 'occult science'—'one of the most pernicious delusions that ever vexed mankind'—as 'mistaking an ideal for a real connexion'.[2] It could be argued that Evans-Pritchard, despite his own excellent criticisms of that school,[3] inherits the same tendency in his distinction between mystical and common-sense notions and his appeal to 'science' 'for a decision when the question arises whether a notion shall be classed as

---

[1] E. Durkheim, *Les formes élémentaires de la vie religieuse*, Alcan, Paris, 1912, pp. 340, 340-1.
[2] E. B. Tylor, *The origins of culture* (Part 1 of *Primitive culture*) (1871), Harper Torchbook, New York, 1958, pp. 112, 116.
[3] E. E. Evans-Pritchard, 'The intellectualist (English) interpretation of magic', *Bulletin of the Faculty of Arts*, Egyptian University (Cairo), 1, 2, 1933.

mystical or common-sense. Our body of scientific knowledge and logic are the sole arbiters of what are mystical, common-sense, and scientific notions'—even though he adds that their 'judgements are never absolute.'[1]

Indeed they are not, and it can be dangerous for the social anthropologist or sociologist to take his own assumptions for granted in classifying the beliefs of others. Above all is this so in the case of social and psychological matters, but it applies quite generally. A particularly striking instance of this is provided by Robin Horton in his discussion of the traditional African diagnosis of disease, which, though reference is made to spiritual agencies, usually identifies 'the human hatreds, jealousies, and misdeeds, that have brought such agencies into play'. Thus Victor Turner 'shows how, in diagnosing the causes of some bodily affliction, the Ndembu diviner not only refers to unseen spiritual forces, but also relates the patient's condition to a whole series of disturbances in his social field'. The idea of the social causation of disease, especially so-called 'organic' disease, was not scientifically respectable when Evans-Pritchard wrote his book on the Azande, and he accordingly classified such hypotheses as 'mystical'. Horton is surely right to urge 'the need to approach traditional religious theories of the social causation of sickness with respect'.[2]

Such respect is obviously methodologically sound and should be applied generally. It underlines the essentially provisional nature of all cognitive judgements. Which is to say that, without embracing any form of epistemological or logical relativism, the sociologist of belief should be as critical of his own beliefs as of the beliefs of others.

[1] *Witchcraft, oracles and magic among the Azande*, p. 12.
[2] Art. cit., pp. 53, 54, 56. The reference to Turner is to his *Ndembu divination*, Rhodes-Livingstone Papers, 31, 1962, and 'An Ndembu doctor in practice', in A. Kiev (ed.), *Magic, faith and healing*, Collier-Macmillan, London, 1964.

Lévy-Bruhl, Durkheim and the Scientific Revolution

Robin Horton

Over the last seventy years, Western intellectuals have shown an increasing interest in the thought patterns of peoples who, though contemporary, have cultures which are at once preliterate, pre-industrial and pre-scientific. One root of this interest is the belief that such thought patterns provide us with a clue to the nature of our own lost heritage—a heritage supposedly destroyed by the advance of science. The other root is the belief that only through the study of pre-scientific thought systems can we get a clear view of the nature of science. Only if we have some idea of what it is like to live in a world into which the scientific outlook has not yet intruded, can we be at all certain as to what are the distinctive features of this outlook and what are simply universals of human thought.

Anyone aiming to enter this momentous field of enquiry can do no better than start with a careful study of the two great French philosopher-sociologists Lucien Lévy-Bruhl and Emile Durkheim. Between them, these two have had an enormous influence on the comparative study of human thought; and even today many of the ideas that dominate the field derive from their work.

In the present paper, I shall begin by comparing the ideas of Lévy-Bruhl and Durkheim on the relation between 'primitive' and 'modern' thought.[1] I shall show that, between them, they have left posterity

---

[1] I have put the terms 'primitive' and 'modern' between quotation marks to express a degree of doubt about their usefulness. Since these are the terms used by our authors, they will recur frequently in the exposition that follows. The reader will be best advised to take it that by 'primitive' our authors mean 'preliterate, pre-industrial, pre-scientific'; and that by 'modern' they mean 'literate, industrial, science-oriented'. For more on this, see note 1 on p. 272.

with two very different conceptions of this relation. I shall also show that, whilst anthropologists and sociologists have since come down very heavily in favour of one of these conceptions, the data point strongly to the other. I shall conclude by suggesting how this curious situation may have come to pass.

In much of what follows, I shall be concerned with the views of the two masters and their disciples on the nature of ideas about spiritual beings and other unobservable influences. The disappearance of such ideas from large areas of human thought has long been regarded as one of the principal indices of the transition from 'primitive' to 'modern'. And it should be clear from what follows that disagreement about the nature of such ideas is an important factor in disagreement about the nature of the scientific revolution.

1. Lucien Lévy-Bruhl

Born in France in 1857, Lévy-Bruhl came to the sociology of thought in middle age, after attaining a considerable reputation as a philosopher. Although grounded in the rich and subtle doctrines of Immanuel Kant, he later opted for the simpler and more clear-cut positivist approach.[1] The latter, as we shall see later, exerted a very strong influence over his sociology.

Lévy-Bruhl's entry into sociology seems to have been inspired by his fellow countryman Emile Durkheim. And though he did not go to work in Durkheim's immediate circle, he was influenced by some of its key ideas. But if Durkheim inspired Lévy-Bruhl, he was also his most perceptive and conclusive critic. So it is appropriate to deal with Lévy-Bruhl first and Durkheim second.

Lévy-Bruhl's work on the sociology of thought falls into two parts: an early period from about 1900 to 1930, and a later period in which he modifies his views in the light of the fieldwork reports of men such as Malinowski and Evans-Pritchard.

The main ideas of the early period are to be found in his *Fonctions mentales dans les sociétés inférieures*, first published in 1910. Four other books belong to this early period; but, by and large, they do little more than produce additional documentation, together with restatements and clarifications.[2]

---

[1] L. Lévy-Bruhl, *Les carnets de Lucien Lévy-Bruhl*, Presses Universitaires de France, Paris, 1949. See preface by Maurice Leenhardt, pp. vi-vii.

[2] L. Lévy-Bruhl, *Les fonctions mentales dans les sociétés inférieures*, Alcan,

Lévy-Bruhl, Durkheim and the Scientific Revolution

Les fonctions opens with a typically Durkheimian statement on the subject matter of a sociology of thought. Lévy-Bruhl takes this subject matter to be 'collective representations'; and these he defines as ideas that are (a) common to all members of a social group, (b) transmitted from generation to generation, and (c) imposed on individuals from an external source, both pre-existing them and surviving them.[1]

This introductory statement is followed by a vigorous critique of the 'English School' of Tylor and Frazer. Lévy-Bruhl accuses members of this school of trying to explain the salient features of primitive thought patterns in terms of a rudimentary, infantile and erroneous use of processes of reasoning found fully developed only in highly educated Westerners. Not only does he take them to task for the obvious fallacy involved in comparing any adult thought with that of an infant. He also gives two reasons for rejecting a programme which starts off from the assumption that primitive thought is primarily concerned with explanation. First, in primitive societies various emotional needs override the need for explanation; and it is these emotional needs that largely determine the content of collective representations. Secondly, the simpler the society, the greater the importance of collective representations in the individual's world-view, and the less the importance of beliefs arrived at by his own exercise of reason.[2]

For a successful theory of primitive thought, then, we must discard all the preconceptions of the English School. We must abandon the idea that primitives are engaged in a fumbling, infantile use of our own canons of logic. And we must cease to think of them as having our own interest in pure, rational explanations. We must be prepared to find their thought obeying laws which are not even *logical* in the strict sense.[3]

According to Lévy-Bruhl, the key to the interpretation of primitive

---

Paris, 1910; *La mentalité primitive*, Alcan, Paris, 1922; *L'âme Primitive*, Alcan, Paris, 1927; *Le surnaturel et la nature dans la mentalité primitive*, Alcan, Paris, 1931; *La mythologie primitive*, Alcan, Paris, 1935. For referential convenience in the exposition that follows, I propose to use the following code of initials in relation to these works: (1) FM; (2) MP; (4) SN & N.

[1] FM, p. 1.
[2] FM, pp. 7–24, 27–31.
[3] FM, pp. 70, 76–93.

251

thought lies not with reason but with emotion.[1] It is the play of emotion which imparts to such thought the following salient characteristics:

(1) Mystical Orientation. Every time primitive man engages in an act of perception, the content of perception is strongly coloured by and invested with emotion. Feelings associated with objects are incorporated into his images, there to form the 'mystical' element. This mystical aspect of experience may be represented in the form of gods or spirits, as in Africa, or in an impersonal form, as in Polynesia. But, whatever the details, it is always represented as an invisible, intangible power.[2]

(2) Lack of Objectivity. As between the strictly perceived and the mystical element of an experience, the latter is the more important. Several consequences follow from this relatively low valuation of perceptual experience. Thus phenomena like dreams and visions, which modern Westerners consider subjective, are admitted to primitive reality on the same footing as ordinary, everyday perceptions. In general, too, the evidence of sight and touch is far from being the sovereign determinant of a belief's survival. A primitive belief is seldom shaken by the sort of observations that a Westerner would take as refuting it.[3]

(3) Participation. In primitive life, the visual and tactual aspect of experience is represented by ideas that correspond to those of Western material-object discourse, whilst the emotional aspect is represented by ideas of mystical influence. But as the visual/tactual aspect is inextricably entwined with the emotional, so objects are inextricably associated with mystical influences. The association, indeed, is so close as to amount to a virtual identity. The object is both itself and a spirit; the spirit both itself and an object. Further, when two objects share the same emotional and hence the same mystical associations, they also become closely associated: so closely, once again, as to be virtually identified. Thus if a man and a parakeet arouse the same emotional associations, a community of mystical essence is established between them, in virtue of which it becomes possible to say that men *are* parakeets and vice versa.

---

[1] FM, pp. 28–9. SN & N, introduction, pp. xx, xxvii–xxxv.
[2] FM, pp. 28–31, 33, 40. SN & N, introduction, pp. xv–xix.
[3] FM, pp. 56–8, 61–7.

This kind of relation, either between a perceptual object and its mystical aura, or between two perceptual objects sharing the same mystical aura, is what Lévy-Bruhl calls a 'participation'. Because the primitive is overwhelmingly mystical in his orientation, his principal way of linking things is in terms of such participation.[1]

(4) Pre-logical Mentality. An important consequence of the prevalence of ideas of participation is a degree of indifference to logical contradictions. Such ideas, as we have just seen, involve affirmations that objects are at once themselves and things other than themselves —at once themselves and not themselves. Hence mystical orientation and participation involve an overriding of the law of contradiction; and it is this that leads Lévy-Bruhl to term primitive thought 'pre-logical'.[2] In using such a term, however, he is at pains to defend himself against misunderstandings. He does not mean that primitive thought actually values contradictions, or that it is incapable of registering and avoiding them. What he does mean is that, where participations are involved, they take precedence over the elimination of contradictions.[3]

(5) Communion with the World. This final characteristic of primitive thought is a consequence of several of the foregoing. In the first place, because primitive man's every perception is so heavily invested with emotion, he does not so much perceive the world around him as feel it. Secondly, because this emotion arises within him as well as investing what he perceives, he himself is involved in a continual participation in the world. Finally, because men, animals, plants and inert things are equally associated with mystical influence, there is a tendency to confront all categories of such objects as though they were in some sense personal—i.e. in some sense fellow subjects. Primitive man, then, is more accurately described as communing with the world about him than as perceiving it.[4]

So much for Lévy-Bruhl's view of primitive thought. What of his view of modern thought; of 'our' thought? Here we come to a rather puzzling feature of his exposition. For although his overriding concern is to establish a strong contrast between 'their' thought and 'ours', he is strangely reticent about the second term in the contrast.

[1] FM, pp. 74–80.
[2] FM, pp. 76–8.
[3] FM, pp. 79–80. MP, p. 12.
[4] FM, pp. 33, 426, 452–4.

Lévy-Bruhl, Durkheim and the Scientific Revolution

I think there are two reasons for this reticence. First, he assumes that he is writing for a modern Western readership, and that this readership is both able to define modern thought for itself and able to agree on a definition.[1] Secondly, his own definition of modern thought is essentially a negative one. Modern thought is above all thought without the various encumbrances of primitive thought.[2] This said, we can go on to summarize what can be read between the lines about his view of the modern mind. Once again, five salient characteristics appear to be involved:

(1) Natural Orientation. The modern thinker is oriented to the natural aspect of his experience, i.e. to what reaches him through his organs of sight and touch. He discounts any emotional accompaniment there may be to input through these organs. In consequence, he perceives objects without any mystical aura, and lives in a world largely unencumbered by unobservable entities and influences.[3]

(2) Objectivity. Since his perception is controlled almost exclusively by input through the organs of sight and touch, modern man sees things as they are in nature, and thus tends automatically toward objectivity.[4]

(3) Induction. Discounting emotion, modern man is free to register naturally occurring conjunctions between events in the visible, tangible world. Objective experience replaces emotion in dictating the links man makes between things. Inductive generalizations are at the core both of common sense and of scientific thought, between which Lévy-Bruhl does not distinguish.[5]

(4) Logical Attitude. Once mystical orientation and participation are banished, man's natural sensitivity to contradiction is free to reassert itself. Modern man is therefore predominantly logical in his attitude.[6]

(5) Separation from and Mastery of the World. In modern life, perception has freed itself from emotional investment. Hence it is possible to talk of man seeing and touching things without feeling them or participating in them. Again, where the various categories of

[1] FM, p. 21.
[2] FM. pp. 39, 116.
[3] FM, p. 39.
[4] FM, pp. 40, 56.
[5] FM, p. 40. SN & N, introduction, p. xvi.
[6] FM, p. 116.

Lévy-Bruhl, Durkheim and the Scientific Revolution

perceptual object are no longer overwhelmingly associated with personalized mystical influence, there is room for discrimination between human and non-human components of the world. So far as the non-human world is concerned, then, man perceives it as something separate and distinct from himself—something to be mastered and controlled rather than something to be communed with.[1]

Let us turn now to what Lévy-Bruhl has to say about the sociology of these two dramatically contrasted thought-syndromes. Here we are on controversial ground, for some reputable commentators complain that he shows little interest in the social factors that underpin this contrast.[2] It is true, in fact, that he does not provide a unified and coherent account. But by putting together what he says in passing at various places in Les fonctions, we can arrive at the rudiments of a sociology of thought.

According to Lévy-Bruhl, the basic societal background to the primitive mentality is a situation in which the individual and his aims are thoroughly subordinated to the community and its aims. In such circumstances, the individual acquires the greater part of his idea-system via the accredited socializing agents of the community. What is more, he acquires it at ceremonies that provide an intense stimulus to the emotions. Hence the emotional aura that clothes his very perceptions of the world around him and gives them their mystical colouring. Again, in circumstances where the individual is thoroughly subordinated to the community, he is unable to think of himself without thinking simultaneously of the community; and this situation furnishes the prototype for all his other ideas of participation.

Now where social life develops in such a way that the individual becomes less and less subordinated to the community, and more and more a person in his own right, the situation becomes greatly changed. In the first place, the individual has less of his idea-system dictated to him by the accredited agents of the community, and thinks more of it out for himself. Hence emotion and mystical orientation give way to perceptual experience and natural orientation. Secondly, the individual becomes more and more able to think of himself as an entity

---

[1] FM, pp. 33, 426, 452–4.

[2] See for instance E. Evans-Pritchard, 'Lévy-Bruhl's theory of primitive mentality', *Bulletin of the Faculty of Arts*, Egyptian University (Cairo), 2, 1934; M. Douglas, *Purity and danger*, Routledge, London, 1966. In chapter 5, Douglas criticizes Lévy-Bruhl for being interested in ideas rather than in institutions.

distinct from his group. Hence the situation which formerly provided the prototype for his ideas of participation no longer obtains, and participation ceases to be a dominant feature of his thought.[1]

In summing up Lévy-Bruhl's early work, then, we can say that it not only provides a bold picture of radically contrasted primitive and modern thought patterns, but also gives some account of the social factors underlying the transition from one to the other.

From the publication of *Les fonctions* onwards, Lévy-Bruhl's thesis attracted great interest in a number of disciplines concerned with the study of man. Among those interested were members of the new generation of anthropologists in Britain and America. Here were people stressing for the first time the importance of a lengthy period of participant observation in any attempt to understand non-Western modes of thought; and they took *Les fonctions* into the field to test its assumptions against the results of such observation. The first of such fieldworkers was Malinowski, who criticized Lévy-Bruhl's views in the light of his experiences in the Trobriand Islands. A little later came Evans-Pritchard, several of whose early publications were examinations of Lévy-Bruhl's position in the light of his experiences amongst such East African peoples as the Azande, Nuer, Dinka and Anuak. His verdict, too, was critical in several respects. Lévy-Bruhl, for his part, lived up conscientiously to his scientific ideal and took account of the field reports of Malinowski, Evans-Pritchard and others. Thus there arose a dialogue between armchair theorist and fieldworkers which was a model of its kind.

Lévy-Bruhl's later books show something of the fruitfulness of this dialogue. Perhaps the main criticism levelled against him by fieldworkers like Malinowski and Evans-Pritchard was that he made primitive peoples much more mystical than they really were. He portrayed them as living continuously upon the mystical plane, whereas in fact they spent much of their time at the level of common sense, where the Western ethnographer could meet them without any difficulty.[2] Lévy-Bruhl's attention to this criticism emerges clearly in his final works. Thus, whereas in *Les fonctions* he does indeed portray primitive man as dominated by the mystical, in *L'expérience mystique*

---

[1] FM, pp. 29–30, 426–32.
[2] See B. Malinowski, 'Magic, science and religion', in J. Needham (ed.), *Science, religion and reality*, Sheldon Press, London, 1925, pp. 27–36; Evans-Pritchard, 1934, op. cit.

Lévy-Bruhl, Durkheim and the Scientific Revolution

et les symboles and in his final *Carnets*[1] he concedes that even primitive man spends only some of his time in the world of mystical influences, and the rest of it in the workaday world of common sense. In these later books, indeed, he speaks of primitive thought as oscillating between the common-sense and the mystical orientation. At ordinary times, such thought is at the level of common sense. But a situation which is in any way unusual or anxiety-provoking triggers a flight to the mystical level. Then, when the situation is past, thought returns once again to the level of common sense. This alternation between one level and another leads Lévy-Bruhl to talk of primitive thought as 'less homogeneous than ours'. By contrast, fully modern thought is a vast expansion and systematization of common sense. It has no room for alternation between the common-sense and the mystical. Hence Lévy-Bruhl refers to it as 'homogeneous'.[2]

A second criticism made by a number of fieldworkers concerned Lévy-Bruhl's use of the term 'pre-logical'. In his *Carnets*, he also deals with this. He admits that the term is a misleading one, with its implication of mental deficiency. He also admits that, in many of the situations where he has applied it, what is at stake is the overriding of physical possibilities rather than of the law of contradiction. Thus a god who is half man, half leopard, or a man who is also a parakeet, is physically impossible yet not logically absurd. So he agrees to drop this most controversial of his characterizations of primitive thought.[3]

These two concessions have led modern commentators to say that Lévy-Bruhl's final works constitute a radical revision of his earlier position.[4] In fact, however, what he retains is more significant than what he withdraws. Thus, although his final picture of primitive thought allows a good deal of common sense in alongside the mystical, and although his final picture of modern thought allows a good deal of the mystical in alongside common sense, his characterization of the

---

[1] L. Lévy-Bruhl, *L'expérience mystique et les symboles chez les primitifs*, Alcan, Paris, 1938; *Les carnets*, 1949.

[2] *L'expérience mystique*, pp. 10, 12–15, 38–49, 47–55, 68, 78–9, 127–8, 169–70; *Les carnets*, pp. 20–2, 33–8, 49–50, 54–6, 69–70, 120–1, 193–8, 223–32, 238–40.

[3] *Les carnets*, pp. 8–14, 47–51, 60–4, 177–82, 228–32.

[4] See for instance R. Firth, 'Problem and assumption in an anthropological study of religion', *Journal of the Royal Anthropological Institute*, 89, 1959, p. 147, n. 4; E. Evans-Pritchard, *Theories of primitive religion*, Clarendon Press, Oxford, 1965, p. 79; G. Lloyd, *Polarity and analogy: two types of argumentation in early Greek thought*, University Press, Cambridge, 1966, pp. 3–6.

mystical remains unrepentantly the same. Again, in his final works we still find common sense lumped together with science, and both of them radically contrasted with the mystical.[1]

One of the enigmas of his later work, indeed, is that for all his positive response to the criticisms of Malinowski and Evans-Pritchard, he seems to have made no response at all to the lone but powerful voice which directed its criticism against these more enduring presuppositions of his thought. The voice in question was that of his colleague Emile Durkheim, to whose views we shall now turn.

2. Emile Durkheim

Durkheim was born a year later than Lévy-Bruhl, and died more than twenty years earlier. Nevertheless, he has left us a much richer and more complex body of thought. Indeed, whereas Lévy-Bruhl spent his sociological career working one compact, consistent and rather simple set of ideas to exhaustion, Durkheim played with and developed several sets of ideas, some of which were inconsistent or even in contradiction with others. This is true above all of his sociology of thought, and makes his views in this sphere a great deal more difficult to present.

As I read Durkheim, the core of his sociology of thought is the thesis that most aspects of human mental life have grown by differentiation and elaboration from a primitive religious basis. By 'most aspects', I mean not only religion as the moderns know it, but the arts, the theoretical constructions of the sciences, and indeed the very categories of logical thought. In the present essay, I shall concentrate my attention on Durkheim's sketch of the way in which primitive religious thought gives rise to the theoretical thought of the sciences.

A first hint of Durkheim's views in this sphere is to be found in his early essay *De quelques formes primitives de classification*.[2] Here, he notes (a) the continuity between primitive religious classifications and the theoretical classifications of the sciences, and (b) the difference

---

[1] In actual fact, the greater part of *Les carnets* is taken up, not with recantation, but with clarification and development of the two key concepts of *Les fonctions mentales . . .*: 'mystical orientation' and 'participation'.

[2] E. Durkheim and M. Mauss, 'De quelques formes primitives de classification: contribution à l'étude des représentations collectives', *Année Sociologique*, 6 (1901–1902), pub. 1903. (Translated by R. Needham as *Primitive classification*, Cohen and West, London, 1963.)

Lévy-Bruhl, Durkheim and the Scientific Revolution

between technical/practical and scientific classifications.[1] These remarks, which show an apprehension of the world of ideas startlingly different from Lévy-Bruhl's, provide a foretaste of the major theme of his *Formes élémentaires de la vie religieuse*.[2]

The basic exposition of this theme is found in chapter 7, book 2 of *Formes élémentaires*. In this chapter, Durkheim begins by giving an account of the origin of ideas about unobservable entities, then follows up with an account of the role of such ideas in human intellectual life. He shows how their role enables them to spread far beyond the context of their birth, and how it gives them a central place both in primitive religion and in modern science.

Durkheim's account of the genesis of these ideas will be familiar to most readers, so we shall not dwell long on it. Briefly, he says that religious ideas are born in the first instance at social gatherings. The impact of the group on the individual at such gatherings gives him the feeling of being transported, of being lifted into thoughts and actions that would be foreign to him were he on his own. Even in the intervals of such periodic gatherings, the presence of the group produces a less intense version of this effect. Now this feeling cannot be accounted for in terms of the particular human beings the individual sees around him: it is too profound to be ascribed to such inadequate causes. In the circumstances, then, the individual has no alternative but to invoke the idea of an all-powerful but unobservable force at work on him.[3]

Initially, says Durkheim, man helps himself to conceive this force by using material symbols or totems. Later, however, he comes to conceptualize it more literally, in ideas of force and influence such as the Polynesian *mana* and the Indian *orenda*, or in ideas of spirits and gods.[4]

Durkheim's account of what it is that gives these ideas of the unobservable a currency so much wider than their context of origin is as little publicized as his account of religious origins is well known. I therefore make no apology for considering it at some length.

---

[1] *Primitive classification*, pp. 81–2.
[2] E. Durkheim, *Les formes élémentaires de la vie religieuse*, Alcan, Paris, 1912. (Translated by J. Swain as *The elementary forms of the religious life*, Allen and Unwin, London, 1915.) References that follow are to the fourth impression of the English translation. For convenience, I refer to the latter as EF.
[3] EF, pp. 205–219.
[4] EF, pp. 219–223.

Lévy-Bruhl, Durkheim and the Scientific Revolution

For Durkheim, the moment at which religion is born is the moment at which the possibility of all higher forms of thought, including science, is also born. As we have already seen, the impact of society on the individual gives rise to the idea of an all-powerful yet unobservable collective force; and to help himself conceive this force, man adopts a material totem as its symbol. Now once this has happened, the invisible force comes to be seen as equally associated, on the one hand with the social group, and on the other with the totem. Group and totem are thenceforth seen as sharing a common essence and as mutually identifiable; and it is the invisible force that has made this identification possible. Again, the double association, with social group and material totem, gives this force a sort of intermediate nature, partly social and personal, partly physical and impersonal. Having acquired such an intermediate or neutral character, the force readily lends itself to association with any phenomenon, no matter what the latter's domain. Hence it becomes the agent of a host of identifications of the kind exemplified by that of the group with its totem—identifications of things which appear to the eye of common sense as drastically distinct.[1]

Now it is these curious identifications that Durkheim considers to be the point of departure for all higher forms of rational thought, the sciences included. Since what he says on this score is so seldom mentioned by his commentators, I shall quote him *in extenso*:

It is true that this logic [of identification] is disconcerting for us. Yet we must be careful not to depreciate it: howsoever crude it may appear to us, it has been an aid of the greatest importance in the intellectual evolution of humanity. In fact, it is through it that the first explanation of the world has been made possible. Of course the mental habits it implies prevented men from seeing reality as their senses show it to them; but as their senses show it, it has the grave inconvenience of allowing of no explanation. For to explain is to attach things to each other and to establish relations between them which make them appear as functions of each other and as vibrating sympathetically according to an internal law founded in their nature. But sensations, which see nothing except from the outside, could never make them disclose these relations and internal bonds; the intellect alone can create the

[1] EF, pp. 236–7.

notion of them. When I learn that A regularly precedes B, my knowledge is increased by a new fact; but my intelligence is not at all satisfied with a statement which does not show its reason. I commence to *understand* only if it is possible for me to conceive B in such a way that makes it appear to me as something that is not foreign to A, and united to A by some relation of kinship. The great service that religions have rendered to thought is that they have constructed a first representation of what these relations of kinship between things may be. In the circumstances under which it was attempted, the enterprise could obviously only attain precarious results. But then, does it ever attain any that are more definite, and is it not always necessary to reconsider them? And also, it is less important to succeed than to try. The essential thing was not to leave the mind enslaved to visible appearances, but to teach it to dominate them and to connect what the senses separated; for from the moment when men have an idea that there are internal connections between things, science and philosophy become possible. Religion opened up the way for them. But if it has been able to play this part, it is only because it is a social affair. In order to make a law for the impressions of the senses and to substitute a new way of representing reality for them, thought of a new sort had to be founded: this is collective thought. If this alone has had this efficacy, it is because of the fact that to create a world of ideals through which the world of experienced realities would appear transfigured, a superexcitation of the intellectual forces was necessary, which is possible only in and through society.

So it is far from true that this mentality has no connection with ours. Our logic was born of this logic. The explanations of contemporary science are surer of being objective because they are more methodical and because they rest on more carefully controlled observations, but they do not differ in nature from those that satisfy primitive thought. To-day as formerly, to explain is to show how one thing participates in one of several others. It has been said that the participations of this sort implied by the mythologies violate the principle of contradiction and that they are by that opposed to those implied by scientific explanations. [A footnote here referring to Lévy-Bruhl's *Les fonctions . . .*] Is not the statement that a man is a kangaroo or the sun a bird, equal to identifying the two with each other? But our manner of thought is not different when we say of heat that it is a movement, or of light that it is a vibration of the ether, etc. Every time that we unite heterogenous terms by an internal bond, we forcibly identify contraries. Of course the terms we unite are not those which the

261

Australian brings together; we choose them according to different criteria and for different reasons; but the processes by which the mind puts them in connection do not differ essentially. . . .

Thus between the logic of religious thought and the logic of scientific thought there is no abyss. The two are made up of the same elements, though inequally and differently developed.[1]

In these paragraphs lies a treasury of profound reflection on the nature of theory and of its relation to common sense. In essence, Durkheim's case is that common sense is a very limited intellectual instrument, and that had we never gone beyond it we could never have started to develop the sciences. Yet we can only go beyond it by making use of ideas about an order of events which lies outside the direct grasp of the senses. By the use of such ideas about an unobservable order of things (what Durkheim calls 'a world of ideals'), we can grasp causal connections which common sense could never have dreamed of. We can grasp unities of process where common sense could have seen only diversity and unrelatedness. But such ideas, so crucial to the development of higher thought, could never have occurred to us had it not been for the primal religious situation in which man was driven to them as the only way of accounting for society's impact on him. So it is that we can find the vital germ of the most elaborate sciences in the first stirrings of the most primitive religions.

Some people, of course, will grant that Durkheim gives a fair account of the intellectual function of unobservable entities in the sciences, but will object that, in drawing a parallel with the spirits and occult influences of religion, he is seizing upon a superficial resemblance which conceals a very deep difference. Such critics will contend that, whilst ideas about atoms and forces refer to the context of the ordinary and the natural, ideas about gods and spirits refer to the context of the extraordinary, the mysterious, the supernatural. Durkheim, however, has already dealt with these objections. For in his first chapter he has given a very cogent dismissal of the attempt to define religion in terms of the mysterious and the supernatural. Several of the things he says there strongly reinforce the passages we have just considered. Thus:

[1] EF, pp. 237–9.

Lévy-Bruhl, Durkheim and the Scientific Revolution

The rites which he [primitive man] employs to assure the fertility of his soil or the fecundity of the animal species on which he is nourished do not appear more irrational to his eyes than the technical processes of which our agriculturalists make use, for the same object, do to ours. The powers which he puts into play by these diverse means do not seem to him to have anything especially mysterious about them. Undoubtedly these forces are different from those the modern scientist thinks of, and whose use he teaches us; they have a different way of acting, and do not allow themselves to be directed in the same manner; but for those who believe in them they are no more unintelligible than are gravitation and electricity for the physicist of today. Moreover, we shall see, in the course of this work, that the idea of physical forces is very probably derived from that of religious forces; then there cannot exist between the two the abyss that separates the rational from the irrational. Even the fact that religious forces are frequently conceived under the form of spiritual beings or conscious wills, is no proof of their irrationality. The reason has no repugnance *a priori* to admitting that the so-called inanimate bodies should be directed by intelligences, just as the human body is, though contemporary science accommodates itself with difficulty to this hypothesis. When Leibniz proposed to conceive the external world as an immense society of minds, between which there were, and could be, only spiritual relations, he thought he was working as a rationalist, and saw nothing in this universal animism which could be offensive to the intellect.[1]

Again:

In whatever manner men have represented the novelties and contingencies revealed by experience, there is nothing in these representations that could serve to characterise religion. For religious conceptions have as their object, before everything else, to express and explain, not that which is exceptional and abnormal in things, but, on the contrary, that which is normal and regular. Very frequently, the gods serve less to account for the monstrosities, fantasies and anomalies than for the regular march of the universe, for the movement of the stars, the rhythm of the seasons, the annual growth of vegetation, the perpetuation of species, etc. It is far from being true, then, that the notion of religions coincides with that of the extraordinary or the unforeseen.[2]

[1] EF, p. 26.
[2] EF, pp. 28–9.

263

Having stressed the continuities which underlie the superficial differences between primitive religious and modern scientific thought, Durkheim does go on to say something about what makes science different from pre-scientific theoretical thinking. But although he makes it clear that the difference is one of profound importance for man's cognitive control of his environment, he nonetheless maintains that it is a difference in degree rather than in kind. In his own words:

> Contrary to all appearances, as we have pointed out, the realities to which religious speculation is then applied are the same which later serve as the subject of reflection for philosophers: they are nature, man, society. The mystery which appears to surround them is wholly superficial and disappears before a more painstaking observation: it is enough merely to set aside the veil with which mythological imagination has covered them for them to appear as they really are. Religion sets itself to translate these realities into an intelligible language which does not differ from that employed by science; the attempt is made by both to connect things with each other, to establish internal relations between them, to classify them and to systematize them. We have seen that the essential ideas of scientific logic are of religious origin. It is true that in order to utilize them, science gives them a new elaboration; it purges them of all accidental elements; in a general way, it brings a spirit of criticism into all its doings, which religion ignores; it surrounds itself with precautions to escape 'precipitation and bias', and to hold aside the passions, prejudices, and all subjective influences. But these perfectionings of method are not enough to differentiate it from religion. In this regard, both pursue the same end; scientific thought is only a more perfect form of religious thought.[1]

As a refined and hence more efficient instrument of explanation, science gradually but inexorably supersedes religion in area after area of human experience. Though it finds least resistance in the area of inert things, and most resistance in the area of 'higher' human behaviour, it seems destined to make inroads even into the latter. At the same time, however, there are certain residual functions of religion which science cannot fulfil. Hence whilst science seems destined to supersede religion in most contexts of life, it cannot do so in all:

[1] EF, p. 429.

Lévy-Bruhl, Durkheim and the Scientific Revolution

Having left religion, science tends to substitute itself for this latter in all that which concerns the cognitive and intellectual functions. Christianity has already definitely consecrated this substitution in the order of material things. Seeing in matter that which is profane before all else, it readily left knowledge of this to another discipline, *tradidit mundum hominum disputationi*, 'He gave the world over to the disputes of men'; it is thus that the natural sciences have been able to establish themselves and make their authority recognized without very great difficulty. But it could not give up the world of souls so easily; for it is above all over souls that the god of the Christians aspires to reign. That is why the idea of submitting the psychic life to science produced the effect of a sort of profanation for a long time; even today it is repugnant to many minds. However, experimental and comparative psychology is founded and to-day we must reckon with it. But the world of the religious and the moral life is still forbidden. The great majority of men continue to believe that there is an order of things which the mind cannot penetrate except by very special ways. Hence comes the active resistance which is met with every time that someone tries to treat religious and moral phenomena scientifically. But in spite of these oppositions, these attempts are constantly repeated and this persistence even allows us to foresee that this final barrier will finally give way and that science will establish herself as mistress even in this reserved region. . . .

Since there is no proper subject for religious speculati onoutside that reality to which scientific reflection is applied, it is evident that this former cannot play the same role in the future that it has played in the past.

However, it seems destined to transform itself rather than to disappear . . .

For faith is above all else an impetus to action, while science, no matter how far it may be pushed, always remains at a distance from this. Science is fragmentary and incomplete; it advances but slowly and is never finished; but life cannot wait. The theories which are destined to make men live and act are therefore obliged to pass science and complete it prematurely.[1]

In other words, in becoming more efficient, science becomes more cautious in its claims to explanatory competence and completeness. But, moving in this direction, it becomes less and less the complete

[1] EF, p. 431.

guide to action which the average man requires to help him live his everyday life. Alongside it, therefore, we tend to find an all-embracing world-view which takes as its point of departure the agreed findings of the sciences, but which goes well beyond such findings to fill in the various gaps left by the scientists.

With all Durkheim's fanatical determination to provide social determinants for every nuance of human behaviour, it is a little surprising to find that *Les formes élémentaires* includes no clear suggestion as to the broad social determinants of the transition from the religious to the scientific consciousness. Probably, his untimely death anticipated a synthesis in which the scheme of social evolution outlined in *La division du travail social* would have been co-ordinated with the scheme of ideational evolution outlined in *Les formes-élémentaires.* From his brief remarks on the subject in *La division du travail social,* one may surmise that he would have made the growth of individualism the crucial variable, but would have shown at the same time how the most individualistic thought could operate only with the aid of devices inherited from collective thought.[1]

In this exposition of what I take to be Durkheim's central thesis, I have tried hard to convey the sustained argument, coherence and panache with which he presents it. However, I should be caricaturing his work if I did not admit that *Les formes élémentaires* contains a subsidiary train of thought which is not merely difficult to reconcile with the main thesis, but is actually in opposition to it.

I am thinking, here, of the contention that in all cultures there is to be found a division of the world into two radically contrasted categories of things sacred and things profane. The sacred, which includes not only gods and spirits but also holy objects and actions, is defined as the category of ideas, objects and actions which are associated with a peculiar attitude of awe and respect in virtue of their being symbols of society. The profane is defined as the category of ideas, objects and actions which have no such symbolic function and hence attract no such attitude of awe and respect.

Associated with this contention is the implication that, as social life becomes more complex, so the sacred declines in importance whilst the profane waxes stronger. Hence the transition from primi-

---

[1] EF, pp. 37–47.

tive to modern involves the decline of one mode of thought and the rise of another strongly contrasted with it.[1]

Quite clearly, this subsidiary train of thought has implications which are very hard to reconcile with Durkheim's main thesis. To have suppressed it in exposition, however, would have meant leaving out what to most modern social scientists is the more familiar aspect of his thought.

Most readers, indeed, are likely to be thoroughly puzzled by my exposition. For they have been brought up to believe that what I call Durkheim's subsidiary thesis is in fact his principal if not his only thesis. As for what I have taken as his principal thesis, this for many will be the first time they have heard of it. Some may even be wondering if it isn't just a figment of my imagination!

Since one of the central questions I shall be going on to tackle in this essay is that of why this very striking aspect of Durkheim's sociology of ideas has been so neglected by posterity, it may be as well at this point to try and whistle up some conclusive evidence that this *is* the central thesis and not just a marginal aberration.

Happily, the strongest possible piece of evidence does exist— nothing less than a review by Durkheim himself, in the *Année Sociologique*, which compares and contrasts Lévy-Bruhl's *Fonctions mentales* with his own *Formes élémentaires*.[2]

In this review, Durkheim notes that both Lévy-Bruhl and himself are concerned to explore the sense of the distinction that is commonly made between 'primitive' and 'modern' thought. Both are in agreement about the social determinants of all thought, and about the essentially religious nature of 'primitive' thought. Beyond this point, however, they part company. Thus Lévy-Bruhl sees 'primitive' and 'modern' thought as antithetical, and the movement from one to the other as the replacement of one pattern by its opposite. Durkheim,

---

[1] E. Durkheim, *De la division du travail social*, Alcan, Paris, 1893. (Translated by G. Simpson as *The division of labour in society*, Macmillan, New York, 1933.) See book 2, ch. 3.

[2] E. Durkheim, Review of *Les fonctions mentales* . . . and *Les formes elementaires* . . ., *Année Sociologique*, 12 (1909–1912), pub. 1913, pp. 33–7.

For this reference, and for both moral support and intellectual stimulus in pursuing the somewhat unusual view of Durkheim's message set out here, I am greatly indebted to Steven Lukes. In a much more intensive study of Durkheim's entire work, he has, quite independently, reached conclusions very similar to the ones advanced here.

on the other hand, sees 'primitive' and 'modern' as two stages in a single evolutionary process, the latter developing out of the former. At many points where Lévy-Bruhl finds contrast and discontinuity, Durkheim claims that a closer look would reveal a fundamental continuity. In this context, he singles out the so-called 'law of participation' for special mention. Lévy-Bruhl sees this 'law' as the exemplar of everything that is most opposed to the spirit of science. Durkheim suggests, to the contrary, that what Lévy-Bruhl calls 'participation' is at the core of all logical life. He ends his review, in fact, by referring the reader back on this matter to the passage in *Les formes élémentaires* which I quoted so extensively earlier on.[1]

Though I hesitate to argue from omission in a very compressed exposition of two substantial books, I think it is noteworthy that this review contains no mention of the sacred/profane dichotomy.

Whatever the significance of this last fact, the review in question leaves us in little doubt that Durkheim regarded the strand of his thinking which I have dwelt on at such length here as being the main burden of his message in the sociology of ideas.

3. Opposing views of the Great Transition

We are now in a position to compare the central views of Lévy-Bruhl and Durkheim on the characteristics of 'primitive' and 'modern' thought patterns, and on the nature of the transition from one type to the other.

Both masters define their field of operation in much the same way, taking sociology to be concerned with 'collective representations' rather than with individual thought-products. Both define collective representations as ideas that are not only shared by most members of the group, but also come to members from outside themselves, having been handed down by the accredited agents of tradition. This second criterion, incidentally, is almost impossibly restrictive of causal analysis; and, not surprisingly, both fall foul of it when offering causal interpretations of thought patterns.[2]

---

[1] EF, pp. 236–7.

[2] For more on the way in which the idea of 'collective representation' inhibits both causal and logic-of-the-situation analyses, see my 'Boundaries of explanation in social anthropology', *Man*, 63, 6, 1963.

Briefly, Durkheim's definition of 'collective' and 'individual' is such that, once one gives an analysis of either kind, one automatically transfers the ideas interpreted from the category of the 'collective' to the category of the 'individual'.

Both masters make the impact of society on the individual responsible for the distinctive features of 'primitive' thinking. Both invoke the growth of individualism in society as the key to the transition from 'primitive' to 'modern' thinking.

For both Lévy-Bruhl and Durkheim, the impact of periods of intense group activity on the individual results in the formulation of ideas about a world of unobservable forces lying behind the world of visible, tangible things. When it comes to the significance of this world of unobservables, however, the two masters take diametrically opposite views.

For Lévy-Bruhl, as we have seen, the essential point about the impact of intense social activity on the individual is the emotion which it provokes. Ideas about unobservables are essentially verbalizations of such emotion. Subjective rather than objective in origin, these ideas are the great obstacles to the emergence of rational thought; for they turn men's minds away from the world as it really is. True, they establish all sorts of links between events in the visible, tangible world. But these links, the notorious participations, do not correspond to anything in reality. Indeed, they distract men's attention from the links that do have an objective foundation. Until men's thoughts are turned away from the world of unobservables, then, science cannot be born.

For Durkheim, on the other hand, ideas about unobservables are an objective response to the impact of society upon the individual. Being objective rather than subjective in origin, they are the *sine qua non* of higher forms of reasoning. Indeed, the day on which they emerge is the birthday of such higher forms. This is so because one can only start to do justice to the patterning of the world when one has escaped from enslavement to common-sense

---

Nonetheless, the notion of 'collective representation', though it is misleading as to the way in which ideas are *actually* transmitted in preliterate, pre-industrial societies, does point to the way in which members of such societies *think* they are transmitted. Thus, as J. Goody and I. Watt ('The consequences of literacy', *Comparative Studies in Society and History*, 5, 3, 1963) have remarked, every individual does his own little bit of reworking of what is handed down to him as 'collective representations'; and it is this reworked material which he hands on to the next generation. Yet while this process of reworking goes on inexorably for generation after generation, all those involved see the process as the handing down of a timeless 'tradition'.

appearances. Far from being a distraction from the world as it really is, the participations created by ideas of an unobservable order are man's most powerful tools for understanding this world.

Although both masters seem to agree that the key social factor in the transition from 'primitive' to 'modern' thinking is the growth of individualism, their diametrically opposed conceptions of the significance of unobservable entities lead them to very different notions as to the nature of this transition. Thus, for Lévy-Bruhl, it involves atrophy of all forms of thought featuring unobservables, and vast expansion of an undifferentiated common sense/science which confines itself to induction from visible and tangible phenomena. One mode of thought gives way before its opposite. For Durkheim, the picture is very different. In the first place common sense, which is as distinct from science as it is from religion, remains on the sidelines, retaining much the same position in 'modern' thought as it enjoyed in 'primitive' thought. Secondly, the essence of the transition lies not in the scrapping of ideas about unobservables, but rather in their progressive specialization as tools of man's explanatory enterprise. To put it in a nutshell, Lévy-Bruhl sees the relation between 'primitive' and 'modern' in terms of contrast, and the transition between them as a process of inversion, whilst Durkheim sees the relation in terms of continuity, and the transition as a process of evolution. For purposes of shorthand, I shall talk in what follows of a contrast/inversion schema as opposed to a continuity/evolution schema.

This comparative summary is, of course, an oversimplification. For, as I said earlier, although there is recognizably one Lévy-Bruhl, there are at least two Durkheims. In choosing which Durkheim to use in the comparison, I have been guided by the master's own opinion. Nevertheless, we should not forget that, in some of Durkheim's remarks about the sacred and the profane, there is implicit a contrast/inversion schema which is difficult if not impossible to reconcile with the evolutionist main line in his thought, and which is reminiscent of Lévy-Bruhl. This conflict within Durkheim's sociology of ideas must be kept in mind if we are to understand fully the peculiar exegesis of the two masters in the work of subsequent generations of Western sociologists and social anthropologists.

4. The masters and the moderns

Before we review the influence of Lévy-Bruhl and Durkheim on the contemporary sociology of thought, we should first pause to note the enormous influence of Durkheim on the social sciences generally. In the context of Euro-American sociology and social anthropology, it is perhaps more than ever appropriate to accord Durkheim the accolade of 'The Master'; for despite new accumulations of data and new theoreticians, people are mining the rich seams of his thought as energetically as ever, and yet these seams show little sign of exhaustion.

The most influential aspect of Durkheim's work is probably his boundary-drawing exercise, designed to establish the autonomy of sociology from psychology and other neighbouring disciplines. Since I have referred earlier to his definition of collective (sociological) facts as a species distinct from individual (psychological) facts, I will not dwell on it further here. Nor, for the same reasons, will I dwell on the difficulty of operating with this definition. I shall rest content with pointing out that the definition has had an enormous appeal to members of a young discipline struggling hard to establish a distinct identity and a distinct institutional existence, and that it is widely, indeed unreflectively, taught to most present-day students.

But Durkheim's general influence rests also on other more solid foundations. His attempt to find variables with which to characterize total organizations (e.g. mechanical versus organic solidarity) has rightly caught the imagination of posterity. So too has his feeling for the relationship between what to the untutored eye seem the most diverse aspects of social life (e.g. broad patterns of socio-economic co-operation, systems of legal procedure, suicide rates).

All these constitute grounds for influence which were established before either Lévy-Bruhl or Durkheim himself had published their main works on the sociology of thought. One reason for the approving reception given to Lévy-Bruhl by social scientists was that his work was sponsored by Durkheim (it was published in the *Année Socio-logique* series), and that he proclaimed the Durkheimian goals of confining the study to the field of collective representations and of dealing with the relation of patterns of thought to types of society. Again, a major reason for the approving professional reception of Durkheim's own *Formes élémentaires* was the nature of the general programme expounded in his earlier works.

271

Lévy-Bruhl, Durkheim and the Scientific Revolution

So much for the factors that have made social scientists broadly receptive to what the two masters have had to say about the Great Transition. Let us now look at some details of their exegesis.

The most striking feature of this exegesis is its emphasis on a contrast/inversion schema and its neglect of the continuity/evolution schema. Where the conceptual framework draws heavily on Lévy-Bruhl, the talk is of 'mystical' versus 'empirical' behaviour, or of 'mystical' versus 'rational' behaviour. Where the framework draws more heavily on Durkheim, the talk is of 'sacred' versus 'profane'. In both cases, religion and art tend to be bundled into one category; common sense, technology and science into the other. In both cases the two categories are seen as radically contrasted. Traditional societies[1] are thought to be strong in the first and weak, though not lacking, in the second. Modern societies are thought to be weak in the first and strong in the second. Hence the movement from traditional to modern is seen as a replacement of one category by its opposite.

The exact terms of the contrast between the categories are usually within the bounds of the possibilities laid down by the two masters; but they vary from scholar to scholar. Thus Radcliffe-Brown and Max Gluckman (who is perhaps his most direct heir) emphasize the contrast between the categories, but do not care to go into much detail about content. For them, the principal interest of the contrast is the indication it provides for different kinds of interpretation. Thus 'mystical' behaviour is to be accounted for in terms of its supposed contribution to social harmony—by 'sociological explanation'. 'Logico-empirical' behaviour, on the other hand, is to be accounted for in terms of ends in the minds of actors, together with objective

---

[1] Faced with the need to find a short, snappy label for societies which are pre-industrial, preliterate, pre-scientific, and which are characterized by a relatively low degree of role and institutional specialization, I prefer the term 'traditional' to the term 'primitive' as used by Lévy-Bruhl, Durkheim, and quite a few more recent scholars. Not only has 'primitive' acquired strong overtones of contempt and opprobrium; it has very few factual connotations to compensate for these overtones. 'Traditional', by contrast, seems to have retained a slight overtone of approval; and, in addition, it does point to an attitude of fundamental importance for the sociology of ideas—the attitude which sees what is handed down to the current generation as an immutable, timeless heritage.

Bringing this topic into relation with that of 'collective representations', one may say first of all that no society really has collective representations of the Durkheimian kind. One may further define 'traditional' societies as those whose members believe that they are living in the light of such representations, and 'modern' societies as those whose members no longer have any such illusion.

272

Lévy-Bruhl, Durkheim and the Scientific Revolution

observation of the conditions sufficient for the attainment of such ends. In Gluckman, especially, there is a strong implication that one of the main concerns of social anthropologists (if not of sociologists) is with 'mystical' behaviour and with 'sociological' explanation. He stresses the link between the two in his characterization of social anthropology as concerned with 'the logic of the irrational'.[1]

Malinowski, though he is one of the main critics of the early Lévy-Bruhl, sticks close to the latter's formulation of the contrast. Thus he talks of magico-religious behaviour as triggered by situations which arouse intense emotion, and as providing a channel for the expression of such emotion. He lumps together common sense, technology and science; and talks of them as concerned with a variety of ends for which the means are chosen by inductive observation.[2]

Roger Bastide, the eminent French Afro-Americanist, develops another facet of Lévy-Bruhl's contrast when he characterizes African traditional thought in terms of a communion between subject and object, and Western thought in terms of the mastery of subject over object. Like Lévy-Bruhl, he sees these two modes of relationship as opposed, and the transition from one to the other as an inversion rather than an evolution.[3] J. V. Taylor, the theologian, missionary sociologist and Africanist, works out a similar scheme in his *Primal vision*.[4]

Among those who claim to derive their inspiration from Durkheim rather than from Lévy-Bruhl, most start out from his contrast between the sacred and the profane. They have tended, however, to pack into the first category not only behaviour symbolic of man's relation to society, but all other symbolic behaviour as well. The second category they reserve for behaviour directed to certain ends and guided by inductive observation of the means appropriate to

---

[1] A. Radcliffe-Brown, *Structure and function in primitive society*, Cohen and West, London, 1952 (see essays on 'Taboo' and 'Religion and society'); M. Gluckman and E. Devons (eds.), *Closed systems and open minds*, Oliver and Boyd, Edinburgh and London, 1964 (see conclusion, pp. 254–9); M. Gluckman, *Politics, law and ritual in tribal society*, Blackwell, Oxford, 1965, pp. 216–67.

[2] Malinowski, 'Magic, science and religion'. The general pattern which emerges from Malinowski's essay is in fact very similar to that which emerges from Lévy-Bruhl's final works.

[3] R. Bastide, 'Religions africaines et structures de civilisation', *Présence Africaine*, 66, 1968.

[4] J. Taylor, *The primal vision*, S.C.M. Press, London, 1963 (see ch. 6, 'The unbroken circle').

those ends. For them, the sacred (or symbolic) includes ritual and art, the profane (or logico-empirical) common sense, technology and science. A further refinement on Durkheim is the thesis that the two categories refer, not to different spheres of behaviour, but to different aspects of every sequence of behaviour. But, whatever the particular reinterpretations they favour, these *soi-disant* followers of Durkheim tend to agree on seeing the sacred and the profane as radically contrasted, and on seeing the transition from 'primitive' to 'modern' as an inversion in which the sacred progressively gives way to the profane. Prominent among this school are Talcott Parsons the sociologist, and Firth, Leach and Beattie the social anthropologists.[1]

Even the great Claude Lévi-Strauss fits, albeit in his own inimitable way, into the contrast/inversion school.

Thus, although at several points in his work he inveighs against Lévy-Bruhl, he perpetuates the latter's radical opposition between religion, which he sees as the domain of confusion and emotion, and science, which he sees as the domain of distinction and reason.[2] And although he largely avoids reference to the religious component of traditional thought patterns, apparently feeling it too distasteful to mention,[3] he seems to agree that one of the features of the move from tradition to modernity is a move from religious to scientific thinking.

Again, in his more positive characterization of the traditional and the modern, a neo-Durkheimian form of contrast/inversion schema is evident. Thus he distinguishes two forms of thought: 'wild thought' (*pensée sauvage*), dominant in traditional cultures, and 'domesticated thought' (*pensée domestiquée*), dominant in modern cultures. He stresses that the two forms are essentially incommensurable, and that they are devoted to different ends. Wild thought attempts to grasp the world through symbol and metaphor. It is non-practical in intent. Domesticated thought is concerned with

---

[1] T. Parsons, *The structure of social action*, 2 vols., Free Press, New York, 1949, pp. 5, 420–5, 431, 721; R. Firth, 1959, op. cit., p. 136; E. Leach *Political systems of highland Burma*, Bell, London, 1954, introduction; idem, 'Virgin Birth', *Proceedings of the Royal Anthropological Institute for 1966*, pub. 1967; J. Beattie, *Other cultures*, Cohen and West, London, 1964, pp. 202–40; idem, 'Ritual and social change', *Man*, N.S., 1, 1966.

[2] C. Lévi-Strauss, *La pénsee sauvage*, Plon, Paris, 1962. See pp. 295–302 for a subtly invidious comparison between totemic and religious thought.

[3] It is remarkable that, in a book entitled *La pensée sauvage*, religion is mentioned in a passage of a dozen pages, and then only grudgingly.

fitting means to ends through the use of literal speech and discursive reason. It aims at achieving practical goals, and its development is controlled by success or failure in achieving these goals.[1]

In many respects, Lévi-Strauss's formulation resembles those of Parsons, Firth and Beattie. But whereas these more sober souls tend to be concerned with the reference of particular symbols to particular phenomena, Lévi-Strauss is concerned with systems of symbols and with their reference, as wholes, to often complex relations between phenomena. To take a somewhat oversimplified example, the sober Anglo-Saxon symbolist may be interested in tracing the symbolic reference of a particular animal to some social group. Lévi-Strauss, in a comparable situation, will be interested in the symbolic reference of a number of different animal species, considered as a set, to the structural relations of a number of different sub-groups within a society. The concern with sets and relations gives his thought an elaborateness and intricacy which seem to distinguish it from the thought of most of his anthropological contemporaries. But this surface difference should not be allowed to obscure its affinities with other variants of the contrast/inversion schema.

A remarkable thing about so many adherents of this schema is the way in which they acknowledge Durkheimian inspiration, yet determinedly ignore the continuity/evolution schema which takes up an important part of their master's great work. This curious combination of attitudes is well exemplified by Talcott Parsons, whose *Structure of social action* is so often recommended to students as the classic exegesis of Durkheim, Pareto and Weber. Early on in this book, Parsons reluctantly notes Durkheim's ideas about the continuity between religion and the sciences, and dismisses these ideas with inadequate argument and an air of embarrassment. By the conclusion of the book, Parsons has managed to pursuade himself that Durkheim never had any such ideas, and extols him as one of those who swept away Victorian ideas about religion as the precursor of science and about the transition from 'primitive' to 'modern' as an evolutionary process.[2]

---

[1] *La pensée sauvage*, passim.
[2] For Parsons's attempt to dismiss Durkheim's continuity/evolution thesis, see pp. 419–25. For his concluding classification of Durkheim with those concerned to sweep away the idea of linear evolution and the idea of religion and magic as pre-science, see p. 721.

To put it briefly, orthodox modern social scientists tend to proclaim themselves disciples of Durkheim in their approach to the study of religion. But, in their actual analyses, they ignore the main theme of their master's work in this sphere, and extol an inconsistent minor theme.

This is a very odd situation. Let us turn to a brief review of the relevant research data, to see whether these can help us to answer the questions it raises.

5. The data

Perhaps we should start by saying that, in the fifty years since the two masters first propounded their theses, no data have emerged that are in any way relevant to the question of ultimate origins. Indeed, it has become clear that such data are unobtainable. So we must conclude that, in providing elaborate accounts of the genesis of ideas about spiritual beings and similar entities, the masters have done no more than give us untestable 'just-so' stories.[1]

However, a great deal of what both Lévy-Bruhl and Durkheim have to say relates not to the ultimate origins of ideas about unobservables, but to the factors that sustain such ideas once they have been launched. Here we are dealing with testable theses. And in the last fifty years enough data have accumulated to allow us to decide between them. Such data are of three kinds. First, there are data on the thought patterns of those preliterate, pre-industrial societies known to the masters as 'primitive' and to ourselves as 'traditional' or 'underdeveloped'. Second, there are data on the thought patterns of the sciences and of the modern industrial societies that support them. Third, there are data on certain features of human thinking which may well be common to all societies, whether traditional or modern.

In dealing with data of the first kind, I shall restrict myself to those thrown up by fieldwork in the traditional societies of Africa. One reason for this self-imposed limitation is that my own research and most intensive reading have been in the African field. The other is that African data have been the most frequently cited by recent theorists of the nature of traditional thought patterns.

---

[1] For this apt expression, I am indebted to Evans-Pritchard, *Theories of primitive religion*, p. 25.

Lévy-Bruhl, Durkheim and the Scientific Revolution

Five outstanding producers of data in this field are Evans-Pritchard, with his monographs on Zande and Nuer thought-systems; Fortes, with his brief but brilliant *Oedipus and Job* (a monograph on Tallensi religion); Lienhardt, with his *Divinity and experience: the religion of the Dinka;* Middleton, with his *Lugbara religion;* and finally Turner, with his host of papers and books on Ndembu religion.[1]

In so far as they have been concerned with making theoretical points, all of these authors have relied on more or less explicit contrast schemes of the 'mystical/empirical', 'sacred/profane' type. But the message that the uncommitted outsider gets from reading these works is not really consistent with such schemata. For in all of them he sees ideas about 'mystical' entities as forming more or less coherent systems of postulates which serve to display the unity underlying the apparent diversity of everyday experience, the order underlying apparent irregularity, the causal enchainment underlying apparent randomness.[2] Again, in all of these works he sees a very subtle relationship between the observable world of people, animals, plants and things, and the unobservable world of the spirits. As Evans-Pritchard and Lienhardt have made particularly clear in their searching phenomenological examinations, the spiritual world is not an immediate datum of experience, but only a situationally invoked interpretation of it. For the African farmer as for the European townsman, the world immediately given and reacted to is the common-sensical world of living and talking men and women, living but uncommunicative animals and plants, and inert water, stone, soil and metal. Through much of life, this common-sensical framework is quite sufficient for the conduct of affairs. Only intermittently, when it fails to provide adequate guidance, is there a resort to ideas

---

[1] E. E. Evans-Pritchard, *Witchcraft, oracles and magic among the Azande,* Clarendon Press, Oxford, 1937, and *Nuer religion,* Clarendon Press, Oxford, 1956; M. Fortes, *Oedipus and Job in West African religion,* University Press, Cambridge, 1959; G. Lienhardt, *Divinity and experience: the religion of the Dinka,* Clarendon Press, Oxford, 1961; J. Middleton, *Lugbara religion,* Oxford University Press, London, 1960; V. Turner—see for example *The forest of symbols,* Cornell University Press, 1967, and *The drums of affliction,* Clarendon Press, Oxford, 1968.

[2] Evans-Pritchard's *Witchcraft, oracles and magic* is perhaps the most striking example of a monograph which starts with the orthodox antithesis between the 'mystical' and the 'empirical', but which goes on to display the 'mystical' in a way which shows its continuity with the 'empirical'.

277

about the spiritual beings who are thought to underpin the common-sensical world and its events. From these works, then, the so-called animist no longer emerges as someone who sees and reacts to animals, plants and inert things as if they were persons, or as someone for whom the boundaries between the personal and impersonal are blurred.[1]

Reviewing the impressions he gets from this work, the uncommitted observer is likely to conclude that traditional ideas about unobservable entities are most appropriately described, neither as symbolic substitutes for literal discourse, nor as expressions of emotion, nor yet as manifestations of some mystic communion between man and nature, but simply as theoretical concepts couched in a slightly unfamiliar idiom. He may even go on, more specifically, to conclude that such ideas form the basis of often highly sophisticated social psychologies.

Since use of the phrases 'theoretical concepts' and 'social psychologies' inevitably implies comparison with thought patterns in the modern West, this seems the appropriate point at which to turn to data of the second kind—i.e. data on the sciences. Here again, there has been a fairly spectacular accumulation since the days of the masters; either in the form of works by philosophers and historians of science on the nature of the scientific enterprise, or in the form of reports by eminent scientists on what they see as the essence of their calling. The main burden of such work has been to show the crucial importance of concepts relating to unobservable or theoretical entities, and the impossibility of giving an account of scientific activity that neglects such concepts. Indeed, a good deal of the debate among philosophers of science during the last two decades seems to have been inspired by Eddington's famous problem of the Two Tables—the hard, solid table of common-sense thought and action; and the largely empty space, peopled by minuscule planetary systems, of theoretical thought and action.[2] The key questions of the debate have been (a) which of the Two Tables is the real one? and (b) is there any sense at all in which both could be real? As the debate

---

[1] See Evans-Pritchard, 'Lévy-Bruhl's theory . . .', and *Theories of primitive religion*, pp. 88–9. See also Lienhardt, *Divinity and experience*, pp. 32–3, 147–8.

[2] A. Eddington, *The nature of the physical world*, University Press, Cambridge, 1928. Although Eddington's views are now considered outmoded, his formulation of the 'Two Tables' problem was certainly fruitful as a stimulus to debate.

stands at the moment, a fair judgement would seem to be that, on the one hand, common-sense discourse and material-object concepts can never be eliminated from thought and life; whilst, on the other hand, the criteria used for deciding the validity of statements about theoretical entities do not differ in essentials from the criteria used for deciding the validity of statements about material objects. Hence we may have to settle for the reality of both tables, and for a mysterious unity-in-duality which holds between them.[1] The homology with 'mystical participation' could hardly be clearer.

Recent writings on the nature of the scientific enterprise have shown up all too clearly the inadequacy of the old inductivist account which ultimately made science out to be nothing more than a vast expansion and systematization of common sense. From now on, common sense and a good deal of technology must be viewed as distinct from science. As Stephen Toulmin pointed out in his study of Western chemistry, this distinction should have been obvious long ago to anyone who cared to consult the historical record. In the case of chemistry, for instance, chemical theory, for all its change and development down the ages, made little difference to the practical use of natural resources until after 1850.[2]

In view of these developments in the history, phenomenology and philosophy of the sciences, it is hardly surprising that their authors, looking across at the growing body of data on 'traditional' thought-systems, have been struck by continuities rather than by contrasts. Thus Polanyi has used Evans-Pritchard's portrayal of the way in which Azande relate their theory of misfortune to the vicissitudes of

---

[1] For defence of the Common-sense Table, see S. Stebbing, *Philosophy and the physicists*, Methuen, London, 1937, chs. 3–4; W. Watson, *On understanding physics*, University Press, Cambridge, 1938. For defence of the Theoretical Table, see N. Hanson, *Patterns of discovery*, University Press, Cambridge, 1958; P. Feyerabend, 'Explanation, reduction and empiricism', in H. Fiegl and G. Maxwell (eds.), *Minnesota studies in the philosophy of science*, 3, Minneapolis, 1962; W. Sellars, *Science, perception and reality*, Routledge, London, 1963, ch. 4. For defence of both Tables, see W. Quine, *From a logical point of view*, Harvard University Press, Cambridge, Mass., 1953, ch. 1; M. Born, *Physics in my generation*, Pergamon Press, London, 1956, pp. 49–54, 105–6, 150–63; R. Harré, *Theories and things*, Sheed and Ward, London, 1961; A. Ayer, *The origins of pragmatism*, Macmillan, London, 1968, pp. 298–336; D. Mellor, 'Physics and furniture' in N. Rescher (ed.), *Studies in the philosophy of science*, American Philosophical Quarterly Monograph No. 3, Oxford, 1969.

[2] S. Toulmin, *The architecture of matter*, Hutchinson, London, 1962, pp. 25, 38, 39, 262; L. White, 'Mediaeval uses of air', *Scientific American*, 223, 2, 1970.

everyday existence as a means of throwing light on the way in which scientists relate theory to experimental data. And although some would say that Polanyi is describing science in an unfortunately conservative mood, the force of the parallel still remains.[1]

Again, Pierre Auger, himself an eminent theoretical physicist, has shown how Lévi-Strauss, in attempting to specify the distinctive features of *pensée sauvage*, has unwittingly succeeded in describing some of the key features of scientific thought. In particular, he points out that the use of analogy and of *bricolage* is central to the development of scientific theory.[2]

Karl Popper, too, has stressed the element of continuity between traditional and scientific theories. He has emphasized that they are to be distinguished, not in terms of content or even in terms of logical structure, but rather in terms of the presence or absence of the critical spirit. And this of course is a matter of degree rather than of kind.[3]

Much the same point has been made more obliquely by Fred Hoyle, who in a rather subtle science-fiction novel has shown that animism, in itself, has much the same status as any other kind of theory, and that, if the facts of the world were a little different, it could be used to provide a scientifically acceptable interpretation of them.[4]

Finally, let me turn to data of the third kind. Here, I am thinking in particular of the experiments performed by Michotte and his Louvain School of psychologists on the perception of causality. Although the subjects of these experiments are European men and women, there is good reason to believe that some of the findings on their behaviour may be universally applicable. The most interesting of these is that people tend to perceive causal connections between phenomena only under certain limited conditions, of which spatio-temporal contiguity and dimensional commensurability seem to be amongst the most important.[5] This finding has momentous implications for the understanding of human cognitive activity; for it

[1] M. Polanyi, *Personal knowledge*, University of Chicago Press, Chicago, 1958, pp. 112–13, 150–9, 286–94.
[2] P. Auger, 'The regime of castes in populations of ideas', *Diogenes*, 22, 1958.
[3] K. Popper, *Conjectures and refutations*, Routledge, London, 1963, pp. 38, 50, 102, 126–31, 187, 190, 257, 319.
[4] F. Hoyle, *The black cloud*, Penguin, Harmondsworth, 1960.
[5] A. Michotte, *The perception of causality*, Eng. trans., Methuen, London, 1963.

enables us for the first time to understand why human beings in all cultures *have* to invoke theory in their attempt to gain cognitive control of their environment. Briefly, what Michotte shows us is that the human being is not an inductive machine capable of automatic registration of all causal connections presented to him in his everyday experience. On the contrary, he has the most limited capacity for registering such connections. And so far in human history, theory, with its apparatus of unobservables underpinning the visible, tangible world, is the only means man has discovered of overcoming this limitation.

In summarizing the implications of these recent accumulations of data for our two opposed schemata, we can say for a start that they are unfavourable to all variants of the contrast/inversion schema.

So far as traditional thought-systems are concerned, variants of the contrast/inversion schema either misdescribe the data, or fail to account for them, or both. Misdescription is evident in the idea of traditional communion with nature. It is equally evident in the classification of statements about spiritual beings as symbolic rather than explanatory. Failure to account for the data is evident in all versions. Thus Lévy-Bruhl's version, in relating 'mystical influences' to an ill-defined and inchoate flow of emotion, is simply trying to dispose of a mystery by enfolding it in a far greater one. Gluckman's version, in seeking to explain ideas of spiritual beings in terms of their contribution to social equilibrium, fails to show why people should get addicted to this particular way of maintaining equilibrium, rather than to any one of a score of others. Why, for instance, should they not take to cathartic football matches rather than to religious rituals? Beattie's version, in seeking to explain ideas of spiritual beings as symbols, fails in a similar way. Beattie makes out quite a good case as to why people may feel the need for personal symbols of events and processes in their environment; but he makes out no case whatsoever as to why they feel the need for persons with the unobservability, omnipresence and other puzzling attributes of spirits. Beattie's version could account for the prevalence of priests in traditional societies. It cannot account for the prevalence of spirits.

So far as modern thought patterns are concerned, variants of the contrast/inversion schema are equally fruitless. Thus their inductivist definition of science completely ignores the crucial role played by theoretical discourse and unobservable entities. It also blurs the distinction between common sense and technology on the one hand, and science on the other. None of the modern versions of this schema even attempts to explain the emergence of science.

When we turn to the continuity/evolution schema, however, we find that recent accumulations of data have given an almost prophetic quality to Durkheim's version of it. His emphasis on the limitations of common sense and on the universal need for theory as a means of extending man's grasp of causal relations not only foreshadows the work of Michotte, but draws out implications from this work which the author himself does not yet appear to have thought of. Durkheim's emphasis on the continuities between traditional religious theory and modern scientific theory foreshadows the work of such avant-garde historians and philosophers of science as Hesse, Popper and Polanyi.[1] In particular, his hint that traditional religious theory may be seen as a precursor of modern social psychology receives striking confirmation in Fortes's work on West African theories of the individual's relation to his society.[2] Again, in stressing that the mysterious relation of unity-in-duality which Lévy-Bruhl christened 'participation' is at the centre not only of religious but also of scientific thinking, he points forward to a topic that has been a prominent feature of the debates of the last decade in the philosophy of science.[3]

In Durkheim's specification of the differences between the traditional and the modern, we find an equally prophetic quality. His emphasis on the critical spirit, on the determination to exclude from the theory-building enterprise all notions other than those involved in the search for explanation, on the refusal to complete a theoretical picture when the data do not warrant it—all these are in line with attempts to define the distinctive character of science by such contemporary philosophers as Toulmin and Popper. His stress on the

---

[1] M. Hesse, *Science and human imagination*, S.C.M. Press, London, 1954; Polanyi, op. cit., pp. 112–13, 150–9, 286–94; Popper, op. cit., pp. 38, 50, 102, 126–31, 187, 190, 257, 379.

Turning from positive to negative evidence, it is interesting to note that references to the personality or impersonality of the content of theory are very rarely found in the current debate about the nature of the scientific outlook. This seems to indicate that most people consider the question of content irrelevant.

[2] Fortes, *Oedipus and Job*.

[3] See note 1 on p. 279.

gradual evolution and differentiation of the scientific outlook from pre-scientific cognitive operations is also in line with the views of such thinkers.

Not only does Durkheim's schema provide the framework for adequate description of the relations between traditional and modern thought patterns. It provides intellectually satisfying explanations of certain crucial features of such patterns, and also points to further possibilities of explanation. Thus, unlike any of the versions of the contrast/inversion schema, it accounts successfully for the universal presence of ideas about a world of unobservables in human cognitive operations. Again, by emphasizing that such ideas have the same function in traditional as in modern cultures, it leads us to look at the considerable amount of work done by Western philosophers on the relation between the forms of scientific theories and their functions, and on the relation between the idioms of these theories and the circumstances under which they are developed. By applying the results of this work to theories generally, we can start to ask and answer some crucial questions about differences of theoretical idiom. Thus we can ask, and answer, the question of why the theoretical idiom of traditional societies tends to be personal, whilst the idiom of modern societies tends to be impersonal.[1]

To sum up, we can say that a survey of recent accumulations of data in this area only deepens the mystery which surrounds the neglect of Durkheim's continuity/evolution schema. To dispel the fog, we shall have to approach the matter from another angle.

6. The contrast/inversion schema as a problem in the sociology of ideas

Three things have emerged clearly from our investigation so far. First, because of his boundary-staking activities on behalf of the subject, as well as because of other more constructive attitudes and insights, Durkheim is regarded down to this day as the founding father of Western sociology and social anthropology. Second, although most members of these disciplines tend to single out his *Formes élémentaires* for special acclaim, the idea of radical contrast between religious and scientific thought, which they purport to derive from this book, is in fact entirely contradictory to his own

---

[1] See my 'African traditional thought and Western science', *Africa*, 37, 1967.

published view of its main theme. Third, the recent accumulations of data, both on traditional and on modern thought patterns, have made the contrast/inversion schema untenable whilst lending over-whelming support to Durkheim's continuity/evolution schema. Yet orthodox sociologists and social anthropologists continue to back contrast/inversion.

Since the outlook of contemporary orthodoxy owes so little either to its professed source of inspiration or to the recent accumulations of data, we can only treat this outlook as a problem in the sociology of ideas. That is, we have to ask ourselves what it owes to the broader ideological trends of the times, and to the social currents which underlie them. In what follows, I shall deal with two trends which seem to me to be highly relevant.

(A) LIBERAL ROMANTICISM

The influence of late nineteenth-century ethos and social life on the founders of British social anthropology is impressed on most students of the subject early in their careers. Thus they are taught to look upon the works of Tylor and Frazer not as dispassionate reflections on the facts about traditional thought patterns as these were then known, but rather as charters for the inflated Victorian self-image, and as typical products of a society engaged in the colonization and exploitation of non-Western peoples. Nor, I think, is this an unfair assessment.

Students, however, are often given the impression that with the advent of fieldwork and participant observation, in the early years of the present century, facts swept away ideology for good. And this is very far from being the case.[1]

It is true, of course, that no British anthropologist returning from two years of participant observation in an African or Polynesian village can ever again give serious consideration to Victorian theories that rest ultimately on a thesis of the childishness and stupidity of non-Western peoples. And thus far, facts *have* swept away ideology. As the present paper has shown, however, the body of

[1] My attention was first drawn to this aspect of anthropological indoctrination by Ernest Gellner's characteristically astringent 'Concepts and society' (*Transactions of the Fifth World Congress of Sociology*, 1, Washington D.C., 1962). Though our diagnoses of what followed upon Victorian ethnocentricity differ considerably, I think we both agree that its demise was *not* followed by a new era of objectivity.

theory which has come to replace these earlier doctrines bears very little more relation to the data than did its predecessors. And the reason is that, whilst facts have helped to sweep away the ideologically based theories of the nineteenth century, they have been overwhelmed again by ideology in the present century. For in Western ideology ethnocentrism and arrogance have given way to collective pessimism and self-questioning; and these are equally powerful and equally distorting in their influence on the study of man.

Some of the roots of this ideological revolution are two or three centuries old; for since their beginnings Western technology and science have generated not only a new confidence in man's power to control and improve his environment, but also an underlying doubt. The balance between confidence and doubt has tilted first to one side and then to the other; and the most one can say is that, through the greater part of the last three centuries, it has tended to come down on the side of confidence.

Here, we are more concerned with the doubt than with the confidence. Such doubt has focused on two themes: the viability of social life, and the viability of reason. In what follows, we shall try to uncover the background to these preoccupations.

The rapid growth of industrial technology has in fact undermined the fabric of Western social life in four ways. First, through ever-changing organizational demands, it has introduced a more or less constant element of uncertainty into expectations about other people's behaviour. Second, through occupational specialization, it has given rise to a multiplicity of only partially overlapping world-views, and thence again to uncertainty in the sphere of role-expectations. Third, through depersonalization of the vast area of occupational relations in the name of efficiency, it has left one or two key relationships (e.g. marriage) with the enormous and all too frequently insupportable burden of fulfilling the entire range of human emotional needs. Fourth, through encouragement of addiction to an impersonal theoretical idiom, it has worked against religious belief and hence weakened an important emotional safety-net.[1] Here, clearly, we have the seeds of deep anxiety about the quality of social and emotional life.

---

[1] Though this statement may seen to contradict the intellectualist approach of the present essay, the contradiction is only apparent. As I have always stressed, we can understand the spirits only if we accept that they are *both* theoretical entities *and* additional members of the human social field.

Equally important has been the undermining of confidence in the discursive thought and the literal speech that we regard as the principal vehicles of human reason. Paradoxically, the loss of confidence in these areas has been largely due to the very factors that have promoted the growth of science.

There is little doubt that many features of the scientific outlook first developed as responses to the proliferation of competing idea-systems in seventeenth-century Europe. One effect of this proliferation was the growth of scepticism, of a readiness to challenge any and every idea regardless of its source. Another effect was the search for explicit criteria of choice in the realm of ideas. The most important outcome of this search was the gradual formulation of the ideal of objectivity: i.e. the rule that ideas which are to be used for purposes of explanation should not be allowed to become instruments of any other end, and that conversely any feature of such ideas which is not relevant to its explanatory purpose should be ruthlessly excised. Since the seventeenth century, scepticism and the search for objectivity have been the negative and positive mainprops of the scientific approach.

But the same proliferation of idea-systems generated another attitude which had very different implications. This was because it confronted men with two possible alternatives to ideas and words. First, they could continue to presume the old, unbreakable link between words and the situations they referred to—in which case they had to face the fact that there was no stable reality to which they could anchor themselves, but only an unpredictable flux. Second, they could accept the transience of the link between words and what they stood for—in which case they could console themselves with the belief in a reality that remained unchanged amidst the flux of ideas and words, a reality to which ideas and words might one day do justice. This second alternative was, of course, the one adopted; for whilst the first could only lead to despair, the second did provide some hope. With it, however, came a certain irreversible loss of confidence in the power of ordinary, literal language.

No one has drawn attention to this loss of confidence more vividly than Jean-Paul Sartre in his novel *La nausée*. As Iris Murdoch puts it in her critical survey of Sartre's work:

The hero of *La Nausée* saw language and the world as hopelessly divided from each other. 'The word remains on my lips: it refuses to go and rest on the thing.' Language was an absurd structure of sounds and marks behind which lay an overflowing and undiscriminated chaos: the word which pretended to classify the infinitely and unclassifiable existent, the political slogan or social label or moral tag which concealed the formless heaving mass of human consciousness and human history.[1]

Here we have an attitude which, though it has been latent for long periods, has always constituted a potential denial of the very possibility of those faculties on which reason itself depends.

These two sources of pessimism have, as I have said, been counterbalanced over the last three hundred years by sources of optimism; and, through much of the nineteenth century, the latter certainly weighed more heavily in the scales.

With the advent of the twentieth century, however, two factors have intervened to push the balance heavily down on the side of pessimism. First, there have been numerous crude yet dramatic demonstrations of the potential horrors of science and technology—the very things on which Western superiority was allegedly based. Acceleration of the Industrial Revolution in the late nineteenth century produced a massive expansion of the urban proletariat and a spectacular deterioration in its living conditions.[2] Then came World War One, with its unprecedented revelation of the destructive power of technology. World War Two, Hiroshima, and the Pollution Era followed in quick succession. Second, there has been a profound and rapid change in the politico-economic relationship between the Western world and the non-West. From the seventeenth century down to the end of the nineteenth, there really was a sense in which European history was world history; for during this period events and policies in Europe had far more effect on events and policies in the rest of the inhabited world than vice versa. With the advent of the twentieth century, however, this has become increasingly untrue.

By the beginning of the century, European statesmen were already seeing many of their best-laid plans upset by events in Asia and America which were completely beyond their control. And in recent

---

[1] I. Murdoch, *Sartre*, Yale University Press, 1963, p. 51.
[2] G. Barraclough, *An introduction to contemporary history*, Penguin, Harmondsworth, 1967, pp. 50–2, 235–7.

years the course of events in the Euro-American West has been increasingly influenced by events in the so-called Third World.[1] The resulting sense that the destiny of their civilization is at the mercy of pressures from outside the walls has led to a profound malaise amongst European intellectuals and leaders. The tail has begun to wag the dog; and the dog naturally feels alarmed.

The combination of these relatively recent disturbing factors with the long-established but latent forces enumerated earlier has been sufficient to evoke a full-blooded ideology of pessimism and self-doubt. Pervasive amongst non-scientific intellectuals, it has even established a partial hold over scientists themselves.

The key to this ideology is given by its attitude to the notion of progress. Of all the guiding notions of the nineteenth century, this is the one that has come in for the most ridicule. In its place have come notions of decline and decay, and of cyclical trends in human affairs. Though most professional historians have ridiculed Spengler and Toynbee for their inordinate explanatory ambitions, there are few who do not share their view of the downward trend in the fortunes of the West.[2]

There is a general despair about the quality of modern Western social life. Although Marxists have been most vociferous in deploring 'alienation', intellectuals at the other end of the political spectrum have been equally obsessed with such things as 'the essential loneliness of modern man'. An obverse of this despair is the cult of communion with nature as a means of 'getting away from it all', and the idea that such communion helps to repair the wounds inflicted on the soul by industrial society. Just as the forces making for dissatisfaction with the quality of Western social life have been gathering strength for several centuries, so too has the cult of communion with nature. In poetry, after all, it has been a prominent theme from Wordsworth onward.[3] Yet it is perhaps only during the last seventy

[1] Barraclough, op. cit., chs. 3–4.
[2] On the unfashionableness of the idea of progress amongst contemporary historians, see J. Plumb, 'The historian's dilemma', in J. Plumb (ed.), *Crisis in the humanities*, Penguin, Harmondsworth, 1964; E. H. Carr, *What is history?*, Penguin, Harmondsworth, 1964, chs. 2 and 5.
[3] For an interesting treatment of Wordsworth's communion with nature, see B. Willey, *Seventeenth century background*, Penguin, Harmondsworth, 1962 (ch. 12, 'Wordsworth and the Locke tradition'); *Eighteenth century background*,

years that this cult has played a major role in Western life, manifesting itself in a dozen ways that Westerners now take for granted but that non-Westerners find strange and distinctive: in the cult of the country hideaway, the lone walk through the woods, the lone scramble up the mountainside, or the lone voyage over the ocean—to name just a few.

Closely allied to the conviction that science and technology are destroying the fabric of society is the conviction that these things are choking the life of feeling. With this have come various movements assuming an antagonism between reason and feeling, and vociferously exalting the latter at the expense of the former. One of the most militant of these was Surrealism, a movement which was at its peak in the Paris of the twenties and thirties, but which created ripples in most Western capitals that have not yet died down. Its devotees displayed a contempt for reason, and for the outside world with which reason claimed to deal most efficiently. They retreated into the inner world of emotion and feeling, and into modes of activity or inactivity which they saw as generating the most natural expressions of this world. Hence their interest in such things as automatic writing and dreaming.[1] Other movements in other Western countries had similar goals. In England, the exaltation of the 'dark, sensual side' of man was launched by D. H. Lawrence. In Germany, the same exaltation of feeling over reason was an important ingredient of Nazism. Though these and other movements have come and gone, the desire that feeling should conquer reason has remained close to the surface of Western life, ready to re-emerge at any time.

A final ingredient of the twentieth-century outlook is an obsession with the inadequacy of literal speech to reality, accompanied by a fascination with all forms of symbolism. Symbols are thought of as

---

Penguin, Harmondsworth, 1967 (ch. 12, ' "Nature" in Wordsworth'). For stimulating exposition of a parallel theme in the visual arts, see K. Clark, *Landscape into art*, Penguin, Harmondsworth, 1956 (ch. 5, 'The natural vision'); *Civilisation*, J. Murray, London, 1969 (ch. 11, 'The worship of nature').

[1] For a very clear statement of both the origins and the doctrines of the Surrealist Movement, see M. Nadeau, *History of surrealism*, Eng. trans., Cape, London, 1968. For a sympathetic, but for an Anglo-Saxon mind less clear, outline of Surrealist philosophy, see F. Alquié, *The philosophy of surrealism*, Eng. trans., University of Michigan Press, Ann Arbor, 1965.

the means of 'saying' everything that is unsayable in terms of literal speech. They are thought to provide a superior means of grasping the particularity of events. Their non-conventional relation to their referents is seen as providing a more direct intuition of reality. Whereas ordinary literal speech gives a self-confessedly poor coverage of the inner world of emotion and feeling, symbolism claims a very extensive coverage of this world.

In their drive to eliminate everything irrelevant to the quest for explanation, scientists have tended to brand symbolism as a dangerous distraction. They have driven it into the licensed but somewhat second-rate enclave of the Arts. From this redoubt, however, its protagonists have waxed strong on those pervasive doubts about the adequacy of literal speech which even their opponents to some extent share with them.

The emergence of this new Western self-image has been closely accompanied by the emergence of a drastically new attitude towards the non-Western world. More specifically, the transition from nineteenth-century self-confidence to twentieth-century self-doubt has been accompanied by the transition from an attitude of contempt and aversion to one of respect and romantic fascination vis-à-vis non-Western cultures. Since the two transitions have occurred at the same times and places often in the minds of the same people,[1] we may legitimately regard the link between them as non-accidental.

A more detailed portrayal of the various components of the new attitude will serve to elucidate the nature of this link.

Amongst Western intellectuals, the first two decades of the present century brought rebirth of respect for non-Western cultures; and this respect has been slowly but surely increasing ever since. It has been expressed in a determinedly sympathetic attitude towards non-Western cultures, in an avowal that each has its own peculiar merits, and above all in an avoidance of invidious comparisons. The resulting complex of attitudes can conveniently be summed up in the phrase 'liberal scruples'.

The influence of collective self-doubt on liberal scruples is not hard to understand. On the one hand, moral self-doubt leads to a heavy load of guilt about past arrogance vis-à-vis non-Western cultures,

---

[1] Dramatic examples are provided by the Surrealists and the Dadaists, both of whom preached that the regeneration of an exhausted Western culture could come only from an injection of non-Western values.

and to a very genuine desire to make amends for it. On the other hand, political self-doubt leads to a more circumspect attitude to powers over whom one would have ridden roughshod fifty years ago, and hence to a desire to maintain friendly relations with them for reasons of sheer expediency.

It is awareness of this dubious mixture of morality and expediency underpinning Western respect for non-Western cultures that evokes non-Westerners' bitter contempt for 'White Liberals'.

Like liberal scruples, the romantic fascination with non-Western cultures first made itself felt in the years just before World War One, and became even more noticeable in the years following the holocaust. Its noisiest propagandists were the Surrealists, who called for the abandonment of European values, and for wholesale importation of culture from Polynesia, China and other faraway places. Alongside them the Dadaists, led by Tristan Tzara, extolled the virtues of African culture.

To start with, the easiest way of getting oneself exposed to the regenerative influence of the traditional cultures was through contact with their material artefacts. Many of these were already lying about in European houses, museums and missionary headquarters, where they had been brought as trophies during the era of colonial expansion and conquest. Given the right price, their possessors were perfectly willing to part with them to people fired with a more positive attitude towards them. Hence the quest for the traditional expressed itself first of all in a cult of 'primitive art'.[1]

Soon, however, other avenues of contact were discovered and utilized—for example, those representatives of traditional culture within the gates, the Negro jazz musicians and blues singers. Later still, scores of holy men poured into Europe from India and points east. Some were real, some bogus, but all provided food for the insatiable appetites of the new West.

Since these early days, detailed tastes have varied with time and place. Sometimes China has been in vogue; sometimes India; sometimes Polynesia; sometimes Africa; sometimes Amerindia. But, whatever the variation in detail, the quest for contact with contemporary traditional cultures has been followed with unabated vigour

[1] For the origins of the European cult of 'primitive art', see M. Leiris and J. Delange, *African art*, Braziller, London, 1968, pp. 1–33.

291

down to the present day. Indeed, it is one of the stronger positive components of the enormously powerful Youth Culture of present-day America.[1]

Having noted this fascination with non-Western cultures, we must go on to ask which of their supposed characteristics provoke it. The following, perhaps, are the most important: the organic community, in which the individual never finds himself set over against his group; communion with nature; predominance of feeling over reason; predominance of symbolism over literal speech; predominance of art over science. One striking thing about this list of supposed salient features of non-Western cultures is its similarity to a list that might be drawn up of the supposed salient features of pre-industrial culture in the earlier West. Given the Western intellectual's awareness of the many parallels between contemporary traditional cultures and earlier phases of Western culture, the desire for contact with such cultures is revealed as being, in essence, a desire to be reunited with one's own lost heritage.[2]

If the reader casts his mind back to what was said earlier about recent accumulations of data relating to the traditional cultures, he will see that the influence of factual information on this image of the 'lost world' is tenuous. Once again, however, the influence of Western pessimism and self-doubt is clear. Thus if we make a list of the various unfulfilled yearnings and malaises of which the modern Western intellectual complains, we shall find that this image displays itself unmistakably as a compensatory fantasy in which every frustrated yearning of the West finds fulfilment and every malaise of the West is banished. Does Western man find himself alienated from his society and lost in an abysmal loneliness? Then traditional culture is the seat of the Organic Community, in which the individual finds it impossible to think of himself as distinct from his group. Does Western man yearn to commune with nature, yet find himself frustrated by his awareness of the unbridgeable difference between people and things? Then traditional culture provides a world-view

[1] See T. Roszak, *The making of a counter-culture*, Faber, London, 1970, ch. 8, 'Eyes of flesh, eyes of fire'.
[2] See Roszak, op. cit. and also F. Perls, R. Hefferline and P. Goodman, *Gestalt therapy*, Julian Press, New York, 1951. On p. 307, the authors contend that the task of anthropology is 'to show what of human nature has been "lost", and, practically, to devise experiments for its recovery'.

which minimizes this difference, and so makes communion fully satisfying. Does Western man suffer from the conviction that reason is killing the life of emotion and feeling? Then traditional culture provides a milieu in which feeling dominates reason. Does Western man despair of the adequacy of words, and attempt to use symbols to 'say' what is unsayable in literal speech? And is he frustrated, in this attempt, by the restricted role allotted to symbolism in the formal structure of Western institutions? Then traditional culture provides a world in which the symbol reigns supreme. Does Western man feel that science is killing art? Then traditional culture provides a world in which art dominates science.

In short, then, the romantic search for a 'lost world' has given rise to an image of traditional culture which can be understood entirely as a reaction to the stresses and strains of life in the modern West.

At this point, we have reached a position from which we can profitably return to deal with our main problem: the vogue of the contrast/inversion schema and the neglect of the continuity/evolution schema by social scientists. For once we have established our right to assume that the attitude to traditional cultures generally current among modern Western intellectuals is also powerfully entrenched amongst social scientists, we shall be in possession of a simple and elegant means of accounting for the situation.

Let us start with the question of 'liberal scruples'. Anthropologists who do fieldwork in the traditional cultures tend to be amongst those most strongly equipped with such scruples. Now that the victims of anthroplogical scrutiny nearly always include a few educated souls who are going to read the resulting report with the sensitive eyes of former colonial subjects, the anthropologist has to develop such scruples, if for no more honourable reason than as part of his basic survival equipment. For the Western anthropologist who not only does fieldwork in a non-Western nation, but who also lives and works in one of the universities of such a nation, the question 'will they be upset by my next paper?' often becomes an overriding obsession.

The main thing for the scrupulous liberal is, of course, to avoid invidious intercultural comparison. Now, in many spheres of traditional culture, the question of such comparison is hardly likely to arise. Take, for instance, the arts. It would be a rash anthropologist indeed who could put his finger on the ends of Art, and who could swear that Western ballet achieved them more perfectly than African

293

masquerade. Again, it would be a rash anthropologist who could bring himself to swear that Western family life was better attuned to the basic emotions of men and women than the family life of the Marquesas, or even that it was morally more elevated. Yet again, the student of traditional political systems is likely to conclude that most of them are as well adapted to the societies they serve as modern British parliamentary government is to the society it serves.

When it comes to the sociology of thought, however, the question of invidious comparison becomes unpleasantly obtrusive. In all known traditional cultures, we find people producing explanations of events, using such explanations to make predictions about the likely consequences of various courses of action, and using the predictions in an attempt to extend their control of the world around them. In the modern West, we find people explaining, predicting and attempting to control the world in just the same sense of these words. However, if the West has done nothing else of indisputable worth, it *has* succeeded in creating an institutional framework that has generated forms of explanation, prediction and control of a power hitherto unrivalled in any time or place. Such cognitive forms, moreover, are known to have developed from earlier and less efficient forms that have recognizable parallels in many contemporary traditional cultures.

Such a situation is deeply embarrassing to our scrupulous liberal. For either he sticks to the facts; and finds himself forced into a comparison strongly unfavourable to the traditional cultures. Or he dodges the comparison; but only at the price of denying the facts.

It is in terms of the latter course of action that we can at last understand the strange antics of the social anthropologist who refuses to take traditional explanations at their face value, and who maintains that at some deeper level of reality these are symbolic statements. For by such antics he converts the data into forms that stand in radical contrast with the explanatory statements of the sciences. Radical contrast means incommensurability, and incommensurability means impossibility of making invidious value-judgements.[1]

That this really is one of the powerful ideological pressures behind the contrast/inversion schema is confirmed by the more or less moral overtones of disapproval expressed against those who, following the

---

[1] On this, see also I. Jarvie and J. Agassi, 'The problem of the rationality of magic', *British Journal of Sociology*, 18, 1967, pp. 62–3.

Lévy-Bruhl, Durkheim and the Scientific Revolution

data, stick to continuity/evolution. Such disapproval finds its most explicit expression in a recent paper by Edmund Leach, entitled 'Virgin birth', in which the author castigates all those who take 'primitive' explanations of the world at their face value.[1] Such people, he says, have an immoral wish to prove that 'primitives' are prone to stupid and childish mistakes. The good anthropologist realizes that, despite appearances, 'primitives' are not even trying to produce explanations, and he therefore avoids such imputations.

A clearer confession of the ideological basis of current anthropological theory could hardly be found!

Let us turn now to the second main component of the modern Western attitude—the romantic fascination with traditional cultures. The modern Western anthropologist who elects to serve his fieldwork apprenticeship in a thoroughly traditional culture can hardly be other than a romantic. As far as intellectual stimulus or professional advancement is concerned, a modern or a transitional community would offer him an equal reward. This being so, his willingness to face two years of unpalliated heat, biting insects, bug-ridden water supply and non-existent sanitation can only spring from a strong expectation of the regenerative effect of encounter with a 'lost world'.

Given the fact that those who have fashioned the generally current romantic image of traditional culture have often scarcely pretended to acquaintance with the relevant data, it is remarkable just how much of this image has tended to reappear in sociological characterizations of traditional thought patterns which *do* purport to be based on the data. Perhaps the most striking instance of this is provided by the Surrealists and Lévy-Bruhl. For the Surrealists, one suspects, would have admitted quite happily to dreaming up most of their ideas about the non-Western world. And Lévy-Bruhl, with equal justice, would have maintained that his ideas on the subject were based on a massive accumulation of data. Yet, although their writings show no explicit cross-references, the resemblance between their respective doctrines is uncanny. Thus, while the Surrealists divide the world of experience into the real and the sur-real, Lévy-Bruhl divides it into the natural and the supernatural. While the Surrealists associate real experience with reason and sur-real experience with feeling and desire, Lévy-Bruhl associates natural experience with reason and supernatural experience with feeling and desire. Both stress the role of feeling and

[1] Leach, 1966, op. cit.

295

Lévy-Bruhl, Durkheim and the Scientific Revolution

desire in creating ideas and objects that are bizarre by the standards of common sense. Both stress the role of feeling and desire in breaking down the separation of man and nature. Both treat the domain of the sur-real/supernatural as something that is subordinate in Western culture, dominant in non-Western culture.[1]

In much the same way, the generally current romantic image of a 'lost world' in which symbolism and art reign supreme turns up again in characterizations of traditional thought patterns favoured by anthropologists like Firth, Leach and Beattie.[2]

[1] At various points in his anthropological works, Lévy-Bruhl stressed that standard Western concepts and categories were virtually useless for the translation of 'primitive' ideas, and that anyone who wished to embark on such translation would have to fashion a new set of concepts for this express purpose. The form taken by such concepts would, of course, be determined solely by the nature of the data under investigation.

Although he clearly saw his own key interpretative concepts as conforming to this requirement, a recent glance at his bibliography, and a re-reading of Leenhardt's introduction to Les carnets as well as of certain passages of Les fonctions mentales, have strengthened my suspicion that the sources of his inspiration may not have been quite what he liked to think they were.

First of all, bibliographic references on the fly-sheet of Les fonctions, together with certain remarks by Leenhardt, suggest that Lévy-Bruhl started with a deep interest in German Romantic 'philosophies de sentiment', and turned to his later rather ascetic positivism by way of reaction.

This view of his personal intellectual development receives some corroboration from his general attitude to the supposed emotional 'mystical' orientation of the traditional cultures with which he deals—an attitude in which fascination vies with impatience. It receives further corroboration from an apparently little-read passage at the end of Les fonctions (pp. 451–5), in which he speaks of the continuing survival of 'pre-logical thought' in the anti-intellectualist doctrines that still wax strong in the modern West, and in which he gets somewhat carried away whilst describing the delights of the 'participation' between subject and object that is so often the central ideal of such doctrines. All this suggests a love-hate relationship with anti-intellectualist creeds which we should expect from a recent convert to rationalism.

Further, the corollary of Lévy-Bruhl's treatment of modern anti-intellectualist doctrines as survivals of a full-blown 'primitive mentality' is the assumption that the categories and concepts of such doctrines can be used as instruments for translating the thought of contemporary 'primitives'.

All in all, the implication is that, like the Surrealists and others of his contemporaries whose romanticism was unaccompanied by any great ethnographic learning, Lévy-Bruhl projected a body of essentially Western ideas and values (with which he still had a lingering identification) on to the traditional cultures.

At present this interpretation of Lévy-Bruhl is of course something of a hunch. However, in the hands of a scholar who is willing to read his early works on the history of Western philosophy with an eye to possible connections with his later anthropological work, I think it might bear fruit.

[2] Firth, Leach, Beattie, op. cit.

Lévy-Bruhl, Durkheim and the Scientific Revolution

This general tendency for 'lost world' fantasies to find their way into anthropological orthodoxy accounts very nicely for the popularity of the contrast/inversion schema. For the 'lost world', being a world in which every frustrated yearning of the West is fulfilled and every malaise of the West banished, is inevitably defined as an inverted image of Western culture.

(B) POSITIVISM

In the conversation of social scientists, one frequently hears glib references to 'Durkheimian Positivism'. Durkheim may have been a positivist in some sense of that word and in some parts of his many-stranded career; but, as he makes clear in the introduction to *Les formes élémentaires*, one of his main concerns is to find a viable alternative to the positivist (or, as he calls it, empiricist) account of human intellectual activity.[1] I believe that it is his anti-positivist bias which has given his sociology of thought much of its prophetic quality vis-à-vis recent accumulations of data. Equally, I believe that widespread adherence to a positivist view of intellectual activity has contributed much to the errors of others in this field.

'Positivism', as a label, has been used in many ways by many people; so I had better preface further remarks with a definition. As I see it, positivism is a two-pronged ideology. First, it is a philosophical outlook which exalts the sciences as providing the only valid tools for acquiring knowledge of the world. Secondly, it is an outlook with a very peculiar conception of the sciences. That is, it holds them to be based largely on the process of induction from occurrences in the visible, tangible world. This process, it maintains, results in descriptive generalizations which show *how* things happen in the observable world. It does not yield explanations of *why* things happen. Such explanations, indeed, are no business of the sciences. For positivism, ideas about unobservable entities, which are so often associated with attempts to explain the workings of the world, are inessential to the process of scientific investigation. At best, they are crutches for thought; at worst, sources of dangerous confusion.[2]

---

[1] EF, pp. 9–20.
[2] Some of the principal sources of this view are E. Mach, *The analysis of sensations*, Open Court Publishing Company, Chicago, 1914; P. Duhem, *The aim and structure of physical theory*, University Press, Princeton, 1954; P. Bridgman, *The logic of modern physics*, Macmillan, New York, 1927; K. Pearson,

Lévy-Bruhl, Durkheim and the Scientific Revolution

As a product of the exuberance of scientists and their sympathizers, the first prong of the positivist ideology is not hard to understand. The second prong is more puzzling; for its conception of scientific activity is so far removed from what scientists actually do. Perhaps the best explanation is that this is a revolutionary ideology. As such, it has followed others of its kind in exaggerating the extent of change and in throwing out a valuable baby with the pre-revolutionary bath-water. Thus because the pre-revolutionary situation gave pride of place to spiritual beings, positivism condemns all ideas about unobservable entities as improper. Again, because the pre-revolutionary situation invoked the sanctions of tradition and authority to override experience, positivism condemns all forms of intellectual operation that are not directly tied to experience.

At this point, I can feel some of my readers getting restless. For I started by telling them that most of the errors of present-day sociology of thought were due to the infection of its practitioners with the ideology of liberal romanticism—an ideology based on a disillusion with science. And now, it seems, I am about to tell them that these errors are also due to infection with the ideology of positivism— an ideology based on excessive enthusiasm for science.

The paradox, though it looks severe, is in fact more apparent than real.

In the first place, members of the present sociological and anthropological establishment received their intellectual formation at a time when most of the generally available accounts of scientific method were positivist in tone. Other more sophisticated accounts were being evolved, but many of these were still confined to the pages of specialist professional journals. Social scientists who cling to positivist accounts of scientific method are therefore rather like historians, classicists and literary men who take Frazer as the last word on traditional cultures. It is all a question of a time-lag in the diffusion of new discoveries and new approaches from their discipline of origin into the general intellectual culture.[1]

The grammar of science, A. and C. Black, London, 1911; R. Carnap, *The unity of science*, Kegan Paul, London, 1934; A. J. Ayer, *Language, truth and logic*, Gollancz, London, 1936.

[1] The only recent work on the history/philosophy of science to have caught the imagination of the wider intellectual public is Thomas Kuhn's *Structure of scientific revolutions*, University of Chicago Press, Chicago, 1962. From the point

Lévy-Bruhl, Durkheim and the Scientific Revolution

But there is also a subtler reason for the amalgamation of liberal romanticism with certain aspects of positivism. Positivism, as I have stressed, is a two-pronged ideology; and it is perfectly possible to use one prong without the other. More specifically, it is perfectly possible to deny that science provides the only means of acquiring valid knowledge about the world, but to affirm that scientific method is largely a matter of induction from observables.

Not only is such a position possible. It fits in very well with an attitude of disillusion or hostility toward the sciences. For it gives the sciences such an extraordinary air of aridity, and assigns them such limited aims, that one can hardly help questioning their claim to a dominant position in Western culture, and wondering whether other ways of grasping reality are not perhaps more important.

Perhaps the first modern thinker to take up this limited form of positivism and use it as a weapon against the overweening claims of science was the great French Catholic physicist Pierre Duhem. The burden of his argument was that the sciences had the very limited function of showing *how* phenomena were correlated in space and time. They therefore presented no challenge to religion, whose function was that of explaining *why* things happened.[1]

If a devout Christian could thus show how one prong of the positivist ideology might be turned against its begetters, what was to stop liberal romantics from following suit? In fact, a positivistic definition of science has been prominent in the views of all the social scientists who have supported the contrast/inversion schema. Lévy-Bruhl, Malinowski, Evans-Pritchard, Gluckman, Firth, Leach and Beattie—all of these in various ways have made it plain that they regard science as an extension of common sense; as based on induction from observables; and as limiting itself to questions of *how* these observables behave.[2]

---

of view of the thesis put forward here, it is perhaps significant that the main reason for the popular success of the book would appear to be the (mistaken) belief that Kuhn demonstrates the essential irrationality of science.

[1] Duhem, op. cit., ch. 1.

[2] See works of these authors referred to in previous footnotes. In particular, see the definitions of 'empirical' and 'mystical' in Evans-Pritchard, 1937, op. cit., pp. 11–12; Gluckman, 1965, op. cit., p. 216; also Leach, 1966, op. cit., p. 39, for a proud acceptance of the label 'vulgar positivist'. For a criticism of the effect of a positivist (or, as he calls it, 'inductivist') stance on the work of social anthropologists generally, see I. Jarvie, *The revolution in anthropology*, Routledge, London, 1964.

Once such a position has been taken up with respect to science, it is inevitable that the magico-religious thinking of the traditional cultures should be seen as radically contrasted with it. For the mysteries of the world of unobservables and of unity-in-duality are then seen as peculiar to magico-religious thinking; and they are certainly poles apart from any simple process of induction from observables.

Again, the prominence of positivist indoctrination gives an alternative explanation of the modern social anthropologist's strange predilection for lumping all ideas that don't look like the results of inductive generalization into the catch-all category of 'symbolism'. For according to some of the better-known versions of positivism, propositions are either scientific (inductively based), or symbolic expressions of emotion.[1]

Not only, then, does a certain limited version of positivism articulate well with the twentieth-century Western ideology of pessimism and self-doubt. Thus articulated in the mind of the social scientist, it also strongly reinforces his support of the contrast/inversion schema.

7. Reconciling fancy and fact

The lesson of this paper is clear. In trying to define the relation between traditional and modern thought patterns, twentieth-century social scientists can hardly be said to have made a notable advance on their nineteenth-century predecessors. Although Durkheim is the ancestral hero of their discipline, although he is one of the few twentieth-century figures who have had something illuminating to say on this topic, and although most of them have quoted him as their authority on it, they have in fact stood his actual teaching on its head. The result, which for brevity I have called the contrast/inversion schema, bears no worthwhile relation to the data.

This strange tale, I have suggested, can be understood only when one has realized that Western social scientists dealing with the non-Western world have escaped from the influence of one powerful ideology only to fall under the influence of another.

Is there any consoling feature to be extracted from this depressing tale? So far as interpretation of the data is concerned, the answer is

---

[1] See R. Carnap, *Philosophy and logical syntax*, Kegan Paul, London, 1935, p. 8; Ayer, 1936, op. cit.

definitely no. The modern contrast/inversion theorists have made no more sense of the data than did Tylor and Frazer. So far as sheer accumulation of data is concerned, the answer is yes. For whilst the Victorian idea of non-Western cultures as childish or half-baked forms of Western culture was surely a deterrent to fieldwork, the modern idea of such cultures as paradisiacal 'lost worlds' is equally surely an inducement to fieldwork. In the case of some of the more thoroughly tradition-oriented cultures, as I suggested earlier, it may even be the *sine qua non* of fieldwork. And although such fieldwork may be inspired by distorting preconceptions, it nevertheless makes for an influx of new and relevant data which may one day be used to overwhelm the preconceptions. Indeed, some of the data which I have used in this paper to show up the inadequacy of contrast/inversion theory have been amassed by exponents of the theory!

Liberal romanticism, clearly, is here to stay; for the factors which nourish it are likely, if anything, to increase in strength. The problem is, how do we harness it so that its interpretations come to run less grossly counter to the data which it helps to produce in such generous quantities?

What we have to try to do, clearly, is show that interpretations which are truer to the data do not necessarily conflict with its most cherished values.

As an example, let us take Durkheim's continuity/evolution schema, which fits the facts of the Great Transition admirably, but which is rejected by Leach and other contemporaries because it offends against their deepest liberal convictions. Let us see whether it really does run counter to these convictions.

The liberal objection to the schema, as we have seen, is that taking traditional explanations at their face value means admitting their inferior cognitive power vis-à-vis explanations produced by the sciences. In terms of liberal values, does this really matter?

In the first place, an erroneous explanation proves nothing about the intellectual capacity of those who put it forward. Indeed, it is in the nature of scientific 'progress by revolution' that today's acceptable explanations are tomorrow's errors. Hence pre-scientific non-Westerners hold no monopoly of erroneous explanations. They share the distinction of being prone to them with the most distinguished scientists.

Secondly, it is becoming more and more apparent that the sciences have made their mark very largely in those areas of human experience least associated with the deepest emotions—i.e. the spheres denoted by the labels 'physics' and 'chemistry'.[1] During the course of their tremendous advances in these spheres, they may well have sacrificed insights into the working of human social life that non-Western cultures still retain. If this is the case, then patient study of non-Western explanations may reveal, not a mere catalogue of errors, but a mixture of much error with a number of significant successes. That this is not fanciful is shown by the case of psychosomatic medicine, which was rediscovered, in the twentieth-century West, partly as a result of reflection on traditional ideas about the social causation of disease and death.[2]

A third consideration involves the past history and probable future development of the sciences. In many ways, the rise of the scientific outlook makes a strange tale. It starts in the Greek overseas colonies during the sixth century B.C., continues first in Alexandria, then in Baghdad, then in southern Italy and Spain, then finally shifts to north-west Europe, the United States and the Soviet Union. One area after another has acted briefly as the home of science before yielding this pride of place to some other. In future, it is true, the tale is unlikely to continue just as before. The sciences have now started to feed the fruits of their activities into the wider culture in the form of benefits which all bearers of that culture can appreciate. So now there is less likelihood that a given area, having once acted as host to the sciences, will lose them again. It is hard to imagine Britain and the United States becoming scientific has-beens in quite the way that ancient Greece and Baghdad did. Nonetheless it is quite possible that, as the sciences spread throughout the world, some of the present centres will lose momentum and new centres overtake them. Already, American occupational psychologists have been asking themselves whether the type of personality thrown up by twentieth-century American culture is the type most likely to produce the creative scientist.[3] And at the other end of the world the Japanese,

---

[1] On this, see Barry Barnes's paper in the present volume.

[2] See, for instance, W. Cannon, 'Voodoo death', *American Anthropologist*, 44, 1942.

[3] R. Cattell, 'The personality and motivation of the researcher from measurements of contemporaries and from biography', in C. Taylor and F. Barron (eds.), *Scientific creativity*, Wiley, New York, 1963 (see pp. 129–31).

relative newcomers to the sciences, have been making extraordinarily vigorous progress in certain key subjects like elementary particle physics.

With ninety per cent of all the scientists who have ever lived still alive and working at the present day, we are clearly at the very beginning of the story. As the tale unfolds, the West may never again find itself without the sciences; but it may well find one day that the peak of creative momentum has passed on to one or more of the non-Western nations.

In this context, I think it is interesting to look at the situation in a country like Nigeria, where the less competent indigenous scientists tend to wax a little lyrical over such figures as native doctors and diviners, whilst the outstanding men tend to take a much more matter-of-fact view of them. I shall always remember one Yoruba medical scientist, an internationally respected leader in his field, who, on being asked at a conference to expatiate on the virtues of native doctors, replied: 'Don't let them give you anything to drink. Don't let them cut you. The rest of the performance is harmless.'

Coming as it does from an iconoclastic innovator, this comment goes to an extreme. But it does suggest that, once the non-Western scientist comes to feel that science really is 'his thing', he also feels free to make comparisons with the cognitive power of his forefathers' methods and generally to look at these methods with an objective eye.

Here, I think, we get close to the root of the liberal sentiment. For is not the inmost reason why the Western liberal feels compelled to allot the non-Westerner a special cognitive province a secret conviction that science can never really be the non-Westerner's 'thing'?

It would seem, then, that we need to convince the liberal of three things.

First, that from an erroneous belief, very little follows, one way or another, about the intellectual capacity of its holder. Second, that traditional theories, considered *as theories*, can in certain spheres of experience be a source of precious insight. Third, that non-Westerners are more than likely to take over the Western lead in some fields of science, and to make these fields 'their thing'. Once convinced of these points the liberal should be free to look at traditional thought patterns with a more objective eye.

What about romanticism, that paradoxical source of bad interpretation and good data? This too, I believe, can be tamed and harnessed.

Personally, I must admit to sharing much of the romantic motivation which I have imputed to supporters of the contrast/inversion schema. I agree that we in the West have paid a heavy price for modernity in general and for the scientific outlook in particular. I share the belief that we in the West can discover something about the quality of our society before it paid this price by looking at contemporary traditional cultures. Finally, I share a conviction as to the regenerative effect of prolonged participation in the life of a culture that has not yet paid the price of modernity.

In these respects, I too am a romantic. But I think it is possible to be a romantic, with all this means in terms of motivation towards anthropological fieldwork, and yet avoid the distorting interpretations that so far have marred twentieth-century Western studies of the traditional. How to do this?

First of all, the romantic in search of his 'lost world' must come to see the impossibility of ever finding a place in which all the frustrated yearnings of the West are satisfied and all the malaises of the West absent. One reason for the impossibility is that many frustrated Western yearnings are the *products* of Western malaises, and do not even arise where such malaises are absent. Such, for instance, is the case with the Western yearning for communion with nature.[1] Another reason is that some Western yearnings are doomed to a degree of frustration in all cultures, human nature being what it is. This is the case with the yearning for the organic community in which the individual can never think of himself as at odds with the group.

However, there are many less simplistic senses in which traditional cultures can offer qualities of life lacking in the West. The romantic should have faith, and wait for the 'lost world' itself to show him what it has to offer.

Secondly, the romantic must come to see that all is not lost if he faces and admits that, in the sphere of explanation, prediction and

---

[1] For more on the idea that the urge towards communion with nature may be the product of certain forms of 'alienation' from modern Western society, see my 'The romantic illusion: Roger Bastide on Africa and the West', *Odu*, N.S., 3, 1970.

control, modern cultures are pursuing the same goals as their traditional counterparts, but are pursuing them with greater efficiency. For the question of the price paid for such efficiency still remains to be asked.

Finally, what about positivism? The cure for this would seem to be more up-to-date reading in the History and Philosophy of Science. Social anthropologists concerned with the study of magico-religious thought in the traditional cultures should become aware of the extent to which their interpretations are coloured by an implicit vision of the nature of Western thought. They should accept the fact that they cannot be effective anthropologists of traditional magico-religious thought without at the same time being anthropologists of modern scientific thought.

Since social scientists still accept everything more easily when it comes to them via Durkheim, they might do well to start their reorientation by re-reading *Formes élémentaires* and acquainting themselves with what the master *really* said.

Frobenius, Senghor and the Image of Africa

J. M. Ita

Leo Frobenius's writings have greatly influenced certain modern analyses (notably by the Négritude writers) of both African culture and, by implication, African thought and non-European thought more generally. An examination of Frobenius's interpretations—and, perhaps even more significant, of some of their sources and the assumptions involved in them—can throw unexpected light on the basic question of this volume.

Leo Frobenius[1] died in August 1938 after a lifetime spent largely in studying the ethnography and history of Africa. 1968, the year of the thirtieth anniversary of his death, has come and gone without eliciting any major comment on his work—at any rate from the English-speaking world.[2] This failure to comment (unless it is based merely on an inability to read German) in itself constitutes an implied judgement that Frobenius's work is so irrelevant to modern research as to be unworthy of mention.

Yet while Anglo-American anthropologists consistently ignore Frobenius, he was, and still is, praised in the highest terms by the African and West Indian writers who initiated the movement of

---

[1] For a bibliography of Frobenius's works up to 1932 see 'Das Schrifttum von Frobenius' compiled by Heinz Wieschoff, contained in *Leo Frobenius, ein Lebenswerk aus der Zeit der Kulturwende*, Koehler und Umelang, Leipzig, 1933, compiled by Rhotert, von den Steinen and others. For a more recent bibliography, see F. Kretschmar, *Leo Frobenius*, cyclostyled, Inter Nationes, 1968.

[2] But for a short review of some of his work on rock art, see C. S. Coon, 'The rock art of Africa', *Science*, 142, No. 3600, December, 27 1963.

Frobenius, Senghor and the Image of Africa

Négritude.[1] Léopold Sédar Senghor, writing as late as the 1960s, says:

> To the first militants of Négritude [Frobenius] was more than a teacher who guided their thoughts; he was a catalyst who uncovered, aroused, strengthened the slumbering energies of the Black Man . . . He spoke to us of the only problem which preoccupied us: the nature, value, and destiny of Black African culture. His books *Kulturgeschichte Afrikas* and *Schicksalskunde* (published in French as *Histoire de la civilisation africaine* and *Le destin des civilisations*) were among the sacred books of a whole generation of African students.[2]

Thus, Senghor sees Frobenius as one who has roused Africans to an awareness of their great cultural heritage and helped to restore dignity and respect to a continent long reputed to possess neither culture nor history. In spite of the very marked contrast between Senghor's view of Frobenius, and that held by Anglo-American anthropologists, the two views have failed to confront each other— though one might have expected such a confrontation in 1968, the anniversary year.

So far, no attempt has been made to judge the relative merits of these conflicting views, or to refute them. The year 1968 did see the publication by Inter Nationes of the monograph by Dr. Freda Kretschmar entitled *Leo Frobenius*.[3] However, Dr. Kretschmar is one of Frobenius's former students and was writing in connection with the anniversary of his death. Understandably, her monograph was a personal tribute rather than a critical assessment of Frobenius's achievement. While she quoted, at length, Senghor's praise of Frobenius, she did not consider the occasion an appropriate one for mentioning hostile views of him, and hence could not attempt to refute them. It is part of my purpose, in this essay, to analyse why these conflicting views of Frobenius have failed to confront each other.

*   *   *

[1] In addition to Senghor, see S. Césaire, 'Leo Frobenius et le problème des civilisations', *Tropiques*, 1, avril 1941.

[2] L. S. Senghor, *Africa and the Germans* (abbreviation AG.), Horst Erdmann Verlag, Tübingen and Basel, 1968, pp. 10–11.

[3] F. Kretschmar, *Leo Frobenius*, 1968.

Frobenius, Senghor and the Image of Africa

Some of the reasons why modern archaeologists and anthropologists dismiss Frobenius's work are straightforward: they object to his historical approach, to the inadequacies of his anthropological fieldwork and his archaeological excavation methods. Frobenius's approach to anthropology (like that of many of his contemporaries) was concerned with origins, and involved hypothetical reconstructions of the past; it was also comparative in that widely scattered cultures were studied in the hope of tracing them back to a common origin.[1]

After the First World War, the theoretical framework of anthropology was revolutionized, largely through A. R. Radcliffe-Brown who rejected all hypotheses about the history of preliterate societies on the grounds that they were incapable of verification. He argued that such societies could be studied only by the synchronic method, by explaining *how they functioned* at a given time—customs being interpreted in terms of their contribution to the maintenance of the total social system.[2] Thus the enquiry into origins was largely abandoned, as there seemed no valid way of conducting it, once the historical and comparative methods associated with it had been discredited.

The 'Functionalist' school, under the influence of Radcliffe-Brown and Malinowski, dominated British anthropology from the thirties. Consequently nearly all British anthropologists have been trained to reject the historical and comparative approach adopted by Frobenius. In America, the historical approach was less discredited than in Britain; but there it was used primarily in investigating Amerindian cultures with which Frobenius had been little concerned.

Frobenius's anthropological fieldwork was hampered by the necessity of working through interpreters. His early expeditions were financed by museums[3] on the understanding that he would collect

---

[1] Audrey Richards, 'Bronislav Malinowski', in T. Raison (ed.), *The founding fathers of social science*, Penguin, Harmondsworth, 1969, p. 189. See also R. Benedict, *Patterns of culture*, Mentor Books reprint, 1953, p. 44.

[2] A. R. Radcliffe-Brown, *The Andaman islanders* (first published 1922), Free Press, New York, 1964, p. vii. See also D. Bidney, *Theoretical anthropology*, Columbia University Press, New York, 1953, p. 248, and J. Beattie, 'A. R. Radcliffe-Brown', in Raison (ed.), op. cit., p. 180.

[3] Frobenius's second expedition was financed not only by the German Colonial Office, but also by the Rudolph-Virchow Stiftung and the Berlin and Leipzig Anthropological and Geographical Museums.

exhibits for them. Thus Frobenius's archaeological methods were, of necessity, often those of a 'collector' rather than of an archaeological scholar.

It is important, however, to see the very real inadequacies of Frobenius's method in their historical context. His first three expeditions began in 1904, 1907 and 1910 respectively, long before the rise of Functionalism with its insistence on fieldwork. At this time most anthropologists were content with second-hand information, and their common practice was to compile and collate notes and observations on 'primitive' peoples which they had received from missionaries and other travellers.[1] Frobenius's earliest works, too, were based on such data and on the study of museum collections.[2] But from the first Frobenius recognized the importance of first-hand observation, and at the earliest opportunity he went into the field. Whatever the defects of his method, the fact that he carried out fieldwork in Africa at all in 1904 and 1907 deserves credit and shows considerable originality of thought. His determination, as early as 1910, to carry out archaeological excavation in Black Africa shows even greater independence of mind. At the beginning of *The Voice of Africa*, Frobenius quotes a German newspaper of 1891 which shows the climate of opinion with which he had to contend. It reads:

> Before the introduction of a genuine faith and a higher standard of culture by the Arabs, the natives had neither political organisation[!] nor strictly spoken, any religion[!] nor any industrial development[!]
>
> Therefore it is necessary in examining the pre-Mahommedan condition of the Negro races to confine ourselves to the description of their crude fetishism, their brutal, and often cannibal customs, their vulgar and repulsive idols and their squalid homes.
>
> If the soil of Africa is turned up today by the colonist's ploughshare, no ancient weapon will lie in the furrow, if the virgin soil be cut by a canal, its excavation will reveal no ancient tomb, and if the axe effects a clearing in the primaeval forests, it will nowhere ring upon the foundations of an old-world palace. Africa is poorer

---

[1] Richards, op. cit., p. 189.
[2] For example, Frobenius's 'Der kameruner Schiffschnabel und seine Motive' in *Nova Acta, Abhandlungen der Kaiserlichen Leopoldinisch—carolinischen Deutschen Akademie der Naturforscher*, 70, 1, 1897 was composed in this way.

in recorded history than can be imagined. 'Black Africa' is a continent which has nor history, nor mystery![1]

It should be emphasized that the ideas expressed in the article quoted do not represent the idiosyncratic vagaries of an individual journalist, but rather a body of opinion in Germany and elsewhere which had been promoted, in considerable measure, by the philosopher Hegel. Hegel's *Philosophy of History*, read by generations of students—both philosophers and historians—was perhaps one of the crucial works in establishing in the minds of the educated classes Africa's reputation as the continent with no history.

Africa, in fact, was not even discussed in the main body of *The Philosophy of History*. It was summarily dismissed from consideration in the introduction. However, before dismissing Africa completely, Hegel found time to observe that the Negroes' consciousness was

> incapable of contemplating any objective entity such as God or Law . . . Nothing remotely human is to be found in their [the Negroes'] character. Extensive reports by missionaries confirm this and Mohammedanism seems to be the only thing which can, in some measure, bring them nearer to a civilized condition.[2]

Hegel repeated a quantity of hearsay, including the following:

> Polygamy among the Negroes generally has the purpose of producing as many children as possible who can then, one and all, be sold as slaves, and often one hears naive remarks such as that of a Negro in London who lamented that he was now a really poor man as he had already sold all his relatives . . . Their condition is capable of neither development nor education. As we see them today, so they have always been.[3]

[1] Quoted in *The voice of Africa* (abbreviation VA.), trans. Rudolph Blind, 2 vols., Hutchinson, London, 1913, I, p. 1 (Frobenius's exclamation marks). This is the English translation *of the first two volumes only* of the German popular edition of *Und Afrika sprach . . .*, Volksausgabe, Vita, Deutsches Verlagshaus, Berlin-Charlottenburg, 1912–13. Most of my other quotations are translated by myself from the German *scholarly edition* in 3 vols. (Wissenschaftlich erweiterte Ausgabe) (abbreviation UAS) of the same publisher. This has been necessary because the English version is incomplete. Apart from one short extract, the whole of the third volume is missing.

[2] G. W. F. Hegel, *Die Philosophie der Geschichte* (abbreviation PG.), Reclam Verlag, Stuttgart, 1961, p. 155.

[3] PG., pp. 159, 162.

He concludes:

> We now leave Africa never to mention it again. For it is not a
> historical continent, it shows neither change nor development, and
> whatever may have happened there (that is in North Africa)
> belongs to the world of Asia and of Europe.[1]

We can thus see that Frobenius's determination to study pre-
Islamic or non-Islamic civilizations in Black Africa was a spirited
challenge to the conception of Africa as the 'continent with no history', which, owing to the enormous prestige and influence of Hegel,
had become so deeply ingrained as to be axiomatic in post-Hegelian
Germany.[2] (Heinrich Barth[3] constitutes only a partial exception to
this statement, for he limited his concern with African history to
those areas which had been profoundly influenced by Islam, and
which, presumably, even Hegel would concede had been 'in some
measure' brought nearer to 'a civilized condition'.)

As we have seen, it is Frobenius's attempt to demolish the Hegelian stereotype of Africa, and to assert the value of indigenous Black
African culture, which has won him the undying gratitude of Senghor
and of certain other writers of the Négritude school.[4] However, we
should not allow Frobenius's merits in this respect to blind us to his
short-comings. For Senghor, it seems, Frobenius's works have
become 'sacred books' in the all too literal sense of being beyond
criticism. The impression conveyed by Senghor is that, since Frobenius placed a high value on Black African culture, therefore everything he said about it must be correct, and the methods by which
he obtained his data must also be impeccable. Whatever Senghor's
generation may have felt about Frobenius, the quasi-veneration in
which Senghor apparently still holds him is of service neither to
Frobenius nor to scholarship. It may, and probably does, repel

[1] PG., p. 163.
[2] It is possible that Frobenius's unreasoning hostility towards Islam is derived
from an over-reaction against the Hegelian belief in Islam as the only civilizing
influence in Africa. For Frobenius's attitude see VA., II, p. 382. 'Oh, how I
loathe these sons of Mecca who have torn to tatters, suppressed, choked and
annihilated so much between Byzantium and Atlantis.' See also VA., II, p. 359.
[3] H. Barth, *Reisen und Entdeckungen in Nord-und Central-Afrika in den
Jahren 1849 bis 1855. Tagebuch seiner im Auftrag der britischen Regierung unter-
nommenen Reise*, 4 vols., J. Perthes, Gotha, 1857–8.
[4] For Frobenius's influence on Aimé Césaire see below.

younger generations of Africans. Indeed, Yambo Ouologuem's somewhat scurrilous satire on an ethnographer transparently named 'Fritz Schrobenius' is probably an example of this reaction.[1]

Senghor ignores the extent to which Frobenius was a man of his day and shared its colonialist assumptions—at least during the time of his earlier expeditions. As I shall show, Frobenius's main interest was in culture, not in race conceived in biological terms. He was not a racialist in the sense of believing in the innate superiority of one race over the others. His occasional contemptuous remarks about Africans are confined to his earlier works; and it is evident that they stem from attitudes which he acquired before leaving Europe, and which he gradually discarded as his work in Africa progressed. That Frobenius imbibed certain of the prejudices of his day is in no way surprising. The significant fact is that he later came to reject them. However, the African whose only knowledge of Frobenius is through Senghor's eulogies of him, and who has thought of him as a vindicator of Black African culture, will be a little disconcerted by some of his remarks. For example, though Frobenius admired the mythology of the Yoruba, his attitude to the people themselves is somewhat contemptuous.

> The life-edifice, world-view and mythology of the Yorubans are spacious, lofty and profound, however unsympathetic, even to repulsiveness may be their character. [2]

Of the Jukun, he writes:

> They went down the swift road to decadence to which all nations and tribes are doomed in the regions of the tropics unless they receive a strong influx from other lands;[3]

and on the state of Liberia:

> Considered as a state, Liberia is such a miserable and imperfect object, such a wretched caricature of our northern cultural circumstances, that it seems completely unworthy of playing any role as a sovereign and administrative power alongside the European colonizing powers. It will be a good thing for Europe, and for this

---

[1] Yambo Ouologuem, *Le devoir de violence*, Editions du Seuil, Paris, 1968, pp. 102–10.
[2] VA., I, pp. 186–7.
[3] VA., II, p. 658.

rich land [Liberia], if the great powers bring about a re-ordering of the state of affairs as soon as possible.[1]

The attitudes expressed in the first two quotations were, as I have said, soon discarded and need concern us no further. But the last quotation shows an attitude that was persistent. Whatever Frobenius may have thought about African culture, there is no indication that he thought that Africans had any right to political independence, or that he doubted that Europeans had a perfect right to colonize Africa. Even his most passionate pleas on behalf of the 'Ethiopians' (i.e. Black African peoples living in acephalous societies) are an attack on *Indirect Rule*, not on colonial rule as such. Frobenius argues that the policy of ruling small so-called 'pagan' tribes through 'state-forming' peoples should be discontinued. He says that such state-forming peoples

> are not the primary producers of crops, on the contrary, they have, for many generations, by their slave-raids deprived the smaller tribes of their manpower. . . . As I now lay this work in the hands of the directors of our colonial task I should like to emphasize the remarkable capacity for work, industry, farming skill, and productive powers of the smaller Ethiopian tribes everywhere in the Sudan, and thus, also, in North Cameroon and North Togo. . . . If we take these able people under our leadership we shall, of course, have to treat them in a way different from that in which they have been treated by the Mohammedan semi-barbarians [i.e. the state-forming peoples].[2]

Frobenius goes on to suggest that the 'Ethiopians' should be re-settled in fertile agricultural areas and given such training as may be necessary

> to make these people an essential part of our valuable and productive colonial empire since they are the most significant labour force of our African colonies.[3]

[1] Frobenius, *Auf dem Weg nach Atlantis. Bericht über den Verlauf der zweiten Reiseperiode der DIAFE in den Jahren 1908–1910* (abbreviation AWA.), Vita, Deutsches Verlagshaus, Berlin-Charlottenburg, 1911, p. 110. (For 're-ordering of the state of affairs' we may, judging from the context, read 'annexation of Liberia by Britain (through Sierra Leone) and France (through Senegal)'.)
[2] UAS., III, pp. 5–6.
[3] UAS., loc. cit.

Frobenius, Senghor and the Image of Africa

It is thus clear that, whatever may be Frobenius's affection for the 'Ethiopians', he nevertheless regards them from the point of view of their potential usefulness to the colonial power. One could read everything Senghor has ever written about Frobenius without being made to realize this fact, and the impression is created that Senghor is so captivated by Frobenius's interest in African culture as to deliberately ignore the colonialist presuppositions with which it is linked. In actual fact, this impression is almost certainly false. It seems, rather, that Senghor has not read *Und Afrika sprach . . .*, vol. III (quoted above), in which these presuppositions are clearly stated, and that his ignorance of them is genuine rather than feigned.[1]

* * *

Although it seems that it is mainly Frobenius's historical approach and his defective field methods that have antagonized anthropologists and archaeologists, there is another aspect of his thought which they would doubtless find repellent if they were more fully aware of it. This is the rigidly schematic, and at the same time mythopoeic, character of Frobenius's explanations. Yet it is precisely their mythopoeic character which has excited the enthusiasm of such writers as Senghor and Suzanne Césaire.[2] Senghor is interested solely in Frobenius's overall interpretation of African culture. Unlike the anthropologists he is not interested in checking Frobenius's empirical data or the methods by which they were obtained. Nor is he concerned with whether Frobenius's conclusions can, in fact, validly be inferred from the empirical data; he is concerned with projecting an image of African culture. While Frobenius's empirical data were, I believe, more accurate than his methods would lead one to expect, his conclusions (as I hope to show in this essay) did not follow from his observations, but were strongly influenced by his reaction to conditions in Germany after the First World War—conditions which had nothing to do with Africa. If this is so, it seems that Senghor risks accepting an interpretation of African culture, which is in itself invalid, because it seems to offer an ideology for Black African nationalism. In this case Frobenius's interpretation has the political

[1] If Senghor has not read this volume, his identification of 'Ethiopian' with 'Black African' as distinct from 'non-state-forming Black African' is also understandable.

[2] S. Césaire, 'Leo Frobénius et le problème des civilisations', *Tropiques*, 1, avril 1941, pp. 27-4.

314

status of a 'useful lie'. On the other hand, as we have just seen, Frobenius's approach to Ethiopian culture presupposed the existence of the colonial system. Frobenius did not envisage the existence of independent African states (except of Liberia, of which he disapproved). In view of this, it seems extremely unlikely that Frobenius should provide an ideology which would be politically 'useful' to independent African states. In so far as Frobenius's interpretation of African culture has been adopted by Senghor as part of his ideology of nationalism, this interpretation calls for careful examination, not only as to its truth, but as to its usefulness (or otherwise) in the post-independence era.

Frobenius's views on African culture underwent some degree of change and fluctuation in the course of his life. But broadly speaking, he describes it in terms of a number of culture areas, or culture circles, which, in turn, rested upon two basic 'world-views' or attitudes to the world. Frobenius calls these the 'Ethiopian' and the 'Hamitic', and they are seen (in theory at least) as being, like the magnetic poles, opposite yet complementary to each other. However, before Frobenius's conception of the underlying polarity is discussed there are some points concerning the culture areas themselves which need to be clarified.

A number of attacks on these 'culture areas' have been misguided in that Frobenius has been regarded as a racialist on the grounds that he allegedly tried to derive all African culture from outside Africa. This accusation is based on a misunderstanding of where Frobenius's main interest lies. Hegel had believed that Africa represented the world of 'Nature' in its raw state, as opposed to that of culture or 'Spirit'. Frobenius, on the contrary, was interested in Africa as a manifestation of human culture. His concern to show the European and Asian connections of African culture was, in essence, an attempt to show that African culture formed an integral part of human culture as a whole—that Africa was not a 'Dark Continent' cut off from the rest of human culture, not part of the 'realms of Nature' in which, as one modern historian puts it, 'barbarous tribes' perform 'unrewarding gyrations' which may be of interest to the sociologist, but cannot possibly concern the historian.[1] Whatever criticisms one may

[1] H. Trevor-Roper, *The rise of Christian Europe*, Thames and Hudson, London, 1964, p. 9.

315

make on other grounds of culture areas as a general concept, or of the particular culture areas proposed by Frobenius for Africa, they do imply the existence, in Africa, of wider connections and larger cultural affinities than the 'Dark Continent of obscure tribes' theory will admit of. Modern scholarship has been more interested in studying the larger political units than the larger cultural connections, but there seems little doubt as to the existence of the latter.[1]

In *Die unsträflichen Äthiopen* Frobenius classified the culture areas in a way that can be summarized as follows:

(i) *The North African* (Eurafrican or Syrtican) cultural area, based on the Mediterranean, with the Sahara, from the Nile to the Senegal as its hinterland, and exerting an influence southwards into the Sudan.

(ii) *The East African* (Asio-African or Eritrean) culture area based on the Upper Nile and Eritrea, extending through the East African savannah, and stretching southwards to include the Zimbabwe culture. This area Frobenius considered to be under the influence of Asiatic civilizations—from Asia Minor through Egypt and the Red Sea, and from India by sea to the East African coast. While the main cultural interchange was thought of as being in a north/south direction, Frobenius also assumed an east/west connection across the savannah belt.

(iii) *The West African* (*or Atlantic*) culture area—including the Ife and Benin cultures and extending as far as the Congo Basin. This culture was regarded by Frobenius as being archaic, and as having been pushed into its present position by pressures from other culture areas.

Frobenius also lists:

(iv) *The Western Sudanic* culture area, which he describes as being 'the heart of the continent'. But on closer examination it becomes apparent that this area was seen, not as a separate area in its own right, but rather as a cultural crossroads, where currents from the other three areas met and mixed.

If the above divisions are to be regarded as the conclusion of an examination of African cultural history, they were premature, since Frobenius certainly did not amass evidence sufficiently methodically

---

[1] What follows is a summary of (not a verbatim quotation from) UAS., III, p. 48.

to demonstrate the existence of these culture areas. However, if the divisions are taken merely as guidelines for further research they can be regarded as useful. Indeed Frobenius's insistence on the cultural importance of the Niger between Timbuktu and the Niger-Benue confluence should have received more attention.

As has already been mentioned, Frobenius claimed to perceive, underlying the culture areas, a more fundamental division of African humanity into two attitudes to life or 'world-views'—the 'Hamitic' and the 'Ethiopian'. It is worth noting that the categories of Hamitic and Ethiopian are for Frobenius not absolute but relative. For example, the Nupe are said to be 'more Ethiopian' than the Hausa, but it is implied that they are less Ethiopian than the Tiv.[1] The rural Hausa are described as lacking some of the Hamitic characteristics displayed by the urban Hausa.[2] Nonetheless, in spite of this qualification, Frobenius's delineation of the 'Hamitic' and 'Ethiopian' characteristics will seem, to most people, arbitrary to the point of being fantastic. It is no doubt this kind of schematism which has caused some scholars to dismiss Frobenius's work as being unworthy of serious attention. We may tabulate a few of the characteristics of the contrasting cultures as shown on page 318.

It will be observed that contrast 5 confuses three entirely different phenomena. Matrilineality has obviously been confused with a dominant position of women in society, although there is no necessary connection between the two. Both have been arbitrarily associated with a high regard for virginity in the bride, though this, again, is not necessarily connected with either. An examination of the context of this contrast will be instructive. Frobenius writes:

and it is in correspondence with the original Hamitic cultural forms of Africa, if even today in a typically Hamitic–Chthonic culture of Europe (for example in France), the bride, however much she may have been corrupted at the intellectual level, at the physical level brings an intact hymen into the marriage, and if society condones the occasional extra-marital adventures of married

---

[1] Frobenius, *Atlantis. Volksmärchen und Volksdichtungen Afrikas* (abbreviation AVV.), 12 vols., Eugen Diederichs, Jena, 1921–8, IX, p. 9. (The title of vol. IX is *Volkserzählungen und Volksdichtungen aus dem Zentral-Sudan*.)

[2] Frobenius, *Erlebte Erdteile; Ergebnisse eines deutschen Forscherlebens* (abbreviation EE.), 7 vols., Frankfurter Societätsdruckerei, Frankfurt, 1925–9, IV, pp. 341–2.

HAMITIC	ETHIOPIAN
1. 'Civilization of the animal'.[1]	'Civilization of the plant'.[2]
2. The 'cave-feeling', i.e. the sense of living within a finite enclosed world. (The attitude of a people who graze their flocks within certain definite boundaries, but whose world has no fixed centre.)[3]	The 'space-feeling', i.e. a sense of the infinity of space and time. (The outlook of a people whose gaze moves outwards from a fixed centre but is limited by no external boundary.)[3]
3. Society involving a rigid caste system, i.e. the individual remains in the caste into which he is born.[3]	Society involving a fluid age-grade system, i.e. the individual progresses through the various age-grades towards seniority.[3]
4. The ('matriarchal') horde as a social unit.[3]	The ('patriarchal') clan as a social unit.[3]
5. 'Matriarchy', i.e. the wife is a virgin at marriage, but is unfaithful afterwards, and the children belong to her.[4]	'Patriarchy', i.e. the wife may not be a virgin at marriage, but is faithful afterwards, and the children belong to the husband's clan.[4]
6. 'Magic', i.e. the attempt to dominate nature by mechanical means such as spells, incantations *or* scientific devices.[5]	'Mysticism', i.e. being in union with Nature, and therefore not trying to dominate her from outside.[6]
7. '*Tatsachensinn*'—a sense of facts.[7]	'*Wirlichkeitssinn*'—a sense of reality or capacity for '*Ergriffenheit*'—an almost untranslatable expression meaning (approximately) total absorption of the whole personality in an experience or 'the gift of emotional spontaneity'.[7]
8. The French and the Anglo-Saxons have the above qualities and are 'Hamitic' in outlook.[8]	The Germans and the Russians have the above qualities and are 'Ethiopian' in outlook.[9]

(Footnotes on p. 319)

women; if the husband is expected to carry the shopping bag to the market in the morning . . . [and so forth].[1]

The use of the term 'original' with reference to the Hamitic cultural forms of Africa hints that these stem from a reconstructed past rather than from anything which is observable in the present. It seems as if Frobenius has derived this whole contrast not from the observation of African society but from his own impression of the behaviour of *French* married women as compared with German. An impression, incidentally, which may be based on literature rather than on social observation.

Contrast 6 is also instructive. It is noticeable that science and magic are equated as both being impious ways of dominating nature. In connection with the idea of dominating the environment, Frobenius says of the Hamites, that their way of life shows

an unheard-of heightening of all those ideas and predispositions which are desirable for 'the struggle for existence' and which condition the nature of their physical existence. . . . 'Ergriffenheit' in the deeper sense is unknown to Hamitic culture. Even those people who have adopted Islam, that is to say, have accepted a religion, know religion only as the sum total of magical formulae and measures [which have to be taken] . . . For Hamitic culture, nothing exists except the secular life governed by the laws of the physical universe.[2]

[1] UnA., p. 79.
[2] KA., p. 240.

Footnotes to table

[1] Frobenius, *Kulturgeschichte Afrikas; prolegomena zu einer historischen Gestaltlehre* (abbreviation KA.), Phaidon Verlag, Frankfurt, 1933, p. 238.

[2] KA., p. 234.

[3] Frobenius, *Das unbekannte Afrika* (abbreviation UnA.), Beck, Munich, 1923, p. 70. See also EE., IV, p. 106.

[4] UnA., p. 79.

[5] KA., pp. 296, 377.

[6] UAS., III, p. 134; KA., pp. 296, 377.

[7] KA., pp. 123, 237-8, 296, 377. See also Frobenius, *Schicksalskunde* (abbreviation Sch.), Frobenius-Institut, Weimar, 1938, p. 162-3.

[8] Sch., p. 163; UnA., p. 79.

[9] Frobenius, *Vom Kulturreich des Festlandes* (abbreviation KF.), Wegweiser Verlag, Berlin, 1923, p. 118.

The fact that Frobenius quotes the expression 'struggle for existence' in English, thus making it an overt reference to Darwin, indicates that this passage is a discussion, in scarcely veiled terms, of the scientific outlook of Western Europe. The 'Ethiopian' values in contrasts 6 and 7 (nature mysticism, and the stress on extra-rational values) are all in the main stream of the German romantic tradition. This is made more apparent by some passages from *Kulturgeschichte Afrikas* (which, incidentally, may help to clarify contrast 7 between 'sense of fact' and 'sense of reality'). Man, Frobenius says,

> can fully comprehend the world of facts . . . but a sense of reality means the ability to abandon oneself totally to the essence of phenomena, that is to say, to abandon oneself, not to the facts, but to the reality underlying them.[1]

As the language and ideas of the quotation are very German, and are probably still obscure to the English-speaking reader, I will try further explanation. Frobenius is contrasting 'the world of facts' which can be fully 'grasped' or 'comprehended' by the rational intellect with 'the world of reality'. By 'reality' he means a 'meta-physical' or 'ultimate' reality which may 'underlie' the facts or 'express itself through' them but which, itself, is not identical with them. This 'reality' cannot be 'comprehended' or 'grasped' by the intellect but can be *experienced* in mystical self-abandonment to it. Exact translation of the quotation has been made difficult by the fact that the German word *begreifen*, to comprehend, or grasp intellectually, has the same basic root as *ergriffen zu sein* which I have had to translate as 'abandon oneself to', but which literally means 'to be grasped' or 'to be seized'. Thus the contrast between the (Hamitic) 'sense of fact' and the (Ethiopian) 'sense of reality' is a contrast between 'grasping' and 'being grasped' or between 'coming to grips with' the facts and 'being held in the grip of' reality. In *Kulturgeschichte Afrikas* Frobenius goes on to say:

> Our own culture, German culture, is one of mysticism, but the life-feeling of the Western peoples [the French and the Anglo-Saxons] was stronger and determined the spirit of the age [of Enlightenment]. . . . We came under the domination of a way of thinking which was originally alien to us, that of . . . rationalism and eventually of materialism. In the nineteenth century we were

[1] KA., p. 25.

playing the part of the Western cultures, but we were only *playing* it . . . [After the first World War] Germany again experienced the 'Ergriffenheit' which corresponds to the inner nature of her being.[1]

It is thus clear from the outset that *Kulturgeschichte Afrikas* is, in part at least, an attempt to reassert 'German mysticism' against what Frobenius regards as French cultural domination of Germany, and there is a danger that the question of whether 'Hamitic' culture is really similar to French culture, and 'Ethiopian' culture to German culture, will be begged rather than answered.

In theory, Frobenius believed that 'Hamitic' and 'Ethiopian' values were complementary to each other, and both necessary to achieve the higher synthesis of the human spirit;[2] in practice, however, the terms which he applies to the Hamites are almost always derogatory:

A large number of their [the Hamites'] customs which are of horrifying cruelty have been known since the days of Herodotus and Agartharcides.[3]

As we have already seen, their women are 'fickle', and as well as being callous and materialistic they are elsewhere described as superficial. All these vices are traditionally attributed to the French by the Germans. It is noteworthy that the record of Frobenius's second expedition (1907–9) which deals with the state-forming peoples of the Niger bend, whom he would class as Hamitic, does not support the image of fickleness and callousness created in his later works. On the contrary their horsemen and bards appear in a romantic aura and are compared to the knights of chivalry and the Minnesänger.[4] We

---

[1] KA., p. 30.
[2] EE., IV, p. 220.
[3] KA., p. 240. See also UAS., III, p. 508: 'For the state-forming peoples are, in general, inferior to the Ethiopians in inner worth. They are much less useful, they are lazier, more deceitful and more fawning [than the Ethiopians].'
[4] KA., p. 240. For Frobenius's earlier high evaluation of the 'Hamites' see particularly the earlier scholarly (as distinct from 'popular') reports, e.g. 'Ethnologische Ergebnisse der zweiten Reiseperiode der DIAFE', Sonderdruck der *Zeitschrift für Ethnologie*, Heft 6, 1909, and 'Kulturtypen aus dem Westsudan; Auszüge aus den Ergebnissen der zweiten deutschen innerafrikanischen Forschungsexpedition nebst einem Anhang über Kulturzonen und Kulturforschung in Afrika', Ergänzungsheft Nr. 166, zu *Petermanns Mitteilungen*, Justus Perthes, Gotha, 1910.

recall that the French and Anglo-Saxons (with whom the Hamites are equated) were Germany's enemies in the First World War; and an examination of Frobenius's works shows that the whole system of Hamitic/Ethiopian contrasts in its crude form was formulated after 1918. Earlier, both the Hamites and the Ethiopians had appeared in a favourable light.

It thus becomes clear that most of what Frobenius has to say about the Hamites after 1918 is based on German resentment of the Anglo-French victory in Europe rather than on empirical observation of any actually existing African people. Although Frobenius did carry out field observations of the peoples he describes as Hamitic, these observations often do not tally with his generalizations, which at least after 1918 are constantly distorted by his hostility to the French. In other words, Frobenius's whole conception of the Hamitic/Ethiopian opposition is largely a projection of German attitudes towards France.

*　　*　　*

At this point, many readers familiar with the relevant literature may feel surprised at my portrayal of Frobenius as an anti-Hamite. For, by and large, the writers who developed the 'Hamitic'/'Ethiopian' scheme (men such as Meinhof, Luschan and Seligman) saw it as a racial dichotomy, between the more light-skinned orthognathous peoples on the one hand, and the more dark-skinned prognathous peoples on the other. They also asserted the innate, racial superiority of the 'Hamites', and tended to credit them with all cultural achievement in Africa.

Now it is true that Frobenius did follow these writers in some minor respects. Thus he largely followed Meinhof and Luschan in allocating particular peoples to one side or other of the dichotomy, for example, in classifying the Hottentots as Hamitic, and also in associating pastoralism with 'Hamites'.[1]

In other respects, however, his approach was totally different. First of all, he saw the dichotomy in cultural rather than racial terms. In his own words

---

[1] For cattle raising as a characteristic of the Hamites see C. G. Seligman, *The races of Africa* (first published 1930), 3rd edition, Oxford University Press, London, 1957, p. 140. For classing of Hottentots see Frobenius, *Erythräa: Länder und Zeiten des heiligen Königsmords*, Atlantis Verlag, Berlin and Zurich, 1931, p. 37.

Now it must be once more emphatically stressed; that the classification which I advance in what follows is a *cultural* classification. It is not based on anthropological classifications according to race.[1]

Secondly, if we compare his views with those of Meinhof and Luschan,[2] we find a radical difference in the valuation of the 'Hamitic'. Luschan, for instance, went to the extreme of asserting the superior value of Hamitic culture even when he could find no specific cultural achievement attributable to a given Hamitic people. Thus when he discussed the Hima, whom he describes as 'without a doubt the tallest people of the earth', he goes on to say that when two races mix

> *the better language, the better grammar, the better religion, and, in so far as there is any question of writing, the better script, will prevail.*[3]

The Hima live in close contact with what Luschan describes as 'their Bantu subjects'. Therefore, in accordance with the rule just propounded,

> we should have expected [the Hima] to preserve their original language. But unfortunately that is not the case, and it appears that they now universally speak the language of their Bantu subjects, from whom, however, they are physically very different.[4]

According to Luschan's own argument, this should prove that the Hima culture was, in fact, not superior to that of their 'Bantu subjects'; but he nowhere accepts this conclusion. On the contrary, his argument runs that since the Hima are orthognathous and taller 'even than the Scots', we should expect them to preserve their own original language[5] and impose it on their subjects. Since this is not the case, we are to conclude merely that the Hima *ought to have imposed* their Hamitic language on their 'Bantu subjects'.

The absurdity of the above argument is too obvious to merit further discussion. But it is a good example of the kind of racialist attitude with which the use of the term 'Hamitic' is often associated.

---

[1] UAS., III, p. 46.
[2] C. Meinhof, *Die Sprachen der Hamiten*, nebst einer Beigabe *Hamitische Typen* von Felix von Luschan, Friedrichsen, Hamburg, 1912.
[3] Meinhof and Luschan, op. cit., p. 247.
[4] Ibid., p. 251.
[5] Ibid., loc. cit.

Moreover Luschan elaborated these beliefs by claiming that the Hamitic races played a civilizing role in Africa similar to that allegedly played by the Nordic races in Europe. He even goes so far as to suggest that the Nordic races and the Hamites are in some way ethnically related, while Southern Europeans, like the Bantu, are to him an object of scorn. 'Of course,' he writes with heavy irony,

> in spite of their small stature, one *could* have said that these dwarfishly small Southern Europeans [viz. the Sicilians] belong to the same group as that to which we assign the North Africans and the North Europeans. . . . but at the same time this was just a supposition, and now it can be said in general terms that the North African Hamites appear to be in some way physically related to the tall dolichocephalic Northern Europeans.[1]

Now if we compare Luschan's scheme with Frobenius's we see that Luschan, equating the Hamites with the 'Nordic' races, thinks they are superior. Frobenius, on the other hand equates the Hamites with the Southern and Western Europeans (in his terms the French) and so thinks them *inferior;* whereas the 'Ethiopians' (in Luschan's terms 'the Bantu and Negroes') are equated by Frobenius with the Germans and are superior. Since the Germans are generally regarded as a branch of the Nordic race, it is now apparent that Frobenius has merely applied the Luschan racial theory to culture and stood it on its head. The relationship of Frobenius's scheme to Luschan's can be tabulated as follows:

LUSCHAN

Hamites	= *Nordic races*	+ *value*
	(*including Germans*)	
Negroes	= Southern Europeans	− value

FROBENIUS

Hamitic culture	= Southern European culture	− value
	(including French)	
Ethiopian culture	= *German culture*	+ *value*

[1] Ibid., p. 246.

Frobenius, Senghor and the Image of Africa

The determining factor in each scheme is Nordic race/German culture. Whichever African people (or culture) is associated with these is preferred.

As has been shown, the whole Hamitic/Ethiopian opposition, as propounded by Frobenius, was based, not on empirical observation in Africa, but on what he, as a German, felt about France. (Frobenius did, of course, make empirical observations in Africa, but these often did not support his major hypotheses.) Since the Hamitic/Ethiopian system was merely a projection on to Africa of European antagonisms, anthropologists were, as we have seen, right to dismiss it. It is, in itself, irrelevant to African studies, but it has gained adventitious relevance to them in that, having been enthusiastically adopted by Senghor, it now has a place in the history of African thought.

While it is not surprising that Senghor should admire Frobenius, because of the interest he showed in Black African culture, it seems at first a little surprising that he should accept every detail of Frobenius's conception of what is 'Hamitic' or 'Ethiopian', including the parallels with French and German culture respectively. Senghor quotes enthusiastically from Frobenius's *Schicksalskunde*:

> The West created English realism and French rationalism.... There is an exact parallel with the corresponding cultures in Africa, a sense of the facts in the French, British, and Hamitic cultures—*a sense of the real in the German and Ethiopian cultures.*[1]

Senghor goes on to comment:

> Frobenius had previously placed North American 'materialism' in the former group, and Russian 'mysticism' in the latter.[2]

Elsewhere in *Schicksalskunde* Frobenius had said:

> The catastrophes of the last decades . . . have revealed the Orient as the bearer of a sense of reality with the emphasis on time and the Occident as that of a space-conscious sense of the facts. The crest of the Vosges mountains can be described as the boundary demarcating the spatial distribution areas of these cultural attitudes.[3]

[1] Senghor, AG., p. 12. See also Senghor, *Liberté I. Négritude et humanisme* (abbreviation L.), Editions du Seuil, Paris, 1964, p. 84 (Senghor's italics).
[2] Senghor, AG., p. 12.
[3] Sch., p. 163.

Thus, Frobenius's system of oppositions is not confined to Africa and Europe, as might have appeared from the terms French/ Hamitic and German/Ethiopian, but is universal. As appears from his quotations from *Schicksalskunde,* one of the features of his system which attracts Senghor is that it enables him to fit the Hamitic/ Ethiopian opposition into what appears to be a universal scheme, and thus assign a definite place to Black African culture in 'la civilisation humaine'.

The contrasts between 'Hamitic' and 'Ethiopian' culture in which Senghor is most interested are those which I have numbered 6 and 7 on my table—that is to say, 'Hamitic sense of the facts' versus 'Ethiopian mysticism and communion with nature'. In *Le message de Goethe aux nègres nouveaux* (1949), speaking of the German and of the Negro soul, Senghor wrote:

> Were they not both born of *Ethiopian culture* which means 'self-abandonment', the gift of emotional spontaneity, a sense of reality, while *Hamitic culture*, to which Western rationalism is related, means the will to dominate, the gift of invention, a sense of the facts?
>
> Leo Frobenius had enlisted us in a new *Sturm und Drang*, had led us to Goethe . . . Like the Rebel . . . we were in revolt against order, against the values of the West, and especially against Reason. . . . Successors to Prometheus, ebony-faced Fausts, we opposed to the platitudes of reason the lofty tree-tops of our forests . . .[1]

The comparison with the *Sturm und Drang* movement, and the emphasis on the revolt against reason, clearly show that Senghor recognized Frobenius's thought as being moulded by the Romantic tradition, and that he quite consciously placed himself in this tradition.

It now becomes clearer why he should so willingly accept the Hamitic/Ethiopian opposition which, as has been shown, has more to do with the European Romantic tradition than with empirical observation in Africa. The Romantic period in Germany was largely the period of the Napoleonic Wars. German national self-consciousness as expressed for example in Fichte's *Reden an die deutsche Nation*, 1808, was forged during the Napoleonic occupation of

---

[1] Senghor, L., p. 84.

Frobenius, Senghor and the Image of Africa

Germany, and as a reaction against it. Indeed, a number of the German Romantic poets were actively engaged in the Wars of Liberation which eventually put an end to the French occupation.[1] As Napoleon, in the German popular mind, was regarded as an heir of the French Revolution, which had enthroned 'universal Reason' in the place of God, the claim that there was a 'universal Reason' had become associated with Napoleon's imperialism. Consequently in the German Romantic ideology 'Reason', generally interpreted as rationalist materialism and godlessness, was identified with France; its claim to universality, with French imperialism; while feeling or 'intuition' and devotion to 'inward spiritual values' (if not to orthodox religion) were identified with German nationalism in revolt or in struggle against France.[2] What could be more natural than that Senghor, a twentieth-century African nationalist, also in revolt against a 'universal' or at least cosmopolitan French empire, should feel drawn to the stereotypes evolved by emergent German nationalism of the previous century? And what could be more opportune to Senghor, than to discover that Frobenius had already equated 'Ethiopian' with German values?

One can understand Senghor's immediate sympathy with German Romantic thought, and his gratitude to Frobenius for having provided him with a useful precedent in ascribing Romantic values to Black African civilization; but the uncritical way in which he has placed himself in the European Romantic tradition gives rise to doubts. Clearly, German nationalism and African nationalism must have *something* in common; otherwise it would be meaningless to describe both as 'nationalism'. But can the details of Frobenius's scheme apply to modern Africa? The important feature which German nationalism and Senghor's brand of African nationalism have in common is that they both grew up in revolt against French imperialism. It is surely obvious that the peoples whom Frobenius describes

---

[1] For example Karl Theodor Körner took part in the wars and was killed in 1813. Friedrich de la Motte Fouqué, who despite the French-sounding name, derived from his probably Norman extraction, was one of the leading figures in the German Romantic movement, took part in the Wars of Liberation, was decorated and reached the rank of major.

[2] See, for example, Thomas Mann, *Betrachtungen eines Unpolitischen* (abbreviation BeU.), in the Stockholmer Gesamtausgabe der Werke von Thomas Mann, S. Fischer Verlag, Frankfurt, 1956. The *Betrachtungen* were written during the First World War as an attempt on the part of the writer to clarify and 'sum up' the 'Germanness' of German culture.

327

as 'Hamitic' are *also* in revolt against French (or British) imperialism, and that their emergent nationalism has *also* been forged in this struggle; it is therefore absurd to lump these peoples together with the French—the very enemy against whom they are revolting. Frobenius himself supported the German colonial effort in Africa. He did not recognize European imperialism in Africa as an evil, but was opposed only to Indirect Rule. Consequently, instead of choosing European imperialism as the negative pole of his opposition within Africa, he was bound to choose some African population group, and he assigned to the Hamites the villain's role, in which, in Europe, he had cast the French. This is a direct result of the fact that Frobenius chose to ignore the colonial situation in Africa; that is, he ignored the fact that, whereas, in Europe, the struggle between France and Germany is two-sided, the African situation was determined by the presence of a third party, the colonial power, against whom *both* 'Hamites' *and* 'Ethiopians' had to contend. One might expect Senghor to see this, and to realize that, even if he wished to accept the values which Frobenius describes as German and Ethiopian, the assignment of the 'French' role to the Hamites did not follow from this, but was merely a reflection of the Europe-based nature of Frobenius's whole scheme, and of the fact that he entirely omitted the colonial powers from his description of African culture.

*　　*　　*

There is another aspect of Frobenius's thought stemming from the Romantic tradition which Senghor seems to have accepted without questioning its implications. Frobenius attributed the characteristics which he described as 'Ethiopian', not to Black African societies in general, but to non-state-forming Black African societies. Black peoples such as the Mandingo and Hausa, who had well-developed states, are classified by Frobenius as 'Hamitic'. Senghor obviously failed to realize this, since he thinks of all Black African civilizations as being 'Ethiopian'.[1] One might at first wonder why, in Frobenius's mind, the non-state-forming Ethiopians should be linked with the

---

[1] AG., p. 11. See also Senghor's allegation that 'magic is not, properly speaking, Negro-African. Frobenius describes it as essentially characteristic of Hamitic culture.' (L., p. 74.) It is obvious from this statement that Senghor misunderstands Frobenius and supposes him to identify 'Hamitic' with 'white [North] African' and 'Ethiopian' with 'Black African'.

Frobenius, Senghor and the Image of Africa

Germans, who, after 1871, had a powerful and unified state. The link between the two peoples is found in the idea of the 'organic' society, which was very prominent in German neo-romantic thought. According to this idea the good society was an 'organic' whole, an 'organism' which had grown up in the course of history. It was argued by German nationalists that the German Empire of 1871 was such a state. The German idea of the 'organic' state was contrasted with the state as an 'organization', i.e. something which is artificially planned. The French democratic state, planned in accordance with the dictates of 'Reason', was regarded as the archetype of the state as 'organization'. America, with its carefully drawn up constitution, was regarded as another such state. Frobenius himself condemns the structure of the post-1918 German state in the following terms:

> Everything was 'organized', and only a few people recognized that all these [new] institutions, which were being zealously fostered both in the state and in private life, no longer represented anything organic, but were symptoms of mechanization. Most typical of all was the constitution which had been 'made' in Weimar.[1]

('Made' has been put in inverted commas by Frobenius to stress the idea that the Weimar constitution was 'made' instead of having 'grown'.)

It is easy to see that the ideal of the 'organic' state in the European context would necessarily be a conservative ideal. Any attempt to change the status quo (once national independence (or unity) had been established) was necessarily associated with definite concrete demands, and thus with 'planning', and so was the antithesis of the ideal of 'organic growth'. The anti-democratic nature of the ideal was made particularly explicit by the German writer Thomas Mann in his book *Betrachtungen eines Unpolitischen*, written during the First World War as a defence of German cultural values. 'An organism', he says with reference to the state, 'is something more than the sum of its parts.'[2] It follows that 'the will of the nation' is not identical with that of its individual citizens added together, and

---

[1] Sch., p. 171.
[2] BeU., p. 272.

consequently one cannot ascertain the 'will of the nation' by consulting the citizens and counting their votes.[1] So democratic government (based on vote-counting) is *by definition* inappropriate to the 'organic state' as this idea was understood in Europe. It is therefore not surprising to find that nineteenth-century Russian and early twentieth-century German nationalists often alleged that the autocratic (or the authoritarian) state was ideally suited to the Russian people (or the German people—as the case might be). The autocratic form of the Russian state (or the authoritarian form of the German state) was commonly defended, not only on the grounds that it was 'organic', but also on the grounds that the Russian (or German) people were an 'inward' or 'spiritual' people, who needed to be freed from the 'burden' of government so that they could devote themselves to their 'inward and spiritual' values.[2] (The great similarity of the Russian and German views is accounted for by the fact that both Russian and German nationalism grew up initially as a reaction against the Napoleonic invasion of the two countries, and under the influence of Hegel's concept of the 'spirit of the nation'.)

If we consider 'Ethiopian' society as described by Frobenius, we can see that it is indeed 'organic', in being based on the natural unit of the extended family or clan. The mysticism attributed by Frobenius to the Ethiopians corresponds to the 'inward and spiritual' values of the Germans and Russians, and contrasts with the 'materialism' attributed to the French and the Hamites. But here the parallel ends; while the Russian and German 'organic' state was authoritarian and anti-democratic, the Ethiopian societies described by Frobenius are, in essence, anti-authoritarian and democratic. This is necessarily so. For if these peoples had recognized a centralized authority, Frobenius would have classified them as 'Hamites' not as 'Ethiopians'. Frobenius's 'Ethiopians' were able to combine an 'organic' social unit (that is one which has 'grown' naturally, without planning) with democracy, because they were *small-scale* societies, small enough for all adult males to take a part in decision-making. The ideology of Négritude, however, is intended for *large-scale*, modern nation-states in which direct democracy is impracticable.

---

[1] BeU., p. 259.
[2] See Konstantin Aksakov's Memorandum to Alexander II, quoted in N. V. Riasanovsky, *Russia and the West in the teaching of the Slavophils*, Harvard University Press, Cambridge, Mass., 1952, p. 152.

Frobenius, Senghor and the Image of Africa

One wonders how Frobenius's conception of 'Ethiopian' society, as organic yet also democratic, can be taken over by African statesmen such as Senghor into the nationalist ideology of new African nations. In any case, most African states are not 'organic' in the sense of having grown. (The present state of Ethiopia is an exception.) So even if such African states are authoritarian they cannot escape being 'planned' and 'organized'. Such planning is necessary both for economic development and for welding together the disparate elements in the state. In other words, Frobenius's stereotype is by definition unsuited to modern African nation-states.

The authoritarian model of the 'organic' state advanced by Aksakov in Russia, and the early Thomas Mann in Germany, was intended to preserve the status quo in their respective countries at the time of writing. But the status quo in a newly independent African state is the status quo of colonialism, and it can hardly be the desire of African nationalists to preserve it. Since the democratic 'organic' model of Frobenius is not suited to large nation-states, it seems that Senghor has, consciously or unconsciously, adopted the authoritarian and conservative model of the 'organic' state advanced by earlier German and Russian nationalists.

* * *

However, if Frobenius's 'Ethiopian' political model has little relevance to the modern African scene, his 'Ethiopian' values of 'mysticism' and 'participation'—the equivalents of the 'inward spiritual values' of the German and Russian nationalists—do seem to have rather more relevance, albeit of an ideological kind.

In modern Africa, as in earlier Germany and Russia, 'mysticism', 'spiritual values' and 'emotional spontaneity' are invoked in an attempt to assert the claims of a people that is in some way disadvantaged—the disadvantage being foreign occupation, economic backwardness, recent or impending defeat in war,[1] or a combination of these. Now it is obvious that if one wants to assert the value of such disadvantaged peoples or underdeveloped nations, against opposition from well-developed and prosperous states, one must

---

[1] 'Foreign occupation', e.g. of Germany and Russia during the Napoleonic Wars; 'economic backwardness', e.g. of Russia before the Revolution and of African countries; 'recent or impending defeat in war', e.g. of Germany during and after the First World War.

331

ascribe to these materially disadvantaged peoples valuable non-material and intangible qualities, which the prosperous states will be said to lack. Thus the similarity of the 'spiritual' values, ascribed to the Germans, Russians and 'Ethiopians' alike, arises from the tactical situation of an emergent nationalism. It does not necessarily imply that these peoples really have any characteristics in common other than that of being materially disadvantaged; it is merely a reflection of the fact that emergent nationalisms tend, out of sheer tactical necessity, to be preoccupied with spiritual or emotional values. This is not to deny the existence of spiritual values, but simply to say that they will be claimed by, or on behalf of, the disadvantaged, whether or not there is any basis in truth for the claim.

There is in fact a widespread popular belief that physical weakness implies moral or spiritual strength, which deserves more serious attention that it usually gets. This belief has probably arisen as follows. An argument on behalf of the weak is necessarily of a non-material or 'moral' nature. That is, it is based, not on what is the case in the materially existent world, but on some conception of what *ought* to be the case. In popular thought, the moral nature of the *argument* is projected on to the people on whose behalf it is advanced, so that intrinsic moral superiority is commonly attributed to the 'poor', the underdeveloped nations or the international proletariat; and the claims of such groups are then taken as arising from this supposed superiority. In actual fact, however, the conception that the disadvantaged have claims as against the powerful and the wealthy exists independently of any superior moral virtue which the disadvantaged may (or may not) have. It rests upon an abstract principle of equality according to which the rights or power of any individual or group should be limited or curtailed as soon as they infringe the rights of other individuals or groups. This conception is aimed at redressing what is perceived as an imbalance, and accordingly the 'poor' or disadvantaged have a claim *by virtue of being disadvantaged*, regardless of their moral virtues. It may sometimes be convenient, as a figure of speech, to attribute special virtues to disadvantaged nations or individuals; but this means only that they 'deserve' that the balance should be redressed in their favour. It is not an expression of literal truth; and even if the existence of these moral virtues is conclusively disproved, the claim for redress is not defeated.

It thus appears that the attribution of special virtues to the

Frobenius, Senghor and the Image of Africa

Germans, Russians and 'Ethiopians' by various nationalists, including Frobenius and Senghor, even if not factually true, is not necessarily a falsehood or a 'useful lie', but can be accepted as the figurative and emotionally compelling formulation of a moral principle, *so long as the national groups concerned are actually disadvantaged by comparison with others.* If, however, a nation which is no longer disadvantaged by comparison with others, but is 'developed', continues to claim special superior qualities (as was the case with Germany after 1936) the claim ceases to be part of a demand for equality, but becomes a demand for special privileges, including a 'right' to curtail the freedom of others not merely relatively but absolutely. (In Germany, this was expressed in the *Anschluss* with Austria, the annexation of Czechoslovakia, the invasion of Poland and also in the attempt to exterminate Jews.) It would therefore appear that the attribution of special moral or spiritual values to one's own nation, which is a tactical requirement for an emergent nationalism, becomes something altogether more sinister if, as was the case in Germany, it is interpreted as a literal truth and advanced as the ideology of a developed nationalism.

*   *   *

It will now be possible to return to the main argument about Senghor and Frobenius. Even if Frobenius had discussed emotional spontaneity and mysticism as being characteristic of the Germans (without mentioning the Ethiopians) his thought would probably have attracted Senghor by virtue of its Romantic stress on non-rational values and because it was geared to expressing the attitudes of an emergent nationalism.[1] It is therefore not true to say that Senghor adopts Frobenius's formulations merely because Frobenius has flattering things to say about Black Africans. However, as I have already suggested, Frobenius's whole formulation is based on German nationalist resentment of France and Britain. Imported into the African situation, it belongs purely to the realm of ideology, being unrelated to Frobenius's actual observation of the African scene. Since the attribution of special moral or spiritual values to underprivileged peoples becomes a danger in the ideology of a

---

[1] See L., p. 134, where Senghor points out that a revolt against Reason was already in progress in Europe at the time when Negro art was 'discovered'.

333

developed state, this aspect of Frobenius's and Senghor's thought will no doubt decrease in usefulness as development takes place. Indeed, other writers of Négritude, whose early work was strongly influenced by Frobenius, have responded to his decreasing relevance. For example, much of the feeling about life expressed in *Cahier d'un retour au pays natal* (1939)[1] is 'Ethiopian' in Frobenius's sense. Indeed, one of the most famous passages in the poem is a transmutation of Frobenius's thought into poetry. Césaire writes:

ma négritude n'est ni une tour ni une cathédrale

elle plonge dans la chair rouge du sol
elle plonge dans la chair ardente du ciel
elle troue l'accablement opaque de sa droite patience

Eia pour le Kaïlcédrat royal!
Eia pour ceux qui n'ont jamais rien inventé
pour ceux qui n'ont jamais rien exploré
pour ceux qui n'ont jamais rien dompté

mais ils s'abandonnent, saisis à l'essence de toute chose
ignorants des surfaces mais saisis par le mouvement de toute chose

insoucieux de dompter, mais jouant le jeu du monde.[2]

We have here a poetic rendering of Frobenius's conception of the plant-like character of Ethiopian civilization which grows downwards into the earth and upwards into the air. We have Frobenius's rejection of the 'Hamitic' attempt to 'master' or 'tame' nature. And in the poem it is given new significance. Frobenius rejected the idea of 'dominating' nature, but described the typical 'Hamitic' achievement as being the domestication of animals. In Aimé Césaire's *Cahier d'un retour au pays natal* the idea of 'domestication' is placed in the context of the slave trade. It is the slaves who have been domesticated, it is men who have been treated like animals.

ceux qui n'ont connu de voyages que de déracinements
ceux qui se sont assoupis aux agenouillements
ceux qu'on *domestiqua* et christianisa.[3]

---

[1] A. Césaire, Présence Africaine, Paris, 1956.
[2] Ibid., p. 71.
[3] Ibid., p. 71.

Frobenius, Senghor and the Image of Africa

And in the context of the slave trade, the condemnation of 'domestication', which had seemed slightly absurd in Frobenius, takes on a new validity.

The words in the passage quoted earlier—'mais ils s'abandonnent, saisis à l'essence de toute chose/ignorants des surfaces mais saisis par le mouvement de toute chose'—contain a direct citation of Frobenius. 'Saisis' is the French translation of the German 'ergriffen', and 'saisissement' is the official French rendering of the 'Ergriffenheit' which Frobenius describes as the essentially Ethiopian characteristic. In the *Cahier*, then, Césaire has made an artistically successful use of Frobenius's concept of what is 'Ethiopian' but he uses it as a poetic not as a political myth.

In politics, however, Césaire adopted an empirical approach. This can be seen in his essay 'Culture et colonisation'.[1] In his drama *Une saison au Congo*,[2] too, he concerns himself, not with the 'essence' of African culture, but with the problems of neo-colonialism in a modern African state. Senghor, by contrast, still goes on quoting Frobenius's formulations of 'Hamitic' and 'Ethiopian' values, despite their decreasing relevance.

Again, regarded purely as the basis of an ideology (i.e. without reference to truth content), the Hamitic/Ethiopian opposition, as formulated by Frobenius, is calculated to be disruptive of African states; for most such states contain both 'Hamites' and 'Ethiopians'. Moreover, as the terms 'Hamitic' and 'Ethiopian' are relative, all the undesirable French/Hamitic qualities could be attributed by the Tiv to the Nupe, by the Nupe to the Hausa, and so forth, while, on the pan-African plane, West African states as a whole could reproach their northern neighbours with the same bad qualities. (The present argument is not intended to deny the existence of cultural differences between African peoples. But diversity need not necessarily imply conflict.)

Yet again, since Frobenius tends to associate 'Hamitic' values with Islam,[3] his formulation would, if used as an ideology for African nations, foster religious as well as ethnic conflict, and would benefit no one except the ex-colonial powers.

---

[1] *Présence Africaine*, 8–9–10, juin-décembre 1956, pp. 190–205.
[2] Editions du Seuil, Paris, 1967.
[3] Sch., p. 89; KA., p. 240.

335

Considered as the basis of an ideology, then, Frobenius's scheme suffers not only from built-in obsolescence, but also from a potential for engendering conflict both within and between African nations.

As I have suggested, there is a hiatus between Frobenius's actual observations in Africa, and the generalizations and conclusions which were supposedly drawn from them, but which, in fact, seem to have been derived from other sources. The generalizations about 'Hamitic' peoples, in particular, were based on German attitudes to France and had little connection with observations in the field. Frobenius's Hamitic/Ethiopian hypothesis seems not only to be false (because European-based) but if used as a political myth may even constitute a threat to the stability of African states. There is also some possibility that theorizing about the essence of Black African culture will be used by some African politicians as a substitute for economic development. Yet if such theories are to be either at all relevant to modern Africa or illuminating for analysing modes of thought more generally, they should be based on verifiable observations made in Africa, not on the Hegelian 'Volksgeist' and the European Romantic tradition.

Religion and Secularism: The Contemporary Significance of Newman's Thought

Hilary Jenkins

One of the main criteria often used when attempting to make a broad contrast between differing modes of thought is the opposition between religious and secular cultures. The normal way of approaching this is to equate secularism, sometimes identified with technology or with rationality, with Western and 'civilized' societies, and religion with non-Western, 'traditional' and 'primitive' societies. However, a similar contrast can be—and often has been—drawn even within our own Western society: religion and secularism can be seen as confronting each other both now and in the course of our historical development.

In this essay the contrast is seen as *within* Western society. The discussion throws light on the terms 'religion' and 'secularism' which are so often used as touchstones in differentiating societies, and reveals that they are perhaps neither so clear nor so unambiguous as at first appears. The opposition between them moreover is a complex and not a clear-cut one, involving both new polarities and a new synthesis as the revaluation of our inherited culture goes on. The analysis here is presented in the form of a discussion of the thought of John Henry Newman, a thinker intimately concerned in the controversies over that revaluation and one almost contemporary in anticipating subversive positions increasingly common among Christian writers today.

*   *   *

337

Religion and Secularism: Newman's Thought

In the last century England ceased to be a confessional society. The old constitution in which Christianity was the law of the land died, and with it the concept of a national conscience enshrined in an established religion. In the universities the transition from one form of society to another, or rather the dislocation, the discontinuity in the transition, was represented in starkly contrasted modes of thought and action. The failure to maintain Oxford as a clerical institution which imposed subscription to the Thirty-nine Articles of the Church of England reflected the failure in Parliament to resist the passage of the acts repealing religious tests and the introduction of franchise reform. Newman's secession from the Church of England in 1845 marked the collapse. Mark Pattison in his *Memoirs* recorded that 'Oxford repudiated at once sacerdotal principles and Kantian logic, for more than a quarter of this century Mill and nominalist views reigned in the schools.'[1] Liberalism, as then understood, replaced theology as the dominant concern; religion ceased to be thought of as the necessary bond of society; a primitive structure of values still recognizably medieval even in the early nineteenth century disintegrated and disappeared. The implications for Christianity and organized religion reach far into our own time and the reconciliation of the traditional Church and the modern world is not yet very far advanced.

Newman was intimately involved in the thinking about the problems of this transition. In his writings he also anticipates radical views common among certain recent Christian writers. Of these Ivan Illich is the most outstanding and the most radical. Illich proclaims the need for a powerless Church. His thesis is that

> only the church can 'reveal' to us the full meaning of development. To live up to this task the church must recognize that she is growing powerless to orient or produce development. The less efficient she is as a power the more effective she can be as a celebrant of the mystery.[2]

Such a viewpoint offends both the clerical bureaucracy and the laymen who speak in terms of social commitment, each seeking a *raison d'être* for the Church in one role or another in modern

[1] Mark Pattison, *Memoirs*, Macmillan, London, 1885, p. 166.
[2] Ivan D. Illich, *Celebration of awareness*, Calder and Boyars, London, 1971, p. 97.

development. Newman also was regarded as 'troppo irreverente', but he was more readily misunderstood when he anticipated this position because he stood at the beginning of the process which Illich vividly describes:

> We stand at the end of a century-long struggle to free man from the constraint of ideologies, persuasions, and religions as guiding forces in his life. A non-thematic awareness of the significance of the incarnation emerges: an ability to say one great 'Yes' to the experience of life. A new polarity emerges: a day-by-day insight into the tension between the manipulation of things and the relationship of persons. We become capable of affirming the autonomy of the ludicrous in face of the useful, of the gratuitous as opposed to the purposeful, of the spontaneous as opposed to the rationalized and planned, of creative expression made possible by inventive solution. We will need ideological rationalizations for a long time to achieve purposefully planned inventive solutions to social problems. Let consciously secular ideology assume this task. I want to celebrate my faith for no purpose at all.[1]

Newman at the onset of this process felt acutely the passing of the older world that was an organic community. 'People say to me', he wrote in 1841, 'that it is but a dream to suppose that Christianity should regain the organic power in human society which it once possessed. I cannot help that. I never said it could. I am not a politician; I am proposing no measures, but exposing a fallacy and resisting a pretence.'[2] As a generic term for the style of life, of language, of social and political relations within which the Church was an integral part, he used the term 'Toryism'. He observed the disintegration of this social pattern with regret but without panic, even with mounting hope of a new system which would give rise to a new polarity between the Church and the world, that is between motives of doing good that good might come, acting in order to succeed, and motives of faith, purposeless, spontaneous, ludicrous, pinned to a verifiable certainty in belief and at last clearly differentiated from and uncompromised by secular associations. For Illich the 'specific function of the church must be a contribution to development

---

[1] Ibid., p. 103.
[2] J. H. Newman, 'The Tamworth reading room', in *Discussions and arguments*, Longmans Green, London, 1907, p. 292.

which could not be made by any other institution.'[1] Newman saw in 1850 that so much that the Church had done in the past, so much that her embattled defenders wished her to take on in the future, was more efficiently and more expertly done by the state or by secular agencies. 'She must, in order to have a meaning, do that which otherwise cannot be done, which she alone can do. She must have a benefit to bestow in order to be worth her existence.'[2] The 'Toryism' that was passed beyond recall elsewhere was fulfilled in the professions of the Catholic Church, heir and successor, as he called her in 1874, to the political and social traditions of the 'free-spoken dauntless Church of old'. Looking back then, when the shape of the new age was very much clearer than it had been, he affirmed that 'this fidelity to the ancient Christian system, seen in modern Rome, was the luminous fact which more than any other turned men's minds at Oxford forty years ago to look towards her with reverence.'[3]

What Newman wanted was a Christianity that was neither an accomplice of the new ideology nor an institutional relic hankering after past domination over society. The Church had both to unlearn an inherent mode of thinking and to reject opportunities for quick success by entering into new alliances. As his experience of Roman authoritarianism and clerical misunderstanding of the cultural changes of the nineteenth century increased, and correspondingly his scepticism about Christian socialist or liberal progressive attempts to assimilate religion to ideology, he sensed the need for a relation of mutual respect between Church and world. It was vital to distinguish between theology and ideology. The confusion between these two grew more rather than less complex.

Newman did not underestimate the problem, essentially one of equipping an old language to meet a new situation. 'I think', he said in 1873,

the trials that lie before use are such as would appal and make dizzy even such courageous hearts as St. Athanasius and St. Gregory, and they would confess that, dark as the prospect of their own day was to them severally, ours has a darkness different

---

[1] Illich, op. cit., p. 97.

[2] J. H. Newman, *Lectures on certain difficulties felt by Anglicans*, Longmans Green, London, 1908, vol. 1, p. 214.

[3] Op. cit., vol. 2, p. 198.

in kind from any that has been before it . . . Christianity has never yet had experience of a world simply irreligious.[1]

Newman grappled with the problem of the Church in an age when the socialization of man was taken out of her hands. After the French Revolution Christianity was confronted for the first time with the baffling encounter not with the age-old opponent of a world organized *against* it but with its own secular mirror-image, a world committed deliberately to making itself good, to the promotion of the well-being of every one of its citizens—in a word with 'secular religion' founded on humanistic reason and equipped, for the first time, with both the industrial revolution and the social sciences to lift mankind into a new era. The implication was clear, modern man had no need for the Gospel as a norm in performing his social miracle. At that early stage in the dénouement of the Gospel's relation to the modern world, a number of equally inadequate and misconceived responses were put forward for the Church. To take two extreme versions, Pius IX from Rome attempted to perpetuate the traditional stance of the Church as supreme oracle in social matters by condemning socialism, liberalism, communism, modern civilization and all its works; Christian socialism with equal maladroitness attempted the opposite gambit, to identify the Gospel with social service. The one by utter repudiation, the other by undiscriminating embrace sought to comprehend an entirely new situation by resorting to traditional precedents. Official Rome represented the old pagan-Christian antithesis; unofficial Anglicanism the old synthesis of medieval Christendom, the consecration of the world. Both were endeavours to give traditional Christianity a further lease of life. It is now clear that social programmes can do without Christianity and in fact do so; equally that the attempt to halt the revolution is futile.

Newman throughout his life was a deadly antagonist to Erastianism and Caesarism, and indeed to ultramontanism. He resisted the pretensions of prevailing ideas. Matthew Arnold admired his insight in perceiving that 'what he called Liberalism . . . was in general, and in the sphere of religion more particularly, quite inadequate, and was

---

[1] M. Spark (ed.), *The Catholic sermons of Cardinal Newman*, London, 1957, pp. 122–3.

not destined to have things forever its own way.'[1] What he wanted was a Church radically independent and a culture that had its own springs of action and no longer needed the leading strings of religion. At the end of his life he could remember an England in which Christianity (as by law established) really was the law of the land, with real penalties for those who abused it or disregarded it. The revolution which had occurred did away with that state of affairs.

> The cause of this great revolution is obvious, and its effect inevitable. Though I profess to be an admirer of the principles now superseded in themselves, mixed up as they were with the imperfections and evils incident to everything human, nevertheless I say frankly I do not see how they could possibly be maintained in the ascendant.

Nor did he ascribe the cause of this inevitable development to a conspiracy or a party, or to any temporary failure of Church power or policy, but simply to the cultivation of intellect, to the general awakening of thought and opinion. He says clearly that it was 'in the nature of things', the necessary accompaniment of human responsibility.[2]

This secular character of modern life no longer surprises us. The best-known discussion of its implication for Christianity is the 'Honest to God' debate provoked by John Robinson.

> I do not believe that this age is wicked (and certainly not wicked above all others) because it is secular. I believe that the process of secularisation represents the same kind of shift in man's whole way of looking at the world as that which marked the transition from the Middle Ages to the Renaissance. That is to say, it is of its nature something towards which the Christian faith is neutral.[3]

Christians are engaged in realizing a new language to fit this altered situation. A novel disposition of the religious mind is fast replacing the closed, defensive and condemnatory disposition of the last century. This is not to say that there is no sense of bafflement but the air is clearing.

[1] David J. de Laura, 'Matthew Arnold and John Henry Newman, the "Oxford Sentiment" and the religion of the future', University of Texas *Studies in Literature and Language*, 6, Supplement 1965, p. 697.

[2] Newman, *Difficulties felt by Anglicans*, vol. 2, pp. 267–8.

[3] J. A. T. Robinson, in D. L. Edwards (ed.), *The honest to God debate*, S.C.M., London, 1963, p. 247.

Religion and Secularism: Newman's Thought

Newman kept up his communications with this distant future. As a result his contemporaries found him difficult to place. He was a disconcerting prophet with a faculty for confusing opponents who were confident they enjoyed a comprehensive grasp of the meaning and direction of the times. His language startled and outraged. He was equally charged with bigotry and scepticism. 'As far as I can understand him' was Charles Kingsley's refrain and he thought Newman utterly blind to the broad meaning of words. Indeed, his employment of language is a fascinating subject recently explored, sympathetically by John Coulson and J. M. Cameron, unsympathetically by T. C. Potts.[1]

The ambiguity and contradiction which contemporaries found in his thought flowed from his penetrating awareness of the provisional character of an age sandwiched between our secularity and past sacrality, in which the role of energizing social myth was in process of transfer from Christianity to purely rational sources. Newman is now much less inexplicable. We have emerged from the half-light of the early phase of secularized man with a dry regard for the great expectations and extravagant claims that were then made for man emancipated from religion. For the Victorians faith in the progressive character of the scientific principle in all fields was an intellectual religion. Newman's confidence was of a different kind. He was prepared to wait on the development of the sciences. In 1854 he wrote:

First let us ascertain the fact—then theologize upon it. Depend upon it, when once the laws of human affairs are drawn out, and the philosophy into which they combine, it will be a movement worthy of the Lawgiver, but if we begin by speaking of Him first of all, we never shall get at His laws.[2]

Faced with the speculations of the hour he thought religious men were nervously impatient to fall in with premature conclusions.[3] He deplored the officious search for scientific or social supports for

[1] See articles by A. M. Allchin and J. M. Cameron in John Coulson and A. M. Allchin (eds.), *The rediscovery of Newman, an Oxford symposium*, S.C.M., London, 1967; John Coulson, *Newman and the common tradition*, Clarendon Press, Oxford, 1970; T. C. Potts, 'What then does Dr. Newman mean?', *Newman-Studien*, 6, Glock und Lutz, Nürnberg, 1964.

[2] Cited in A. Dwight Culler, *The imperial intellect*, Yale University Press, New Haven, 1955, p. 269.

[3] J. H. Newman, *On the scope and nature of university education*, Everyman, London, 1915, p. 252.

Christianity. For him the firm foundation lay in the facts of revelation, in devotion to the objects of faith, safeguarded by authority that found its continuance not only in the historic teaching Church but in the conscience of the faithful. He saw the process of scientific hypotheses rising and falling, knowledge proceeding by fits and starts: 'we live in a wonderful age; the enlargement of the circle of secular knowledge just now is simply a bewilderment, and the more so, because it has the promise of continuing and that with greater rapidity, and more signal results.'[1] What alarmed him was the tendency to confound what ought to be distinct. His message was 'to be patient with appearances, and not be hasty to pronounce them to be really of a more formidable character'.[2] To him the ultramontanist seeking refuge in authoritarian reaction was as much subject to panic as the liberal who jettisoned all doctrine. He was not disturbed to admit that atheism could well be as consistent with the phenomena of the physical world as the doctrine of a creative power. He could reply in kind that unbelief, though it considered itself especially rational, really went upon presumptions and prejudices as much as faith does.[3] He never forgot that life is for action, and expected the Church to fight for her place as an aggressive power among others in an era of increasingly dynamic change. The rational principle could take care of itself, the intellect would go its own way. 'This is no day for what are popularly called "shams". Many as are its errors, it is aiming at the destruction of shadows and the attainment of what is either sensible or intellectually tangible.'[4] He did not grudge this new independence, nor did he want to fasten the Church upon it as if her continuing life could find no other foundation.

Illich expresses this confidence when he says that social innovation has become a sophisticated and complex business.

> I believe that this innovative action will increasingly be taken by groups committed to radically humanist ideals, and not gospel authority, and should therefore not be taken by the churches. The modern humanist does not need the gospel as a norm.[5]

[1] J. H. Newman, *Apologia*, Clarendon Press, Oxford, 1967, p. 233.
[2] Cited in Culler, op. cit., p. 270.
[3] J. H. Newman, *Sermons . . . preached before the University of Oxford*, London, 1843, pp. 186, 223, 224.
[4] Newman, *Difficulties felt by Anglicans*, vol. 1, p. 212.
[5] Illich, op. cit., p. 102.

He makes the point that I think Newman anticipates, that the Christian wants, or ought to want, not to interfere in or control the process of development, but the freedom to go further, to give the benefits that could not come from any other institution.

Newman saw the chief error of the day in the notion that

> our true excellence comes not from within, but from without; not wrought out through personal struggles and sufferings, but following upon passive exposure to influences over which we have no control.[1]

(Hence his notorious preference for the Irish beggar woman who had the theological virtues of faith, hope and charity.) New liberalism was old Pelagianism. The Church was the school of holiness, the only antagonist capable of meeting the unbridled intellect of modern man in its suicidal excesses.[2] A situation altogether novel had arisen since the French Revolution inaugurated the secular age. There was, to use Lionel Trilling's phrase, a change in the 'hum of implication'. Language was bound to be confused in the transition from one culture, underpinned by Christian sanctions, to a new culture dependent on its own rational principles. In such circumstances Newman fought a battle on two fronts; first against the mischief of the liberal spirit in religion, which interfered in the sphere of faith, reducing belief to a mere sentiment, a personal taste, a private opinion—the natural end of which seemed to him to be the worship of self, of one's own consciousness; and second against the erection of quasi-religious ideologies which sought to substitute themselves for Christian orthodoxy and to supersede the role of the Church. In a word he opposed doctrinaire secularism as an ersatz rival of religion and liberal theology as an emasculation of Christianity. The one was condemned by its insufficiency; the other by its claim to be all-sufficient. It was precisely in what his own age called controversial divinity, in proclaiming the Gospel, that the Church could contribute to development, and precisely in trying to halt, impede or control the social and political field that she would confuse and compromise her mission.

In the upset of old values and the extravagant claims made for new ones, ambiguity and confusion were inevitable. The protagonists

---

[1] Newman, *Discussions and arguments*, p. 264.
[2] Op. cit., pp. 260–6; idem., *Apologia*, pp. 219–20.

did not understand each other in the moment of crisis. Newman was at pains to find definitions.

> Nor do I aim at more than ascertaining the sense in which the words Faith and Reason are used by Christian and Catholic writers. If I shall succeed in this I shall be content, without attempting to defend it. Half the controversies in the world are verbal ones; and could they be brought to a plain issue, they would be brought to prompt termination. Parties engaged in them would then perceive, either that in substance they agreed together, or that their difference was one of first principles. This is the great object to be aimed at in the present age, though confessedly a very arduous one. We need not dispute, we need not prove—we need but define. At all events let us, if we can, do this first of all; and then see who are left for us to dispute with, what is left for us to prove. Controversy at least in this age, does not lie between the hosts of heaven, Michael and his angels, on the one side, and the powers of evil on the other; but it is a sort of night battle, where each fights for himself, and friend and foe stand together. When men understand what each other mean, they see, for the most part that controversy is either superfluous or hopeless.[1]

Confusion was compounded by the inadequacy of theology and the premature state of the sciences. Science was supposed by enthusiasts for the new knowledge to lead by itself to belief in a beneficent Being, not, as Newman held, to have a natural and proper predilection for atheism. What, Newman asked, does the word 'God' mean in *their* mouths? 'Let me not be thought offensive, if I question, whether it means the same thing on the two sides of the controversy.' The fashion of the day spoke of Physical Theology, a jejune study that was really no science at all; or of the Evidences of Religion; or of the Christian law of the land, 'if there is any man alive who can tell what that is'; or of acquaintance with the Scripture, but to Newman neither historical reading nor religious feeling were theological science.[2]

Argument for want of precision led to wasteful controversy. In the transition from implicit faith and unconscious tradition to rational grounds for action, tested experience and demonstrable proofs,

[1] Newman, *Sermons . . .*, op. cit., pp. 192–3.
[2] J. H. Newman, *The idea of a university*, Holt, Rinehart and Winston, London, 1968, pp. 27–8, 45–6.

words were acquiring new meanings. Ivan Illich considers the process as he sees it now:

> The Christian response has been deeply affected by the acceleration of time; by change, development, by growth having become normal and permanence the exception. Formerly the king could be at the opposite pole from the priest, the sacred from the profane, the churchly from the secular, and we could speak about the impact which one would have on the other.[1]

In the early stage of this process intellectuals adopted a sacerdotal role; there were positivist, Comtist prophets and mystagogues; ethical religions grew up; and clergy attempted to insert the Gospel into social programmes so as to acquire the new justification of utility. Even agnosticism attempted to throw a religious glow over moral duty.

The principle upon which most of Europe had organized its religious and social arrangements since the Reformation had been that of national establishments; up until the shock of the French Revolution the Church, or the Churches, had operated as part of the apparatus of the state. Even the revolutionaries had been slow to move towards total separation of the two and after the failure of the Civil Constitution of the Clergy had experimented with civic religions. Underlying the earlier system had been the assumption of a believing people, held together and civilized by established Christian institutions. The theory presupposed a mutual dependence of religion and government and the necessity for religious restraints and sanctions. In Newman's youth such had been the position in England but the admission to Parliament of Dissenters and Roman Catholics initiated a constitutional revolution. The structure of government was no longer commensurate with the National Church. If the nation any longer had a Christian conscience, what was its form and context when religious pluralism was recognized by statute?

In such circumstances of crisis Dr. Arnold offered the extreme liberal solution, that the Church of England should become a department of state for social and ethical truths. Newman came closer to the demands and opportunities of the new dispensation. He regretted the passing of 'Tory' values. In fact he never viewed the advent of democracy with enthusiasm. He could not share the

---

[1] Illich, op. cit., p. 103.

optimism, to him specious and superficial, of the liberal bourgeois state. He saw society moving from loyalty to persons to the arrangement of things and commodities, and adopting the maxim that 'utility and expedience, or, in other words, what tends to produce wealth, is the only rule on which laws are to be framed.' Old instinctual morality had an affinity with the believing disposition. Now universal education would encourage a critical rational attitude. Respect, reverence, awe, strong emotional attachment, the myths that move men to action, sprang from spontaneous life, from the genius of irrational prejudice, from historic national character. Reason and utilitarian philosophy would dry these up at their source. In this sense he believed, and shocked his auditors by saying, that England would be much healthier if it were more superstitious. Rationalism was a cause of atrophy. He doubted the permanent ability of the liberal state built on self-interest to control the masses. The march-of-mind men, the long-headed radicals, were irresponsibly yet inevitably eroding the deeply human resources of the old organic culture. He feared the undifferentiated mass society and the destruction of national and local idiosyncrasy. Reason, he thought, was a puny instrument on which to rely once authority and custom were displaced. Human nature remained prone to act from belief rather than from dialectic. Deprived of religion people would seek other creeds.[1] High-minded rationalism could not be other than a creed for an élite. Masses of men were unlikely to wait upon proven conclusions, either for good or ill.

> On such philosophy as this were it generally received, no great work ever would have been done for God's glory and the welfare of man. The 'enthusiasm' against which Locke writes may do much harm, and act at times absurdly; but calculation never made a hero.[2]

Nevertheless the old state of relationships was irrecoverable. Liberal philosophy for the moment triumphed. What had been a mere party or school in the early part of the century came to be, as

[1] See G. Sorel, *Reflections on violence*, English trans. by T. E. Hulme, Allen and Unwin, London, 1916, pp. 5, 32 and 115–16; also Terence Kenny, *The political thought of J. H. Newman*, Longmans, London, 1957.
[2] J. H. Newman, *Essay on the development of Christian doctrine*, Sheed and Ward, London, 1960, pp. 236–7.

Religion and Secularism: Newman's Thought

Newman recognized, the whole educated lay world. The toryism of his youth had passed away and in its place had come a liberal, individualistic, tolerant and pluralist world. Observing the predicament of Gladstone who struggled to maintain the position of a Christian statesman, Newman saw the force of the argument that no government could be formed in England in the last quarter of the century if religious confession were a condition. In 1883 he thought the petition against the bill to admit atheists to Parliament 'a piece of humbug'. The new state was already accomplished fact. By then it was futile to prevent the consequences of the earlier admission of liberal principles. 'The whole theory of Toryism, hitherto acted on, came to pieces and went the way of all flesh.'[1] Pius IX's syllabus of modern errors was equally futile. Newman left that problem to the future. Such decrees were ultimately subject to the interpretation of developing theology. What one pope could do another pope could undo. The fallacies of Progress could then be distinguished from real advances.

> And thus, in centuries to come, there may be found out some way of uniting what is free in the new structure of society with what is authoritative in the old, without any base compromise with 'Progress' and 'Liberalism'.[2]

The advance of the secular society would itself expose impostures. In this sense the Church could be neutral. God surely had not created the visible Church as the nurse of natural principles.

Newman's historical sense was strongly developed. Like Sorel it is the fluid character of reality that strikes him. He was early in coming to terms with the process of progressive disenchantment whose end was the expulsion of religion from the organization of human affairs, a de-mythologized and de-sacralized world. He did not produce a systematic analysis of social behaviour but he frequently adverted to the nature of social change. He anticipates later sociology in his ideal types of barbarous and civilized societies; the former grounded in superstition, belief in persons and families, in patriarchalism and papalism, having an affinity with a vivid and forceful religion; the latter mundane, matter-of-fact, functional and rational,

---

[1] Newman, *Difficulties felt by Anglicans*, vol. 2, pp. 266–8.
[2] Op. cit., pp. 262–9.

conducive to scepticism and unbelief.[1] He grasped the character
of the nineteenth-century transition, a bourgeois liberal society
proclaiming its modernity at the very moment when its values were
being challenged by a democratic mass society with which it was
unable to cope, clinging to the vestiges of the older society from which
it was only partially separated. The extravagant claims of the ideo-
logues witnessed to their descent from the chiliastic, millenarian social
protest of the sixteenth-century anabaptists. 'All political movements',
Marx wrote in *The eighteenth brumaire*, 'have been slaves to the
symbols of the past: thus Luther donned the mask of the Apostle
Paul, the Revolution of 1789 to 1814 draped itself alternately as the
Roman Republic and the Roman Empire.' As the century wore on
ideology increasingly wore the mask of religion. 'There was', writes
Daniel Bell,

> a 'built-in' compulsion for the free-floating intellectual to become
> political. The ideologies, therefore, which emerged from the nine-
> teenth century had the force of the intellectuals behind them.
> They embarked upon what William James called 'the faith ladder',
> which in its vision of the future cannot distinguish possibilities
> from probabilities, and converts the latter into certainties.[2]

Raymond Williams's analysis in *Culture and society* helps to place
Newman's attitude of reserve, his refusal to endorse a premature
commitment of Christianity to any side in the ideological battle.

> We project our old images into the future . . . We do this as con-
> servatives, trying to prolong old forms; we do this as socialists,
> trying to prescribe the new man. A large part of contemporary
> resistance to certain kinds of change . . . amounts to an inarticu-
> late distrust of this effort at domination. There is the hostility to
> change of those who wish to cling to privilege. There is also the
> hostility to one's life being determined, in a dominative mood
> masked by whatever idealism or benevolence. This latter hostility
> is valuable, and needs to be distinguished from the former with
> which it is often crudely compounded. It is the chafing of any
> felt life against the hands which seek to determine its course, and

---

[1] See Werner Stark, in H. Tristram et al., *Newman centenary essays*, Burns
Oates, London, 1945, p. 159.
[2] See Karl Mannheim, *Ideology and Utopia*, Kegan Paul, London, 1936,
pp. 190–7; and Daniel Bell, *The end of ideology*, Collier Books, New York,
1961, p. 397.

this, which was always the democratic impulse, remains essential within the new definitions of society. There are still major material barriers to democracy, but there is also this barrier in our minds, behind which, with an assumption of virtue, we seek to lay hands on others, and, from our own constructions, determine their course. Against this the idea of culture is necessary, as an idea of the tending of *natural* growth.[1]

Newman despised social and political dogmatism as shams. He looked to a mutual autonomy of culture and religion to allow for freedom and creative life. But in the night battle all were thrown together, a congeries of overweening expectations for man's secular aspirations and of panic on the part of churchmen overtaken by unprecedented changes in the relation of their religion to the world. In England, his contemporaries endeavoured to throw a divine glow over purely secular phenomena. Education, social reform, the new sciences, war, imperialism, the civilizing mission of the superior races, were assimilated to religious chiliasm in a backward-looking effort to compete with or to emulate religion. Newman looked forward to a relation of natural and regenerate man, of the Church and contemporary culture, that would allow for new alliances between identities that were properly themselves and whose appropriate languages were finally disentangled.

In 1841, high-tide for liberal capitalist optimism in England, he mocked scientific unions, free trade, railroads and industrial exhibitions as agencies for the regeneration of humanity. Posterity would be able to judge their success. The notion that Useful Knowledge would inspire moral virtue struck him as silly. Sir Robert Peel's confidence that lending libraries would be the temples of natural religion was mere portentous language that Bentham, arch-apostle of utilitarianism, would have despised. This was liberalism at its most brash, led on by the habit of the pulpit into creating a human providence and temporal satisfactions for the inward yearning of the heart. In France Comte deified humanity and in England Frederic Harrison produced the bizarre positivist religion of rationalist sacraments and pilgrimages. Equally extreme reactionary Catholic ultramontanism, Newman's other antagonist, sought to project old images and lay hold on the future.

[1] Raymond Williams, *Culture and society*, Penguin, Harmondsworth, 1961, pp. 322–3.

For Newman the ultramontanists were an aggressive and insolent faction, power-seekers ignorant of holiness. The claims of the liberals on the other hand were sophistry. Their error was the notion that in knowing more a man necessarily became better.

> Does popular education act as a dose or a charm, do physics lead to moral improvement?. . . Who was ever consoled in real trouble by the small beer of literature and science?. . . Does Sir Robert Peel mean to say. . . you have but to drench the popular mind with physics, and moral or religious advancement follows?

Such nostrums were being offered to the labouring classes as a substitute for Faith—'we will say, for instance, in a severe winter, snow on the ground, glass falling, bread rising, coal at 20d. the cwt., and no work.' Human nature demanded an inward change and was offered only a change of external objects, diversion and excitements, a philosophy of expedients and palliatives. True excellence came not from without but from within. It is not education to which he objects, but education dressed up to produce the goods of religion. Those things that previously had been looked for in the old Faith would now be better achieved by the vigorous new principle of knowledge, decked out with a pantheon of saints and a litany of virtues. What was intended was the supersession of religion.

> To have recourse to physics to make man religious is like recommending a canonry for gout. . . The ascendancy of Faith may be impracticable, but the reign of Knowledge is incomprehensible. The problem for statesmen of this age is how to educate the masses (i.e. morally), and literature and science cannot give the solution.[1]

In 1832 he had said that 'the country seems to me to be in a dream, being drugged with this fallacious notion of its superiority to other countries and other times.' By the midcentury the humiliations of the Crimean War saw a turning away from the ideal of individual liberty towards the ideal of the efficient state, more democratic, professional, competent and chauvinist. Newman's response was to underline that the peculiar virtue of the British constitution was that 'instead of making a venture for the transcendant, it keeps fast by a safe mediocrity.'[2] His principle was that in every human work there

---

[1] Newman, *Discussions and arguments*, pp. 266–8, 292, 299.
[2] Op. cit., p. 308.

is a maximum of good short of the best possible. But the myths that were to inspire later imperialism were in the making. To Newman it was all a 'temerarious proceeding', a temptation to national conceit. The course of the century justified his view that the inordinate claims of doctrinaire progress were themselves a betrayal of reason. The only result was to reintroduce theology by the back door. It was not to the drift of the age that he objected. On the contrary he was foremost in recognizing that the proper and logical consequence of rationalism was a most *plausible* scepticism. (He predicted universal unbelief as the authentic condition of modern man.) It was the cant of the age that was objectionable intellectually and morally dangerous. The classical bourgeois state existed in the shadow of the historic religious state. Habit encouraged the notion of a civil religion. Newman insisted on the distinction between the life of faith and the life of reason. 'Knowledge is one thing, virtue another, good sense *is* not conscience, refinement is not humility, nor is largeness and justness of view faith.'[1]

Newman was very much his own man. Lord Acton as well as Manning found him exasperatingly unpredictable in his attitude to current developments. He was truly an inopportunist in his century, isolated alike from progressives and reactionaries. Writing in the 1860s to his friend T. W. Allies—whose own assessment was 'J.H.N. is a queer man. Who can understand him?'[2]—Newman analysed different modes of the relation of Christianity to society. Medieval Christendom he saw as another illustration of blurred definitions. 'I do not see my way to hold that "Catholic civilization" (i.e. Christendom) . . . is *in fact* (I do not say in the abstract), but in fact, has been, or shall be, or can be, a good or per se desirable.' The tendency of Christianity to impress itself on the face of society was a mixed good. It could lead to secularization of the Church and corruption of the clergy. His basic conviction was St. John's: *mundus totus in maligno positus est*. Such a permanent evil required a great antagonist. He doubted the real value of past submission of states and rulers to the Church. He saw the medieval type of society as not more than 'the shadow of Christianity visible from the accidental character of a certain stage in human affairs'. Christianity under that system

---

[1] Newman, *The idea of a university*, discourses II–IV.
[2] Wilfred Ward, *The life of John Henry Cardinal Newman*, Longmans, London, 1927, vol. 1, p. 20.

was so far contaminated that salvation had to be sought through a cloistered retreat from the world.

In all historical contexts the Church had need to be vigilant. Each age had its own human expedients. Newman questioned whether more souls were saved under such arrangements as theocracy, legal establishment of religion, or the Erastian state and rejected the suggestion of a providential sequence of stages in the relation of the Church to the world.

> The conclusion I am disposed to acquiesce in is this:—that certain ages, i.e. . . . the ages of barbarism, are more susceptible of religious impressions than other ages; and call for, need, the visible rule of religion; that, as every animal knows its own wants, and distinguishes by instinct between food and poison, so a ruder people ask for a strong form of religion, armed with temporal sanctions, and it is good for it; whereas other ages reject it, and it would be bad for them . . . in matter of fact, it was a good thing for men thus to be compelled to become Christians, and a bad thing for them now. I don't say that it made *more* true Christians, but it was the way by which Christians were they more or fewer, were to be made. A mediaeval system now would but foster the worst hypocrisy—not because this age is worse than that, but because imagination acts more powerfully upon barbarians, and reason upon traders, savants and newspaper readers.[1]

Historical relativism of this kind outraged the peculiarly a-historical notions of his liberal opponents and the a-historical theology of the reactionary Catholic party. Allies thought the Church should stick tooth and nail to the consecration of the world and cited *The Times*—than which he could see no more sagacious exponent of the heretical mind!—as eager for its *desecration*. For Newman when the state gave it would also take.

> The question is not whether the particular provision is or is not good, but whether the whole state of legislation, the mediaeval organisation, the system did not necessarily *de facto*, and, in virtue of its containing much that is Christian, also contain much that is unChristian.

His position is most sharply illustrated in his denial that even the legal establishment of Catholic marriage (on which the Roman

---

[1] Mary H. Allies, *Thomas William Allies*, Burns and Oates, London, 1907, pp. 111–14.

Catholic Church was then, and is now, hypersensitive) was actually and in fact a benefit: 'You cannot have it by itself and not other things with it.'[1] Each provision therefore carried its own practical corruption; none was divinely ordained; no temporal condition could nullify the force of St. John's words.

By the time Newman received the cardinalate in 1879 the progressive socialization of man on a basis other than religion was already well advanced, but its character had greatly altered. Liberalism as a doctrinaire ideology could be separated from real and beneficial change. He said in Rome:

> There is much in the liberalistic theory which is good and true; for example, not to say more, the precepts of justice, truthfulness, sobriety, self-command, benevolence . . . and the natural laws of society . . . It is not until we find that this array of principles is intended to supersede, to block out, religion, that we pronounce it to be evil.[2]

A universal and *thoroughly secular* education might reasonably be looked to as an answer to promoting an orderly, industrious and sober population. Such a mild programme contrasted starkly with the earlier wild predictions; with the reign of universal peace to be expected from free trade or the civilizing mission of imperialism.

Amidst such quasi-religious notions Newman denounced a new ideological idolatry and pointed to a future that is perhaps clearer for us: the meaning of the advent of a purely secular world was that society should be open, tolerant and creative, averse to grand designs, a de-mythologized world of free and responsible men, to whom the polarities of nineteenth-century controversy would indeed appear as Matthew Arnold's darkling plain where ignorant armies clashed by night. The night battle, his own image for these confused conflicts, where friend and foe stood together, would, he thought, be succeeded by a climate of thought in which a new polarity and a new synthesis could emerge between a religion *semper eadem* and a permanently changing world:

> What is uncertain, and in these great contests commonly is uncertain, and what is commonly a great surprise, when it is

---

[1] Ibid., pp. 120–2.
[2] Ward, op. cit., vol. 2, pp. 459 ff.

witnessed, is the particular mode by which, in the event, Providence rescues and saves His elect inheritance. Sometimes our enemy is turned into a friend; sometimes he is despoiled of that special virulence of evil which was so threatening; sometimes he falls to pieces of himself; sometimes he does just so much as is beneficial, and then is removed. Commonly the Church has nothing more to do than to go on in her own proper duties in confidence and peace; to stand still and to see the salvation of God.[1]

[1] Ibid., vol. 2, p. 462.

Basic Differences of Thought

Sybil Wolfram

This essay, although wide in subject matter, is narrow in conception. I am concerned with only one question, namely, what kind of difference in societies' thought or thinking could qualify as a 'basic' one.

This is not a simple problem. In the first place, it is not obvious what makes a difference a 'basic' one; and, in the second, it is far from clear which items are supposed to be different or what the nature of the difference between them is supposed to be. The question of what constitutes a single society is itself a vexed one, and neither societies nor thought can easily be classified in a convincing manner, let alone one in which it is even minimally plausible that the societies so classified are characterized by the modes of thought so distinguished.

One example is enough to give a glimpse of the difficulties involved. Scientific thinking is sometimes supposed to characterize our society. What however does this mean? We might take 'scientific thinking' to be, let us say, the acceptance of evidence or, more narrowly, the attempt to discover natural laws, or perhaps, more narrowly still, the attempt to discover those natural laws which will enable us to manipulate nature. But perplexities arise on every side. Is 'our' society to be conceived of as a single society covering what is sometimes loosely referred to as the 'Western world', or as just one member of this set of related societies, or as an instance of a type of society marked off by certain characteristics and such that Ancient China, for example, belongs to the same type? Then, what allows us to say that a society thinks scientifically? Is it that there should be a body of knowledge which can in some sense be said to belong to the society, as we may be said to have a body of knowledge about the natural world although many of us do not have it? Or is it rather that the society should conduct its affairs on a scientific basis, or that its members on the whole think in a scientific manner, or merely that they have a penchant for 'scientific' support for beliefs they may hold, as others perhaps appeal to tradition? Again, we may enquire in what way classifications, which have played so large a part in social anthropology of late, may be said to be either scientific or not. Is a classification scientific when it is conceived for the purposes of framing general laws, or is there some other standard?

When I say that this discussion is narrow in conception, I have in mind in part that I am not so much concerned to pursue questions like these as to try to see what different sorts of claims the umbrella of a 'basic difference in the thinking of societies' could cover, or, in other words, to engage in a kind of critique of classifications of societies and their thoughts from this point of view. But I also have another point in mind. Social anthropologists not infrequently speak of two major classes of society, of primitive and civilized societies, for example, or traditional and modern ones, but for the most part they do so incidentally, in the course of discussing particular subject matters or of contrasting some other particular society with 'ours'. Few, if any, would probably seriously commit themselves to any such all-embracing divisions of societies and thought as I shall, in most cases, be dismissing, and many, notably Evans-Pritchard, would undoubtedly regard the attempt to reach such divisions as at best premature and at worst misconceived and stultifying. The merit of arriving at any conclusions on the question I propose to discuss is partly negative: to rule out of court certain, perhaps tempting, generalizations suggested by the terms in which particular comparisons are drawn. Its positive aspect is more nebulous and probably confined to opening up one or two channels of enquiry.

*   *   *

It is not, as I have remarked, very clear how the notion of a 'basic difference' should be construed. Some questions concerning basic differences are requests to know what principle of differentiation is employed: enquiry into the basic difference between a horse and a pony, a plant and an animal or a primitive and a civilized society are, or may very well be, enquiries concerning the use of the terms. 'What is the basic difference between . . .?' here means 'What is the basis of the division (we make) between . . .?' Such questions are directly answerable, or if we like well-formed, only where we do make a division on a single basis, and the terms in fact mark categories of a mutually exclusive and exhaustive division based on a single differentiating characteristic, or what logicians have called determinates under a single determinable. 'Is there a basic difference between . . .?' may sometimes correspondingly be understood to ask whether the terms referred to mark two or more such categories. That is, it may be paraphrased: 'Is there a basis of the division we make between . . .?' The answer 'no' will then be appropriate where the terms are used in a fashion so varied that they cannot be said to mark a single division, where they mark one of degree and not of kind, as with 'rich' and 'poor', 'large' and 'small', or where there is not a single principle of differentiation as in the case of 'incest' and 'adultery'. In some contexts we may also like to answer 'no' because the categories are distinguished not in terms of characteristics but in terms of a unique relation between their members, as with animal species, or, for instance, according to periods of manufacture or location.

When it is asked whether there is a basic difference in the thinking of primitive and civilized societies, or Western and non-Western ones, the question is clearly not of this sort. It is not whether the basis of the division we make between 'primitive' and 'civilized' or 'Western' and 'non-Western' is in terms of thought. Or at least the answer to this question is so evidently 'no' that it would be a surprising one to ask. Rather it seems to be whether there is a differentiation of thought which will serve to distinguish societies already grouped after some other fashion. This question is clearly one of great latitude. We are tied neither to a specific division of thought nor to just one division of societies. We do not even seem necessarily restricted to divisions of either which have already been made. What is at issue, at least in the first instance, appears to be whether any division of thought can be found which supplies a principle for differentiating societies. But this formulation of the question is ambiguous, and also incomplete. It could mean: 'Is there a way of classifying thoughts or thinking such that all thoughts, or all those attributable to societies, fall into two or more mutually exclusive and exhaustive categories and societies may be distinguished according to which they possess?' Or it could mean merely: 'Can we construct a division of societies into two or more classes according to a difference in their thought?'

The incompleteness of the question or questions lies in the fact that no distinction is made between basic and non-basic differences. This is particularly evident in the second, which is suspiciously easy to answer in the affirmative. All we need to do is to select a thought which can be ascribed to societies and divide societies into those which possess it and those which do not. The chances are that 'our' or 'Western' society has some thought or other which is shared by no other known society, and indeed that, however exactly societies are demarcated, the same is true of every one of them. We should probably be unlucky too if we could not single out any thought possessed by all the members of one set of known societies and none of the members of another, no matter how membership of the sets were determined, just as we should be if we could not find some feature distinguishing at least many pairs of finite sets of persons. If however the thought concerned the latest pop singer or the efficacy of toothpaste, the whole matter would be of little interest. That a society or set of societies is alone in believing in toothpaste might be a difference between it and other societies, but, as things are, it would hardly qualify as a basic difference between them. Of course, if a society believing in toothpaste were called a 'squidge society' and one not doing so a 'squodge society', it would be correct to say that the basic difference between squidge and squodge societies is that the one believes in the efficacy of toothpaste while the other does not.

But where we are inventing classifications, and sometimes even when we are not, the question 'Is there a basic difference between . . .?' or 'Is such and such a basic difference between . . .?' calls for another interpretation. On being told that the basic difference between a horse and a pony is that the former is over, and the latter under, 14hh., we might go on to ask whether there is really a basic difference between the two. We are not then enquiring into the basis of the distinction between a pair of terms, but rather whether this difference generates others. The term 'generate' is here to be taken seriously. What is in question is not merely a matter of correlation, such that if it turned out that toothpaste societies keep pets and wear shoes, and non-toothpaste societies do not, believing/not believing in toothpaste automatically becomes a basic difference. For it to become so it would have to be discovered that it is a difference which brings about others, or, in other words, that we have reason to suppose that if a society comes to believe in toothpaste other changes will follow. These must probably also be of a certain nature if the term 'basic' is to be applied. When a social anthropologist seeks for basic differences in the thinking of societies, his quest is for a way of explaining or classifying certain features of their behaviour, and only differences in thought which are the basis of differences in these are likely in his eyes to qualify as basic.

On this criterion, there are a large number of diverse differences of thought which have a claim to be called 'basic'. The belief that what we term coincidences or matters of luck are caused by personal agencies is in this sense a basic difference of thought between the Azande and ourselves. The same may be said of ourselves and certain other societies on the strength of, for example, the different basis employed for dividing relationships into kinship and affinal ones. This too generates differences in behaviour of a kind to interest the anthropologist. Any one of these features could, of course, be employed in a twofold division of societies by the single expedient of distinguishing societies according to whether they possess or lack this or that view, do or do not believe that everything is caused, do or do not regard marriage as a tie between unilinear lines. Whether this would be a useful procedure is another matter. If societies not believing that everything is caused, or not regarding marriage as a tie between unilinear lines, differ widely in what they do believe concerning the causation of events or the nature of the marriage tie, it does not seem particularly impressive. It becomes very much more interesting if there is some uniformity of belief and conduct within the negative category, or alternatively kinship structures or views concerning causality can be divided into a larger number of categories along a single line of differentiation, each generating distinguishable conduct. And I shall try to show later how the notion of a basic difference can be tightened up accordingly.

The point I want to make at the moment is that, whatever refinements we introduce, classifications like these need to be sharply distinguished from ones which would supply a satisfactory affirmative answer to the first question I mentioned, that is: 'Is there a way of classifying thoughts such that all those ascribable to societies fall into mutually exclusive and exhaustive categories, and societies may be distinguished according to which they possess and the behaviour in each attributed to the category of thought characterizing it?' One way of expressing the difference is to say that the former are classifications of societies according to individual thoughts they have, and not, as would be required for an answer to this question, according to a *sort* of thought or thinking. These certainly do not amount to the same, and it obviously cannot be taken for granted that because societies differ in individual thoughts, therefore they also differ in the kind of thoughts which they possess, or in the nature of the thinking which leads to them. There is no *a priori* reason to suppose that all the individual thoughts of any one society have a feature in common distinguishing them from all the individual thoughts of another, or that they all derive from a single specifiable kind of thinking.

This is not in any way to denigrate classification in terms of individual thoughts. Rather the reverse. The discovery that societies are distinguishable by modes of thought would be one of incomparably greater magnitude, on a par perhaps with discovering that different kinds of living things are distinguishable by different kinds of chromosome or different kinds of substance by a different kind of atomic structure. And that it may be so is not something which can be ruled out in advance or on the strength of our present knowledge. On the other hand, there is little evidence that it is so. There are of course ways of classifying thoughts into kinds more or less satisfactorily, and classifications of thinking which at least approximate to this model. But, as I want now to show, their prospects as the basis of a classification of societies and their practices are not particularly rosy, and probably far less so than those of individual thoughts.

* * *

I shall not say a great deal about divisions of thoughts into kinds. They can be divided up in a variety of ways: into affirmative and negative, for instance, or into those which concern definite particulars and those which do not, into thoughts about how things are, thoughts about how they might be, ones about how they ought to be, or, again, into correct, incorrect and untestable ones. But the trouble about divisions like these is that there is not the slightest reason to suppose that any, let alone every, society's thoughts are wholly of one kind and never of another. For any definite candidate there is always ample evidence the other way, whether we treat a society having thoughts of one kind or another as meaning that members of the society have them or their language provides a way of expressing them, or, more restrictively, as meaning that individual thoughts of these categories can be ascribed to the society as a whole because they are shared by virtually all its members. Certainly we have thoughts of all these kinds, so that the most that could plausibly be suggested is that other societies lack one or another type, and differ from us not so much in having thoughts of a different kind, as in having fewer kinds. It seems almost inconceivable that members of a society should altogether lack, let us say, thoughts concerning definite particulars; and although possible, it is hardly probable that there are societies which have no single thought comparable to our belief that the earth is round or that the Egyptians married their sisters. Similarly, there is a patent absurdity in supposing that in some societies people have or share no correct thoughts, while in others they have or share only correct ones, or that there should be societies with only untestable or no untestable thoughts. One interpretation of the suggestion that Western society is characterized by its scientific thinking is that it possesses a body of scientific knowledge; and it might perhaps seem that we could at least lay claim to a larger number or higher proportion of correct beliefs than other societies. Apart from the difficulty of finding a way of enumerating beliefs so that this becomes a testable hypothesis, a division like this would clearly be one of degree and not of kind. And it is not even altogether certain that Western society would come out on top. Social anthropologists have been at pains to point out that other societies often have knowledge which we lack. Literate societies' scores are of course swelled if their recorded knowledge is added to that currently possessed by some or all their members; and they will do better, the more able and determined they are to preserve their records. But it is difficult to get round the fact that this goes for their incorrect, as well as their correct, beliefs, and that the number of these which have gained currency in our society, even for long periods of time, not to mention those of which there are written or other records, is very great, and might even, on any count, possibly exceed the number of correct ones.

Divisions of thinking merit a little more scrutiny. I shall confine myself to what is I think the most popular candidate, that between scientific and unscientific thinking. This looks more hopeful at first sight, and it is worth devoting proportionately more space to showing that it suffers in fact from similar defects.

When we mark off scientific from other thinking, such as artistic or practical, we sometimes do so initially by its object, that is, to discover and establish truths. We should probably also distinguish it within this category by the nature of the truths which are sought, namely, that, unlike those which are the principal object of the historian, they are of a general and not a particular nature, and, unlike those with which mathematicians occupy themselves, they are contingent and not necessary, and so require observation, and not only deduction, for their discovery. Clearly these are not promising categories for distinguishing societies. And when the scientific thinking of our society is opposed to thinking in other societies, rather than to other thinking in our own, the more usual contrast is with such species of thinking as magical or religious. In other words, the comparison is between that portion of our thinking which concerns generalization about the world and a similar portion in other societies. In our society, observation of the world would be regarded as the only good foundation of a general belief about it, and the possession of well-founded general beliefs as in turn the only sound basis for beliefs about particular things when we lack the evidence of direct observation of them, as we do for instance in the case of events which have not yet occurred. Beliefs to the effect that events of an X sort cause ones of a Y sort could be justified only by evidence that whenever events of an X sort occur, ones of a Y sort follow. Similarly, justification of doing X in order to achieve Y requires good evidence that Xs are regularly followed by Ys. Lack of scientific thinking in a society presumably consists of not forming general beliefs, or ones concerning unobserved events, on the basis of observed regularities, that is of not forming such beliefs or else not basing them on this foundation. Division of societies into those thinking scientifically and those not doing so is thus not based on a differentiation of thinking in general but on that of only a section of it. And correspondingly, one could not expect to achieve a division of all thoughts which could be ascribed to societies in this way but, at best, only of that portion of them which concerns classes of particulars and those not currently observed.

Basic Differences of Thought

There is an intrinsic extreme improbability about the notion that there are societies in which there are no beliefs at all about these subjects, or none which are based on observation of regularities. Survival is so unlikely in such a case that the suggestion seems not worth considering. But one might entertain the more restricted, although still exceedingly ambitious, proposal that in some societies and eras, like our own, beliefs always or typically depend on observed regularities, while in others they frequently or primarily have a different source. They may be founded on tradition, or the Word of God, or of Marx, instead of on facts, or else set against no standard of truth. A differentiation of thinking along such lines as these could, if it worked, explain differences both in the scientific and technological development of societies and in their social practices. Founding one's beliefs on observation is plainly a prerequisite of science and technology, and it might also be supposed to issue in a different set of beliefs, and so a different set of social practices, than any other method of arriving at them. Attractive, or even plausible, as this may seem at first sight, it is fairly obvious that it does not, and could not really be expected to, work. There are two main reasons for this.

The first is that it is not at all evident that societies can be divided into those thinking scientifically and those failing to do so. A society or era in which a statement was held true, whatever observation suggested, simply on the grounds that it had always been believed, or occurred in the Bible, could certainly be said to think unscientifically, and, indeed, in a way unintelligible to ourselves. So it is fortunate for our credulity, if not for the prospects of a division of societies on this basis, that citing, or even relying on, such sources does not amount to so radical a difference in the treatment of facts. This is easy to see in the case most familiar to us, the Protestant type treatment of God's Word, but, *mutatis mutandis*, the same is almost certainly true of the rest.

There is, in the first place, an obvious and important distinction between an accepted manner of justifying beliefs and their actual basis. That someone seeks to justify his view that X is Y by bringing forward evidence E does not entail that his view rests on E in the sense that he has formed it because of E or would relinquish it should E turn out to be incorrect. And it cannot be taken for granted that whatever is the socially acceptable sort of evidence to give is what forms the basis of all, or even most, commonly or individually held

365

beliefs. What I have in mind is not so much that members of a soceity may typically cite the Word of God in support of beliefs they hold and at the same time hold ones directly contravening it, but rather that their beliefs may not always have a direct dependence on what the Bible says. In some cases, indeed, it is impossible that they should. There are likely to be vast numbers of questions on which any written source is silent, and few statements or commands so clear that there can be no doubt about their meaning. The treatment of God's Word on the question of which relatives should not marry is a pleasing and typical illustration of the well-known possibilities of interpretation. Leviticus chapter 18 contains a detailed list of these relatives. But in eighteenth and nineteenth century England for instance there were no less than four favoured views of what God intended. Some held that He meant the list literally; the law took the line that the relatives mentioned are examples and all those 'like' them obviously included; others again proffered the view that He was laying down a marriage law appropriate to the ancient Jews' state of society; and, finally, a more select circle maintained that the word translated as 'marry' was mistranslated and the chapter did not concern the question of prohibited marriages at all. While directly textual evidence was employed, so was the notion of God's consistency and good sense, and, in effect, this meant that controversy about what the marriage law should be, turned on what it would be consistent or good sense to do.[1] God's Word, although always cited and in good faith, could thus scarcely be said to be the foundation of the beliefs expressed. The form of the argument was that God must have meant P since P is true, and not that P is true because God said it, a view which received perhaps its most delightful expression in Berkeley's theory that natural laws are God's sign language.[2]

It is equally easy to see how a people may not only cite, but also rely on, the Word of God for at least some of its beliefs without

---

[1] For details, and the part played by God's Word in the controversy concerning the legalization of marriage with a deceased wife's sister, 1842–1907, see S. Wolfram, 'Le mariage entre alliés dans l'Angleterre contemporaine', *L'Homme*, 1, 1961.

[2] Touched on in G. Berkeley, *An essay towards a new theory of vision*, 1709, secs. 147, 152, and *A treatise concerning the principles of human knowledge*, 1710, secs. 44, 65–6, and developed e.g. in *The new theory of vision or visual language shewing the immediate presence and providence of a Deity vindicated and explained*, 1733, secs. 38 ff.

having a way of thinking different in kind from that of the scientist. It may, for instance, be believed that the study of God's Word is a better way of arriving at the truth in complicated matters than reliance on such evidence as it is in our power to assemble. Argument in favour of this view can very well be of an inductive kind rather than the deductive kind preferred by Descartes. When, for example, Bishop Butler condemns the attempt to maximize happiness, instead of doing what God, through the medium of our consciences, prompts, as a mistake 'than which . . . none can be conceived more terrible', this is not because he regards the object as mistaken, but because he thinks observation goes to show that the means are more seldom attended by success.[1] If this were so, then it would of course be 'unscientific' not to follow God's Word (or, at any rate, our inner voice) in our endeavours to do right. Faith in our competence to assess the effects on happiness of our actions, or refusal to accept the reliability of our consciences because we believe them to be induced by our upbringing, may be less at odds with what we now think we know than insistence that our consciences guide us right because given to us by an all-good and omniscient being; but it is obviously no more scientific in itself.

Whether we treat reliance on God's Word as evidence of unscientific thinking or regard it merely as the outcome of a mistaken theory, perhaps of a peculiarly disastrous, because peculiarly pervasive, nature, depends on whether the facts which we think show it to be mistaken were known to those holding it. But, either way, it is difficult to deny that very similar thinking also occurs in our society at the present time. Beliefs are of course now typically justified by reference to facts or what scientists have discovered, and many of them are doubtless better founded than many of those held in societies not exposed to modern science or technology. But it obviously does not follow from this that all of them are founded on fact or even that none are held in the face of known facts which strongly suggest their falsity. And indeed we need look no further than social anthropology itself to find plenty of examples to the contrary. The various theories competing to explain so-called incest prohibitions, to mention one such set, owe a far more obvious debt to writings of

[1] J. Butler, 'Of the nature of virtue', sec. 10, Dissertation 2 appended to *The analogy of religion, natural and revealed, to the constitution and course of Nature*, 1736.

the pre-scientific era than to observation, and display a dexterity in avoiding contrary evidence rivalling that of any theological doctrine.[1] The lack of social currency, and likely lack of influence on legislators, of such theories makes it improbable that they have had much effect on social practices; but they are evidence, if evidence is needed, that the dependence of beliefs of a testable nature on fact is not ubiquitous in our society and age, any more than it is absent in others.

But even if it were, and differentiation of thinking into scientific and unscientific supplied a better division of societies than it seems to do, there is another, and, in my opinion, more powerful reason, why it would be unlikely to yield a division of societies' practices. This is that there exists an important section of social practices which cannot be thought of as dependent upon what true or false beliefs a society holds; and this section includes a very considerable portion of, if not all, those practices in which social anthropologists have shown a special interest.

What a society chooses to do, or requires to be done, in order to secure a particular end certainly depends upon what is believed, whether on good or on bad evidence, to secure that end. And there are of course rules of conduct of this kind in our society, as no doubt in others. Rules of the road, for example, are very likely chosen in the belief that these are good, or the best means to secure such specific objects as speed and safety, and the beliefs on which they rest are probably based on observation and susceptible of alteration as circumstances change or new facts come to light. Again, it may well be the case that many prevalent views about what it is morally, as opposed to socially, right or wrong to do stem from beliefs, correct or otherwise, of what on the whole in our society leads to human happiness.[2] But equally there is little doubt that many formalized and unformalized rules of conduct in our society,[3] as in others, are not of this kind, and do not depend on beliefs which either are, or could be,

[1] See S. Wolfram, 'The explanation of prohibitions and preferences of marriage between kin', unpublished D.Phil. thesis, University of Oxford, 1956, chs. 4–6, for substantiation of these claims.

[2] I am not of course denying untestable components such as that all human beings have equal rights to happiness; but only suggesting that inductive generalizations concerning the effects on happiness (so construed) e.g. of lies likely to deceive, are both required and employed in assessing acts from what would be considered a moral point of view.

[3] Where I mention specific instances of these, 'our society' refers to England.

based on evidence in this way. Sometimes there is a socially accepted justification which makes it appear as if the rules in question are purposive in the same way as rules of the road, as when our prohibitions of marriage between relatives are ascribed to the ill effects of the in-breeding which would otherwise occur. But the cited belief is, as in this case, apt to be badly supported, or even contradicted, by known facts, so that if it were the basis of the prohibition, this would be the result not of scientific but of unscientific thinking. And, more important, our practice does not conform to it. We neither consistently prevent marriages likely to have genetically bad results nor confine ourselves to forbidding marriages of relatives which, according to our beliefs, might. Prohibitions of marriage between in-laws have always been, and still remain, if in amputated form, an integral part of the law relating to prohibited marriages.[1] In other cases there is no equally favoured justification. If asked, we might produce some hygienic reason for not eating animals we keep as pets, or explain the propriety of giving them names by its convenience. But we should be hard pressed to justify our taxation of husband and wife as one,[2] now that Biblical support for their unity would be unacceptable, let alone such practices as men taking off their hats in church or our habit of giving flowers and other presents to the sick. Where we have either no belief purporting to be based on observation to justify our rules of conduct, or none which can seriously be supposed to do so, we are prone to fall back on a more general socially accepted belief, namely, that they conform to, or are relics of ones which did conform to, Utilitarian principles.

The cases I have mentioned, and many others which have been, or could be, adduced, suggest that if we insist on this theory, we must ascribe some remarkably ill-founded beliefs, and a good deal of unscientific thinking, to ourselves to account for the ill-chosen

---

[1] At present a person is forbidden in any circumstances to marry ascendants and descendants of a wife or husband and correspondingly a wife or husband of an ascendant and descendant. Until 1960 he continued to be forbidden to marry blood relatives of a divorced husband or wife to the same degree as his own although Acts of 1907, 1921 and 1931 permitted them in the case of a deceased husband or wife. For the earlier position and history of the change see S. Wolfram, 1961, op. cit., where I tried to show that the gradual disappearance of restrictions of marriage with affines is probably part and parcel of a whittling down of the doctrine of the unity of husband and wife.

[2] Written in 1969 when husband's and wife's earnings were taxed virtually as one person's.

nature of many of the means we adopt towards our ends. It seems, on the whole, more likely that the theory is wrong, and more in accordance with the evidence to consider the social practices of which I have been speaking not as means to ends but rather as ways of marking socially made assimilations and distinctions.[1] When we require particular conduct of or towards people distinguished by one or another feature, demarcate sorts of occasion by behaviour appropriate on them or prescribe this or that to those standing in relationships differentiated in this or that way, there is then no test of the correctness or otherwise of what we are doing. If it is not the object of these rules to bring about particular results, they clearly cannot be classed as the outcome of scientific or unscientific thinking according to their effectiveness as means. Nor can it be thought that the existence of such unpurposive rules of conduct in a society is itself the sign of an unscientific society. The associations of particular conduct with particular classes of people, occasions or relationships can be compared in form to scientific theories, and contrasted to them because, unlike these, they are not subject to assessment for truth and falsity. We may certainly, if we wish, label them 'non-scientific', and so distinguish social practices which stem from non-scientific thinking from ones which, like those designed to secure particular ends, require scientific thinking for their success. This may yield a distinction between social practices such as giving the sick flowers on the one hand and making them rest on the other. But there does not seem the slightest reason to suppose that it is a distinction which will also yield a division between societies. The associations on which practices like the former rest are not a curious and ineffectual variety of natural law, any more than natural laws are a curious and ineffectual variety of communication which God has chosen to employ, *faute de mieux*. We might possibly expect good science to oust bad, or a society which has discovered correct theories to throw out mistaken ones; but there seems no more reason to suppose that a society which engages in science will cast off practices of the kind I have been describing than that taking up carpentry leads to giving up the piano.

*   *   *

[1] See C. Lévi-Strauss, *La pensée sauvage*, Plon, Paris, 1962, trans. into English as *The savage mind*, Weidenfeld and Nicolson, London, 1966, *passim*—to which, in spite of some difference of opinion, I am greatly indebted in this passage.

None of this of course proves that there could be no division of thoughts or thinking into categories which could serve to distinguish societies and their practices as a whole. Nevertheless it seems worth retreating to, and briefly reconsidering the question of, divisions of societies on the basis of individual thoughts, especially those untestable ones which seem to generate many of the social practices of interest to the anthropologist.[1] There is a good deal to be made of the notion of 'basic differences of thought' in this direction, whether or not a single division of societies is attainable.

To group societies' practices on the basis of individual thoughts from which they emanate is itself obviously to do something in particular, different, for example, from grouping them in terms of ends they secure. And suggestions to the effect that such and such practices are members of a set resulting from such and such an individual thought are equally clearly ones of substance. Bringing together the impropriety of eating pets and the propriety of naming them as a set of practices emanating from the thought that pets are like people, or the income tax inspector's treatment of husband and wife and such practices as ascribing the same domicile to them or requiring them to take on each other's relationships as a set resulting from the thought that a married couple is more like one person than two, effects some ordering of social practices, even if many such thoughts and practices can be attributed to every society. Hence the justifiability of claiming a 'basic difference of thought' whenever a difference in two societies' practices can be ascribed to the presence in the one of a thought which is absent in the other.

Still, often when there is said to be a basic difference of thought between two or more societies, or sets of societies, something more than this is intended, as something more ambitious is sought. I shall mention just two such additional requirements. The first, on which I touched earlier, turns on the distinction between the presence of a rule of conduct and its absence. A rule of conduct must take the form: do X, do not do Y; and it can be said to concern a class of items only if it applies to all of them. 'Non-relatives may marry' is not a rule of conduct, nor is 'Some persons not related by blood

---

[1] Whether this is partly accidental or not it is hard to say. These beliefs may have attracted more attention because they seem less readily explicable or because the anthropologist is interested precisely in untestable beliefs due to their likely variety.

must not marry' one concerning the class of all those not related by blood. We may like to restrict the use of 'a basic difference of thought' to those cases where two societies not only have incompatible thoughts, but each of these also generates rules of conduct. For reasons of space, I shall not argue the point, but merely state that it is only thoughts of a universal and affirmative form, ones to the effect that all such and suches are so and so, which can generate rules of conduct: absence of the belief that all kinship ties are created by descent in the male line, or belief that it is not so, results in the absence of rules of conduct concerning patrilineal kin, not in the presence of these or any others. The only thoughts which, on this more stringent criterion, are candidates for ones basically different from the thought that all kinship ties are created by male descent are ones both incompatible with it and of the form 'All kinship ties are so and so'; 'All kinship ties are created by descent in the female line (and so none by descent in the male line)' or 'All kinship ties are created by descent indifferently through either sex (and so some not by descent in the male line)' fill this bill in a way that merely not thinking something particular about kinship ties cannot. The virtue of restricting the notion of a basic difference of thought in this way lies in the terminological underpinning it gives to a separation of wheat from chaff. Only classifications of societies in terms of subjects about which all of them have general thoughts of a positive nature will count as ones in terms of basic differences of thought; mere divisions of them into those which do and those which do not think, for instance, that pets are like people will no longer qualify for this distinction.

The requirements can be pitched yet higher. It may be claimed that if one society considers that all kinship ties are created by descent in the male line, and another that they are all created by descent in the female line, this is not a basic difference of thought between them. The grounds for this are that they must then also have views in common: that all kinship ties are created by descent through one sex, that 'being related by kinship to' is a transitive relation; so they exhibit a basic similarity of thought. There is a contrast, of possible promise, between differences with a common denominator like this, and ones of which the same is not true. If society A thinks that all kinship ties are created by descent through one sex and society B that all of them are created by descent through either or both sexes indifferently, they must also have thoughts in common, e.g. that some kinship ties are created by descent through one sex, but these are not of a form to lead to requirements of conduct distinguishing one set of items from another. And whereas A makes 'being related by kinship to' a transitive relation, B makes it a non-transitive one. In other words, if x is related by kinship to y, and y to z, then in society A x must be related by kinship to z, while in B he may or may not be. This in turn means that rules of conduct distinguishing kin can take a form in society A which they cannot in society B: being kin to someone cannot in B, as it can in A, be set apart by entailing having to behave, or be, the same as he in some respect or belonging to the same clan as he, for these are transitive relations, and only such non-transitive relations as 'behaving in such and such a manner towards' can single out a set of persons defined in terms of a non-transitive relation between them. In our society 'being (close) kin to' could be marked off by being required to go into mourning or being forbidden to marry but not, as in some societies, by living in the same place or having special customs. When there is a difference of thought as 'basic' as this we may expect those rules of conduct which serve to mark socially made assimilations and distinctions not only to affect different sets of persons, but also to take a somewhat different form.

That there will remain some cases in which all societies have either basically similar or basically different thoughts in this sense seems probable. It is at least likely that one could find classes of items concerning which all societies think, and divide societies into groups on the basis of whether their beliefs about these items can be specified as a single belief or not. How many basically different thoughts there would be about any one such class of items, it would obviously be impossible to say in advance. To what extent division of societies according to thoughts about one such class of items correlates with that according to those about another, or whether the whole group of those of a society's thoughts which result in rules of conduct of the kind under consideration could ever, or always, be reduced to a single thought of great generality such as 'all relations between persons (or better: items) are asymmetrical and transitive (and hence hierarchical)', seem equally questions decidable only by investigation. Differentiation of societies by individual thoughts generating social practices of the kind in question might yield a single division of them, even if divisions of thinking do not; and it might even

373

divide them into just two classes. One might back spatial and temporal proximity, if not wealth or scientific prowess, as a breeder of similarity in thoughts like these, and for this or other reasons speculate that the societies comprising the Western world would fall on the same side of a fence like this. But that it should be alone there and all other societies, past and present, hand in hand on the other, is something on which I, for one, should not care to put my money.

Notes on Contributors

BARNES, STANLEY BARRY, M.A. Lecturer, Science Studies Unit, Edinburgh University. First degree in Natural Sciences, M.A. in Sociology, Essex. Editor of Penguin Reader in Sociology of Science, and author of several papers in the area. Particularly interested in relating the culture of science to general sociological (anthropological) theories.

COLBY, BENJAMIN N., B.A., Ph.D. Professor of Anthropology, University of California, Irvine. Main writings: 'A partial grammar of Eskimo folktales', 1973; *Ixil country: a plural society in highland Guatemala* (with Pierre van den Berghe), 1969; *Ethnic relations in the Chiapas highlands*, 1966. Main interests: narrative analysis; experimental anthropology; psychobiology; the creation of pro-life cultures.

COLE, MICHAEL, Ph.D. Associate Professor of Ethnographic Psychology, The Rockefeller University, New York. Main publications: *The new mathematics and an old culture*, 1967 (with John Gay); *Handbook of Soviet psychology* (edited, with Irving Maltzman); *The cultural context of learning and thinking* (with John Gay, Joseph Glick and Donald Sharp); and various papers on animals', children's and adults' learning. Main interests: the experimental study of the relation between culture and thought processes; studies in the development of learning skills in children.

FINNEGAN, RUTH, M.A., D.Phil. Senior Lecturer in Comparative Social Institutions, The Open University. Main publications: *Survey of the Limba people of Northern Sierra Leone*, 1965; *Limba stories and story-telling*, 1967; *Oral literature in Africa*, 1970; and various papers. Main interests: sociology of literature (particularly oral literature); philosophy of the social sciences. Background in classical studies (including history and philosophy) and social anthropology/sociology.

GELLNER, ERNEST, M.A. (Philosophy, Politics and Economics), Ph.D. (Social anthropology). Professor of Philosophy with special reference to Sociology, London School of Economics. Main publications: *Words and things*, 1959; *Thought and change*, 1965; *Saints of the Atlas*, 1969; *Arabs and Berbers* (ed.), 1973. Main interests: sociology, anthropology, philosophy.

HORTON, ROBIN, M.A. Professor of Social Anthropology, Faculty of Social Science, University of Ife, Nigeria. Main publications: *The gods as guests: an aspect of Kalabari religious life*, 1960; *Kalabari sculpture*, 1965; and many papers on religion and traditional belief systems. Main interests: African traditional thought and religion, and the philosophy of science. Background in philosophy, psychology and natural sciences.

Notes on Contributors

ITA, J. M., M.A., Ph.D. Lecturer in Modern Languages, University of Ife, Nigeria. Main writings: 'The significance of Russian literature for the work of Thomas Mann' (unpublished doctoral thesis); 'Laye's "Radiance of the king" and Kafka's "Castle" ', *Odu*, 1970. Main interests: twentieth-century German studies, comparative literature. Background in modern languages (German and Russian).

JENKINS, HILARY, M.A. (Cambridge), Ph.D. Lecturer in History, University College, Dublin. Previous experience teaching history and political theory in University College of Rhodesia. Main interests: religious and political thought in the nineteenth century, contemporary theology and ecumenism.

LUKES, STEVEN, M.A., D.Phil. Fellow and Tutor in Politics, Balliol College, Oxford. Main publications: *Emile Durkheim*, 1973; *Individualism*, 1973; (edited with Anthony Arblaster) *The Good Society*, 1971; and various papers, including 'Some problems about rationality', *European Journal of Sociology*, 1967 (repr. in B. Wilson (ed.), *Rationality*, 1970). Main interests: social and political theory; sociology of knowledge and sociology of morality; political sociology. Background in philosophy, politics and economics.

NAGASHIMA, NOBUHIRO, M.A. Associate Professor in Cultural Anthropology, University of Saitama, Japan. Publications: (in English) 'Historical relations among the central Nilo-Hamites: an analysis of historical traditions', University of East Africa Social Science Conference Paper, 1969; also various papers in Japanese. Main interests: anthropology of communication (particularly ritual); interdisciplinary work in anthropology/humanities. Background in biology and social anthropology.

TAMBIAH, S. J., M.A., Ph.D. Lecturer in Social Anthropology, University of Cambridge, and Fellow of King's College, Cambridge. Main publications: *Buddhism and the spirit cults in northeast Thailand*, 1970, and several papers. Main interests: religion, myth and ritual; kinship; economic institutions; the sociology of literacy and of oral traditions; and the relevance of history, philosophy of religion, and economic theory for social anthropology.

WHITELEY, W. H., B.A., Ph.D. Late Professor of Bantu Languages, University of London. Died April 1972. Main publications: *The tense system of Gusii*, 1960; *A selection of African prose* (compiler), 1964; *A study of Yao sentences*, 1966; *Swahili: the rise of a national language*, 1969; *Language use and social change* (ed.), 1971. Main interests: linguistic theory, current problems in social anthropology, and language in society. Original training in social anthropology with subsequent research mainly within linguistics.

WOLFRAM, SYBIL, M.A., D.Phil. Fellow and Tutor in Philosophy, Lady Margaret Hall, Oxford, and University Lecturer. Publications: papers in Moral Philosophy and on English Kinship. Other main interests: philosophical logic, methodology in the social sciences. Background in philosophy, politics and economics, and social anthropology.

Bibliography

(*English translations of Japanese titles in this bibliography are by N. Nagashima*)

ALLIES, M. H., *Thomas William Allies*. Burns and Oates, London, 1907.
ALQUIÉ, F., *The philosophy of surrealism*. Eng. trans., University of Michigan Press, Ann Arbor, 1965.
ANDRZEJEWSKI, B. W., and LEWIS, I. M., *Somali poetry: an introduction*. Clarendon Press, Oxford, 1964.
ARGYLE, W. J., 'Oedipus in Central Africa'. University College London Seminar Paper, 1966 (unpublished).
AUGER, P., 'The regime of castes in populations of ideas'. *Diogenes*, 22, 1958.
AUSTIN, J. L., *How to do things with words*. Clarendon Press, Oxford, 1962.
AYER, A. J., *Language, truth and logic*. Gollancz, London, 1936.
AYER, A. J., *The origins of pragmatism*. Macmillan, London, 1968.
BABALQLA, S. A., *The content and form of Yoruba ijala*. Clarendon Press, Oxford, 1966.
BANTON, M. (ed.), *Anthropological approaches to the study of religion*. A.S.A. Monographs 3, Tavistock, London, 1966.
BARNES, S. B., 'Paradigms—scientific and social'. *Man*, N.S., 4, 1969.
BARRACLOUGH, G., *An introduction to contemporary history*. Penguin, Harmondsworth, 1967.
BARTH, H., *Reisen und Entdeckungen in Nord- und Central-Afrika in den Jahren 1849 bis 1855*. 4 vols. J. Perthes, Gotha, 1857–8.
BARTLETT, F. C., *Remembering*. Cambridge University Press, London, 1932.
BASTIDE, R., 'Religions africaines et structures de civilisation'. *Présence Africaine*, 66, 1968.
BATESON, G., 'Social planning and the concept of deutero-learning'. *Symp. Sci. Phil. Relig.*, 2, 1942.
BEATTIE, J., *Other cultures*. Cohen and West, London, 1964.
BEATTIE, J., 'Ritual and social change,' *Man*, N.S., 1, 1966.
BECKER, H. S., *Sociological work: method and substance*. Allen Lane, London, 1971.
BEIDELMAN, T. O., 'Right and left hand among the Kaguru: a note on symbolic classification'. *Africa*, 31, 1961.
BEIDELMAN, T. O., 'Pig (Guluwe): an essay on Ngulu sexual symbolism and ceremony'. *Southwestern Journal of Anthropology*, 20, 1964.
BEIER, U. (ed.), *Introduction to African literature*. Longmans, London, 1967.
BELL, D., *The end of ideology*. Collier Books, New York, 1961.
BELL, D., 'Soviet ideology'. *Slavic Review*, 24, 1965.

Bibliography

BEN-DAVID, J., 'Roles and innovations in medicine'. *American Journal of Sociology*, 65, 1960.

BEN-DAVID, J., and COLLINS, R., 'Social factors in the origins of a new science: the case of psychology'. *American Sociological Review*, 31, 4, 1966.

BENEDICT, R., *Zuni mythology*. 2 vols. Columbia University, New York, 1935.

BENEDICT, R., *Patterns of culture*. Mentor books, reprinted 1953.

BENSON, L. D., 'The literary character of Anglo-Saxon formulaic poetry'. *Publications of the Modern Language Association*, 81, 1966.

BERGER, P. L., and LUCKMANN, T., *The social construction of reality*. Anchor Books, New York, 1967, and Allen Lane, London, 1967.

BERGER, P. L., *The social reality of religion*. Faber, London, 1969.

BERKELEY, G., *An essay towards a new theory of vision*. 1709.

BERKELEY, G., *A treatise concerning the principles of human knowledge*. 1710.

BERKELEY, G., *The new theory of vision or visual language shewing the immediate presence and providence of a Deity vindicated and explained*. 1733.

BERLIN, B., 'Speculations on the growth of ethnobotanical nomenclature', *Cognition*, 1, 1971.

BERLIN, B., and KAY, P., *Basic color terms: their universality and evolution*. University of California Press, Berkeley, 1969.

BEST, E., *The Maori school of learning*. Dominion Museum monograph 6, Wellington, 1923.

BEST, E., *The Maori as he was*. Dominion Museum, Wellington, 1934.

BIDNEY, D., *Theoretical anthropology*. Columbia University Press, New York, 1953.

BITÔ, M., 'Hôken shakai to Jugaku' (The feudal society and Confucianism), in K. Ishida (ed.), *Nihon Bunkashi Gairon*, Tokyo, 1968.

BOHANNAN, P., *Social anthropology*. Holt, Rinehart and Winston, New York, 1963.

BORN, M., *Physics in my generation*. Pergamon Press, London, 1956.

BOUSFIELD, W. A., 'The occurrence of clustering in the recall of randomly arranged associates'. *Journal of General Psychology*, 49, 1953.

BOWEN, E. S., *Return to laughter*. Doubleday, New York, 1964.

BOWRA, C. M., *Heroic poetry*. Macmillan, London, 1952.

BOWRA, C. M., *Primitive song*. Weidenfeld and Nicolson, London, 1962.

BRIDGMAN, P., *The logic of modern physics*. Macmillan, New York, 1927.

BROWN, R. W., and LENNEBURG, E. H., 'A study in language and cognition'. *Journal of Abnormal and Social Psychology*, 49, 1954.

BRUNER, J. S., 'The course of cognitive growth'. *American Psychologist*, 19, 1964.

BUTLER, J., 'Of the nature of virtue', appended to *The analogy of religion, natural and revealed, to the constitution and course of Nature*. 1736.

BUXTON, J., 'Animal identity and human peril: some Mandari images'. *Man*, N.S., 3, 1968.

CAESAR, J., *De bello gallico*.

CANNON, W., 'Voodoo death'. *American Anthropologist*, 44, 1942.

CARNAP, R., *The unity of science*. Kegan Paul, London, 1934.

CARNAP, R., *Philosophy and logical syntax*. Kegan Paul, London, 1935.

CARNEIRO, R. L., 'Ascertaining, testing and interpreting sequences of cultural development'. *Southwestern Journal of Anthropology*, 24, 4, 1968.

CARR, E. H., *What is history?* Penguin, Harmondsworth, 1964.

CATTELL, R., 'The personality and motivation of the researcher from measurements of contemporaries and from biography', in C. Taylor and F. Barron (eds.), *Scientific creativity*, Wiley, New York, 1963.

378

Bibliography

CÉSAIRE, A., *Cahier d'un retour au pays natal*. Présence Africaine, Paris, 1956.
CÉSAIRE, A., 'Culture et colonisation'. *Présence Africaine*, 8/9/10, 1956.
CÉSAIRE, A., *Une saison au Congo*. Editions du Seuil, Paris, 1967.
CÉSAIRE, S., 'Léo Frobénius et le problème des civilisations'. *Tropiques*, 1, avril, 1941.
CHADWICK, H. M., and N. K., *The growth of literature*. 3 vols. University Press, Cambridge, 1936–40.
CHADWICK, N. K., 'The distribution of oral literature in the Old World. A preliminary survey'. *Journal of the Royal Anthropological Institute*, 69, 1939.
CHADWICK, N. K., and ZHIRMUNSKY, V., *Oral epics of Central Asia*. University Press, Cambridge, 1969.
CHAYTOR, H. J., *From script to print*. Heffer, Cambridge, 1945.
CHOMSKY, N., *Aspects of the theory of syntax*. M.I.T. Press, Cambridge, Mass., 1965.
CLARK, K., *Landscape into art*. Penguin, Harmondsworth, 1956.
CLARK, K., *Civilisation*, J. Murray, London, 1969.
COFER, C. N., 'Does conceptual organization influence the amount retained in immediate free recall?' in B. Kleinmuntz (ed.), *Concepts and the structure of memory*, Wiley, New York, 1967.
COFER, C. N., BRUCE, D. R., and REICHER, G. M., 'Clustering in free recall as a function of certain methodological variations'. *Journal of Experimental Psychology*, 71, 1966.
COHEN, B., 'Recall of categorized word lists'. *Journal of Experimental Psychology*, 66, 1963.
COHEN, S. (ed.), *Images of deviance*. Penguin, Harmondsworth, 1971.
COLBY, B. N., 'A partial grammar of Eskimo folktales', *American Anthropologist*, 75, 1973.
COLE, M., GAY, J., and GLICK, J., 'Some experimental studies of Kpelle quantitative behavior'. *Psychonomic Monograph Supplements*, 2, 10 (whole no. 26), 1968.
COLE, M., GAY, J., GLICK, J., and SHARP, D., *The cultural context of learning and thinking*. Basic Books, New York, 1971.
COLE, M., GAY, J., GLICK, J., and SHARP, D., 'Linguistic structure and transposition'. *Science*, 164, 1969.
CONKLIN, H. C., 'Hunanóo color categories'. *Southwestern Journal of Anthropology*, 11, 1955.
COON, C. S., 'The rock art of Africa'. *Science*, 142, No. 3600, 1963.
COPE, T., *Izibongo. Zulu praise-poems*. Clarendon Press, Oxford, 1968.
COULSON, S. J., *Newman and the common tradition: a study in the language of Church and society*, Clarendon Press, Oxford, 1970.
COULSON, S. J., and ALLCHIN, A. M. (eds.), *The rediscovery of Newman, an Oxford symposium*. S.C.M., London, 1967.
CROSBY, R., 'Oral delivery in the Middle Ages'. *Speculum*, 11, 1936.
CRYNS, A. G. J., 'African intelligence: a critical survey of cross-cultural intelligence research in Africa south of the Sahara'. *Journal of Social Psychology*, 57, 1962.
CULLER, A. D., *The imperial intellect*. Yale University Press, New Haven, 1955.
DEESE, J., 'Serial organization in the recall of disconnected items'. *Psychological Reports*, 3, 1957.
DELARGY, J. F., 'The Gaelic story-teller'. *Proceedings of the British Academy*, 31, 1945.
DE LAURA, D. J., 'Matthew Arnold and John Henry Newman, the 'Oxford sentiment' and the religion of the future'. University of Texas *Studies in Literature and Language*, 6, Supplement 1965.

Bibliography

DILLON, M., *Early Irish literature*. Chicago University Press, Chicago, 1948.

DILLON, M. (ed.). *Early Irish society*. Radio Eireann, Dublin, 1954.

DORE, R. P., *Education in Tokugawa Japan*. Routledge, London, 1965.

DORSON, R. M., 'Oral styles of American folk narrators', in T. A. Sebeok (ed.), *Style in Language*, John Wiley and Sons, New York, 1960.

DOUGLAS, M., *Purity and danger*. Routledge and Kegan Paul, London, 1966.

DOUGLAS, M., (ed.), *Witchcraft confessions and accusations*. A.S.A. Monograph 9, Tavistock, London, 1970.

DUHEM, P., *The aims and structure of physical theory*. University Press, Princeton, 1954.

DURKHEIM, E., *De la division du travail social*. Alcan, Paris, 1893. (Trans. by G. Simpson as *The division of labour in society*. Macmillan, New York, 1933, and Free Press, Glencoe, 1960.)

DURKHEIM, E., Review of Lévy-Bruhl, *Les fonctions mentales dans les sociétés inférieures*, and his own *Formes élémentaires de la vie religieuse*. *Année Sociologique*, 12 (1909–12), publ. 1913.

DURKHEIM, E., *Les formes élémentaires de la vie religieuse*. Alcan, Paris, 1912. (Trans. by J. Swain as *The elementary forms of the religious life*. Allen and Unwin, London, 1915.)

DURKHEIM, E., *Sociology and philosophy*. Trans. D. F. Pocock. Cohen and West, London, 1953.

DURKHEIM, E., and MAUSS, M., 'De quelques formes primitives de classification: contribution à l'étude des représentations collectives'. *Année Sociologique*, 6 (1901–1902), publ. 1903. (Trans. by R. Needham as *Primitive classification*. Cohen and West, London, 1963.)

DYSON-HUDSON, N., *Karimojong politics*. Clarendon Press, Oxford, 1966.

EBISAWA, A., 'Kirishitan-shû no shinkô to shisô' (The belief and thought of Christianity), in K. Ishida (ed.), *Nihon shisôshi gairon*, Tokyo, 1963.

EDDINGTON, A. *The nature of the physical world*. University Press, Cambridge, 1928.

EDWARDS, D. L. (ed.), *The Honest to God debate*. S.C.M., London, 1963.

EINARSSON, S., *A history of Icelandic literature*. Johns Hopkins Press, New York, 1957.

ELIADE, M., *The myth of the eternal return*. Pantheon Books, New York, 1954.

ENTWISTLE, E. J., *European balladry*. Clarendon Press, Oxford, 1939.

EVANS-PRITCHARD, E. E., 'The morphology and function of magic, a comparative study of Trobriand and Zande ritual and spells'. *American Anthropologist*, 31, 1929.

EVANS-PRITCHARD, E. E., 'The intellectualist (English) interpretation of magic'. *Bulletin of the Faculty of Arts*, Egyptian University (Cairo), 1, 2, 1933.

EVANS-PRITCHARD, E. E., 'Lévy-Bruhl's theory of primitive mentality', *Bulletin of the Faculty of Arts*, Egyptian University (Cairo), 2, 1934.

EVANS-PRITCHARD, E. E., 'Imagery in Ngok Dinka cattle-names'. *Bulletin of the School of Oriental (and African) Studies*, 7, 1934.

EVANS-PRITCHARD, E. E., 'Zande theology'. *Sudan Notes*, 19, 1936 (reprinted in his *Essays in social anthropology*, Faber and Faber, London, 1962).

EVANS-PRITCHARD, E. E., *Witchcraft, oracles and magic among the Azande*. Clarendon Press, Oxford, 1937.

EVANS-PRITCHARD, E. E., *The Nuer*. Clarendon Press, Oxford, 1940.

EVANS-PRITCHARD, E. E., *Kinship and marriage among the Nuer*. Clarendon Press, Oxford, 1951.

EVANS-PRITCHARD, E. E., *Social anthropology*. Cohen and West, London, 1951.

Bibliography

EVANS-PRITCHARD, E. E., *Nuer religion*. Clarendon Press, Oxford, 1956.
EVANS-PRITCHARD, E. E., 'Anthropology and history' in his *Essays in social anthropology*. Faber and Faber, London, 1962.
EVANS-PRITCHARD, E. E., *Theories of primitive religion*. Clarendon Press, Oxford, 1965.
EVANS-PRITCHARD, E. E., *The Zande trickster*. Clarendon Press, Oxford, 1967.
EVANS-PRITCHARD, E. E., (ed.), *The institutions of primitive society*. Blackwell, Oxford, 1954.
FESTINGER, L., *A theory of cognitive dissonance*. Stanford University Press, Stanford, Calif., 1957.
FEYERABEND, P., 'Explanation, reduction and empiricism' in H. Fiegl and G. Maxwell (eds.), *Minnesota studies in the philosophy of science*, 3, Minneapolis, 1962.
FILLIOZAT, J., *The classical doctrine in Indian medicine. Its origin and Greek parallels*. Munshiram Manoharlal, Delhi, 1964.
FINNEGAN, R., 'Early Irish kingship'. Unpublished B.Litt. thesis, University of Oxford, 1960.
FINNEGAN, R., *Limba stories and story-telling*. Clarendon Press, Oxford, 1967.
FINNEGAN, R., 'Attitudes to speech and language among the Limba of Sierra Leone'. *Odu*, N.S., 2, 1969.
FINNEGAN, R., 'How to do things with words: performative utterances among the Limba of Sierra Leone'. *Man*, N.S., 4, 1969.
FINNEGAN, R., *Oral literature in Africa*. Clarendon Press, Oxford, 1970.
FIRTH, R., *We the Tikopia: a sociological study of kinship in primitive Polynesia*. Allen & Unwin, London, 1936.
FIRTH, R., 'Problem and assumption in an anthropological study of religion'. *Journal of the Royal Anthropological Institute*, 89, 1959.
FIRTH, R., 'Twins, birds and vegetables'. *Man*, N.S., 1, 1966.
FISHMAN, J. A., 'A systematization of the Whorfian hypothesis'. *Behavioural Science*, 5, 1960.
FORDE, D., and JONES, G. I., *The Ibo and Ibibio-speaking peoples of south-eastern Nigeria*. International African Institute, London, 1962.
FORTES, M., *Oedipus and Job in West African religion*. University Press, Cambridge, 1959.
FORTUNE, R. F., *Sorcerers of Dobu*. Routledge and Kegan Paul, London, 1932.
FRAKE, C. O., 'The disgnosis of disease among the Subanum of Mindanao'. *American Anthropologist*, 63, 1961.
FREUCHEN, P., *Book of the Eskimos*. Arthur Barker Ltd., London, 1962.
FROBENIUS, L., 'Der kameruner Schiffschnabel und seine Motive'. *Nova Acta, Abhandlungen der Kaiserlichen Leopoldinisch—carolinischen Deutschen Akademie der Naturforscher*, 70, 1, 1897.
FROBENIUS, L., 'Ethnologische Ergebnisse der zweiten Reiseperiode der DIAFE'. Sonderdruck der *Zeitschrift für Ethnologie*, 6, 1909.
FROBENIUS, L., 'Kulturtypen aus dem Westsudan; Auszüge aus den Ergebnissen der zweiten deutschen innerafrikanischen Forschungsexpedition nebst einen Anhang über Kulturzonen und Kulturforschung in Afrika'. Ergänzungsheft Nr. 166 zu *Petermanns Mitteilungen*, Justus Perthes, Gotha, 1910.
FROBENIUS, L., *Auf dem Weg nach Atlantis*. Vita, Deutsches Verlagshaus, Berlin-Charlottenburg, 1911.
FROBENIUS, L., *The voice of Africa*. 2 vols. Hutchinson, London, 1913 (Eng. trans. of first 2 vols of *Und Afrika sprach . . .*, Volksausgabe, Vita, Deutsches Verlagshaus, Berlin-Charlottenburg, 1912–13).

Bibliography

FROBENIUS, L., *Atlantis. Volksmärchen und Volksdichtungen Afrikas*. 12 vols. Eugen Diederichs, Jena, 1921-8.

FROBENIUS, L., *Das unbekannte Afrika*. Beck, München, 1923.

FROBENIUS, L., *Vom Kulturreich des Festlandes*. Wegweiser Verlag, Berlin, 1923.

FROBENIUS, L., *Erlebte Erdteile; Ergebnisse eines deutschen Forscherlebens*. 7 vols. Frankfurter Societätsdruckerei, Frankfurt, 1925-9.

FROBENIUS, L., *Erythräa; Lander und Zeiten des heiligen Konigsmordes*. Atlantis Verlag, Berlin and Zurich, 1931.

FROBENIUS, L., *Kulturgeschichte Afrikas*. Phaidon, Frankfurt, 1933. French trans. as *Histoire de la civilisation africaine*. Gallimard, Paris, 1936.

FROBENIUS, L., *Schicksalskunde*. Frobenius-Institut, Weimar, 1938.

Leo Frobenius, ein Lebenswerk aus der Zeit der Kulturwende. Dargestellt von seinen Freunden und Schülern. Koehler und Umelang, Leipzig, 1933.

FURUTA, K., 'Shin bukkyô no seiritsu' (The establishment of new Buddhism) in K. Ishida (ed.), *Nihon bunkashi gairon*, Tokyo, 1968.

GAY, J., and COLE, M., *The new mathematics and an old culture*. Holt, Rinehart and Winston, New York, 1967.

GELLNER, E., 'Concepts and society'. *Transactions of the Fifth World Congress of Sociology*, 1, Washington, D.C., 1962.

GLADWIN, T., 'Cultural and logical process', in Ward H. Goodenough (ed.), *Explorations in cultural anthropology*, McGraw-Hill, New York, 1964.

GLUCKMAN, M., *Politics, law and ritual in tribal society*. Blackwell, Oxford, 1965.

GLUCKMAN, M. (ed.), *Essays on the ritual of social relations*. University Press, Manchester, 1962.

GLUCKMAN, M., and Devons, E. (eds.), *Closed systems and open minds*. Oliver and Boyd, Edinburgh and London, 1964.

GOODY, J., and WATT, I., 'The consequences of literacy'. *Comparative Studies in Society and History*, 5, 3, 1963 (reprinted in J. Goody (ed.), *Literacy in traditional societies*, 1968).

GOODY, J. (ed.), *Literacy in traditional societies*. University Press, Cambridge, 1968.

GOSLING, N., 'On the drawings of L. da Vinci'. *The Observer Review*, 1.6.1969.

GOUGH, K., 'Implications of literacy in traditional China and India', in J. Goody (ed.), *Literacy in traditional societies*, 1968.

GREENFIELD, P. M., and BRUNER, J. S., 'Culture and cognitive growth'. *International Journal of Psychology*, 1, 1966.

GRIMBLE, A., *Return to the islands*. Murray, London, 1957.

HAGA, K., 'Zen no shisô to Muromachi bunka no seishin' (The Zen philosophy and the spirit of Muromachi culture), in K. Ishida (ed.), *Nihon shisôshi gairon* Tokyo, 1963.

HANSON, N., *Patterns of discovery. An inquiry into the conceptual foundations of science*. University Press, Cambridge, 1958.

HARRÉ, R., *Theories and things*. Sheed and Ward, London, 1961.

HASKINS, C. P., 'Report of the President 1966-67'. Carnegie Institution, Washington, 1968.

HAYLEY, A., 'Symbolic equations: the ox and the cucumber'. *Man*, N.S., 3, 1962.

HEGEL, G. W. F., *Die Philosophie der Geschichte*. Reclam Verlag, Stuttgart, 1961.

HERTZ, R., *Death and the right hand*. Eng. trans. by R. and C. Needham, Cohen and West, London, 1960.

HESSE, M. B., *Science and human imagination*. S.C.M., London, 1954.

HESSE, M. B., *Forces and fields: the concept of action at a distance in the history of physics*. Nelson and Sons, London, 1961.

Bibliography

HESSE, M. B., *Models and analogies in science*. Sheed and Ward, London, 1963; expanded edn., University of Notre Dame Press, Indiana, 1966.

HOLLIS, M., 'The limits of irrationality'. *European Journal of Sociology*, 8, 1967.

HOLLIS, M., 'Reason and ritual'. *Philosophy*, 42, 165, 1968.

HORTON, R., 'The Kalabari *Ekine* society: a borderland of religion and art'. *Africa*, 33, 1963.

HORTON, R., 'Boundaries of explanation in social anthropology'. *Man*, 63, 6, 1963.

HORTON, R., 'African traditional thought and Western science. Part I. From tradition to science. Part II. The "closed" and "open" predicaments'. *Africa*, 37, 1967.

HORTON, R., 'Neo-Tylorianism: sound sense or sinister prejudice?' *Man*, N.S., 3, 1968.

HORTON, R., 'The romantic illusion: Roger Bastide on Africa and the West'. *Odu*, N.S., 3, 1970.

HORTON, R., 'Lévy-Bruhl among the scientists', *Second Order*, 2, 1, 1973.

HOYLE, F., *The black cloud*. Penguin, Harmondsworth, 1960.

HUBERT, H., and MAUSS, M., *Sacrifice. Its nature and function*. Eng. trans. by W. D. Halls, Cohen and West, London, 1964.

HYMES, D. H., 'Functions of speech: an evolutionary approach', in F. C. Gruber (ed.), *Anthropology and education*, University of Pennsylvania Press, 1961.

IENAGA, S., 'Kokka no keisei to tairiku bunka' (The formation of the nation and the continental culture), in K. Ishida (ed.), *Nihon bunkashi gairon*, Tokyo, 1968.

IENAGA, S., 'Kodai kokka no shûkyô, shisô, bungei (Religion, thought and literature in the ancient Japanese state), in K. Ishida (ed.), *Nihon bunkashi gairon*, Tokyo, 1968.

ILLICH, I. D., *Celebration of awareness*. Calder and Boyars, London, 1971.

INOUE, M., *Shinwa kara rekishi he* (From myth to history). History of Japan, Series 1, Chuôkôron-Sha, Tokyo, 1965.

INOUE, M., *Nihon kodai kokka no kenkyû* (The study of the ancient Japanese state). Iwanami-Shoten, Tokyo, 1965.

ISHIDA, E., 'Minzoku bunka no keisei' (The formation of the folk culture), in K. Ishida (ed.), *Nihon bunkashi gairon*, Tokyo, 1968.

ISHIDA, K., 'Bunkashigaku to Nihon bunkashi' (Culturology and the history of Japanese culture), in K. Ishida (ed.), *Nihon bunkashi gairon*, 1968.

ISHIDA, K., 'Zen no shisô to bungei bijutsu' (Zen philosophy and literature and fine arts), in K. Ishida (ed.), *Nihon bunkashi gairon*, 1968.

ISHIDA, K. (ed.), *Nihon shisôshi gairon* (An introduction to the history of Japanese thought). Yoshikawa-Kobunkan, Tokyo, 1963.

ISHIDA, K. (ed.), *Nihon bunkashi gairon* (An introduction to the history of Japanese culture). Yoshikawa-Kobunkan, Tokyo, 1968.

ITÔ, T., 'Nihon kenkyu to seiyô gakujutsu no juyô' (Japanese studies and the acceptance of Western disciplines), in K. Ishida (ed.), *Nihon bunkôshi gairon*, Tokyo, 1968.

JARVIE, I., *The revolution in anthropology*. Routledge, London, 1964.

JARVIE, I. C., and AGASSI, J., 'The problem of the rationality of magic'. *British Journal of Sociology*, 18, 1967.

JESPERSON, O., 'Mankind, nation and individual', in *A linguistic point of view*, Oslo and Cambridge, 1925.

JOCHELSON, W., *Peoples of Asiatic Russia*. American Museum of History, New York, 1928.

383

Bibliography

JONES, J. H., 'Commonplace and memorization in the oral tradition of English and Scottish popular ballads'. *Journal of American Folklore*, 74, 1961.

JORAVSKY, D., 'Soviet ideology'. *Soviet Studies*, 18, 1, 1966.

JORDAN, Z., *Philosophy and ideology*. Reidel, Dordrecht, 1963.

KAGAME, A., *La poésie dynastique au Rwanda*. Institut Royal Colonial Belge, Brussels, 1951.

KENNY, T., *The political thought of J. H. Newman*. Longmans, London, 1957.

KIRK, G. S., *Myth: its meaning and functions*. University Press, Cambridge, 1970.

KIRK, G. S. (ed.), *The language and background of Homer*. Heffer, Cambridge, 1964.

KNOTT, E., *Irish classical poetry*. Colm Ó Lochlainn, Dublin, 1957.

KRETSCHMAR, F., *Leo Frobenius*. Cyclostyled, Inter Nationes, 1968.

KUHN, T. S., *The structure of scientific revolutions*. Chicago University Press, Chicago, 1962 (revised edn., 1970).

KUHN, T. S., 'The function of dogma in scientific research', in A. C. Crombie (ed.), *Scientific change*, Heinemann, London, 1963.

LAKATOS, I., and MUSGRAVE, A., *Problems in the philosophy of science*. North-Holland Publ. Co., Amsterdam, 1968.

LEACH, E., *Political systems of highland Burma*. London School of Economics and Political Science and Bell and Sons, London, 1954.

LEACH, E., 'Virgin birth'. *Proceedings of the Royal Anthropological Institute for 1966* (pub. 1967).

LEACH, E., *Lévi-Strauss*. Fontana, London, 1970.

LEACH, E. (ed.), *The structural study of myth and totemism*. Tavistock, London, 1967.

LEACH, MACE. (ed.), *The ballad book*. Yoseloff, London, 1955.

LEIRIS, M., and DELANGE, J., *African art*. Braziller, London, 1968.

LÉVI-STRAUSS, C., *La pensée sauvage*. Plon, Paris, 1962. (Trans. as *The savage mind*, Weidenfeld and Nicolson, London, 1966.)

LÉVI-STRAUSS, C., *Le totémisme aujourd'hui*. Presses Universitaires de France, Paris, 1962. (Eng. trans. by R. Needham as *Totemism*, Penguin, Harmondsworth, 1969.)

LÉVI-STRAUSS, C., 'The story of Asdiwal', in E. Leach (ed.), *The structural study of myth and totemism*, Tavistock, London, 1967.

LÉVY-BRUHL, L., *Les fonctions mentales dans les sociétés inférieures*. Alcan, Paris, 1910, and Presses Universitaires de France, Paris, 1951.

LÉVY-BRUHL, L., *La mentalité primitive*. Alcan, Paris, 1922. (Eng. trans. *Primitive mentality*, Beacon Press, New York, 1966.)

LÉVY-BRUHL, L., *L'âme primitive*, Alcan, Paris, 1927.

LÉVY-BRUHL, L., *Le surnaturel et la nature dans la mentalité primitive*. Alcan, Paris, 1931.

LÉVY-BRUHL, L., *La mythologie primitive*. Alcan, Paris, 1935.

LÉVY-BRUHL, L., *L'expérience mystique et les symboles chez les primitifs*. Alcan, Paris, 1938.

LÉVY-BRUHL, L., *Les carnets de Lucien Lévy-Bruhl*. Presses Universitaires de France, Paris, 1949.

LIENHARDT, G., *Divinity and experience: the religion of the Dinka*. Clarendon Press, Oxford, 1961.

LIENHARDT, G., *Social anthropology*. Oxford University Press, London, 1964.

LLOYD, G. E. R., *Polarity and analogy: two types of argumentation in early Greek thought*. University Press, Cambridge, 1966.

Bibliography

LORD, A. B., *The singer of tales*. Harvard University Press, Cambridge, Mass., 1960; and Atheneum, New York, 1965.

LOVEJOY, A. O., 'The meaning of romanticism for the historian of ideas'. *Journal of the History of Ideas*, 2, 1941.

LUKÁCS, G., *Histoire et conscience de classe*. Fr. trans. by K. Axelos and J. Bois, Editions de Minuit, Paris, 1960.

LUKES, S., Review article on D. Bell, 'Soviet ideology'. *New Society*, 16 June 1966.

LUKES, S., 'Some problems about rationality'. *European Journal of Sociology*, 8, 2, 1967 (reprinted in B. R. Wilson (ed.), *Rationality*, Blackwell, Oxford, 1970).

MACH, E., *The analysis of sensations*. Open Court Publishing Company, Chicago and London, 1914.

MACINTYRE, A., 'Is understanding religion compatible with believing?' in J. Hick (ed.), *Faith and the philosophers*, Macmillan, London, 1966.

MACINTYRE, A., 'A mistake about causality in social science', in P. Laslett and W. Runciman (eds.), *Philosophy, politics and society* (2nd series), Blackwell, Oxford, 1967.

McLUHAN, M., *Understanding media, the extensions of man*. Routledge and Kegan Paul, London, 1964.

MAGOUN, F. P., 'Oral-formulaic character of Anglo-Saxon poetry'. *Speculum*, 28, 1953.

MALINOWSKI, B., 'Magic, science and religion', in J. Needham (ed.), *Science, religion and reality*, Sheldon Press, London, 1925.

MALINOWSKI, B., *Coral gardens and their magic*. Indiana University Press, Bloomington, 1965.

MANDLER, G., 'Organization and memory', in K. W. Spence and J. T. Spence (eds.), *The psychology of learning and motivation*, Academic Press, New York, 1966.

MANN, T., *Betrachtungen eines Unpolitischen*. S. Fischer Verlag, Frankfurt, 1956.

MANNHEIM, K., *Ideology and Utopia*. Kegan Paul, London, 1936; Routledge, London, 1960.

MARANDA, P. and E. K. (eds.), *Structural analysis of oral tradition*. University of Pennsylvania Press, Philadelphia, 1971.

MARX, K., *Introduction to the critique of political economy* (1857) in *A contribution to the critique of political economy*, trans. N. I. Stone, Kerr, Chicago, 1913.

MASUDA, Y., *Junsui bunka no jôken* (Conditions for a homogenous culture). Kodan-Sha, Tokyo, 1967.

MAUSS, M., *The gift*. Trans. by I. Cunnison, Cohen and West, London, 1954.

MAYER, P., *The lineage principle in Gusii society*. International African Institute Memorandum 24, Oxford University Press, London, 1949.

MAYER, P., *Gusii bridewealth law and custom*. Rhodes-Livingstone Papers, 18, Oxford University Press, Cape Town, 1950.

MAYER, P., 'Gusii initiation ceremonies'. *Journal of the Royal Anthropological Institute*, 83, 1953.

MBITI, J. S. *Akamba stories*. Clarendon Press, Oxford, 1966.

MEEK, C. K., *Law and authority in a Nigerian tribe*. Oxford University Press, London, 1937.

MEINHOF, C., *Die Sprachen der Hamiten*. Friedrichsen, Hamburg, 1912.

MELLOR, D., 'Physics and furniture', in N. Rescher (ed.), *Studies in the philosophy of science*, American Philosophical Quarterly Monograph No. 3, Oxford, 1969.

MICHOTTE, A., *The perception of causality*. Eng. trans., Methuen, London, 1963.

MIDDLETON, J., *Lugbara religion*. Oxford University Press, London, 1960.

MILNER, G. B., 'Siamese twins, birds and the double helix'. *Man*, N.S., 4, 1969.

Bibliography

MIYAMOTO, T., *Minzokugaku heno michi* (A way to folklore). Mirai-Sha, Tokyo, 1968.

MURDOCH, I., *Sartre*. Yale University Press, 1963.

NADEAU, M., *History of surrealism*. Eng. trans. Cape, London, 1968.

NEEDHAM, J., *Science and civilisation in China*. University Press, Cambridge, 1954.

NEEDHAM, J. A. (ed.), *Science, religion and reality*. Sheldon Press, London, 1925.

NEEDHAM, R., 'The left hand of the Mugwe: an analytic note on the structure of Meru symbolism'. *Africa*, 30, 1960.

NEWMAN, J. H., *Sermons, chiefly on the theory of religious belief, preached before the University of Oxford*. London, 1843.

NEWMAN, J. H., *Essay on the development of Christian doctrine* (1845). Sheed and Ward, London, 1960.

NEWMAN, J. H., *Lectures on certain difficulties felt by Anglicans* (1850). Longmans, Green, London, 1908.

NEWMAN, J. H., *The idea of a university* (1852). Ed. M. Svaglic, Holt, Rinehart and Winston, London, 1968.

NEWMAN, J. H., *On the scope and nature of university education* (1852). Everyman, London, 1915.

NEWMAN, J. H., *Apologia* (1864). Ed. M. Svaglic, Clarendon Press, Oxford, 1967.

NEWMAN, J., 'The Tamworth reading room', in *Discussions and arguments* (1872). Longmans, Green, London, 1907.

NISBET, R. A., *The sociological tradition*. Heinemann, London, 1970.

NISHIO, Y., 'Kyûtei seikatsu no shisô to bungei' (Thought and literature of private life in the royal court), in K. Ishida (ed.), *Nihon bunkashi gairon* (An introduction to the history of Japanese culture), Tokyo, 1968.

NKETIA, K., 'Akan poetry'. *Black Orpheus*, 3, 1958.

NORRIS, H. T., *Shinqiṭī folk literature and song*. Clarendon Press, Oxford, 1968.

O'RAHILLY, T. F., 'Irish poets, historians and judges'. *Proceedings of the Royal Irish Academy*, 36, 1922.

OSSOWSKI, S., *Class structure in the social consciousness*, trans. S. Patterson, Routledge, London, 1963.

OUOLOGUEM, Y., *Le devoir de violence*. Editions du Seuil, Paris, 1968.

PARSONS, T., *The structure of social action*. 2 vols. Free Press, New York, 1949.

PARSONS, T., *Societies. Evolutionary and comparative perspectives*. Prentice-Hall, Englewood Cliffs, 1966.

PATTISON, M., *Memoirs*, Macmillan, London, 1885.

PEARSON, K., *The grammar of science*. A. and C. Black, London, 1911.

PEEL, J. D. Y., 'Understanding alien belief systems'. *British Journal of Sociology*, 20, 1969.

PERLS, F., HEFFERLINE, R., and GOODMAN, P., *Gestalt therapy*. Julian Press, New York, 1951.

PHILLPOTTS, B., *Edda and saga*. Thornton Butterworth, London, 1931.

PIAGET, J., 'Nécessité et signification des recherches comparatives en psychologie génétique'. *International Journal of Psychology*, 1, 1, 1966.

PLUMB, J., 'The historian's dilemma', in J. Plumb (ed.), *Crisis in the humanities*, Penguin, Harmondsworth, 1964.

POCOCK, D. F., *Social anthropology*. Newman history and philosophy of science series, Sheed and Ward, London, 1961.

POLANYI, M., *Personal knowledge*. University of Chicago Press, Chicago, 1958 (2nd edn. Harper Torchbooks. New York, 1964).

POPPER, K., *Conjectures and refutations. The growth of scientific knowledge*. Routledge, London, 1963.

Bibliography

POUND, L., *Poetic origins and the ballad*. Macmillan, New York, 1921.
PROPP, V., *Morphology of the folktale*, trans. L. Scott, Indiana University Research Center in Anthropology, Folklore and Linguistics, Bloomington, 1958.
QUINE, W., *From a logical point of view*. Harvard University Press, Cambridge, Mass., 1953.
RADCLIFFE-BROWN, A. R., *The Andaman Islanders* (1922). Free Press, New York, 1964.
RADCLIFFE-BROWN, A. R., *Structure and function in primitive society*. Cohen and West, London, 1952.
RADIN, P., *The trickster. A study in American Indian mythology*. Routledge and Kegan Paul, London, 1956.
RADIN, P., *Primitive man as philosopher*. Dover Publications, New York, revised edn., 1957.
RADLOV, V. V., *Proben der Volkslitteratur der türkischen Stämme und der dsungarischen Steppe*. St. Petersburg, 1866–1904.
RAISON, T. (ed.), *The founding fathers of social science*. Penguin, Harmondsworth, 1969.
RASMUSSEN, K., *The Netsilik Eskimos. Social life and spiritual culture*. Gyldendalske Boghandel, Copenhagen, 1931.
RAWSON, E., *The Spartan tradition in European thought*. Clarendon Press, Oxford, 1969.
REISMAN, D., *The oral tradition, the written word and the screen image*. Antioch Press, Yellow Springs, 1956.
RAISANOVSKY, N. V., *Russia and the West in the teaching of the Slavophiles*. Harvard University Press, Cambridge, Mass., 1952.
RIVERS, W. H. R., *Medicine, magic and religion*. (The Fitzpatrick lectures before the Royal College of Physicians of London in 1915 and 1916.) Kegan Paul, London, 1924.
RIVIÈRE, P., *Marriage among the Trio*. Clarendon Press, Oxford, 1970.
ROBINSON, F. N., 'Satirists and enchanters in early Irish literature', in *Studies in the history of religion presented to C. H. Toy*, Macmillan, New York, 1912
ROSENBERG, B. A., 'The formulaic quality of spontaneous sermons'. *Journal of American folklore*, 83, 1970.
ROSS, J., 'Formulaic composition in Gaelic oral poetry'. *Modern Philology*, 57, 1, 1959.
ROSZAK, T., *The making of a counter-culture*. Faber, London, 1970.
RUSSELL, B., *My philosophical development*. Allen and Unwin, London, 1959.
SCHON, D. A., *Invention and the evolution of ideas*. Tavistock, London, 1967.
SCHUTZ, A., *Collected papers*. Nijhoff, The Hague, 1962–4.
SEARLE, J. R., *Speech acts. An essay in the philosophy of language*. University Press, Cambridge, 1969.
SELIGMAN, C. G., *The races of Africa* (1930), 3rd edn., Oxford University Press, London, 1957.
SELLARS, W., *Science, perception and reality*. Routledge, London, 1963.
SENGHOR, L. S., *Liberté I. Négritude et humanisme*. Editions du Seuil, Paris, 1964.
SENGHOR, L. S., *Africa and the Germans*. Horst Erdmann Verlag, Tübingen and Basel, 1968.
SIMMONS, D. C., 'Tonal rhyme in Efik poetry'. *Anthropological Linguistics*, 2, 6, 1960.
SKOLIMOWSKI, H., *Polish analytical philosophy*. Routledge, London, 1967.
SMITH, M. G., 'The social functions and meaning of Hausa praise-singing'. *Africa*, 27, 1957.

Bibliography

SOREL, G., *Reflections on violence*. Eng. trans. by T. E. Hulme, Allen and Unwin, London, 1916.

SPARK, M. (ed.), *The Catholic sermons of Cardinal Newman*. London, 1957.

SPINDEN, H. J., *Songs of the Tewa: preceded by an essay on American Indian poetry*. The Exposition of Indian Tribal Arts, Inc., New York, 1933.

SPIRO, M. E., 'Religion: problems of definition and explanation', in M. Banton (ed.), *Anthropological approaches to the study of religion*, Tavistock, London, 1966.

STEBBING, S., *Philosophy and the physicists*. Methuen, London, 1937.

STEINER, F., 'Chagga truth'. *Africa*, 25, 1954.

SWADESH, M., 'Origén y evolucíon del lenguaje humano'. *Anales de Antropología Universidad Nacional Autónoma de Mexico*, 2, 1965.

TAMBIAH, S. J., 'The magical power of words'. *Man*, N.S., 3, 1968.

TAYLOR, J., *The primal vision*. S.C.M., London, 1963.

THOMAS, K., 'History and anthropology'. *Past and Present*, 24, 1963.

THOMAS, K., *Religion and the decline of magic: studies in popular beliefs in sixteenth and seventeenth century England*. Weidenfeld and Nicolson, London, 1971.

TOULMIN, S., *The architecture of matter*. Hutchinson, London, 1962.

TRASK, W. T., *The unwritten song. Poetry of the primitive and traditional peoples of the world*. 2 vols. Jonathan Cape, London, 1969.

TREVOR-ROPER, H., *The rise of Christian Europe*. Thames and Hudson, London, 1964.

TRISTRAM, H., et al., *Newman centenary essays*. Burns Oates, London, 1945.

TSUJIMURA, A., *Nihon bunka to communication* (The Japanese culture and communication). N.H.K., Tokyo, 1968.

TULVING, E., 'Subjective organization in free recall of "unrelated" words'. *Psychological Review*, 69, 1962.

TULVING, E., 'Theoretical issues in free recall', in T. R. Dixon and D. L. Horton (eds.), *Verbal learning and general behavior theory*, Prentice-Hall, Englewood Cliffs, 1968.

TULVING, E., and PEARLSTONE, Z., 'Availability versus accessibility of information and memory for words'. *Journal of Verbal Learning and Verbal Behavior*, 5, 1966.

TURNER, V., *Ndembu divination*. Rhodes-Livingstone Papers, 31, University Press, Manchester, 1962.

TURNER, V., *Chihamba the white spirit. A ritual drama of the Ndembu*. Rhodes-Livingstone Papers, 33, University Press, Manchester, 1962.

TURNER, V., 'Three symbols of *passage* in Ndembu circumcision ritual: an interpretation', in M. Gluckman (ed.), *Essays on the ritual of social relations*, University Press, Manchester, 1962.

TURNER, V., 'An Ndembu doctor in practice', in A. Kiev (ed.), *Magic, faith and healing*, Collier-Macmillan, London, 1964.

TURNER, V., 'Colour classification in Ndembu ritual', in M. Banton (ed.), *Anthropological approaches to the study of religion*, Tavistock, London, 1966.

TURNER, V., *The forest of symbols*. Cornell University Press, 1967.

TURNER, V., *The drums of affliction: a study of religious processes among the Ndembu of Zambia*. Clarendon Press, Oxford, 1968.

TYLOR, E. B., *The origins of culture* (Part 1 of *Primitive culture*) (1871). Harper Torchbook, New York, 1958.

UNESCO. *World congress of ministers of education on the eradication of illiteracy, Teheran 1965. Speeches and messages*. UNESCO, 1966.

Bibliography

WALDRON, R. A., 'Oral-formulaic technique and Middle English alliterative poetry'. *Speculum*, 32, 1957.

WALLACE, A., and ATKINS, J., 'The meaning of kinship terms'. *American Anthropologist*, 62, 1960.

WALLACE, W. L., *Sociological theory*. Heinemann, London, 1969.

WARD, W., *The life of John Henry Cardinal Newman*. Longmans, London, 1927.

WATSON, W., *On understanding physics*. University Press, Cambridge, 1938.

WETTER, G., *Soviet ideology today*, trans. P. Heath, Heinemann, London, 1966.

WHITE, L., 'Mediaeval uses of air'. *Scientific American*, 223, 2, 1970.

WHORF, B. L., *Language, thought and reality: selected writings of Benjamin Lee Whorf*, ed. J. B. Carroll. M.I.T. Press, Cambridge, Mass, 1964.

WILLEY, B., *Seventeenth century background*. Penguin, Harmondsworth, 1962.

WILLEY, B., *Eighteenth century background*. Penguin, Harmondsworth, 1967.

WILLIAMS, R., *Culture and society*. Penguin, Harmondsworth, 1961.

WILSON, B. R. (ed.), *Rationality*. Blackwell, Oxford, 1970.

WINCH, P., *The idea of a social science and its relation to philosophy*. Routledge, London, 1958.

WINCH, P., 'Understanding a primitive society'. *American Philosophical Quarterly*, 1, 4, 1964.

WINCH, P., 'Understanding a primitive religion', in D. Z. Phillips (ed.), *Religion and understanding*, Blackwell, Oxford, 1967.

WOLFRAM, S., 'The explanation of prohibitions and preferences of marriage between kin', unpublished D.Phil. thesis, University of Oxford, 1956.

WOLFRAM, S., 'Le marriage entre alliés dans l'Angleterre contemporaine'. *L'Homme*, 1, 1961.

YAMAGUCHI, M., 'Africa no chiteki kanôsei (An intellectual possibility of Africa). Koza tetsugaku (Philosophy series), 18, Iwanami, Tokyo, 1967.

YAMAGUCHI, M., 'Ushinawareta sekai no fukken' (For the restoration of the lost world). Mikai to bunmei, Gendaijin no shisô (Primitive and civilized, Modern thoughts series), 15, Heibon-Sha, Tokyo, 1968.

YAMAGUCHI, M., 'Bunka to kyôki' (Culture and delirium: Homo delirus). *Chuô-Kôron*, Tokyo, Jan. 1969.

ZIMAN, J. M., *Public knowledge. An essay concerning the social dimension of science*. University Press, Cambridge, 1968.

Index

aborigines, Australian, 96, 115
Abuuga, Erasto, 149n
accretion picture, 175
Acton, Lord, 353
Adali-Mortty, G., 119n
administration, territorial, 66
Africa, free recall experiments, 74–80
  influence on Western culture, 291
  lack of writing, 115
  Négritude, 59, 93, 306–36
  traditional thought pattern, 276–83
Agassi, J., 182n
Akamba stories, 125
Akan, oral literature, 123
Aksakov, Konstantin, 330n, 331
Allchin, A. M., 343n
Allies, Mary, 354n
Allies, T. W., 353, 354n
Alquié, F., 289
Americans, free recall experiments, 75–81, 91
Amerindia, *see* Indians, American
analogies, definition, 209
  and Greek philosophy, 206, 207 9
  magical acts and, 199–206, 208, 212–218, 222
  scientific, 183–4, 194, 196–7, 199–200, 208–13
  types of, 209–12
Andrzejewski, B. W., 128n
animals, colour-words for, 152–6
  use in African stories, 120–1
anomalies, and belief-systems, 22, 182–98
Arabic, 115
Ardener, E. W., 156n
Argyle, J., 58
Arianhdit, 47
Aristotle, 64, 118, 208

Arnold, Matthew, 341–2, 355
Arnold, Thomas, 347
arts, 289, 290, 291, 293–4
  see also literature
Atkins, J., 69n
attraction, analogy of, 206–8, 209, 213, 215–16
Auger, Pierre, 280
Austin, J. L., 34, 219–20
Australia, aborigines, 115
awarè, 99
Ayer, A. J., 279n, 298n
Azande, 31, 32, 37–42, 48, 52–4, 121, 166–7, 185, 187, 200–26, 239, 243
azmaris, 141

Babalǫla, S. A., 123n, 127n
Bacon, Francis, 209
Barnes, S. B., 41, 185n, 230n, 302n
Barraclough, G., 287n
Barth, Heinrich, 311
Bartlett, F. C., 72, 83
Bastide, Roger, 273
Bateson, Gregory, 68, 70, 73
Beattie, J., 48n, 182n, 187, 274, 275, 281, 296, 299, 308n
Becker, Howard S., 32n
Beidelmann, T. O., 145, 146–7
Bell, Daniel, 243n, 350
Ben-David, J., 197
Benedict, R., 136n, 308n
Benin culture, 316
Bennett, Mrs L. V., 93n
Benson, L. D., 136n
Bentham, Jeremy, 351
Berger, P. L., 28n, 61n, 231n
Bergson, Henri, 41
Berkeley, G., 177n, 366n
Berlin, B., 68, 146n, 161

391

Index

Index

recluses, 96
Reicher, G. M., 76n
religious ideas, and origins of modern thought, 258, 259–66
and secularism in Western society, 20–1, 337–56
renga, 97, 99–100, 102
reversed world, 29, 92–111
Riasanovsky, N. V., 330n
Richards, Audrey, 219, 308n
Riesman, D., 71
rites, magical, 20–2, 119–206, 208, 212–29, 239, 243
rituals, belief in the efficacy of, 193
and colour concepts, 146–7, 148, 156, 157–60
Rivière, P., 244n
Robinson, F. N., 134n
Robinson, John, 342
role specialization, 23, 49–50, 162, 169, 173–7, 194
Roman literature, 136
romanticism, *see* liberal romanticism
Rosenberg, B. A., 136n
Ross, J., 117n, 136n
Roszak, T., 292n
rote memory, 23, 73–3, 88
Ruanda, oral literature, 120, 123, 139
Russell, B., 239n
Russia, *see* Soviet Union
Ryô-nin, 100

sacred/profane schema, 272–5, 277
Sapir, 67
Sartre, Jean-Paul, 286–7
scepticism, growth of, 286
Scheler, Max, 236n
Schleicher, August, 67
Schon, Donald A., 184n
Schutz, Alfred, 32n
scientific thought, analogies in, 183–4, 194, 196–7
delimiting of, 171–2
differentiated structure of, 17–19, 194–8
origins of, 259–66
paradigms, 51, 165, 184–5, 188–92, 195–8, 234–5, 243
and preliterate belief-systems, 162–181, 186–94, 246–7
presupposition and commitment in, 184–6

Scotland, oral literature in, 117
scripts, development in Japan, 105, 106
Sea Dyaks, 117
Searle, J. R., 221n
secularism, and religious thought, 20, 337–56
Seligman, C. G., 322
Sellars, W., 279n
Senegambia, griots, 134n
Senghor, Léopold Sédar, 307, 311–15, 325, 326–8, 331, 333
sensations, 64
Sharp, D., 67n
Shin-Kokin-Shû, 99
Shintoism, 100, 105, 109
Shunzei, Fujiwara, 99
Siberia, oral literature, 116–17
Simmons, D. C., 127n
Skolimowski, H., 231n
Smith, M. G., 120n
social classification, and belief-systems, 191–4
social relevance, and memory, 72
societies, classification of, 14–16, 90–1, 112, 144, 249n, 358–62, 371–4
Somali, love poetry, 117, 128
songs, epic, *see* oral literature
sorcery, *see* magical acts
Sorel, G., 348
Sorokin, P., 236n
Soviet Union, ideology, 243, 245
nationalism, 330–3
as an open society, 41
Spain, trade with Japan, 107
Spark, M., 341n
Sparta, 30
speech, and magical acts, 220–2
predominance of symbolism over, 289–90, 292
Spengler, O., 288
Spinden, H. J., 133n
Spiro, M. E., 239
Stark, Werner, 350n
Stebbing, S., 279n
Steiner, Franz, 240–1
story-telling, 120, 121, 123, 125, 129, 130, 136
see also oral literature
Sudan, 313, 316
supreme being, 45–7
surrealism, 30, 289, 290n, 291, 295, 296n
Swadesh, M., 68

398

Index

Swazi, 72
symbolism, twentieth-century fascination for, 289–90, 292, 293

taboo, 190, 192
Tambiah, S. J., 115n, 204n, 217n
Tanzania, cattle terms of the Cushitic Iraqw, 155n
Tatar, saga-tellers, 120
Taylor, J. V., 273
Tewa, 132–3
thinking definition, 63–4
Thomas, K., 57n
Thorn, Richard, 44n
thought, content, 25–7, 65
  modes of, see 'modes of thought'
  processes, 25–7, 65–6
Tien Shan, 117
Tikopian Islanders, oral literature, 122
Tiv, 317, 335
Togo, North, 313
Toryism (Newman), 339, 340, 347, 349
Tosa nikki, 107
totems, 259, 260
Toulmin, Stephen, 279, 282
Toynbee, 288
translation, inter-cultural, 32–4
Trask, W. R., 117n, 125n
Trevor-Roper, H., 315n
trickster tales, 52–4
Trilling, Lionel, 345
Trobrianders, 217, 218, 219, 222
Truk Islands, 68
truth, social determination of, 19–20, 27, 230–48
Tsujimura, A., 98n
tsukiai, 95
Tulving, E., 71, 78, 79
Ture, 52–4
Turner, V., 145, 146, 147, 156, 160, 161, 217n, 248, 277
Two Tables (Eddington), 278–9
Tylor, E. B., 34, 231, 247, 251, 284, 301
Tzara, Tristan, 291

ultramontanism, 341, 344, 351–2
United States, see Americans, and Indians, American
Uzbek, epic singers, 123

validity, social determination of, 230–148
Vedic ritual, 228

verbal learning processes, 71
verse, see poetry
Vlahovljak, Mumin, 87

waka, 97–100, 106, 107
Wakabayashi, M., 93n
Waldron, R. A., 136n
Wallace, A., 69n
Wallace, W. L., 236n
Ward, Wilfred, 353n
Watson, 279n
Watt, Ian, 54n, 109n, 112n, 114, 269n
Weber, Max, 229
Wetter, G., 243n
White, L., 279n
Whorf, B. L., 67, 161, 231, 233–4, 235, 238
Wieschoff, Heinz, 306n
wild thought (Lévi-Strauss), 274–5, 280
Willey, B., 288n
Williams, Raymond, 350–1
Winch, Peter, 33n, 183n, 231, 233, 235, 238
Winnebago, oral literature, 133
witchcraft, see magical acts
Wolfram, S., 366n, 368n, 369n
Wolofs, 70
Wood, David, 230n
Word of God, 365–7
Wordsworth, William 288
written communication, and Zen Buddhism, 102

Xavier, Francisco, 107

Yakushkov, 142
Yamaguchi, M., 102n, 110
Yamamoto Tsunetomo, 102, 103
Yoruba, mythology of, 312
  oral literature, 123
  poetry, 127
Youth Culture, 292
yu-gen, 99
yugenism, 102
Yugoslavia, epic songs, 85, 91, 123, 125, 127, 133
Yukagirs, 116–17

Zande, see Azande
Zeami Motokiyo, 102, 103
Zen Buddhism, 101–2
Zhirmunsky, V., 123n, 139
Ziman, J., 41
Zulus, oral literature, 116, 120, 127

399

www.ingramcontent.com/pod-product-compliance
Lightning Source LLC
Chambersburg PA
CBHW070715280326
41926CB00087B/2153